Union with Christ

Union with Christ
Adolf Schlatter's Relational Christology

Michael Bräutigam

Foreword by
Andreas J. Köstenberger

James Clarke & Co

James Clarke & Co
P.O. Box 60
Cambridge
CB1 2NT
United Kingdom

www.jamesclarke.co
publishing@jamesclarke.co

ISBN: 978 0 227 17573 6

British Library Cataloguing in Publication Data
A record is available from the British Library

First published by James Clarke & Co, 2015

Copyright © Michael Bräutigam, 2015

Published by arrangement
with Pickwick Publications

Unless otherwise indicated, all Scripture quotations are from the ESV® Bible (The Holy Bible, English Standard Version®), copyright © 2001 by Crossway, a publishing ministry of Good News Publishers. Used by permission. All rights reserved.

Material in chapter 6 of this work has previously appeared in my essay, "Good Will Hunting: Adolf Schlatter on Organic Volitional Sanctification," Journal of the Evangelical Theological Society 55.1 (2012) 125–43. Used by permission of the editor and publisher.

All rights reserved. No part of this edition may be reproduced, stored electronically or in any retrieval system, or transmitted in any form or by any means, electronic, mechanical, photocopying, recording, or otherwise, without prior written permission from the Publisher (permissions@jamesclarke.co).

Contents

Foreword by Andreas J. Köstenberger | vii
Acknowledgments | xiii
Abbreviations | xv

Introduction | 1

Part 1: The Genesis and Context of Schlatter's Christology | 15

1 Who was Adolf Schlatter? Biography and Theology | 17
2 Where was Adolf Schlatter? | 32

Part 2: The Shape of Schlatter's Christology | 105

3 The *Sehakt:* Empirical-Critical Realism and the Unified Christ | 107
4 The *Denkakt* (I): Jesus in Relation to God | 124
5 The *Denkakt* (II): Jesus in Relation to God and Humanity | 145
6 The *Lebensakt:* Organic Volitional Union with Christ | 173
    Epilogue: Christology after Schlatter | 196

Bibliography | 201
Subject Index | 221
Name Index | 233

Foreword

Andreas J. Köstenberger[1]

A COUPLE YEARS AGO, I came upon a new publication by Adolf Schlatter, *Einführung in die Theologie*, published by Calwer in 2013.[2] Not only was I greatly interested in what Schlatter has to say about the study of theology, I was intrigued by the fact that Schlatter, who went to be with the Lord in 1938, managed to publish yet another book—with the help of prolific Schlatter scholar Werner Neuer and the publisher, of course! The fact that Schlatter material continues to be published over seventy-five years after his death constitutes a fitting tribute to his remarkable caliber as a scholar.

While some, in his day as well as in ours, write him off variously as a conservative, as non-scholarly, or as inelegant in his prose, Schlatter's work as the whole has truly stood the test of time and continues to be relevant for theological and biblical research. For this reason, I am delighted at the publication of Michael Bräutigam's important new study, *Union with Christ: Adolf Schlatter's Relational Christology*. Bräutigam's work is part of a Schlatter renaissance that is discovering, or rediscovering, his contribution for a new generation of scholarship.[3]

---

1. Andreas Köstenberger is the translator of Adolf Schlatter's *New Testament Theology* and the co-translator (together with Robert Yarbrough) of Schlatter's final work, *Kennen wir Jesus? (Do We Know Jesus?)*. See *The History of the Christ: The Foundation of New Testament Theology*; *The Theology of the Apostles: The Development of New Testament Theology*; *Do We Know Jesus? Daily Insights for the Mind and Soul*. Köstenberger is Senior Research Professor of New Testament and Biblical Theology at Southeastern Baptist Theological Seminary in Wake Forest, North Carolina, USA, and the founder of Biblical Foundations™.

2. Schlatter, *Einführung in die Theologie*. This volume includes Schlatter's previously unpublished lecture, "Einführung in die Theologie" (1924), and it also contains his 1931 farewell message to his students after fifty years of teaching activity, "Erfolg und Misserfolg im theologischen Studium."

3. See Dintaman, *Creative Grace*; Walldorf, *Realistische Philosophie*; Rieger, *Adolf*

ESSENTIAL CONTENT

In his study of Schlatter's Christology, Bräutigam shows that Schlatter's work in this area reveals a distinct relational trajectory which offers new perspectives for today's Christological discussions. The work is divided into two major parts. Part 1 examines Schlatter's Christological agenda against the backdrop of his biography and the central theological developments of his time, exploring his critique of Kantian Christology and his engagement with the revival movement, the Ritschlian school, and dialectical theologians, most importantly his compatriot Karl Barth.

This sets the scene for the more systematic-theological discussions in Part 2. Instead of pursuing exclusively the classic two-nature treatment, Schlatter is shown to develop a relational account of Jesus Christ that is embedded in a trinitarian framework in which Father, Son, and Spirit share a communion of will and of love that creates, shapes, and upholds the life and story of Jesus the Christ.[4] Within this framework, Schlatter regards Jesus' action on the cross as the pre-eminent relational movement, first and foremost toward the Father and also toward human beings.

At the cross, Jesus reveals his divinity as he maintains fellowship with God in the Spirit despite his God-forsakenness. He reveals his humanity by maintaining close communion with sinners, transforming and gathering the redeemed into the new community of faith. Schlatter's relational perspective thus offers a sustainable Christology that provides not only a balanced view of Jesus' divinity and humanity but also offers a creative way of investigating Jesus' essential and relational being.

ANCILLARY CONTRIBUTIONS

This first rigorous attempt dedicated to chiselling out the distinct shape of Schlatter's Christology offers much food for thought for today's theological discussions. In particular, the work will prove to be of interest to *Barth and Bonhoeffer scholarship* as Schlatter at one point taught both of them and both witness to Schlatter's strong formative influence on them. By delineating Schlatter's characteristic and unique theological program, this work contributes not only to our understanding of Schlatter's thought but to that of Barth's and Bonhoeffer's theological development as well.

Schlatters Rechtfertigungslehre; Rüegg, *Der sich schenkende Christus*.

4. This strongly resonates with my own work in this area, particularly with regard to Johannine studies: see volume co-authored with Scott R. Swain, *Father, Son and Spirit*.

Not only does this study contribute to Christological discussions and Barth and Bonhoeffer scholarship, it also amplifies one of my favorite Schlatter contributions, that to *hermeneutics*. Specifically, Schlatter conceives of the core concept of *Anschluß an Christus* (union with Christ) through three distinct yet related theological and hermeneutical movements: the *Sehakt* (act of seeing); the *Denkakt* (act of thinking); and the *Lebensakt* (act of living).[5] In this way, the present work contributes also a case study of Schlatter's hermeneutic as applied to Christology.

The present work also informs *historical Jesus research* in the vein of both New Testament studies and Christological systematic exploration. As can be seen clearly in his two-volume *New Testament Theology*, according to Schlatter there is no rift between the historical Jesus and the Christ of faith.[6] Rather, there is the one person of Jesus Christ who accomplishes his salvific cross-work in concrete space and time. This is surely a remarkable proposition, given that it was originally set forth in a day when the German theological air was rife with the likes of Martin Kähler and Rudolf Bultmann.[7]

PRIMARY CONTRIBUTION

But the primary contribution of this work is its scrutiny of Schlatter's *Christological thought*. While Schlatter subscribes to classic formulations such as *homoousios* or the hypostatic union, he believes that these devote insufficient attention to the relational dimension of New Testament Christology. As a being in action and communion, Jesus sustains a twofold relationship with God and humanity: in relation to God, he is the Son of God who acts in perfect volitional union with God (*Denkakt* #1); in relation to humanity, he is the Christ who possesses the will to save humanity (*Denkakt* #2).

Based on his creative, relational reconstruction, Schlatter offers an alternative interpretation of the classic notions of Jesus' divinity and humanity. According to Schlatter, Jesus demonstrates his divinity as he obeys the Father perfectly and remains in unbroken communion of will with him

---

5. My indebtedness to Schlatter's hermeneutic is evident in Köstenberger and Patterson, *Invitation to Biblical Interpretation*; idem, *For the Love of God's Word*.

6. This is evident already in the title of volume 1: *Die Geschichte des Christus* (*The History of the Christ*). I have translated Schlatter's *Geschichte des Christus* into English, *The History of the Christ: The Foundation of New Testament Theology*; See also my translation of Schlatter's *Theologie der Apostel*, published in English as *The Theology of the Apostles: The Development of New Testament Theology*.

7. See Kähler, *Christ of Faith*. Note in particular Bultmann's contention that the "message of Jesus is a presupposition for the theology of the New Testament rather than a part of that theology itself." Bultmann, *Theology of the New Testament I*, 3.

even on the cross while also sharing in our human nature and thus fulfilling his role as the Christ, with the ultimate goal of establishing the new community of God of which he is the head. Thus the Jesus of history is also the Christ of faith who reconciles humanity with God through his work on the cross.

Yet Schlatter, and Bräutigam, are not done yet. In characteristic fashion, Schlatter weds biblical study and dogmatics with ethics: orthopraxis must accompany orthodoxy.[8] A study of Schlatter's Christology is thus incomplete without a discussion of how Christology impacts the individual believer and the community. In this regard, Schlatter stresses faith in the person and work of Christ as the means through which humans are brought into relation with God and with each other in the new community of faith. Individuals enter into volitional union with Jesus (*Anschluß an Jesus*), a union that is mediated by the Holy Spirit and leads to a communion of will with God that in turn triggers ethical action.[9]

FINAL COMMENDATION

Along with established Schlatter scholars such as Werner Neuer and Robert Yarbrough, this work places its author, Michael Bräutigam, on the vanguard of Schlatter scholarship in the twenty-first century.[10] With astute treatments such as these, it is entirely possible, if not likely, that Schlatter may emerge as more influential in the twenty-first century than he was in the twentieth century. While at times overshadowed by theological giants such as Bultmann or Harnack, Schlatter's refusal to follow scholarly trends in his day may yet reap rich dividends from which we all can benefit.[11]

It has been a joy and privilege to summarize the contents and potential contribution of this remarkable volume. I cannot emphasize strongly enough the generative potential of the present work for New Testament

---

8. Note the fact that Schlatter followed his 2-volume *New Testament Theology* with volumes on dogmatics and ethics. See Schlatter, *Das christliche Dogma*, and, *Die christliche Ethik*.

9. Toward the end of Schlatter's lifetime, the term *Anschluß* took on ominous overtones owing to its use in the Third Reich as designating the forceful annexation of my native country of origin, Austria, in 1938 by Nazi Germany under Adolf Hitler.

10. See in particular Werner Neuer's monumental Schlatter biography, *Adolf Schlatter: Ein Leben für Theologie und Kirche*. Neuer's more popular biography (*Adolf Schlatter*, 1988) has been translated into English by Robert W. Yarbrough, *Adolf Schlatter: A Biography of Germany's Premier Biblical Theologian*. See also by Yarbrough, "Adolf Schlatter," in *Dictionary of Historical Theology*, 505–7.

11. For a comparative study, see Köstenberger, "T. Zahn, A. von Harnack, and A. Schlatter," in *Pillars in the History of New Testament Interpretation: Old and New*.

research and Systematic theology. I recommend it very highly as a suggestive and fruitful exploration of a heretofore neglected aspect of Schlatter's multifaceted scholarly output, namely his relational Christology, which is yet to be taken up and incorporated in today's discussions of the person and work of our Lord and Savior Jesus Christ.

Acknowledgments

I GLADLY ACKNOWLEDGE THE help and support of a wide range of people, none of whom can be charged with any deficiencies of this work. First of all, I wish to thank my doctoral supervisor, Paul T. Nimmo, whose attention to detail was matched by a genuine enthusiasm for the dissertation on which this book is based. Paul's scholarly excellence and constant drive for clarity and precision remain exemplary to me and made me a more careful thinker and theologian. I also want to thank my doctoral examiners, Johannes Zachhuber and David Reimer, for their stimulating feedback and encouragement. During my previous postgraduate studies, I have had the privilege of studying under Donald Macleod, whose lectures in systematic theology fuelled my passion for Christology. In many ways, this project is an extrapolation of these sublime classroom encounters.

Back in 2008, on a beautiful day in Louisville, KY, I discussed the viability of this project with Andy McGowan, who remained a loyal supporter for which I am very grateful. Andreas J. Köstenberger has been very generous in taking time to discuss significant questions with a view to translating Schlatter's prose during my visit at Southeastern Baptist Theological Seminary in 2010, and he was also kind enough to provide the foreword to this book.

With a view to the publication of this book, I would like to register my gratitude to K. C. Hanson and the editorial team at Pickwick Publications for their enthusiasm and support. Thanks are also due to Werner Neuer who offered more than once helpful clarification with a view to biographical and historical questions. I also wish to thank the Kirk Session and the congregation of Buccleuch & Greyfriars Free Church of Scotland in Edinburgh, among whom I had the privilege of serving as an elder in the past few years, a constant reminder that theology is a function of the church (a truly Schlatterian premise). I have been helped along the way by stimulating conversations with my friends, Bill Schweitzer, Fiona Christie, James

Eglinton, John Scoales, Eric Mackay, Andrew Kloes, and Christian Sturm. I am very grateful to Bob Yarbrough, Thomas Wehr, and Hans Burger who read parts of the manuscript and offered constructive feedback and counsel.

Finally, I wish to thank my family for their enduring care and support. I am indebted to auntie Thea, who patiently helped me decipher Adolf Schlatter's intricate handwriting in his unpublished documents. To my parents, my sister, and to Jenni: *Herzlichen Dank für Eure Unterstützung*! All errors and shortcomings remain my own.

Michael Bräutigam
Edinburgh, March 2015

Abbreviations

Andachten Schlatter, Adolf. *Daß meine Freude in euch sei: Andachten*. 3rd ed. Stuttgart: Calwer, 1957

B-Schl Br Neuer, Werner, ed. "Der Briefwechsel zwischen Karl Barth und Adolf Schlatter: Ein Beitrag zum 100. Geburtstag Karl Barths." *Theologische Beiträge* 17 (1986) 86–100

Dogma Schlatter, Adolf. *Das christliche Dogma*. 2nd ed. Stuttgart: Calwer, 1923

Ethik Schlatter, Adolf. *Die christliche Ethik*. 3rd ed. Stuttgart: Calwer, 1929

RGG *Religion in Geschichte und Gegenwart: Handwörterbuch für Theologie und Religionswissenschaft*. Edited by H. E. von Campenhausen and K. Galling. 3rd ed. 7 vols. Tübingen: J.C.B. Mohr, 1957–65

"Selbstdarstellungen" Schlatter, Adolf. "Adolf Schlatter." In *Die Religionswissenschaft in Selbstdarstellungen*. Edited by Erich Stange. Leipzig: Felix Meiner, 1925

Introduction

WHY ADOLF SCHLATTER?

WHO WAS ADOLF SCHLATTER (1852–1938), and why should we care, in particular, about his Christology? The answer that there is no study on Schlatter's Christology yet might be true but not entirely satisfactory. While, for example, a study with the title "The Correlation between Excessive Preaching Habits and Congregational Sleeping Patterns: The Example of Eutychus in Acts 20:9," might be unique and perhaps even remotely interesting, its relevance is certainly arguable. The present work, however, claims to be both unique and relevant for the following reasons. First of all, Adolf Schlatter is an important theologian who has for too long suffered a wrongful neglect. Whilst he contributed crucially to the development of twentieth-century Protestant theology, endeavors with a view to examining his influence more closely are still scarce. This study represents one step towards closing this gap in scholarly research. Secondly, Schlatter's theology is highly promising as it opens avenues of ecumenical understanding. Careful to avoid any confessional bias and always determined to examine Scripture as objectively as possible, Schlatter's "theology of facts" (Werner Neuer) offers an ideal basis for a constructive dialogue not only between Reformed and Lutherans but also, more broadly, between Protestants, Roman Catholics and Eastern Orthodox traditions. It seems, thirdly, that Schlatter's dogmatic trajectory has so far successfully escaped scholarly attention. Although Schlatter is still recognized as an important New Testament theologian, the scientific community would do well to unearth Schlatter's dogmatic legacy, which offers promising insights for our theological discussion today. This project focuses on what we consider to be the most fascinating aspect of Schlatter's dogmatics, namely his relational approach to Christology. Before we turn in more detail to the character and scope of this study, the abovementioned incentives for a resurgence in Schlatter scholarship deserve a fuller explanation and we shall look at each of those in the following section.

Schlatter's Influence on Protestant Theology

Adolf Schlatter's influence is generally underrated. Markus Bockmuehl refers to Schlatter as "brilliant but widely ignored,"[1] and Robert Yarbrough names Schlatter "one of Christianity's truly seminal (and neglected) post-Enlightenment thinkers."[2] Although one observes a growing interest in Schlatter during the past fifteen years or so—in particular after the publication of Werner Neuer's extensive Schlatter biography in 1996—he is still very much a forgotten theologian, both in the German-speaking world and in the Anglo-Saxon context. In John E. Wilson's *Introduction to Modern Theology: Trajectories in the German Tradition* (2007), Adolf Schlatter is merely worth a footnote and he is, strangely enough, mistakenly portrayed as representing an anti-Semitic position.[3] In the Blackwell Compendium to *The Modern Theologians: An Introduction to Christian Theology since 1918* (2005), Schlatter is only mentioned in passing, namely as one of Karl Barth's teachers.[4] This fact alone, one would think, should have sparked academic interest in the past (particularly in the Barth community), yet Schlatter's influence on Barth is still one of the black spots of theological research. Worse still, the 2003 edition of the *Biographical Dictionary of Evangelicals* omits Schlatter altogether.[5] Given Schlatter's significant influence in theology, this notorious Schlatter-neglect is certainly a conundrum, calling for a new generation of scholars to rediscover his lasting contribution.[6]

During his career, Schlatter lectured for a hundred consecutive semesters in Bern (1881–88), Greifswald (1888–93), Berlin (1893–98), and Tübingen (1898–1930), influencing several generations of pastors and theologians. A short listing of some of Schlatter's students reads like a who's who of twentieth century German Protestant theology: Alongside the already mentioned Karl Barth, there were Dietrich Bonhoeffer, Rudolf Bultmann, Erich Seeberg, Paul Althaus, Paul Tillich, Ernst Käsemann, and

---

1. Bockmuehl, *This Jesus*, 218n1.

2. Yarbrough, "Translator's Preface," 9.

3. Wilson, *Introduction to Modern Theology*, 21n72. We shall return to this issue in the next chapter.

4. Hardy, "Karl Barth," 22.

5. Larsen, *Biographical Dictionary of Evangelicals*.

6. Andreas J. Köstenberger offers some explanations for this neglect, in "Preface," 13–22.

Otto Michel, to name but a few. While one cannot speak of a characteristic Schlatter-school, he certainly left a distinct mark on his students. In many ways the exact nature of this influence is still theological *terra incognita*, awaiting its discovery today. Adolf Schlatter lived in turbulent times, both historically and theologically. His particular historical position at the interface of two centuries and the context of the then increasing diversification of the theological landscape make Schlatter research fascinating and promising for today, at the outset of a new century. Growing up in rural Switzerland, Schlatter was immersed in Wilhelmine Prussia during his time in Greifswald and Berlin; he lived through the First World War where he lost a son; he then became a citizen in the Weimar Republic, and subsequently witnessed in Tübingen the rise of National Socialism, until he passed away on the verge of the Second World War. Theologically, he was raised and rooted in Protestant Reformed orthodoxy; he was influenced by German philosophical idealism, had to answer liberal claims around the fin de siècle, and was finally in dialogue with 1920s dialectical theology. At times of paradigmatic theological change, Adolf Schlatter challenged his contemporaries by formulating a fresh, yet conservative theological design. Advocating an observative, empirical approach to theology, Schlatter roots the historical and systematic disciplines in the perceived reality of God's revelation in creation, in Scripture, and, supremely, in Jesus Christ. With this angle, he aimed to provide an alternative to the liberal critique of Scripture and theology, while at the same time avoiding the uncritical adoption of a conservative, biblicist theology.[7] Occupying this unique position, Schlatter's contribution promises to be stimulating for our theological conversation today and one cannot but agree with Wuppertal dogmatician Johannes von Lüpke, who notes that "[i]t is time to return to Schlatter's theology in order to make progress in today's discussions."[8] This applies not only to the present debate on Christology as we shall see later, but also to our ecumenical exchange.

Schlatter's Ecumenical Perspective

In a time of increasing segmentation and specialization, and some would add, confessional isolation, Adolf Schlatter stands out as a fascinating polymath

---

7. Schlatter was clearly not a biblicist (more on this in chapter 2). Still, the stereotype seems alive and well, even in his former domain Tübingen. Clemens Hägele observes that readers interested in Schlatter's dogmatic opus will have to look for his books in the Tübingen *Theologicumsbibliothek* under the shelfmark biblicists. Hägele, *Schrift als Gnadenmittel*, 33n102.

8. Lüpke, "Vorwort," 9.

with a holistic theological and confessional agenda. Covering virtually all the disciplines of theological scholarship, he brings together a remarkable grasp of original languages, exegetical skills, as well as philosophical and experiential power. Paired with his intrinsic confessional openness, which could be attributed to the special circumstances of his upbringing (his mother was a lifelong member in the Swiss Reformed Church, whereas his father was one of the founding members of a Free Evangelical Church), it makes Schlatter an ideal conversation partner in today's attempts to overcome confessional barriers.[9] Originally ordained in the Swiss Reformed Church, Schlatter showed no reservation working closely alongside Prussian Lutheran theologian Hermann Cremer (1834–1903) in Greifswald, or later, in Berlin, with the liberal Adolf von Harnack (1851–1930), all the while retaining strong connections with the conservative pietist movement.[10] In one of his autobiographical reflections, Schlatter insists that while he was "in Switzerland a part of the Reformed [Church], in Prussia [a member] of the united [Church] and in Tübingen part of the Lutheran Church, it did not have any influence on my inner position."[11] Schlatter also enjoyed the works of Catholic theologian Franz von Baader (1765–1841) who exerted an important influence on him. Long before the initiation of the ecumenical dialogue, Schlatter makes clear that he intended to work towards "overcoming the severe abyss that separates the Protestant and Catholic Churches."[12] In this sense, it is not surprising that his contribution is in fact appreciated not only among Protestant readers but also within the Catholic context. In his *Geleitwort* to the 1985 reprint of Schlatter's commentary on the Epistle of James, Catholic New Testament theologian Franz Mussner remarks that Schlatter's exegetical works are highly significant for the ecumenical dialogue, as they exhibit a paradigm of obedience to the text which could

---

9. On Schlatter's ecumenical perspective see Neuer, "Die ökumenische Bedeutung," 71–92.

10. See Neuer, *Adolf Schlatter*, 428–40. The term "pietism" is notoriously difficult to define. See Wallmann, *Der Pietismus*, 7–8. In general, scholars agree in defining pietism broadly as a religious movement of renewal of the seventeenth century, which had its prime of life in the eighteenth century. Together with Anglo-Saxon Puritanism, it is considered to be the most important religious movement within Protestantism since the Reformation. The main concern of early pietism was a reform of the Protestant churches in Germany under Philipp Jakob Spener (1635–1705) in Frankfurt (1670s), picked up by August Hermann Francke (1663–1727) in Halle (1690s). Other noteworthy representatives of pietism are Johann Albrecht Bengel (1687–1752) and Friedrich Christoph Oetinger (1702–82).

11. Schlatter, *Rückblick*, 19–20.

12. Ibid., 236.

work as a common denominator for both traditions.[13] Protestant theologian Hans-Martin Rieger's dissertation on "Adolf Schlatter's Doctrine of Justification and the Possibilities of Ecumenical Understanding," recently received an award from the Catholic faculty at the University of Regensburg.[14] Moreover, Pope emeritus Benedict XVI considers Schlatter a noteworthy conversation partner,[15] and it is surely not coincidence that Schlatter scholar Werner Neuer is the only Protestant enjoying the honor of being a permanent member of the Ratzinger *Schülerkreis*.[16] As we shall see throughout this work, Schlatter's contribution indeed possesses significant potential to build bridges in our current attempts at interdenominational dialogue.

Schlatter's christological Contribution

It is mainly Schlatter the New Testament theologian who has been in the spotlight of scholarly interest so far. While there occasionally appeared studies on Schlatter's dogmatic outline in the first decades after his death,[17] scholarship in general focused mainly on Schlatter's New Testament legacy.[18] His New Testament theology was not only critically acclaimed in Germany,[19] but was also well received in the English-speaking world, through translation work by Robert Morgan,[20] and more recently, Andreas J. Köstenberger,

---

13. Mussner, "Geleitwort," xii.

14. In 2000, the Catholic theological faculty awarded Rieger the first prize of the Dr Kurt Hellmich Trust which promotes research in ecumenical theology.

15. Commenting on Schlatter's dispute with Adolf von Harnack, Ratzinger notes that Schlatter was right in his assessment that what separated their theologies was not merely the question of miracles, as Harnack argued, but in fact the question of Christology. See Ratzinger, *Truth and Tolerance*, 132n17.

16. Vieweger, "Der protestantische Papst-Schüler."

17. The studies mainly focused on basic prolegomena to Schlatter's systematic approach. See for example Fraas, "Die Bedeutung der Gotteslehre fur die Dogmatik bei Adolf Schlatter und Reinhold Seeberg"; Dymale, "The Theology of Adolf Schlatter with Special Reference to His Understanding of History"; Bailer, *Das systematische Prinzip*; Egg, *Adolf Schlatters kritische Position: Gezeigt an seiner Matthäusinterpretation*; Meyer-Wieck, "Das Wirklichkeitsverständnis Adolf Schlatters"; Kindt, *Der Gedanke der Einheit: Adolf Schlatters Theologie und ihre historischen Voraussetzungen*.

18. For an overview see Yarbrough, "Modern Reception," 417–23.

19. Schlatter students Wilhelm Lütgert, Otto Michel and Ernst Käsemann were significantly influenced by Schlatter as Neuer observes (*Adolf Schlatter*, 790). Leonhard Goppelt (1911–73) saw Schlatter as a forerunner of his own New Testament theology and Peter Stuhlmacher (1932–) followed closely in Schlatter's footsteps. See Stuhlmacher's own comments in his essay, "Adolf Schlatter's Interpretation of Scripture," 433–46.

20. Schlatter, "Theology of the New Testament and Dogmatics," 117–66.

6   Union with Christ

who translated Schlatter's two-volume New Testament Theology, *The History of the Christ* (1997), and *The Theology of the Apostles* (1999). Among Anglo-Saxon New Testament scholars who are currently rediscovering Adolf Schlatter's exegetical legacy are—in addition to Schlatter translators Andreas Köstenberger and Robert Yarbrough—Donald Guthrie, Brevard Childs, Hendrikus Boers,[21] N.T. Wright,[22] Markus Bockmuehl,[23] and Thomas R. Schreiner.[24] While these developments suggest a slight Schlatter renaissance, Schlatter the dogmatician is still largely unknown to the wider audience. Perhaps this could be attributed to the rise of dialectical theology which somewhat overshadowed Schlatter's dogmatic heritage.[25] About half a century after Schlatter's demise, Werner Neuer lamented that his systematic approach had until that point not been adequately processed.[26] In 1996, Neuer presented his comprehensive Schlatter biography, "Adolf Schlatter: A Life for Theology and the Church" (*Adolf Schlatter: Ein Leben für Theologie und Kirche*). This milestone publication fuelled a fresh interest in the Swiss scholar, together with the publication of two reprint collections of some of his most influential theological writings a few years later.[27] Recent sources on Schlatter's dogmatic opus explore his take on the doctrine of Scripture,[28] his understanding of the sacraments,[29] and his view of justification.[30] Major English-language systematic treatments however are still scarce, which could be attributed to the lack of translations of Schlatter's dogmatic works (such as his *Dogma* and *Ethik*)—noteworthy exceptions are Stephen Dintaman's monograph,[31] and Andreas Loos' doctoral thesis.[32]

21. On Guthrie, Childs, and Boers, see Yarbrough, "Modern Reception," 423–26.

22. Wright, *New Testament*, 121, 194, 344, 373.

23. Bockmuehl refers to Schlatter in his *Seeing the Word*, and commends Schlatter's theology and method (74, 88).

24. Note extensive references to Schlatter in the index of Schreiner's *New Testament Theology*, 947.

25. As Stuhlmacher suggested, in "Adolf Schlatter," 219. Other scholars come to the same conclusion; see Neuer, *Zusammenhang von Dogmatik und Ethik*, 22; Walldorf, *Realistische Philosophie*, 12; Gasque, "Promise of Schlatter," 20; Morgan, "Introduction," 29.

26. Neuer, *Zusammenhang von Dogmatik und Ethik*, 25.

27. Neuer, *Die Bibel verstehen*, and von Lüpke, *Adolf Schlatter*.

28. Hägele, *Schrift als Gnadenmittel*.

29. Rüegg, *Der sich schenkende Christus*.

30. Rieger, *Schlatters Rechtfertigungslehre*.

31. Dintaman, *Creative Grace*.

32. Loos, "Divine Action, Christ."

Considering the status quo, it is most surprising that Schlatter's significant christological angle has until this day not attracted adequate attention. This is a serious neglect insofar as Schlatter's theology is, as Paul Althaus put it, "through and through christocentric."[33] So far, there are only a few studies available which examine certain facets of Schlatter's Christology. While Johannes H. Schmid carefully analyses Schlatter's picture of the historical Christ,[34] he, however, misunderstands basic prolegomena to Schlatter's dogmatic thinking, which limits his study to a certain extent.[35] Werner Neuer touches upon certain aspects of Schlatter's Christology when discussing Schlatter's atonement theology.[36] In his examination of Schlatter's doctrine of justification, Hans-Martin Rieger refers to some important christological foundations in Schlatter's dogmatic thinking, and he rightly points to the characteristic relational feature in Schlatter's Christology.[37] Finally, Andreas Loos provides significant insight into the Trinitarian structure of Schlatter's Christology, while his special focus on "Divine action" in general prevents him from offering a more elaborate christological discussion in particular.[38]

While those recent scholarly endeavors might be promising, one still looks in vain for rigorous attempts dedicated to chisel out the distinct shape of Schlatter's Christology. Some years ago, Jürgen Moltmann pointed out that "[i]n face of today's theological questions, A. Schlatter's 'Jesus' Divinity and the Cross' [*Jesu Gottheit und das Kreuz*] deserves to be snatched away from oblivion."[39] The findings presented in this study suggest that Moltmann is right. Of course, the goal cannot be to offer an exhaustive account of Schlatter's Christology. Rather, this work aims to expose the foundational building blocks of Schlatter's Christology. More precisely, it will be argued that the central and most significant feature of Schlatter's Christology is its relational orientation. That is, on the one hand Schlatter is critical of the traditional way of approaching Christology merely speculatively "from above"; yet on the other hand, he also rejects the path "from below" as the only valid way towards a Christology proper. Instead, Schlatter suggests a relational approach to Christology, which, as this study shows, is a robust and creative approach that can adequately describe and integrate the person and work

33. Althaus, "Adolf Schlatters Wort," 103.

34. See Schmid, *Erkenntnis des Geschichtlichen Christus*.

35. We agree with Walldorf's observations, which suggest that Schmid in particular neglects Schlatter's philosophical-theological realism, while also denying an underlying ontological concept in Schlatter. See Walldorf, *Realistische Philosophie*, 18–19.

36. Neuer, *Zusammenhang von Dogmatik und Ethik*, 198–227.

37. Rieger, *Schlatters Rechtfertigungslehre*, 306–26.

38. See Loos, "Divine Action, Christ."

39. Moltmann, *Der gekreuzigte Gott*, 187.

of Jesus Christ. Before we proceed to present a more detailed outline of this project, we must not forget to point to the overall character of this work and certain challenges associated with Schlatter research.

CHALLENGES AND CHARACTER OF THIS STUDY

When investigating Schlatter's theology, one is faced with several challenges. We shall briefly look at three major difficulties which deserve to be mentioned at the outset, namely first, the problem of our overall theological terminology to be used in this study, secondly, Schlatter's lacking interaction with secondary sources, and finally, the sheer size of Schlatter's works and his often difficult language.

Terminology

There is, first of all, the problem of terminology, and this applies not only to Schlatter, but to every study concerning nineteenth- and twentieth-century theology. Evidently, Adolf Schlatter's lifespan overlaps with a fascinating diversification of the theological landscape at that time. Usually linked with the branch of *positive theology*, Schlatter witnessed the hegemony and the collapse of so-called *liberal theology*, while he also observed the irenic attempts of the *mediating theologians*, who sought to break middle ground between these two poles. In the second half of his career, Schlatter was also in close dialogue with the *dialectical movement* of post-World War I Germany. One obviously needs to take into account this intriguing kaleidoscope of theological movements and schools as they explicitly and also implicitly contributed to the characteristic shape of Schlatter's christological outlook. The complexity of the different theological streams of that time renders our task both stimulating and challenging. Joachim Weinhardt, for example, laments that "a standard description of the 19th century [theological] schools is not available," while adding that it will be impossible to reach any agreement in the future.[40] This certainly does not sound auspicious. Theologians usually resort to the abovementioned fourfold division of liberal theology, mediating theology, positive (or confessional/conservative) theology, and dialectical theology, in order to systematize the different theological approaches and ideas. These terms, however, are fuzzy and unpropitious for several reasons.[41] It is difficult, for example, to find a consensus on what

40. Weinhardt, *Wilhelm Herrmanns Stellung*, 7.
41. See ibid., 5–15.

liberal theology is.[42] One would ideally need to add a qualification, that is, one would have to define in which ways a theology is liberal in relation to another theology. On the whole, scholars disagree in their labelling of different theologians as liberal,[43] mediating,[44] positive/confessional,[45] or dialectical.[46] It seems almost impossible to categorize clearly the complex

42. The term "liberal" in itself seems to be highly problematic, as Weinhardt suggests. According to Weinhardt, the term was first used to describe a certain stance on church politics (for example in relation to the *Apostolikumsstreit*, see chapter 2). Later, the term made its way into the theological vocabulary when it was used by confessional theologians, conservative Ritschlians, and dialectical theologians to designate the leftwing Ritschlians Harnack and Herrmann. See Weinhardt, *Wilhelm Herrmanns Stellung*, 13-15, 18; cf. Axt-Piscalar's definition, in "Liberal Theology in Germany," 468-69.

43. According to Axt-Piscalar, liberal theology stands (narrowly defined) for the theology from around 1870 to 1918 and includes Albrecht Ritschl (1822-89) and his successors, such as Adolf von Harnack (1851-1930), Julius Kaftan (1848-1926), Wilhelm Herrmann (1846-1922), Martin Rade (1857-1940) and Ernst Troeltsch (1865-1923). It also includes representatives of the *religionsgeschichtliche Schule* (history of religion school), such as Wilhelm Bousset (1865-1920), Hermann Gunkel (1862-1932), Johannes Weiss (1863-1914), Alfred Rahlfs (1865-1935), Heinrich Hackmann (1864-1935), William Wrede (1859-1906), Albert Eichhorn (1856-1926), and Richard Reitzenstein (1861-1931). In the wider sense, she claims, liberal theology refers to those "ways of thinking which constructively take up Enlightenment principles and try to render them theologically" (Axt-Piscalar, "Liberal Theology in Germany," 469). This includes then Johann S. Semler (1725-91), as well as the approaches by Schleiermacher, Strauss, Baur and the Tübingen school. On the history of religion school see Chapman, "History of Religion School," 434-54.

44. Scholars generally agree that proponents of mediating theology sought to mediate between the two poles of liberal and positive theology, that is, they clearly intended to remain faithful to the Scriptures (without being rigid biblicists), while also taking into account the findings of modern science. Mediating theology began to prosper with the foundation of the journal *Theologische Studien und Kritiken* in 1828. Lists of mediating theologians usually include Isaak A. Dorner (1809-84), whom Eckhard Lessing, however, counts among the free theologians (see his *Geschichte der deutschsprachigen*, 1:141-44), Carl Ullmann (1796-1865), Friedrich W. C. Umbreit (1795-1860), Johann K. L. Gieseler (1792-1854) and Carl I. Nitzsch (1787-1868). See Matthias Gockel's essay on "Mediating Theology in Germany," 301-7. Apparently, depending on how broadly or narrowly one defines liberal, or positive, theology, one ends up with different lists of mediating theologians.

45. Lessing defines positive theology as a conservative theological stream which is closely tied to the church. Influential positive theologians are the Beck students Martin Kähler (1835-1912), Hermann Cremer (1834-1903) and Adolf Schlatter, who were the main heads of the positive Greifswald school (more on this in chapter 2). To this school belonged also Schlatter's student Wilhelm Lütgert (1867-1938), Erich Schaeder (1861-1936), Ernst Cremer (1864-1922), Karl Bornhäuser (1868-1947), Friedrich Bosse (1864-1931), and Julius Kögel (1871-1928). Closely affiliated with the Greifswald school are Samuel Oettli (1846-1911), Christoph Riggenbach (1818-90) and Otto Zöckler (1833-1906). See Lessing, *Geschichte der deutschsprachigen evangelischen Theologie*, 1:116-32. With regard to this term, one also observes the lack of a scholarly consensus.

46. Karl Barth's theology, for example, has one often been labelled dialectical, which,

10   Union with Christ

theological programs of the (equally complex) theological individuals. One easily runs the risk of doing an injustice to the scholars' own theological idiosyncrasies.

Thus, when referring in this study to these classical terms liberal, mediating, positive/confessional theology, and dialectical theology, one needs to bear in mind their inherent shortcomings. While we make, for the sake of simplicity, use of these terms in the following first chapter, they will be employed only tentatively in the remainder of this study and crucially in instances where Schlatter himself uses these terms. In light of these conceptual vulnerabilities, the most elegant solution then, it seems, is to focus on Schlatter's own theological characteristics and of the different individuals he encounters in the context of his life and work. For, only when one takes the theological personality seriously, against the backdrop of his or her historical context, will one be able to probe the theological matter more deeply.

Schlatter's Lacking Interaction with other Scholars

Second, Schlatter's hesitation to interact with other scholars in his works presents a particular obstacle to the reader. Only on rare occasions does one find clear references to other theologians and movements, and this might be another reason for the Schlatter-neglect mentioned earlier. "I neither had the time nor the inclination," writes Schlatter, "to refute my colleagues' views."[47] While this might sound quite harsh and even slightly condescending, one needs to put this statement into perspective in order to understand Schlatter's basic intention. In one of his autobiographical works, Schlatter himself wonders whether he should not have listened more carefully to fellow New Testament theologian Bernhard Weiss (1827–1918), who once encouraged him to pursue to a greater extent "conversation with colleagues."[48] However, Schlatter makes clear that his reluctance in this respect was not a reflection of his ignorance. Rather, it was an essential part of his empirical realist method of focusing exclusively on the theological facts (*Tatsachen*) as he perceived them in his reading of the New Testament. Schlatter writes:

> It was not the desire for originality which prompted me to be more reserved in my references to [secondary] literature; it was rather a sign of a diffident anxiety. . . . [F]or I needed protection for my own thinking, so that the thoughts of the others

---

however, does not reflect all of the different stages of Barth's theological development.

47. Schlatter, "Entstehung der Beiträge," 54; cf. 71.
48. Schlatter, *Rückblick*, 116.

would not confuse me; [I needed] protection for my own eye, so that it would remain capable [*sehfähig*] to discern the facts [*Tatbestände*].[49]

Schlatter's main intention then was to focus the reader's attention on the content of the New Testament as the foundation for dogmatics. To interact with secondary literature would only have distracted him (as well as the reader) from this goal. Whether or not this approach is helpful in terms of encouraging academic debate remains to be seen. However, a careful reading of Schlatter reveals that he indeed closely interacts with contemporary ideas, movements and even colleagues, although he is generally hesitant to name names—which might be due to his difficult frontline position between positive and liberal theology, as we shall see in due course. At any rate, one is required to read Schlatter very carefully, thus between the lines, as it were, in order to identify his hidden, but surely existent, critique of ideas and movements.

Schlatter's Output and Language

There is, thirdly, the sheer volume and the difficult language of Schlatter's works. As the number of his publications exceeds the four hundred mark,[50] the key to a successful study is to select the most significant material in the Schlatter corpus. For our purposes, a focus on Schlatter's major New Testament theology (*Glaube im Neuen Testament*, *The History of the Christ*, and *The Theology of the Apostles*), and his dogmatic opus (*Das christliche Dogma* and *Die christliche Ethik*) is advisable, insofar as Schlatter unfolds in these fundamental works both the characteristics of his New Testament picture of Christ and the foundations of his overall Christology. One will also need to consult crucial monographs, relevant journal articles and speeches, as this additional material provides a substantial insight into the distinctive features of Schlatter's christological approach.[51] Schlatter's *Do We Know Jesus?*, though originally composed as a devotional, contains significant christological information, and, last but not least, Schlatter's unpublished documents demand careful attention, in particular his 1884 Bern lecture, "Christologie und Soteriologie." Schlatter's unpublished works are handwritten in an outdated German writing-style, the *Sütterlinschrift*, which

---

49. Ibid.
50. For an overview, see Neuer, *Adolf Schlatter*, 832–41.
51. Such as *Jesu Gottheit und das Kreuz*, "Das Bekenntnis zur Gottheit Jesu," in *Gesunde Lehre*, by Adolf Schlatter, 32–48; "Der Zweifel an der Messianität Jesu," 7–75; and *Das Gott wohlgefällige Opfer*.

renders a transcription at times challenging, and only very little material has as yet been transcribed.[52]

Finally, one must mention the particular challenge presented by his sometimes convoluted and labyrinthine language. "Schlatter's theology is difficult to comprehend," William Baird laments, "written in a convoluted style that defies comprehension even by native German intellectuals."[53] Similarly, Schlatter student Otto Michel notes that Schlatter is an "opinionated, in no way easily accessible theological thinker."[54] Peter Stuhlmacher complains about Schlatter's "monstrous phrases,"[55] and remarks that it is "virtually impossible" to translate Schlatter's prose into English.[56] While these comments are certainly not encouraging, they are surely somewhat exaggerated. As it is often difficult to provide a literal translation of Schlatterian key terms without losing important connotations, the meaning of the German term will be explained and used alongside when appropriate. Unless otherwise indicated, translations are my own. Having briefly discussed both the promise and the challenge of Schlatter research, we conclude our introductory remarks by offering the overall roadmap of this work.

THE ROADMAP: CHAPTER CONTENTS

This book consists of two major parts. The first half of this work is dedicated more to Schlatter's biographical-historical background, which sets the stage for the major dogmatic-christological analysis in the second half. The first part on "The Genesis and Context of Schlatter's Christology," is to a great extent an exercise in narrative theology, paving the way for the second, systematic-theological part, which focuses on "The Dogmatic Shape of Schlatter's Christology." The following section offers a brief summary of the chapter contents.

Part one: The Genesis and Context of Schlatter's Christology

Chapter 1 deals with the basic question: Who was Adolf Schlatter? As Adolf Schlatter is no household name among scholars, this introductory chapter

52. Unpublished documents and manuscripts by Adolf Schlatter are accessible in the Adolf Schlatter archive in Stuttgart, Germany [Bestand D 40].

53. Baird, *History of New Testament Research*, 2:374.

54. Michel, "Schlatter als Ausleger der Schrift," 227; cf. Bailer's summary of challenges with a view to Schlatter research in *Das systematische Prinzip*, 11–20.

55. Stuhlmacher, "Zum Neudruck," xi.

56. Stuhlmacher, "Foreword," x.

provides a brief sketch of Schlatter's life and theology. Retracing Schlatter's individual history also raises one's awareness of the underlying reasons for his characteristic theological development, and, in particular, of his unique christological outlook. In chapter 2, we focus on the question: Where was Adolf Schlatter? In this threefold section we examine in more detail the complex theological-historical landscape of Schlatter's time, determining how it contributed to the *Sitz im Leben* of his theology. In a first step, we trace several noteworthy stimuli for Schlatter's theological development, such as his encounters with the revival movement (*Erweckungsbewegung*) at home and with pietism through his teacher Johann T. Beck, which stood in stark contrast to idealist positions the young Schlatter was faced with in school and at the university. We analyze, secondly, Schlatter's critical position towards certain Christologies he came across during his career in Bern, Greifswald, and Berlin, in particular focusing on his critique of Albrecht Ritschl and his pupils Wilhelm Herrmann and Adolf von Harnack. Moving chronologically to Schlatter's time in Tübingen, we shall thirdly, discuss Schlatter's critique of his former student Karl Barth more closely. In outlining Schlatter's theological exchange with major figures of his time, we are able to identify both significant aspects of his christological critique and his alternative suggestions. These important considerations set the stage for the ensuing dogmatic discussion in part 2.

Part two: The Dogmatic Shape of Schlatter's Christology

Chapters 3 to 6 form the dogmatic heart of this study, based on Schlatter's threefold distinction of seeing-act (*Sehakt*), thinking-act (*Denkakt*), and life-act (*Lebensakt*). The goal is to investigate first the methodological foundation of Schlatter's Christology (chapter 3), moving then to an analysis of the dogmatic core of his relational Christology (chapters 4 and 5), while the final part looks at the existential-ethical ramifications of his christological account (chapter 6). The following paragraphs offer a more detailed outline. Chapter 3 deals with the seeing-act, in which we seek to demonstrate how Schlatter arrives with his empirical realist method at a unified account of Jesus Christ. According to Schlatter's New Testament observation, there is no rift between the historical Jesus and the Christ of faith. Rather, there is only one unified Jesus Christ who performed the salvific deed on the cross in concrete space and time. Chapters 4 and 5 focus on the dogmatic implications of the christological picture described in the seeing-act, what Schlatter calls the thinking-act. While Schlatter subscribes to classic christological formulae, such as *homoousios* or the hypostatic union, he feels that these ignore the significant relational aspect he observes in the New Testament documents. In Schlatter's view, a relational understanding of Jesus Christ is more in touch with the New Testament witness as it shows Jesus Christ as a being in action and in communion. Schlatter sees Jesus in a twofold relationship, a double communion as he calls it, namely with God and with humanity. In relation to God (*Denkakt* I), Jesus is the Son of God who acts in perfect union of will with God. And in relation to humanity (*Denkakt* II), Jesus is the Christ, the Son of Man, who possesses the will to salvation for humanity. Based on his creative, relational framework, Schlatter offers an alternative interpretation of the classic notions of Jesus' divinity and humanity. According to Schlatter, Jesus demonstrates his divinity as he obeys the Father perfectly and remains in unbroken communion of will with him even on the cross, while he also shares in our human nature and thus fulfils his role as the Christ with the ultimate goal of establishing the new community of God of which he is the head. Chapter 6 discusses the implications of Schlatter's relational Christology for the Christian life. For Schlatter, dogmatics has to go hand in hand with ethics: orthodoxy remains incomplete without orthopraxy. It is thus essential for a correct reading of Schlatter to examine how Christology impacts the individual believer and the community. We will thus consider how Schlatter emphasizes faith in the person and work of Christ as the means through which human beings are brought into an existential relation with God and with each other in the new community of faith. The individual completes her[57] volitional "union with Jesus" (*Anschluß an Jesus*),[58] mediated by the Holy Spirit, which leads to a communion of will with God that in turn triggers ethical action. In this respect, it will also be assessed whether Schlatter accomplished his goal of a completion of the Reformation (*Vollendung der Reformation*). The study concludes by offering a summary of our findings while also pointing to the lasting value of Schlatter's relational Christology for today's discussions.

---

57. The University of Tübingen had opened its doors for female students in 1904. In contrast to some of his colleagues, Schlatter welcomed and supported female theology students, and he showed no reservations about leading bible studies at the Tübingen "Deutsche Christliche Vereinigung studierender Frauen" (DCVSF). See Neuer, *Adolf Schlatter*, 556–59. Kierkegaard biographer and Schlatter student Anna Paulsen, together with other Schlatter students, later expressed their gratitude to Schlatter in an open letter in the *Festschrift* for his seventy-fifth birthday, in Bender et al., *Vom Dienst an Theologie und Kirche*, 5–6. Our use of gender-inclusive language in this work clearly reflects Schlatter's openness in this respect.

58. *Anschluß* (or *Anschluss*) *an Jesus* is a key concept in Schlatter's work; it refers to one's union, connection, and allegiance with Jesus Christ.

PART 1

The Genesis and Context of Schlatter's Christology

"THEOLOGICAL HISTORY" WRITES MÜNSTER systematician Eckard Lessing is "personal history."[1] While this is certainly correct, one could add that the converse is also true: personal history is theological history.[2] Lessing points to the various autobiographical accounts by German Protestant theologians of the latter half of the nineteenth century, and claims that their theological agendas were meant to be read against the backdrop of their personal and general history. This is certainly true in the case of Adolf Schlatter. When studying Schlatter, one needs to take into account his own life context, the "unity of [his] biblically rooted theology and [his] biography," as Peter Stuhlmacher remarks.[3] Schlatter himself penned several autobiographical volumes with the declared intention to disclose what shaped his theological thinking.[4] He clearly points out that his theological outlook and particular method were given to him through his history.[5] To neglect Schlatter's biographical context then would be an unwise move as he himself, as it were,

---

1. Lessing, *Geschichte der deutschsprachigen evangelischen Theologie*, 1:25.
2. See McClendon, *Biography as Theology*, 67–88.
3. Stuhlmacher, "Adolf Schlatter," 231.
4. Among these are his "Entstehung der Beiträge zur Förderung christlicher Theologie" (1920), *Erlebtes: Erzählt von D. Adolf Schlatter* (1924, rev. ed. 1929), the *Rückblick auf meine Lebensarbeit* (published posthumously in 1952), as well as his autobiographical chapter in "Selbstdarstellungen," 145–71 (1925). One also finds an unpublished autobiographical manuscript in the Schlatter archive in Stuttgart, "Der Idealismus und die Erweckung in meiner Jugend" (n.d., probably 1926).
5. Schlatter, "Selbstdarstellungen," 145.

expects the readers of his theological *œuvre* to be familiar with his own story, his *Geschichte*. For Schlatter, theology and life, thinking-act (*Denkakt*) and life-act (*Lebensakt*), form an inseparable union. As it is impossible to do justice to Adolf Schlatter's theology without adequately taking into account his personal historical context, this study is thus not merely a task in dogmatic theology but also a historical and, if you will, a psychological exercise. Understanding Schlatter's life, to which we now turn, is the key to unlocking the overarching elements of his theological, and in particular, christological agenda.

1

Who was Adolf Schlatter?
Biography and Theology

THE *SITZ IM LEBEN* OF SCHLATTER'S THEOLOGY (1852-75)

ADOLF SCHLATTER WAS BORN in St. Gallen, Switzerland, on August 16, 1852, the seventh child of Hektor Stephan Schlatter (1805-80) and Wilhelmine, née Steinmann (1819-94). In the following nearly eighty-six years of his life as pastor, professor, author and speaker, Adolf Schlatter would continue the family's Protestant tradition, his family line being traceable to the fifteenth century reformer Joachim Vadian (1484-1551). To a great extent, Schlatter's theology has its *Sitz im Leben* in the Christian home of his youth. "The power with which we children were embraced by our parents' faith," remembers Schlatter later, "was the presupposition and root from which my own story [*Geschichte*] grew."[1] His parents lived out the union of faith and love, the unity of orthodoxy and orthopraxy, which would leave an indelible impression on their son. Still, despite their close fellowship in faith, Schlatter's parents were confessionally divided. Complaining of a lack of church discipline, Stephan Schlatter left the Reformed Church, joined an Evangelical Free Church, and was re-baptized. Even though his wife had sympathies for the Free Church, she could not follow her husband and remained with the children in the established Reformed Church. Obviously, this painful

1. Neuer, *Adolf Schlatter: A Biography*, 24 [Schlatter, *Rückblick*, 12].

split affected the young Schlatter.[2] It might explain why he never became a clear-cut confessional theologian, rather embodying a lifelong ecumenical openness. Overall, however, for Schlatter's parents personal allegiance to Jesus Christ by faith was paramount and took priority over any denominational affiliations.[3] This has undoubtedly contributed to Schlatter's strong Christocentric focus. An irenic theologian, he would throughout his career labor for the unity of the church, seeking fellowship with those with whom he knew himself united by faith in Christ, regardless of their different ecclesial backgrounds.[4] His father, a trained pharmacist, inspired Schlatter with his love for nature, for the natural sciences, and for botany in particular.[5] "My eyes, therefore," remembers Schlatter, "were opened to nature at an early age, for God had given me parents who praised him with earnest faith as the Creator of nature."[6] This early exposure to the natural realm[7] set the course for his later philosophical-realist stance against any contemporary Kantian approaches and contributed to his development of an empirical "theology of facts."[8] Overall, in his boyhood home, Schlatter was equipped with a view for the broad range of God's revelation in creation, which certainly influenced his overall theological perspective, the "impetus towards the whole" (*Richtung auf das Ganze*), as he would later describe it in his "Christian Dogmatics."[9]

In secondary school, Schlatter was exposed to a world quite different from home. In various ways, his time in secondary school foreshadowed the important questions Schlatter would struggle with as a theologian later in

2. For instance, Schlatter's father did not witness his son Adolf's *Konfirmation*, or his ordination, nor did he attend his own daughter's funeral service, as all these occasions took place in the *Landeskirche*. See Schlatter, *Rückblick*, 19, and "Idealismus und Erweckung," 43.

3. Schlatter explains: "For my parents, the superiority of Jesus over the church was certain [*stand fest*]. Their communion was established in that both saw in their allegiance to Jesus [*Anschluß an Jesus*] the rule that governed them." Schlatter, *Erlebtes*, 32; see also *Rückblick*, 20–21, and "Entstehung der Beiträge," 28.

4. Having grown up in the Swiss Reformed Church, he had later no reservations about becoming a member of the United Church in Prussia and of the Lutheran Church in Württemberg. See Schlatter, *Rückblick*, 19–21, 26 and *Erlebtes*, 57–58. For Schlatter's view on ecumenical dialogue see for example, Schlatter, "Das Evangelium und das Bekenntnis," 21–31; and "Die Grenzen der kirchlichen Gemeinschaft," 3–20.

5. See Schlatter, "Entstehung der Beiträge," 24.

6. Neuer, *Adolf Schlatter: A Biography*, 27; see also Schlatter, *Rückblick*, 14–15; *Erlebtes* 121–2; "Idealismus und Erweckung," 37–39.

7. His *Anschluß an die Natur* as he calls it in "Selbstdarstellungen," 155.

8. As Werner Neuer labelled it; see Neuer, *Zusammenhang von Dogmatik und Ethik*, 44–49; see also Dreher, "Luther als Paulus-Interpret," 112.

9. Schlatter, *Dogma*, 13, 19.

life. In religious education, Schlatter was challenged by liberal theology, and in the philosophy classroom he was confronted with Hegelian and Kantian abstract thought. School, with its critical, liberal outlook, was a stark contrast to his parents' home and challenged the young Schlatter's faith. His decision to take up theological studies was therefore marked by a sincere interest in clarifying and consolidating his faith, an attempt to reconcile home and school, faith and science. "Not the clerical office, but the clarification of the question of truth, not the acquisition of skills, but the acquisition of knowledge were his goals when Schlatter took up his studies in May 1871," observes his biographer Werner Neuer.[10]

In 1871, when the German Empire was proclaimed in Versailles, Schlatter moved to Basel to begin his theological studies.[11] The first semesters were dominated by philosophical lessons. Schlatter found Friedrich Nietzsche's (1844–1900) lectures disturbing[12] and was much more impressed by Karl Steffensen (1816–88) with his "religious manner of thinking" (*religiöse Art des Denkakts*),[13] together with his notion of the historical conditionality of philosophical ideas which supported Schlatter's suspicion of Kant's "pure reason."[14] Rudolf Eucken (1846–1926) introduced Schlatter to Aristotle, which clearly had an effect on Schlatter, who would later, in Aristotelian manner, emphasize the reality-based character of human perception and thought—in both his philosophical and his theological works.[15] Schlatter moved to Tübingen in 1873, where he hoped to gain further theological clarification from the systematician Johann Tobias Beck (1804–78).[16] Beck was certainly *the* formative figure of his years of study. "Every sentence

---

10. Neuer, *Adolf Schlatter*, 53. Schlatter himself emphasizes the existential importance of his decision to study theology in that he identifies it with his conversion. "To those, who ask me for the day of my conversion, I am inclined to answer that my decision to study theology was my conversion." Schlatter, *Rückblick*, 37; see also "Entstehung der Beiträge," 34.

11. Schlatter studied in Basel from spring 1871 until spring 1873, and then, after three semesters in Tübingen, again in the winter semester of 1874/5.

12. Schlatter attended Nietzsche's lectures on Platonic dialogue (1871/72) and remembers, "He treated his listeners like a despicable mob [*verächtlichen Pöbel*]." Schlatter, *Rückblick*, 42; see also "Entstehung der Beiträge," 38.

13. Schlatter, "Entstehung der Beiträge," 37.

14. "Through Steffenson, 'pure reason' died for me," writes Schlatter, "as it came to light through which historical processes it was generated." Schlatter, *Rückblick*, 39; "Entstehung der Beiträge," 35.

15. Neuer points to the Aristotelian influence in Schlatter's theology. Neuer, *Zusammenhang von Dogmatik und Ethik*, 128; see also Walldorf, *Realistische Philosophie*, 38, 55n18.

16. Schlatter studied in Tübingen from spring 1873 until autumn 1874.

I utter reminds me of him," remembers Schlatter: "he unlocked the New Testament for my life."[17] We will return to the significant influence of Beck's teaching on his student Schlatter at a later stage. Schlatter returned to Basel in 1874 and achieved in all theological exams the highest possible score (*sehr gut*). Although he found fulfilment in academic work, Schlatter felt the call for practical church service, which led him to his first post as a theological graduate in training for the ministry (*Vikariat*).

THEOLOGY AND CHURCH: THE PASTORATE (1875–80)

In the spring of 1875, Adolf Schlatter was ordained at the St. Laurenzen Church in St. Gallen, and for the following five years he worked in the ministry in Switzerland, first, for a few months, as a vicar in the parish of Kilchberg on Lake Zürich, then as an interim assistant to a liberal minister in Neumünster and finally, for three years, as minister in Kesswil on Lake Constance. In Neumünster, Schlatter was asked to balance the liberal teaching with positive theology to the satisfaction of the conservative part of the congregation. This was obviously not an easy task for the young pastor Schlatter. Later in life, he was continually exposed to the challenge of defending his own position among liberal colleagues in the university. During his diaconate, several churches approached him with the request to fill their vacancies and Schlatter was open to different confessional ministry options. Whilst he was even prepared to become a Free Church minister, he finally felt the strong urge to support the established national Reformed Church. Thus Schlatter agreed at the end of 1876 to respond to the call to the Church in Keßwil on Lake Constance (which included the congregations in the villages of Uttwil and Dozwil), at the request of his predecessor Paul Jung, father of the psychoanalyst Carl Gustav Jung (1875–1961).

Ahead of Schlatter lay three pleasant years in rural Switzerland, from January 1877 until April 1880, "filled richly with what is most delightful and spiritually enriching in the pastoral work."[18] Living as a bachelor in a large manse, he took the opportunity to court a young lady from Dozwil. Schlatter successfully proposed to Susanna Schoop (1856–1907) shortly after their first encounter, and they married on January 15, 1878. Susette, as Schlatter called his wife, was a faithful and loyal partner, bearing five children and following her husband through the ups and downs of German university life before her sudden and untimely death in 1907. Schlatter would never remarry. For the children in his congregations, Schlatter drafted a curricu-

17. Schlatter in Neuer, *Adolf Schlatter*, 72.
18. Schlatter, *Rückblick*, 68.

lum for the confirmation class that already revealed the structure of his later dogmatic opus.[19] At that time, however, Schlatter would have been far away from any thought of entering academia, were it not for friends who encouraged him to pursue an academic career and for the Bern pietist circles who tried to recruit him for a university post in Bern.[20] This was not an easy decision for Schlatter. "Giving up my pastorate," he explains, "was a serious sacrifice for me personally."[21] In the end, Schlatter decided in favor of Bern, under the conviction that the church called him to the post: "Indeed, here acted the church," he notes.[22] According to Schlatter, theology and church belonged together. Whether as pastor or as theology professor, he considered himself to work constantly in the service of the church.

CHRISTOLOGICAL DISPUTES IN BERN, GREIFSWALD AND BERLIN (1880-98)

Having arrived in Bern in May 1880, Schlatter was immediately confronted with the conflict between the positive pietists and the liberal faculty. Belonging to neither one of the two camps, Schlatter was isolated from the outset, with Old Testament scholar Samuel Oettli (1846–1911) as his only ally. "I had to rely therefore," writes Schlatter, "from the very beginnings of my work only on myself."[23] Mark Noll sheds some light on the reasons for Schlatter's isolated position:

> Schlatter was far too conservative in his approach to the New Testament, and to Christian theology in general, to win a reputation in the university world in which he labored so earnestly. Yet he was also far too scholarly in his approach to problems of theological method and far too willing to engage the leading

---

19. Schlatter did not use the Heidelberg Catechism in his class and drafted his own curriculum in order to contextualize the gospel, thus making it available in contemporary language and fashion. In a similar manner to his later *Dogma*, the material begins with God's revelation in creation, conscience and history, followed by anthropology, then Christology, soteriology, and ecclesiology. See Neuer, *Adolf Schlatter*, 126.

20. Schlatter's friends, for instance his student friend Adolf Bolliger (1854–1931), who became later theology professor in Basel, suggested he should take up academic research. Basel professor Hans Konrad von Orelli (1846–1912) asked Schlatter to contribute to the journal *Der Kirchenfreund*, and in 1879 Schlatter's first essay was published, tellingly on Christology—"Christologie der Bergpredigt" ("Christology of the Sermon on the Mount").

21. Schlatter, *Rückblick*, 72.

22. Ibid., 76; see also "Entstehung der Beiträge," 17.

23. Schlatter, *Rückblick*, 91; see also "Entstehung der Beiträge," 21.

thinkers of his day to make much of an impact on the popular pietism of the German-speaking world with which he shared so much.[24]

Looking back, Schlatter describes his experience as being caught in the crossfire of the two warring factions repeatedly as a "struggle for Jesus' sake" (*Kampf um Jesu willen*).[25] The personal challenge consisted in his aim to mediate[26] between the two positions in order to arrive at fellowship (*Gemeinschaft*).[27] This was obviously a very ambitious goal as the liberal camp labelled Schlatter a "biblicist without criticism" (*kritiklosen Biblizisten*), whereas the positive party referred to him as a "faithless critic" (*glaubenslosen Kritiker*).[28]

In order to receive permission to teach theology, Schlatter had to compose a doctoral dissertation and sit several exams.[29] Having completed the dissertation on John the Baptist, Schlatter complained that the Bern faculty still denied him the doctorate since they thought his "book did not have any scientific worth."[30] Moreover, to frustrate Schlatter's professorial aspirations, the faculty raised the bar for the exams to a level that would never again be applied. Yet Schlatter succeeded in all his *vivas* and written exams,

---

24. Noll, "Foreword," 7.

25. See Schlatter, *Rückblick*, 80–81, 92, 97, 99, 114, 140, and "Selbstdarstellungen," 149. Schlatter also describes his struggle as a "fight with a dual front," directed against a "restorative confessionalism" on the one hand and a "polemical 'science of religion'" on the other hand. Schlatter, *Rückblick*, 171; see also "Entstehung der Beiträge," 18; "Ein Wort zum Preise meines Amtes," 97–98; *Metaphysik*, 18.

26. This does not mean that Schlatter was a mediating theologian. The definition of mediating theology presented earlier does not suggest any overlap with his own viewpoints (we return to this issue in chapter 2).

27. Schlatter consistently held fast to his irenic approach. He expressed his optimism that unity was achievable, as the Scriptures—in that they contain Jesus' word, who calls all people to God—had the power to establish unity. See Schlatter, *Rückblick*, 82, and "Selbstdarstellungen," 157.

28. Schlatter, "Entstehung der Beiträge," 19. For Schlatter's rejection of the label "biblicist," as understood by many of his colleagues, see Schlatter, "Briefe über das Dogma," 56–58. See *Rückblick*, 124 for his own, positive definition of "Biblizismus."

29. Schlatter's dissertation on John the Baptist, penned in only one month, was thought to have been lost until it was rediscovered in 1952 and subsequently published by Wilhelm Michaelis as *Johannes der Täufer*.

30. Schlatter, "Entstehung der Beiträge," 61. Although the Bern Protestant faculty denied Schlatter the doctorate, Hermann Cremer later managed to convince the theological faculty at the University of Halle to award Schlatter the title. The *Doktortitel*, which Schlatter finally received in November 1888, was a formal requirement for Schlatter to take up his work as a professor in Greifswald. See Neuer, *Adolf Schlatter*, 250.

and finally, after a long waiting period, he received the *venia legendi* for New Testament and the history of dogmatics. In early 1881, Schlatter began lecturing as a private lecturer (*Privatdozent*), covering in his eight years in Bern an extensive range of topics, from Old and New Testament and church history to systematic theology and the history of philosophy. In his *Habilitationsvorlesung* in spring 1881, as well as in his dogmatic lectures, Schlatter delineates his concept of an empirical theology of facts that he would adhere to throughout his career.[31] The first and foremost task of the theologian is thus to perform the seeing-act (*Sehakt*), where one simply observes the New Testament documents with faithful objectivity. With his lectures and speeches, as well as his publications—especially the prize-winning "Faith in the New Testament" (*Der Glaube im Neuen Testament*)—Schlatter soon won a positive reputation among even his liberal-minded colleagues.[32]

The 1885 publication of "Faith in the New Testament" meant for Schlatter an academic breakthrough. He received calls to the faculties of Halle, Kiel, Greifswald, Basel, Heidelberg, Marburg, and Bonn.[33] In response, the Bern faculty in fact now tried to keep Schlatter, promoting him to associate professor for New Testament and systematic theology. Yet it was Lutheran theologian Hermann Cremer (1834–1903) who was finally able to head-hunt Schlatter. Cremer convinced him to join him in his work in the north of Germany, in Greifswald. Schlatter appreciated the uniformly positive theological faculty and looked forward to a lecture hall "that was incomparably larger and more efficient than the one Bern could offer."[34] In August 1888, Schlatter, together with his wife Susanna and their now two children, left Switzerland for good and moved to Greifswald.

After his inaugural lecture delivered in Latin on December 29, 1888, Schlatter began teaching New Testament and dogmatics in Greifswald. He offered daily consultation hours (*Sprechstunden*) for his students and invited them to his weekly open evenings at his home, as he had done previously in Bern.[35] He published an "Introduction to the Bible" (1889), and after a lengthy journey through Palestine, Schlatter summarized his findings in a monograph.[36] Schlatter again received calls from esteemed German universities, such as Heidelberg and Marburg, but he declined as he

31. See for example his "Wesen und Quellen der Gotteserkenntnis" (summer 1883).

32. The prize was awarded by the Hague Society for the Defence of Christianity (1883).

33. See Stupperich, "Adolf Schlatters Berufungen," 100–17.

34. Schlatter, *Rückblick*, 126; "Entstehung der Beiträge," 69.

35. Schlatter's work, *Aus meiner Sprechstunde* (1929), allows for a unique insight into the kind of discussions he had with his students in those consultation hours.

36. Schlatter, *Zur Topographie und Geschichte Palästinas* (1893).

was satisfied with the working environment at Greifswald and in particular with the fruitful collaboration with Cremer. Even so, his time in Greifswald would soon come to an end as Schlatter was caught up in the events of the so-called struggle over the Apostles' Creed, which shall be examined more closely in the following chapter. In short, in 1893, the Prussian ministry of culture established a new chair for systematic theology at the University of Berlin in order to counterbalance the influence of Adolf von Harnack (1851–1930), and the call was finally issued to Schlatter, who made sure that he would be entitled to teach not only dogmatics, but also New Testament theology, as he considered the two subjects as intricately connected. In August 1893, Schlatter delivered his last lecture in Greifswald, and a month later, he moved with his wife and by then five children to Berlin, where he would teach for the next five years.

In Berlin, Schlatter lectured alongside influential colleagues such as Julius Kaftan (1846–1926), Otto Pfleiderer (1839–1908), and Bernhard Weiss (1827–1918); he taught Christian ethics, the "history of Jesus" and New Testament theology. Alongside his teaching activity, Schlatter was engaged in ecclesial, evangelistic and missionary work. He joined a Christian homegroup (*Bibelkränzchen*), held regular bible studies in the Berlin YMCA, and became one of the directors of the East-Africa Mission. His friendship with Friedrich von Bodelschwingh (1831–1910) resulted in the establishment of the biannual Bethel Theological Week (*Betheler Theologische Woche*). While in Berlin, Schlatter developed a closer relationship with Harnack and the two scholars engaged in regular debates on Christology. In autumn 1897, Schlatter was offered the newly established chair for New Testament theology in Tübingen. Looking forward to more suitable conditions for doing theology, Schlatter accepted the call, while again ensuring that he would also be entitled to lecture in systematic theology.

AN IMPETUS TOWARDS THE WHOLE: TÜBINGEN (1898–1938)

During his first few years in Tübingen, Schlatter had difficulty in warming to his faculty colleagues and students. The friendship with Tübingen systematician Theodor Haering (1848–1928) that he wished to establish was not gaining momentum, which could perhaps be attributed to their difference in character and to theological controversy, as Schlatter was critical of Haering's mediating approach.[37] However, Schlatter developed a closer relationship with church historian Karl Holl (1866–1926) whom he knew from his

37. See Neuer, *Adolf Schlatter*, 377.

time in Berlin.[38] Considering Schlatter's biography, such as his exchange with Harnack in Berlin, for instance, it seems safe to say that Schlatter particularly enjoyed fellowship with scholars of opposing views, as he there had the opportunity for stimulating exchange and creative interaction, which suited his rather lively temperament.[39] To Schlatter's astonishment, the Swabian students welcomed him only with reserve, labelling Schlatter as too orthodox and unscientific.[40] To a great extent, such stereotypes grew out of the *Stiftsstudenten*'s exposure to liberal teaching in Tübingen, as Schlatter student Paul Althaus remarks.[41] Many of Schlatter's fellow lecturers were strongly influenced by Ferdinand Chr. Baur (1792–1860) and advocates of the Ritschl-school.[42] Schlatter's empirical-realist method of "seeing what is there" differed considerably from his colleagues' approaches. In his lecture series, "The Philosophical Work since Descartes" (*Die Philosophische Arbeit seit Cartesius*), Schlatter critiqued the influence of German idealism on theology.[43] The lectures, which were also later published, laid out the epistemological basis for his empirical-realist approach, highlighting that "every true theologian is an observer."[44]

In due course, Schlatter's lectures were described as "events,"[45] not least as he lectured without manuscript and apparently knew the whole Greek New Testament by heart.[46] Thus, the former skepticism gave way to a growing appreciation among the Württemberg students.[47] Several of Schlatter's students would later rise to prominence: Rudolf Bultmann, Paul Althaus, Paul Tillich, Erich Seeberg, Karl Barth, Ernst Käsemann, Otto Michel, Karl-

---

38. Holl, who described himself as a liberal pietist, taught in Tübingen from 1900 until 1906. The two theologians enjoyed a deep personal friendship (Schlatter baptized Holl's daughter Elly and became her godfather) and theologically fruitful relationship that was continued in a letter exchange after Holl's move to Berlin in 1906. See Neuer, *Adolf Schlatter*, 380–83 and Stupperich, "Briefe Karl Holls an Adolf Schlatter," 169–240.

39. Schlatter was not only spirited but oftentimes quite brusque in theological discussions. "Dear colleague, this is crap [*Blech*]!" was apparently one of Schlatter's favorite expressions. Neuer, *Adolf Schlatter*, 378.

40. See ibid., 385–91.

41. Althaus, "Adolf Schlatters Wort an die heutige Theologie," 96–97.

42. As, for instance, the already mentioned Karl Holl and Karl Müller (church historian in Tübingen from 1903 to 1922).

43. Winter semester of 1905/6 lectures (and again 1908), "Die Philosophische Arbeit seit Cartesius. Ihr ethischer und religiöser Ertrag."

44. Schlatter, *Philosophische Arbeit*, 27.

45. Neuer, *Adolf Schlatter*, 602.

46. Ibid., 603.

47. See for example Paul Althaus's reminiscences in "Adolf Schlatters Wort an die heutige Theologie," 95.

Heinrich Rengstorf, Gustav Stählin, and Dietrich Bonhoeffer, to name but a few. During his first Tübingen decade, Schlatter lectured in New Testament and systematic theology, and he regularly gave speeches, many of them with a clear christological focus.[48] His literary output covered New Testament studies, Bible commentaries,[49] and christological monographs.[50] However, Schlatter's activities in Tübingen were not limited to the academy. Theology and church were in his view inseparable. Schlatter was thus involved in the Württemberg Church, as well as in various church-related groups and activities. He regularly preached from the pulpit at the Tübingen Stiftskirche,[51] and in 1912 he was elected a member of the Württemberg Synod. Schlatter organized and participated in various Christian meetings and gatherings, and in theological conferences and societies. He supported the "Tübingen German Christian Student Union" (*Deutsche Christliche Studentenvereinigung*, DCSV) and he was involved in the "Jünglingsverein," later called CVJM (*YMCA*), which he presided over from 1912 until handing the chair over to his son Theodor seven years later.

The sudden death of his wife on July 9, 1907 marked a turning point in Schlatter's life. Left with five children, Schlatter was supported by his two eldest daughters, Hedwig (1887–1946) and Dora (1890–1969).[52] Now a widower, Schlatter devoted the remaining thirty years of his life to the completion of his theological life's work and to further ecclesiastical engagement. Between 1908 and 1914, Schlatter published a broad range of exegetical and Judaistic studies,[53] while also summarizing his previous theological

---

48. "Christi Versöhnen und Christi Vergeben" (1898), "Die Gottheit Christi" (1902), and "Die Messianität Jesu in ihrer Geschichtlichkeit und Bedeutung" (1907).

49. After twenty-five years of work he completed in 1910 the thirteen volumes of "Annotations to the New Testament" (*Erläuterungen zum Neuen Testament*), covering virtually every book of the New Testament.

50. Such as "Jesu Gottheit und das Kreuz" (1901), which is particularly relevant for our analysis of Schlatter's theology of the cross in chapters 4 and 5.

51. On Schlatter as preacher see Wurster, *Aus Schrift und Geschichte*, 207–19.

52. Schlatter's three other children were his daughter Ruth (1893–1962) and his sons Paul (1888–1914) and Theodor (1885–1971). Theodor Schlatter followed in his father's footsteps, becoming a professor at the Bethel Theological School, then dean at Esslingen and later prelate in Ludwigsburg. Over eight hundred letters between Schlatter and his son Theodor bear witness to an intimate relationship.

53. Schlatter points out that a clear understanding of Pharisaical and rabbinnical Judaism is the prerequisite to an adequate New Testament interpretation. See Schlatter, "Selbstdarstellungen," 16–21. His ground-breaking studies in Palestinian Judaism made him a pioneer in this area. Schlatter was "an historian who laid a firm foundation for the study of the background of New Testament literature by acquiring a first-hand knowledge of contemporary Jewish life and thought," remarks Levertoff, in "Translator's Note," xii. See also Stuhlmacher's comments in "Zum Neudruck von Schlatters *Glaube*

drafts in four major works which reflect the broad range of his teaching activities. He arranged his New Testament studies in two volumes, namely, "The Word of Jesus" (*Das Wort Jesu*, 1909), and "The Teaching of the Apostles" (*Die Lehre der Apostel*, 1910). His systematic program was published in 1911 as "The Christian Dogma" (*Das christliche Dogma*), followed a few years later by an ethic (*Die christliche Ethik*, 1914).[54] Schlatter later renamed the second revised edition of his "Word of Jesus" as *The History of the Christ* (*Die Geschichte des Christus*, 1920), thereby emphasizing the concrete historical setting of Jesus' being in action. In his *Dogma* he unfolds his theology of facts in more detail, insisting that theological assertions have to be rooted in observable reality. Still, the facts are not only observed in the seeing-act (*Sehakt*) and analyzed in the thinking-act (*Denkakt*) but they must also be assimilated, passing into the ownership of the individual's life-act (*Lebensakt*). Schlatter thereby underlined that that exegesis and dogmatics are inseparably connected with ethics. It was therefore only natural of Schlatter to publish, shortly after his New Testament works and his dogmatics, a Christian ethics. In the second part of this work we shall deal with the three acts, seeing-act, thinking-act, and life-act, in more detail, in particular as they provide a useful framework for our exploration of Schlatter's overall christological program.

The First World War marked a deep incision in Schlatter's life. Only a few years after his wife's death, Schlatter had to suffer another heart-rending loss. In September 1914, Schlatter's youngest son Paul, then a promising academic historian, was hit by a shell splinter on the battlefield and subsequently died of his injuries in a German hospital. The years after his son's death proved to be a period of despondency and depression for Schlatter. The pace of his written output slowed down. Still, in 1915, Schlatter penned his most abstract work, "Metaphysics" (*Metaphysik*), with the intention of explaining his empirical philosophy as an alternative to Kantian speculative reason.[55] Perhaps still due to his despondency, however, Schlatter was not satisfied with the finished product and decided against its publication; only several decades later, in 1987, would his *Metaphysik* become available to the public. It is worth mentioning that in spite of the war and his tragic

---

im Neuen Testament," x. Leonhard Goppelt claims to be strongly influenced by Schlatter in this respect, praising his "immense and superior history of religion/philological investigation of the New Testament." Goppelt, *Theology of the New Testament*, 1:278.

54. Both works are unfortunately still untranslated. Translations of his dogmatic opus into English are desirable in order to establish Schlatter's importance as a systematic theologian in the English-speaking sphere as well.

55. For a concise discussion of Schlatter's work, see Walldorf, "Aspekte einer realistischen Philosophie," 74–85.

personal losses, Schlatter did not feel compelled to modify his theology.[56] Thus, theologically, his post-1914 writings do not differ substantially from his pre-War writings.[57]

With the end of the First World War Schlatter regained new strength, and the period between 1918 and 1930 marks the high point of his career as a university professor when he lectured up to sixteen hours a week in a lecture hall filled with up to six hundred students, while also publishing over a hundred works. In the summer semester of 1922, Schlatter delivered for the last time a dogmatic lecture, as systematician Karl Heim (1874–1958) was called to the Tübingen faculty. In August of the same year, Schlatter retired officially from his teaching activity at the age of seventy; however, he decided to continue lecturing in New Testament for fifteen more semesters, until 1930, as he was suspicious of his successor, the Bonn exegete Wilhelm Heitmüller (1869–1926), a representative of the history of religion school.

In the last decade of his teaching activity, Schlatter mainly lectured in New Testament theology while also publishing revised editions of his New Testament Theology (1920 and 1922), his *Dogma* (1923), and *Ethik* (1924 and 1929), together with several essays, bible studies, sermons and autobiographical works. With the rise of dialectical theology in the 1920s, Schlatter was particularly interested in his former student and son of his successor in Bern, Karl Barth (1886–1968). Schlatter's fascinating theological interaction with Barth, in particular with a view to Christology, is in the focus of our considerations in the following chapter. Schlatter's last decade, with an output of almost ninety publications between 1929 and 1937, can surely be regarded as active retirement. As major projects, Schlatter pursued several scientific commentaries on the New Testament, such as on Matthew,[58]

---

56. Except for revising the chapter on war in his ethics in a subsequent edition; without becoming a pacifist, he had now a stricter view on war, arguing that it should only be viewed as the *ultima ratio* of politics, rather than one of its ordinary means.

57. Robert Yarbrough observes that "the Schlatter corpus documents a theological development that grew in breadth, depth, nuance and grounding. There are no radical shifts or new directions." Yarbrough, "Adolf Schlatter," 506. Wilhelm Michaelis notes that the 1880 dissertation of the "young Schlatter" was already a "true Schlatter." Michaelis, "Nachwort des Herausgebers," 168.

58. Schlatter, *Der Evangelist Matthäus*.

John,[59] Luke,[60] James,[61] the Corinthian Letters,[62] Mark,[63] Romans,[64] the Pastoral Epistles,[65] and First Peter.[66] Schlatter also published his translation of the New Testament (1931),[67] although it did not satisfy him entirely as he still thought Luther's translation was better.[68] While Schlatter worked on his New Testament commentaries, the political situation in Germany changed for the worse. The rise of National Socialism culminated in Hitler's rise to power in 1933 and concerned Schlatter deeply. He opposed the Nazis' racist ideology, criticized the "German Christians" (*Deutsche Christen*) and was highly suspicious of the leadership cult around Hitler that was slowly but steadily gaining ground in Germany.[69] At an early stage he raised his concerns publicly as a speaker and writer, and was later personally involved in the Württemberg church struggle (*Kirchenkampf*), during which he published several statements opting for a clear independence of the church from the state.[70] As the church struggle grew more intense, he had to witness his son Theodor's displacement as dean of Esslingen and could not prevent the repeated house arrests of his friend and fellow countryman, the bishop Theophil Wurm (1868–1953). One must certainly lament that Schlatter did not as emphatically reject the Aryan Paragraph as the Confessing Church for instance. Nonetheless, this does not immediately make Schlatter an anti-Semite, as some scholars suggest.[71]

Do We Know Jesus? (*Kennen wir Jesus?*). That was Schlatter's challenging question in 1937 to the National Socialists and the German population in his last publication.[72] Knowing Jesus, what he wants and does, was accord-

59. Schlatter, *Der Evangelist Johannes*.
60. Schlatter, *Das Evangelium nach Lukas*.
61. Schlatter, *Der Brief des Jakobus*.
62. Schlatter, *Paulus, der Bote Jesu*.
63. Schlatter, *Markus, Der Evangelist für die Griechen*.
64. Schlatter, *Gottes Gerechtigkeit*.
65. Schlatter, *Die Kirche der Griechen im Urteil des Paulus*.
66. Schlatter, *Petrus und Paulus*.
67. Schlatter, *Das Neue Testament, übersetzt*.
68. See Neuer, *Adolf Schlatter*, 694.
69. See Schlatter's essay, "Die neue deutsche Art in der Kirche."

70. Schlatter, "Das Evangelium und das Bekenntnis," 21–31; "Grenzen der kirchlichen Gemeinschaft," 3–20; see also Neuer, *Adolf Schlatter*, 725–45.

71. This view is in particular propagated by McNutt in his various essays, "A Very Damning Truth," 280–301; "Vessels of Wrath, Prepared to Perish," 176–90; "Adolf Schlatter and the Jews," 353–70. For a more balanced account see Neuer, *Adolf Schlatter*, 725–80, and Gerdmar, *Roots of Theological Anti-Semitism*, 253–326.

72. Schlatter, *Kennen wir Jesus?* Recently made available in English as *Do We Know*

ing to Schlatter the only answer to the precarious anti-Christian atmosphere in Germany at that time. In his final months, at the beginning of 1938, he worked on a second edition of *Kennen wir Jesus*, thereby dedicating his remaining strength to the task that was most important to him: to portray the words and works of Jesus Christ. On May 18, 1938, eighty-five-year-old Schlatter died peacefully in his home in Tübingen. Friedrich von Bodelschwingh Jr. (1877–1946) remarked in his speech at the funeral, "For me personally and for many of my co-workers he became a leader to Christ."[73]

CONCLUSION

Who then was Adolf Schlatter? How can one best characterize his life and theology in a nutshell? This short biographical-theological sketch reveals that Schlatter escapes any spontaneous attempts at theological labelling. Nonetheless, looking at Schlatter's life and work, two characteristics seem to stand out: Schlatter was an *irenic theologian* with a clear *Christocentric perspective*. Schlatter was an irenic theologian. What makes it difficult to locate Schlatter on the theological map of his time is his eclectic and at the same time irenic and holistic approach.[74] Somehow, Schlatter stood between idealism and the revival movement, between the Ritschl school and orthodox confessionalism. Although born and raised in the Reformed tradition, Schlatter remained confessionally open, showing no reserve towards representatives of any theological *couleur*. He also rejected the increasing specialization and prevalent mentality of departmentalization in the academy. Eager to unite the oftentimes estranged departments, Schlatter, as New Testament scholar, systematic theologian, lecturer in Old Testament, church history and philosophy, demonstrated in his own life how cross-theological work could look like. His theology was distinctly designed to be a "comprehensive theology,"[75] and in the end, life itself, argues Schlatter, has to be envisaged as an organic whole.

Where others saw disunity and dualisms, Schlatter perceived unity and harmony between faith and reason, nature and grace, church and academy, God and humanity. In one of his autobiographical memories, Schlatter points out that he was always both scholar *and* believer, church member *and* member in the academy, pupil *and* teacher, part of the state *and* part of

---

Jesus?

73. Neuer, *Adolf Schlatter*, 820.

74. Schlatter, *Rückblick*, 197; "Selbstdarstellungen," 157.

75. Schlatter to Cremer, 25 November 1901, in Stupperich, *Wort und Wahrnehmung*, 93.

nature.[76] As parish minister, university professor, speaker, author, and social activist, Schlatter, with his life, his diverse interests and activities, sets an example of theological *and* cultural engagement, combining theory *and* practice, always with the perspective of the whole of human experience. Furthermore, Schlatter was a Christocentric theologian. Taking into account Schlatter's biography, one easily detects the clear christological leitmotif that pervades his life and work. Both his first and his last publications focused on Jesus Christ, the divine-human person in action who offers an existential union (what Schlatter calls *Anschluss*) with him. Unlike many of his contemporaries, Schlatter saw no rift between the historical Jesus and a Christ of faith. For Schlatter, the two are one as Jesus' person and work displays one harmonious unit. The unified Jesus Christ is the one who also brings about unity by uniting human beings with God and with each other in the new community of faith. In Schlatter's view, Jesus Christ performs his unifying work against the backdrop of concrete *history*, with a determined *volition*, and always in *relation* with his heavenly Father (through the Holy Spirit) and with us.

These three terms, *history*, *volition*, and *relation*, are key to an adequate understanding of Schlatter's Christology and they will appear consistently throughout this work. Given then the prominence of the christological motif in Schlatter's life and work, its neglect in Schlatter studies is surprising. It leaves a serious gap in Schlatter scholarship insofar as Schlatter's methodology and philosophy serve exactly the purpose of observing and understanding the being and action of Jesus Christ. We shall now, as a first step, turn to the genesis and the context of Schlatter's Christology, tracing important factors that influenced Schlatter and shaped his christological thinking.

---

76. See the chapter headings in Schlatter, *Erlebtes*, 7–8.

2

Where was Adolf Schlatter?

THUS FAR WE HAVE answered the question, *Who* was Adolf Schlatter, by providing a brief overview of his life and theology. In this chapter, we will now direct our attention to the question, *Where* was Adolf Schlatter? The goal is to trace the genesis and development of Schlatter's Christology within the intellectual and theological context of his day and age. Hence, questions such as these demand answers: Who were Schlatter's theological allies? With whom did he interact? Whose christological positions did he share (and why)? With whom could he not agree (and why)? This foundational, and thus rather extensive, chapter seeks to portray Schlatter in interaction with significant representatives of diverse movements in order to identify the stimuli which contributed to his own Christology. As one might expect from what has been outlined in the previous biographical section, Schlatter's position is unique and certainly not easy to pin down. He was neither a convinced idealist nor a fervent pietist, and he was neither a Ritschlian nor a biblicist. Rather, Schlatter was somewhat "in between," as we shall discover in more detail in the following three sections. In delineating the development of his Christology, we will proceed chronologically, first looking at Schlatter "Between Idealism and the Revival Movement," secondly tracing his position "Between Ritschlianism and Confessionalism," and thirdly focusing on his interaction with Karl Barth in "Schlatter *Zwischen den Zeiten*." This historical-theological overture sets the scene for our dogmatic reflections in part two. With this outline in mind, we now turn to our first point.

BETWEEN IDEALISM AND REVIVAL MOVEMENT

Adolf Schlatter was born right in the middle of the nineteenth century, and in many ways these were exciting times, both historically, with revolutions in Europe and the rise of nationalist imperialist states, and also with a view to the intellectual *Zeitgeist*, when one thinks of the flourishing of German idealism,[1] romanticism or Marxism, for example. Theology, of course, was not excluded from these developments. David Fergusson is certainly right when he calls the nineteenth century the "most diverse and creative period in the history of Christian theology."[2] Now what was it that made this period so diverse and creative as Fergusson suggests? Before focusing in more detail on Schlatter, it is fitting to answer first this important question as it allows us to understand the rich intellectual context of his time.

Some historians consider the nineteenth century to have been an era where increasing secularization and scientific progress led to a collapse of religious belief in Western Europe. Jürgen Osterhammel describes this period as a time of de-Christianization in Europe,[3] and Owen Chadwick points to the "secularisation of the European mind."[4] On the one hand, it is certainly true that the nineteenth century witnessed a general attack on religion. Earlier Enlightenment and idealist critical thought had contributed to an erosion of belief in the supernatural, thereby fuelling a general anti-religious mind-set, which was susceptible to Ludwig Feuerbach's (1804–72) reduction of religion to anthropology, and Karl Marx's (1818–83) denunciation of religion as the "opiate of the people." Accordingly, Hugh McLeod observes a significant devaluation of personal faith and a decrease in attendance in religious practices and events in nineteenth century Germany.[5] This, however, is only one part of the whole picture. For, on the other hand, one must not overlook a certain resurgence of religion in the nineteenth century. As a

---

1. When referring to idealism in this work, we always mean philosophical idealism (in contrast to the notion of idealism where one intends to pursue certain ideals in one's life), and in particular German idealism. It is difficult to offer a succinct definition for the term, as its interpretation differs slightly depending on whether one talks about Kant's transcendental idealism or Fichte's, Schelling's or Hegel's transformation of Kant's thoughts into absolute idealism. It is for this reason that we refer to individual philosophers and their particular concepts in this study. For an introduction to German idealism see Ameriks, "Introduction," 1–17.

2. Fergusson, "Preface," xi.

3. Osterhammel, *Die Verwandlung der Welt*, 1248.

4. Chadwick, *Secularisation of the European Mind*.

5. McLeod notes that the intellectual bourgeoisie (influenced by Darwinism) in particular showed an increase of hostility towards those who took their Christian faith seriously. McLeod, *Secularisation in Western Europe*, 182.

matter of fact, "the nineteenth century," Christopher A. Bayly contends, "saw the triumphal reemergence and expansion of 'religion.'"[6] Indeed, religion, as an antithesis to Enlightenment rationalism, was very much in the focus of this era. The nineteenth century saw a significant increase in missionary activities,[7] and in revivals (*Erweckungen*) in the continental Protestant[8] and Catholic churches.[9] Records also show a new growth of evangelicalism in Great Britain, which influenced to a great extent the French-speaking Protestants in Switzerland, leading to an awakening (*Réveil*) in Geneva.[10] This was then a time of severe cultural discrepancy: a critical, even antireligious mindset leading to a decline of religious observance and tradition on the one hand and powerful religious awakenings on the other hand. This was the air the young Schlatter breathed, and his Christology grew out of his exposure to the two main opposing movements in the nineteenth century, namely modern idealist critical thought and the revival movement (*Erweckungsbewegung*).[11] Church historian Kurt Dietrich Schmidt calls this the "primordial dichotomy" (*Urzwiespalt*) of the nineteenth century.[12] "Idealism and the revival movement," notes Schlatter, "were in the first part of the nineteenth century the most powerful and fruitful processes that gave us Germans our history."[13] In spite of their inherent differences, the con-

---

6. Bayly, *Birth of the Modern World*, 325.

7. The nineteenth century has thus rightly been called the century of missions. Shortly before the turn of the century, Protestant missionary societies were established in England (London, 1795), Scotland (1796), and the Netherlands (1797), reaching the apex of their impact in the nineteenth century. In Germany and Switzerland, still influenced by the missionary activities of the *Herrnhut Brüdergemeinde* under Count Zinzendorf (from 1732 onwards), missionary societies were founded in Berlin (1800) and Basel (1816, *Basler Missionsgesellschaft*). See Renkewitz, "Erneuerte Brüderunität," 1439–43. For a short overview from a historical perspective see Osterhammel, *Die Verwandlung der Welt*, 1261–8, and from a theological perspective, see Wellenreuther, "Pietismus und Mission," 166–93.

8. See Benrath, "Die Erweckung innerhalb der deutschen Landeskirchen," 150–271; cf. Kupisch, *Die Deutschen Landeskirchen*, 49–97. One also thinks of the related Protestant revival in North America, the *Second Great Awakening* (1785–1810). In this revival, one of Schlatter's ancestors, Michael Schlatter (1718–90), was instrumental in that he propagated the new pietism among the German immigrants. See Noll, "Evangelikalismus und Fundamentalismus," 474–80.

9. Weigelt, "Die Allgäuer katholische Erweckungsbewegung," 87–111.

10. Scottish Congregationalist Robert Haldane's (1764–1842) visit to Geneva in 1816 had a significant impact on the *Réveil*. Gäbler, "Evangelikalismus und Réveil," 43, 51–2.

11. For a brief overview of the revival movement in nineteenth-century Europe, see Beyreuther, "Erweckung," 621–9, and Schmidt in his *Kirchengeschichte*, 459–69.

12. Schmidt, *Kirchengeschichte*, 470.

13. Schlatter, "Idealismus und Erweckung," 1. This quote alludes to Schlatter's

tours of the two movements were not clear-cut; the careful observer will note significant overlaps. Many pietists, for example, held Enlightenment views, and many idealists had pietist roots and affinities.[14] Ulrich Gäbler thus points out that the "discontinuity between Enlightenment and Revival [movement] was less deep than the revivalists pretended and as research supposed until recently."[15] Likewise, Hartmut Lehman maintains that "[the] pious [people] who engaged in the works of the new pietism were . . . paradoxical as it might seem at first glance, as much as their opponents, 'children of the Enlightenment.'"[16]

This applies to Adolf Schlatter as well. He was certainly a child of his own time, and in what follows, we will explore the implications of this important synergy of idealism and *Erweckung* on Schlatter's theological development in more detail. As noted earlier, we shall do so from Schlatter's own perspective, which means that we will refer constantly to his own autobiographical accounts, where he explains how his theological thinking emerged out of the friction between his pietist background and his subsequent exposure to idealist teaching in school and at university. Proceeding chronologically, we will first take a closer look at the contrast of Schlatter's pietist background and the idealist philosophical-theological mind-set to which he was exposed at school and at university. In a second step, we shall trace how this tension culminated in a serious existential crisis for the young theology student. Influential figures such as Johann T. Beck and Franz von Baader contributed to a consolidation of his theology, as shall be discussed in the third section. Taking then this whole range of experiences and influences into account, we will, fourthly and finally, be in the position to carve out the characteristic Schlatterian response to idealist Christologies.

Early Antagonisms: Idealism vs. *Erweckung*

Adolf Schlatter was deeply rooted in the theological and spiritual background of his family and its circle of friends from the Swiss revival movement.

---

strong identification with the German people. Hence, in his memorial address, Gerhard Kittel calls Schlatter "the Swiss man, who was completely German! [*der Schweizer, der ganz Deutscher war!*]" Kittel, "Adolf Schlatter: Gedenkrede," 16.

14. Pietist Friedrich Christoph Oetinger (1702–82), a representative of Württemberg pietism, shows affinities with speculative, idealist philosophy (see in particular his *Theosophische Werke*, 6 vols., 1858–63). Idealist poet and thinker, Gotthold Ephraim Lessing (1729–81), on the other hand, grew up in an orthodox Lutheran home (his father was a clergyman), not far away from the pietist Herrnhut community.

15. Gäbler, *Auferstehungszeit*, 165.

16. Lehmann, "Die neue Lage," 8.

Schlatter's hometown, St. Gallen, was along with Zürich and Bern one of the main centers in Switzerland where pietist ideas had already gained a foothold at an early stage.[17] While the French-speaking cantons in Switzerland were touched by the Genevan *Réveil*,[18] the German-speaking regions, such as St. Gallen, were mainly under the influence of the German Society of Christianity (*Deutsche Christentumsgesellschaft*), which was founded in 1780 in Basel.[19] The *Christentumsgesellschaft* had a substantial impact on the Swiss revival as it gave rise to the establishment of the Basel Bible Society (1804)[20] and the Basel Missionary Society (1815), as well as the creation of several charitable institutions.[21] Adolf Schlatter's family history is deeply interwoven with the Swiss revival movement. Schlatter's grandmother Anna, née Bernet (1773–1826), was a key figure in the movement at the turn of the century. "[O]ne of the most noble representatives of the new pietism,"[22] she stood in close connection with several heads of the Swiss and German revival movement, not only with those of the Protestant persuasion, like Johann Kaspar Lavater (1741–1801),[23] but also with Roman Catholics, like Martin Boos (1762–1825), main partisan of the Allgäu Catholic revival movement in south Germany.[24] Anna Schlatter enjoyed a lively exchange of letters with both of them,[25] and welcomed to Adolf Schlatter's later house

---

17. Heike Bock argues this in her review of *Der frühe Zürcher Pietismus (1689–1721)*, by Kaspar Bütikofer. Schmidt simply defines the revival movement as the awakening of a renewed pietism. "Pietismus," 378.

18. Gäbler, "Evangelikalismus und Réveil," 43, 51–52.

19. This took place through the initiative of the Augsburg minister Johann August Urlsperger (1728–1806). The *Deutsche Christentumsgesellschaft* aimed to thwart rationalist Enlightenment ideas by affirming traditional orthodox Protestant doctrines. From its Basel headquarter the movement grew to an international network of like-minded circles and personalities. See Staehelin, *Christentumsgesellschaft*, 3–13; cf. Beyreuther, "Christentumsgesellschaft," 1729–30; and Weigelt, "Die Diasporaarbeit der Herrnhuter Brüdergemeine," 113–49.

20. Around that time, several other bible societies were established in Switzerland, such as those in Bern (1805), Schaffhausen (1809) and Zürich (1812).

21. Such as the formation of the Beuggen Institution for the Education of Schoolteachers for the Poor (*Armen-Schullehrer-Anstalt*, 1820), the Beuggen Social Welfare Institutes (*Diakonischen Anstalten Beuggen*, 1820), and the Deaf-Mute Foundation in Riehen (*Taubstummenanstalt Riehen*, 1838). Staehelin, *Christentumsgesellschaft*, vii; cf. Gäbler, "Erweckungsbewegungen," 1081–88; and Pfister, *Kirchengeschichte der Schweiz*, 171–259. On the connection between the revival movement and social-charitable action see Kuhn, *Religion und neuzeitliche Gesellschaft*, 14–41.

22. Hadorn, *Geschichte des Pietismus*, 401.

23. Neuer, *Adolf Schlatter*, 5.

24. See Jehle-Wildberger, *Anna Schlatter-Bernet*, 87–104.

25. Neuer, *Adolf Schlatter*, 8. See also Zahn, *Anna Schlatters*, lxii–lxxiii.

of birth well-known figures of the revival movement.[26] She had also no reservations in enjoying fellowship with rather revolutionary theologians, such as Friedrich D. E. Schleiermacher (1768–1834) and Wilhelm M. L. de Wette (1780–1849), for instance, who were also both among her guests.[27] "Through her Christocentric and bible-oriented piety," observes Schlatter biographer Werner Neuer, "Anna Schlatter knew herself to be joined with all Christians who tried to bring their lives into line with the living Christ and the Scriptures—a trait that would later also characterize her grandson Adolf Schlatter."[28] Though Schlatter never met his grandmother personally, the theological parallels between grandmother and grandson—particularly in terms of Christocentricity and ecumenical openness—are indeed striking and can be attributed to the continuation of her legacy in the Schlatter household.

The revival movement continued to leave its mark on the Schlatter family in the next generation. As Adolf Schlatter recalls, his mother Susanna represented the Protestant Reformed type and his father Stephan the pietist revival type.[29] The harmonious combination of Reformed theology and pietistic piety in his parents left a deep impression on the young Schlatter. "The revival," he notes, "has moved my adolescence much more effectively and fruitfully than idealism."[30] Schlatter describes his parents' influence as such:

> Our parents brought us up in such a way that they shared with us their whole possession [*Besitz*] and experience . . . [I] saw from the very beginning what a life lived before God looks like. The power with which we were as children embraced by the faith of our parents was the prerequisite and the root from which my own story grew.[31]

26. These included Karl F. A. Steinkopf (1773–1859), then secretary of the *Christentumsgesellschaft*, Christian H. Zeller (1779–1860), the inspector of the *Armenkinderanstalt Beuggen*, Aloys Henhöfer (1789–1862), leader of the Baden revival, and Gottfried Daniel Krummacher (1774–1837), leader of the Lower Rhine Revival (*niederrheinische Erweckungsbewegung*). See Neuer, *Adolf Schlatter*, 5.

27. Ibid.

28. Ibid., 7.

29. See Schlatter, "Entstehung der Beiträge," 23; cf. *Rückblick*, 12. Schlatter himself notes that his mother's influence upon him, particularly in ecclesial aspects, was greater than his father's, which is also reflected in his extensive letter exchange with his mother. See Neuer, *Adolf Schlatter*, 30. On the other hand, Schlatter highlights that he followed his father in spiritual and theological matters. Neuer, "Idealismus und die Erweckung in Schlatters Jugend," 70.

30. Schlatter, "Idealismus und Erweckung," 24.

31. Schlatter, *Rückblick*, 12.

Looking back, Schlatter is grateful that he never felt the "overbearing attitude of ecclesial dogma" in his parental home, and that he "did not belong to those who were tantalized in their youth by orthodoxy."[32] From the very beginning Schlatter thus learned that theology was not a dry discipline but that it influenced every aspect of life, and that dogmatics and ethics were inseparably connected, an important insight he would expand on in his later career. Schlatter's father Stephan, who as a young boy was instructed at an institution of the Brethren movement,[33] had helped to build a home for children from troubled family backgrounds,[34] and was one of the seven founding members of the first Free Evangelical Church in St. Gallen (1837).[35] Schlatter's uncle, his father's brother-in-law Daniel Schlatter (1791–1870), travelled as a missionary to the Muslim Tatars in the Crimea and became known as the Tatarenschlatter. Appreciative of his uncle's missionary activity, Schlatter refers to his uncle as a "man of the will," in contrast to the rather passive idealists.[36] This notion of the "will" is important as it points to Schlatter's later theological-volitional emphasis, one of the key characteristics of his theology and, especially, Christology as we shall discover in due course. The young Schlatter then was clearly impressed with the kind of lived ethics he observed in both his father and his uncle. From an early age, Schlatter was affected by the key features of the revival, namely the combination of heart and hand, faith and works.

In school, as highlighted earlier, Schlatter met the revival's antagonist. In the classroom, he remembers, he had to cope with a different, rather anti-Christian and anti-pious atmosphere.[37] During his time in secondary school, Schlatter was introduced to German Enlightenment and idealist thought. His philosophy teacher, the Hegelian Johann Jakob Alder (1813–82), tried to warm Schlatter to Hegelian thought, yet Schlatter was reluctant to adopt Hegel's abstract philosophical system and rather preferred the speculative character and the moral emphasis of Kantianism.[38] While Schlatter clearly appreciated the selfless and determined "moral power of Kantianism" with

32. Ibid., 13.

33. The *Knabenanstalt der Königsberger Brüdergemeinde*.

34. In 1840, Schlatter's father, together with his cousin Ambrosius Schlatter, set up the *Rettungsanstalt* in St. Gallen, which looked after neglected children. Schlatter, "Idealismus und Erweckung," 31–32.

35. See Schlatter, *Rückblick*, 23. Schlatter's father left the Reformed Church due to what he considered a damaging influx of theological liberalism in the Reformed Landeskirche. See Neuer, *Adolf Schlatter*, 7, 13–14, 32.

36. Schlatter, "Idealismus und Erweckung," 26.

37. Schlatter, *Rückblick*, 34.

38. See Neuer, *Adolf Schlatter*, 41–42.

its focus on the performance of the moral duty,[39] he was convinced that Kant had built his philosophical house on sand, as we shall discuss below. Alder, as a former minister, also taught religious education, which meant that Schlatter came in contact with the kind of liberal Reformed theology that dominated the St. Gallen Reformed Church at that time (and which was one of the reasons why his father had left the church).[40] For a total of six years, Schlatter thus listened to a liberal theologian who questioned the historical reliability of the Scriptures, who emphasized primarily the ethical value of Jesus' teachings, and who was suspicious of traditional dogmatics in general.[41] There was, then, obviously a considerable contrast between what the young Schlatter had learnt at home and what he was confronted with in the classroom. It seems plausible that this created a tension for Schlatter, and from this perspective, it is understandable why Schlatter chose to study theology in the first place, namely, as an endeavor to examine the "broad ditch" between the piety of his parental home and the critical attitude of liberal theology at school.

Reading Spinoza with Glowing Head

Schlatter moved to Basel in May 1871 and his first four semesters in university focused mainly on philosophy. At first, the young student proved to be very open towards critical philosophy, thus, he sat "with delight in the philosophical lecture theatre," and it was Schlatter's intention to reflect as critically as possible upon his theological position against the backdrop of his pious upbringing.[42] In the winter semester of 1871/2, the philosophy professor Karl Steffensen (1816–88) introduced Schlatter to the writings of Benedict de Spinoza (1632–77), which had a significant impact on Schlatter, as his Spinoza studies led to a serious crisis of faith for him around Christmas 1871.[43] Spinoza's writings had obviously not only triggered a crisis in Schlatter's life, but had also, much earlier and on a much larger scale, changed the post-Reformation theological landscape with the first major attempt at what we today call modern historical criticism.

Historian Jonathan Israel argues that in the period from 1650 to 1750 Spinoza was "the chief challenger of the fundamentals of revealed religion,

39. Schlatter, "Idealismus und Erweckung," 11.
40. Neuer, *Adolf Schlatter*, 13–14.
41. Ibid., 43.
42. Schlatter, "Idealismus und Erweckung," 10.
43. See Neuer, *Adolf Schlatter*, 59.

received ideas, tradition, [and] morality."[44] Assuming that Schlatter was familiar with Spinoza's *Theological-Political Treatise* (1670), he saw himself confronted with an attack on almost everything in which he had been taught to believe. Influenced by Cartesian rationalism and Jewish medieval thought, Spinoza rejected the notion of a personal God and introduced a pantheistic worldview with God, or nature, as the one single, supreme reality.[45] The son of Jewish immigrants from Portugal, Spinoza not only provided a new hermeneutical method, paving the way for modern historical criticism of the bible, but also challenged the traditional post-Reformation view on Christology.[46] As regards the latter, Spinoza did not subscribe to the traditional doctrine of Jesus' incarnation,[47] and he was convinced that Jesus did not perform miracles, which would have been incompatible with the laws of nature.[48] Moreover, he did not consider Christ a prophet,[49] nor did he believe that he was divine,[50] or that the resurrection had occurred in the literal sense.[51] Ultimately, the sole significance of Jesus Christ, according to Spinoza, lay in his abilities as a moral and religious teacher, a humanistic role model to be imitated. Jesus Christ, then, in Spinoza's view, was the philosopher *par excellence*, the *summus philosophus*.[52] With his radical thoughts, Spinoza influenced later Deist and skeptical authors,[53] and he opened the door for subsequent Enlightenment and idealist thinkers. German idealist Georg W. F. Hegel (1770–1831) once remarked that "Spinoza is the main center of modern philosophy: either Spinozism or no philosophy at all."[54] After Spinoza, then, theism was increasingly overshadowed by rational Deism and by Enlightenment philosophy and theology. Gotthold E. Lessing

44. Israel, *Radical Enlightenment*, 159.

45. See Donagan, "Spinoza's Theology," 343–82.

46. See Israel, "Introduction," ix; cf. Harrisville and Sundberg, *Bible in Modern Culture*, 37.

47. "As to the additional teaching of certain Churches, that God took upon himself human nature, I have expressly indicated that I do not understand what they say." Spinoza, *The Letters* (Letter #73), 333.

48. See Spinoza, *Theological-Political Treatise*, 91; cf. Israel, "Introduction," xviii-xix.

49. Spinoza, *Theological-Political Treatise*, 63.

50. See Israel, "Introduction," xviii.

51. Spinoza argued that the resurrection had to be interpreted allegorically. Spinoza, *Letters* (Letter #78), 348; see also ibid., 338–39 (Letter #75).

52. Hoping, *Einführung in die Christologie*, 135.

53. Such as John Toland (1670–1722), Pierre Bayle (1647–1706) and others; see Israel, "Introduction," xvii.

54. Hegel, *Werke*, 20:163–64.

(1729–81) admired Spinoza,[55] and the "Reimarus fragments," which Lessing published in the 1770s, are clearly anticipated by Spinoza's thought.[56] Albert Schweitzer (1875–1965) was thus mistaken when he argued in his investigation of the *Quest for the Historical Jesus* that "Reimarus had no predecessors."[57] One can clearly trace the quest for the historical Jesus to the seventeenth-century criticism of Spinoza.

Still, one wonders whether it was in fact Spinoza's christological critique which seriously challenged Schlatter's faith. Perhaps it was rather Spinoza's close identification of God and substance, together with what Schlatter later called Spinoza's "new concept of nature," which attracted him at first.[58] While it is certainly debatable whether Spinoza was a pantheist, Schlatter presumably found this close linking of God, substance and nature both intriguing and unsettling. Intriguing, as he himself grew up developing a high view of nature, as we have seen earlier, but also unsettling as Spinoza's god had not much in common with the personal creator-God Schlatter was introduced to in his parental home. Schlatter reflects on his crisis as follows: "There was a time," he writes, "when I read Spinoza with glowing head, far into the night, in order to figure out whether I could become a follower of Spinoza [*Spinozist*] instead of being a Christian."[59] "Even today," he adds, "I could point to the place in Basel where I came . . . close to blasphemy: 'God, if you exist, reveal yourself to me.'"[60] Schlatter eventually managed to overcome this existential crisis, particularly with the support of his family and a clear focus on the Scriptures. "What sustained me," Schlatter is convinced, "was the fact that I remained in constant association with the bible."[61] In retrospect, this critical life-event actually helped to consolidate his theological convictions and it would remain his one and only major crisis of faith. In his continuing intellectual struggle with critical philosophical thought, Schlat-

55. Bubser, "Spinoza," in *RGG* 6:251.

56. Between 1774 and 1778, Lessing published altogether seven fragments ("Wolfenbüttel fragments," *Fragmente des Wolfenbüttelschen Ungenannten*), originally by Hermann Samuel Reimarus (1694–1768), which appeared as "Apologie oder Schutzschrift für die vernünftigen Verehrer Gottes" in the journal *Zur Geschichte und Literatur aus den Schätzen der herzoglichen Bibliothek zu Wolfenbüttel*. This led to the so-called fragment controversy (*Fragmentenstreit*) between Lessing and representatives of Lutheran orthodoxy. Finally, Lessing was banned from publishing works on religion. Lessing, however, continued the discussion by poetic means, for example in his drama, *Nathan der Weise* (published 1779).

57. Schweitzer, *Quest of the Historical Jesus*, 24.

58. Schlatter, *Philosophische Arbeit*, 58.

59. Schlatter, *Rückblick*, 39.

60. Ibid., 53.

61. Ibid.

ter gained substantial support from influential teachers and thinkers, such as Johann T. Beck and Franz von Baader. It is to these significant figures that we turn next.

Beck-Enthusiasm

Johann T. Beck, who was born in 1804, the year Kant died, disapproved of the influx of Enlightenment and idealist thought on theology in his time.[62] With the support of the *Christentumsgesellschaft*, Beck was called to his first university post in 1836 in Basel, in order to balance what the pietists considered the critical teaching of Wilhelm M. L. de Wette.[63] The year before, David Friedrich Strauss (1808–74) had published his *Life of Jesus Critically Examined*, which rapidly gained influence in German theological departments—Beck, obviously, responded critically to Strauss' work.[64] Later, Beck moved to Tübingen, where he shared the lecture hall with Strauss' teacher Ferdinand Christian Baur.[65] Beck, the "pietist biblicist,"[66] could not agree with the mythical viewpoint and the historical skepticism of his liberal adversaries, a view that his student Schlatter was happy to share.

When Schlatter arrived in Tübingen in 1873, Beck was in his final years of teaching, yet still lecturing at the age of seventy.[67] Schlatter had less than two years in Tübingen and he intended to focus mainly on Beck, thus attending all the lectures delivered by him, in dogmatics, hermeneutics and in ethics.[68] Such was his early "Beck-enthusiasm" (*Beck-Begeisterung*), as

---

62. For an overview of Beck's theology, see Hake, *Bedeutung der Theologie Johann Tobias Becks*, 27–84.

63. Köberle, "Beck," *RGG* 1:953. Beck taught in Basel from 1836–43 and de Wette from 1822–49.

64. With his mythical view outlined in *Das Leben Jesu kritisch bearbeitet*, Strauss treated the New Testament storyline not "as true history, but as a sacred legend." Strauss, *Life of Jesus*, 32. Strauss' mythical approach and his historical skepticism influenced notable theologians after him, such as Wilhelm Bousset of the history of religion school, and the later student of Schlatter, Rudolf Bultmann. Beck, whose life-span overlaps with that of Strauss, clearly rejected Strauss' mythical critique of the Scriptures. See Riggenbach, *Johann Tobias Beck*, 135–36; cf. Hoffmann, *Verständnis der Natur*, 132–39.

65. Beck taught in Tübingen from 1843–78 and Baur from 1826–60.

66. Beck was, Schlatter notes, heavily influenced by the Swabian pietists, not only by Oetinger, but also by Bengel, Roos, and Rieger. Schlatter, "Becks theologische Arbeit," 28.

67. Schlatter studied in Tübingen from spring 1873 until autumn 1874.

68. In the summer semester of 1873, Schlatter attended the following lectures by Beck: "Christliche Glaubenslehre, erster Theil," "Erklärung der Briefe von Timotheus," and "Erklärung der kleinen Propheten." In the winter semester of 1873/74, Schlatter

Schlatter biographer Werner Neuer observes,[69] that his mother feared he would become a so-called "Beckite."[70] The then twenty-one year old student was fascinated by the personality and the charisma of his teacher and his style of lecturing. Commemorating Beck's one hundredth birthday three decades later, Schlatter, then himself professor in Tübingen, explains what attracted his attention:

> [H]e has a genuine, a real God! Not an idea of God that he processed dialectically, not a God-consciousness, from which he drew his sentiment; frankly and openly in the lecture hall, not in a chamber in the back, but from within the professor himself this marvelous event came to light: having a God whose word he heard, whose will he did, in whose service he stood with his whole labor.[71]

One can easily recognize how, in Schlatter's eyes, Beck's realist theology differed substantially from idealist theologians who borrowed Hegelian philosophy and processed their thoughts dialectically (Schlatter has perhaps Strauss in mind, here) and how it was also different from any tendencies, where the sentiment was central to our knowledge of God. This was very much to Schlatter's liking. He clearly preferred Beck's theological realism which emphasized God's concrete revelation in creation over any theological speculation that remained abstract.[72] Beck thereby reinforced what Schlatter had already learned at home, and later, Schlatter encouraged his students—much like Beck—to an independent observation of the Scriptures.[73]

---

attended "Glaubenslehre, zweiter Theil," "Erklärung des Epheserbriefs," and in the summer semester of 1874, "Christliche Ethik" and "Erklärung der Petribriefe." I am grateful to Dr Michael Wischnath, director of the archive of the University of Tübingen, for the kind provision of this information (e-mail message to author, November 16, 2010).

69. Schlatter's student letters to his family are marked by a strong enthusiasm for Beck. Neuer, *Adolf Schlatter*, 71.

70. Schlatter to his parents, 13 February 1874, in Neuer, *Adolf Schlatter*, 74. Beck's influence on Schlatter is treated elsewhere in more detail. See Neuer, "Das Verhältnis Adolf Schlatters zu Johann Tobias Beck," 85–95.

71. Schlatter, "Becks theologische Arbeit," 25–26.

72. See Schlatter's notes in his *curriculum vitae*, "Rückblick auf meinen Entwicklungsgang," 6 (in Neuer, *Adolf Schlatter*, 81); cf. Schlatter, "Becks theologische Arbeit," 37–39. Similarly to Schlatter's father, Beck, the "friend of analogies" as Schlatter called him, emphasized creation as the locus of God's revelation ("Becks theologische Arbeit," 30). Beck's "lively devotion to nature [*lebhafte Naturandacht*]" worked as a catalyst for his student's emphasis on a personal *Anschluss an die Natur*. Schlatter, "Becks theologische Arbeit," 30; see also "Selbstdarstellungen," 155. For Beck's theological understanding of nature, see Hoffmann, *Verständnis der Natur*.

73. See Schlatter, *Erlebtes*, 98–100.

44   Part 1: The Genesis and Context of Schlatter's Christology

In fact, later, Schlatter regarded his own lectures as "seeing-aids" which should facilitate the students' own seeing-act (*Sehakt*),[74] and enable them to "hear God in Scripture."[75] The student of Beck was convinced that one of the foundational tasks of theology (as of any other science) was observation:

> We, as members of the *universitas litterarum* [full-scale university that comprises the entirety of the sciences], are therefore called, in the scope of the work appointed to us, to see, to observe with chastity and cleanness. . . . This is the *ceterum censeo* [necessary requirement] for every labor within the university. Science is first seeing, and secondly seeing, and thirdly seeing and again and again seeing.[76]

In addition to Beck's realism, his clear emphasis on unity, and in particular, the inner cohesion of Scripture impressed Schlatter. Beck could not concur with his liberal contemporaries, such as Strauss, de Wette and Baur, who for his taste went too far as they unduly separated the teaching of Jesus from that of his apostles.[77] Schlatter very much followed suit. Beck's emphasis on theological unity,[78] in particular on Scriptural unity, resonates in Schlatter's works, for instance in his *History of the Christ* and in his *Theology of the Apostles*, and also in his published lecture on "Jesus and Paul" where he makes the case for the intrinsic unity and continuity of Jesus' and the apostles' teaching. "I saw . . . no rift between Jesus' work and that of his messengers," Schlatter asserts in Beckian fashion, "between the work of Peter in Jerusalem and that of Paul among the Greeks, but I possessed a unified New Testament."[79] Furthermore, Beck also helped Schlatter to reconcile faith and science, a particularly important aspect for Schlatter's later development as a university professor. Beck personified, in Schlatter's view, the vision of a (literally) faith-ful scientist. In the lecture hall, remembers Schlatter, Beck

---

74. Schlatter, *Rückblick*, 208; see also Neuer, *Adolf Schlatter*, 605–6.

75. Neuer, *Adolf Schlatter*, 391. "I showed the young folks who came to me how I dealt with the text, set myself before them as an example and lent them my eyes so that they learned to see." Schlatter, *Erlebtes*, 102.

76. Schlatter, "Atheistische Methoden," 240. Elsewhere, Schlatter notes: "I remained . . . what I always have been, a realist, and I required the seeing-act of the student, by which he opened himself in observation of the subject matter." Schlatter, *Rückblick*, 208, see also 52–53, 240; "Atheistische Methoden," 139; "Christus und Christentum, Person und Prinzip," 24; "Becks theologische Arbeit," 32; "Religiöse Aufgabe der Universitäten," 72.

77. Beck, *Miscellaneum Pastorale*, 93 in Hoffmann, *Verständnis der Natur*, 106.

78. See Neuer, *Adolf Schlatter*, 68–71; see also Beintker, "Johann Tobias Beck und die neuere evangelische Theologie," 230.

79. Schlatter, *Rückblick*, 233–34.

was a "confessing Christian and researcher at the same time,"[80] exemplifying how one could stay true to the biblical tradition while at the same time performing theology as science. Schlatter later emulated his teacher's example by emphasizing the scientific character of theology, a subject that in his view had its rightful place at the university.[81] The requirement of "faith" for the pursuit of theology was for him not an obstacle to true theological science, as some of his contemporaries suggested,[82] but was demanded by the subject-nature of theology itself (see our discussion in chapter 3).

Although one notices then indeed significant overlaps between Beck and Schlatter, the student did not follow the teacher in every respect. Unlike Beck, Schlatter was, as noted earlier, no biblicist in the strict sense Beck was.[83] Moreover, Schlatter could also not agree with Beck's interpretation of the doctrine of justification[84] and his overall systematic approach[85] with

80. Ibid., 45.

81. This is, in fact, one of the few overlaps between the convictions of Schlatter and his Berlin colleague Adolf von Harnack. Both Schlatter and Harnack argued consistently for theology's status as an academic subject at the university. See Schlatter, "Religiöse Aufgabe der Universitäten," 61–79 and Harnack, "Die Aufgabe der theologischen Fakultäten und die allgemeine Religionsgeschichte nebst einem Nachwort," 159–87. See also my "A Queen without a Throne? Harnack, Schlatter and Kuyper on Theology in the University," 104–18.

82. As Paul Jaeger, for instance, argued in "Das 'atheistische Denken' der neueren Theologie," 577–82. Schlatter offered a critical review of Jaeger's arguments in "Atheistische Methoden," 228–50.

83. In contrast to Beck, Schlatter was more open to a critical approach to the New Testament. For Schlatter, faith *and* critique of the Scriptures—rightly understood—were not at odds but close allies in New Testament research. In Schlatter's view, "[the] critique of the Bible becomes our vocation on two levels, namely as historical and as dogmatic critique." Schlatter, *Dogma*, 373; see ibid., 372–80 for Schlatter's position on the authority, infallibility and perspicuity of Scripture. In this context, see also my essay, "Adolf Schlatter on Scripture as *Gnadenmittel*," forthcoming. On the theological differences between Schlatter and Beck on the Scriptures see Hägele, *Die Schrift als Gnadenmittel*, 216–33.

84. Schlatter complained that Beck deviated too much from Luther as he highlighted ethical renewal at the expense of the forensic aspect of justification. Schlatter, *Rückblick*, 46–47. Thus, God's action in making us righteous, Schlatter laments, is pitted against his act of declaring us righteous. This creates an unhealthy dualism which Schlatter intends to avoid with his own account of justification by faith. See Schlatter's essay, "Von der Rechtfertigung" (1883). For a more detailed comparison of Beck's and Schlatter's positions on the doctrine of justification, see Rieger, *Schlatters Rechtfertigungslehre*, 20–33. We return to this aspect at a later stage when discussing the life-act in chapter 6.

85. From Schlatter's perspective, Beck's dogmatic system was too strict as it was exclusively based on Scripture. Schlatter preferred to develop a broader dogmatic framework by including extra-biblical sources such as history, linguistics, and anthropology. Altogether, Schlatter concludes that "Beck was indeed a determined dogmatician, but

its ahistorical bent.[86] This latter point is particularly important. With his own emphasis on concrete history, and on the general historical context of the New Testament events, Schlatter clearly moved beyond his teacher.[87] Taking into account the historical context, specifically when dealing with Christology, is a crucial aspect of Schlatter's theological thinking that will surface time and again in this work. Still, taken as a whole, Beck's influence on Schlatter was considerable. Evidently, Schlatter himself admits that he was in many ways a "follower of Beck."[88] Beck's theological realism, his focus on the unity of the Scriptures and his synthesis of faith and science provided a solid basis for Schlatter's theological *vita*. Schlatter left Tübingen a changed student, equipped for the theological and christological debates that lay ahead.

Franz von Baader

If Beck was *the* significant figure during his studies, the most important influence on his "theological and personal development during his time in the diaconate in Neumünster" was Catholic philosopher, physician, engineer and social reformer Franz von Baader (1765–1841).[89] Schlatter was fascinated by Baader's works.[90] Not only in the course of his pastorate, but also during his first years in Bern as a *Privatdozent*, Schlatter extensively read and excerpted Baader's works. He waded through two-thirds of Baader's complete works, sixteen volumes in total, as one can gather from the unpublished documents in Schlatter's estate.[91] What was it that Schlatter

---

he grounded his system on a basis that was not accessible for me." Schlatter, *Rückblick*, 51; cf. "Becks theologische Arbeit," 38.

86. Schlatter speaks of Beck's "fear of history." Schlatter, *Rückblick*, 44; see also "Entstehung der Beiträge," 44.

87. While Beck acknowledged the importance of biblical history and one's own, individual *Geschichte*, he neglected, in Schlatter's view, the significance of the general historical context. As a result, Schlatter complains, Beck's approach "remains in a peculiar way confined [*begrenzt*]," primarily due to the fact that Beck "rejected and ignored general history [*Gesamtgeschichte*], which creates societies, peoples, states and churches." Schlatter, "Becks theologische Arbeit," 31, 37. This was, according to Schlatter, the crucial point "where his [Beck's] work was separated by a wide distance from what theological research is moved by today." Ibid., 37.

88. Schlatter, *Rückblick*, 46, 200.

89. Neuer, *Adolf Schlatter*, 100.

90. Baader himself was deeply influenced by Louis Claude de Saint-Martin (1743–1803). Baader's works were published between 1851 and 1860 as *Franz von Baader's sämmtliche Werke*.

91. Neuer, *Adolf Schlatter*, 106. These unpublished documents include "Biblische,

found stimulating in Baader's writings? At least three aspects deserve closer attention.[92] Schlatter appreciated Baader's holistic concept of theological unity based on empirical observation, his relational-volitional emphasis, and his balanced appraisal of orthodox pietism. We shall briefly look at each of these points in turn.

First of all, Baader's approach of taking into account the whole of reality in regards to the theological enterprise strengthened what Schlatter had already learned from Beck a few years earlier. Schlatter welcomes Baader's "movement of thinking towards unity that seeks to examine the totality of events."[93] Baader also echoes a theological realism Schlatter had encountered similarly in Beck, namely a clear focus on God's revelatory action in creation.[94] "The insight that knowledge [*Erkenntnis*] is impossible without congruent observation [*Schauen*]," Baader writes, "and that the manner of the one corresponds to the other, has completely disappeared from the newer philosophy."[95] Schlatter could not agree more. The Beckian-Baaderian conviction, namely that observation is the prerequisite for unified knowledge (*Erkenntnis*) is *the* foundation for Schlatter's theological realism as outlined in his later works. The God who is one, and who creates unity, also ensures that the observer of his works obtains unified knowledge. "As it was God's work that I was supposed to observe," Schlatter writes, "I was assured that my thinking would arrive at unity."[96] Theology is thus concerned with the perception of the whole of God-created reality. In Schlatter's own words:

> The territory that the theological task has to stride across ranges over the whole revelatory work of God. That endows it with an impetus towards the whole [*Richtung auf das Ganze*].... In the idea of God [*Gottesgedanke*] is included the sentence that all being stands in relation to God and that it somehow visualizes his power and his will.[97]

---

theologische und philosophische Begriffe bei Franz von Baader," "Sentenzen aus Franz von Baader," and his lecture, "Baaders Verhältnis zu den wissenschaftlichen Bestrebungen seiner Zeit." In the winter semester of 1884/5, Schlatter devoted a series of lectures to Franz von Baader's theology and philosophy, "Einführung in die Theologie Franz von Baaders."

92. For a more comprehensive account see Kindt, *Der Gedanke der Einheit*, 62–122.

93. Schlatter, "Idealismus und Erweckung," 20.

94. See Lütgert's comments in "Adolf Schlatter als Theologe," 22.

95. Baader, *Werke*, 1:306, 276; cf. 8:348–49.

96. Schlatter, "Entstehung der Beiträge," 63. Schlatter argues that as we are the creation of a God who works unity, the drive for unity is therefore basically implanted in our consciousness. See Schlatter, *Ethik*, 251.

97. Schlatter, *Dogma*, 13; see also "Entstehung der Beiträge," 82–83.

These sentences from his "Christian Dogma," written in the early twentieth century, are clearly rooted in his early encounter with Baader. "Wherever Baader looked," Schlatter later remarks, "whether he described nature or read the Scriptures, whether he dealt with the movement of thinking or of volition, he was always concerned with the work of the One, from whom and to whom everything is."[98] By applying the idea of unity through observation to Christology, Schlatter arrives at a unified picture of Jesus Christ, as we shall discuss in more detail in part 2.

Schlatter was, secondly, also sympathetic to Baader's focus on volition and relation.[99] Baader underscores volition as a central human capacity, coining the expression "act of the will" (*Willensakt*),[100] a term Schlatter added to his own theological dictionary.[101] Moreover, Baader stresses the reality of concrete volition in our relationship with God. He speaks of the soteriologically relevant "union of will" (*Willenseinigung*)[102] between God and us, through which we receive through Christ a "new will" (*neuer Wille*).[103] As we shall see later, Schlatter uses the exact Baaderian vocabulary as he develops his own relational-volitional agenda with a view to Christology. Put briefly, Schlatter points to Jesus as being in volitional union with the Father and with us, acting according to his strong will towards the cross (*Kreuzeswille*), through which he unites his will with the Father's will to salvation (*Heilandswille*), and thus paves the way for our volitional union with God. Thirdly, Schlatter also developed through Baader a more balanced appreciation for his revival and pietist heritage. "Baader's critical power . . . in the appraisal of pietism and of the Reformation," writes Schlatter, "were of great help to me."[104] Studying the writings of the Catholic philosopher, Schlatter was encouraged to take a step back and reflect critically on his own theological tradition, in particular with a view to social ethics. As early as 1835, Baader had published a work on "The Situation of the Proletariat" *(Die Lage des Proletariats)*, through which he established himself as one of the earliest nineteenth-century social reformers.[105] Given Baader's strong social engage-

---

98. Schlatter, "Idealismus und Erweckung," 19–20.

99. See Kindt, *Der Gedanke der Einheit*, 78–79 and 87–88.

100. Baader, *Werke*, 13:213.

101. See Schlatter, *Rückblick*, 93, "Christologie und Soteriologie," 25.

102. Baader, *Werke*, 1:191.

103. Ibid., 8:156.

104. Schlatter, "Selbstdarstellungen," 151.

105. The full title of this work is: *Über das dermalige Mißverhältnis der Vermögenslosen oder Proletairs zu den Vermögen besitzenden Klassen der Sozietät in betreff ihres Auskommens, sowohl in materieller Hinsicht, aus dem Standpunkte des Rechts betrachtet.*

ment on behalf of the socially disadvantaged, Schlatter wondered whether the contemporary pietist movement might perhaps lag behind, having lost its originally active impetus. "Baader's rich doctrine of love stood next to the poor evangelical tradition," Schlatter remarks. In his own time, he observed what he called a "degeneration [*Verkümmerung*] of our evangelical ethic."[106] Dissatisfied with what was in his view a passive pietism, Schlatter opted for an active ethics of love that was rooted in dogmatics, calling for nothing less than a completion of the Reformation. This important aspect of Schlatter's work will be discussed in chapter 6 on the life-act.

Taken together, Schlatter received significant stimulation in his theological development through his encounters with Beck and Baader. He was encouraged to bring together faith and scientific theological research; as in any other science, critical observation was crucial and Schlatter's development of a faith-based theological realism is to a great extent rooted in the ideas of Beck and Baader. Through his empirical seeing-act Schlatter observed, as did his teachers, unity and harmony in Scripture, creation, and, of course, Jesus Christ's words and works, his being and action. We also noted how Schlatter's concern for Jesus' concrete historical context, his volition and relation with God and us, was inspired by these two figures, equipping him to meet the challenges of idealist christological ideas. Having illustrated both Schlatter's upbringing in the context of the revival movement and the considerable impact of Beck and Baader, one is now able to trace Schlatter's critical interaction with the christological challenges post-Reformation Protestantism faced at the nineteenth century.

Responding to Idealist Christologies

At the outset, one must point to some characteristics of Schlatter's consideration of idealist approaches to theology. First of all, Schlatter sees the origins of idealist theological critique mainly in Greek philosophy. According to Schlatter, a specific array of philosophical concepts ranges "from Plato in an unbroken tradition through Kant down into the present."[107] Thus one needs to keep in mind that "Schlatter's philosophical argument with 'Greek thought,'" as Werner Neuer claims, "is first and foremost a dispute with idealism."[108] "Descartes, Spinoza, and Kant," Schlatter states, "are comparatively small modifications of the same type, namely the Greek type: the

106. Schlatter, "Idealismus und Erweckung," 22.
107. Schlatter, "Briefe über das Dogma," 18; see also *Rückblick*, 40.
108. Neuer, "Idealismus und Erweckung in Schlatters Jugend," 67. See also Neuer, "Einführung," 10–11, and Walldorf, *Realistische Philosophie*, 214–24.

human being is reason; its life consists of thinking; and the same applies to the world, because it is thought [*gedacht*], it exists."[109] While these statements allude to one of Schlatter's main criticisms, namely the attempt to use pure reason (*reine Vernunft*) to conceive of the world apart from empirical observation, they also suggest that Schlatter tends not to be very succinct with regard to philosophical concepts and movements. In fact, he does not seem to distinguish clearly enough between terms such as Enlightenment, Kantianism, idealism, and the like. This oversimplification in his treatment of philosophical concepts obviously limits the validity of his discussion to a certain degree.[110] Nevertheless, one has to admit that Schlatter was first and foremost a theologian and only secondly a philosopher, and as such, he could obviously not have been equally an expert on each and every thinker.[111] Rather, the Swiss theologian took a "bird's eye view" of philosophy—always having in mind the whole picture, the *Richtung auf das Ganze*.[112] Taking this into account, we turn to Schlatter's critique of idealist theology, considering it from his own perspective. In doing so we shall first concentrate on Schlatter's criticism of Kant's rationalism from the vantage point of his own empirical realism. We focus, secondly, on Christology as the center of gravity, since Schlatter saw a serious discrepancy between the Jesus he encountered in the New Testament and the Jesus of Kant and Hegel. The latter versions reflect in his view Ebionite tendencies as they stress Jesus' human side as a teacher of morals, while neglecting, and this is our third and final point, the soteriological dimension of Jesus' person and work.

First of all, then, Schlatter saw a fundamental conflict between his own empirical approach and the rationalism of the idealists. Now this does not mean that Schlatter was opposed to reason or rigorous theological thinking. On the contrary, he certainly welcomed Kant's call, *Sapere aude!* (Dare to know!), as his own focus on the theological thinking-act (*Denkakt*) shows.[113] Yet Schlatter disagrees with what he considers Kant's skepticism towards our perceptive abilities and his overconfidence in the capacity of our reason.[114] Thus, Kant could not be further away from Schlatter's empirical realist position, as the former pursued "a pure metaphysics without any

---

109. Schlatter, *Philosophische Arbeit*, 212.

110. See Walldorf's comments in *Realistische Philosophie*, 282–84.

111. Ibid., 283.

112. This is how Walldorf describes it in ibid., 282.

113. See Schlatter, "Briefe über das Dogma," 15 and Neuer's comments in "Idealismus und Erweckung in Schlatters Jugend," 70.

114. For Schlatter's critical interaction with Kantian epistemology see his *Philosophische Arbeit*, 115–51 and "Idealismus und Erweckung," 16–19. See also *Dogma*, 90–92.

intermixture of sense perception."[115] In this sense, Schlatter was certainly correct in assuming a close link between Kant and Platonism.[116] Though Kant certainly tried to make room for a substantiated belief in God, the *perfectio noumenon*, he opines—other than Schlatter—that this belief cannot be based on knowledge (*Erkenntnis*) but is rooted in the subjective "longing of our reason" (*Bedürfnis der Vernunft*).[117] In this way, Kant intends to "deny knowledge in order to make room for faith" (*das Wissen aufheben, um zum Glauben Platz zu bekommen*).[118] This was, in Schlatter's view, a philosophical (and theological) cul-de-sac. Thus, Schlatter demurs that

> for Kant, it was certain that the conditions which enabled our thinking were rooted exclusively in reason [*Vernunft*] itself . . . The thinking-process arises within ourselves. . . . We thus abide with Leibniz' *Monas* which produces its imaginations from within itself.[119]

Schlatter asserts that every theology that tries to eke out an existence within the boundaries of mere reason and neglects the observation of concrete reality renders itself absurd.[120] As soon as theology bids farewell to the close observation of the given facts in creation and the events presented in the New Testament, it deteriorates, becoming "abstract scholasticism,"[121] and losing its scientific character.[122] "A dogmatician," contends Schlatter, "who no longer observes but only reasons . . . is at best a poet and at worst a dreamer [*Phantast*]."[123] "Attention to abstraction," he laments, "replaced en-

---

115. Kant to J. H. Lambert, 2 September 1770, in Kant, *Philosophical Correspondence*, 60.

116. Schlatter, *Philosophische Arbeit*, 145; see also "Entstehung der Beiträge," 37.

117. Kühn, *Kant*, 304.

118. Kant, *Critique of Pure Reason*, 117 [*Kritik der Reinen Vernunft*, Bxxx].

119. Schlatter, *Philosophische Arbeit*, 109.

120. Schlatter's Dutch contemporary, the theologian Herman Bavinck (1854-1921), argues similarly, "A philosophy which, neglecting the real world, takes its start from reason, will necessarily do violence to the reality of life and resolve nature and history into a network of abstractions. . . . If this be unwilling to take revelation as it offers itself, it will detach it from history and end by retaining nothing but a dry skeleton of abstract ideas." Bavinck, *Philosophy of Revelation*, 25.

121. Schlatter, "Theologie des NT und Dogmatik," 77.

122. Ibid., 79. See also his critique in *Philosophische Arbeit*, 112. Again, Bavinck agrees here with Schlatter in noting that "the starting point of all human knowledge is sense perception. . . . Truth must not be drawn from books but from the real world. Observation is the source of all real science." Bavinck, *Reformed Dogmatics*, 1:226.

123. Schlatter, "Theologie des NT und Dogmatik," 13. In Schlatter's view the church needed dogmaticians who "desired nothing but observation in its austere and sober seriousness." Schlatter, "Entstehung der Beiträge," 83.

tirely the observation of reality."[124] Following Aristotle's dictum that "there is nothing in the intellect which is not first in the senses,"[125] Schlatter is convinced that Kant's endeavor of attaining knowledge without relying on empirical observation is destined to failure. The implications for the notion of faith are in Schlatter's view particularly perilous. Whereas Kant, according to Schlatter's reading, grounds religion and rational faith in practical reason (*praktische Vernunft*), independent of history, Schlatter explicitly intends to ground faith in God's revelation against the backdrop of concrete history. Whilst Kant had to deny knowledge in order to make room for faith, Schlatter is emphatic that empirical knowledge is in fact the basis and the prerequisite for faith. The Swiss theologian was not only unhappy with the Königsberg philosopher's epistemology and its implications for faith, but also disapproved of the corollaries of Kant's approach for Christology, as we shall see next.

Schlatter concluded, secondly, that the abyss between idealism and *Erweckung* was unbridgeable, in particular with a view to Christology. If sixteenth-century Reformation brought into focus matters of ecclesiology, and of course the question of justification, the focus shifted with the rise of the Enlightenment to Christology. "Now, the struggle is about Christ," claims Schlatter.[126] Much to his dismay, post-Reformation Protestantism was ill-prepared for a profound christological debate.[127] Protestant theology was—much more than Roman Catholicism—caught off guard by the challenges of the Enlightenment critique. Alister E. McGrath attributes this susceptibility to the relative weakness, at least in comparison to the Roman Catholic Church, of the Protestant ecclesiastical institutions.[128] Still, the major challenges came not from the outside but from the inside, from the Protestant camp itself. As already mentioned, many an Enlightenment philosopher descended from a Protestant, often pietistic, background, and the maxim of protest and the call for a constant reformation (*Ecclesia semper reformanda*), had always been a central pillar of Protestantism, thus allowing—and even encouraging—a philosophical critique of theology.[129] It is thus no coincidence that the critical lives of Jesus (by Reimarus, Strauss and others) and the overall quest for the historical Jesus originated from within Protestantism itself. "It is in the nature of things," writes Schlatter,

124. Schlatter, *Philosophische Arbeit*, 111.
125. Aristotle, *De anima*, III, 4, 430 a 1; cf. Aquinas, *Summa contra gentiles*, II, c. 66.
126. Schlatter, *Philosophische Arbeit*, 93.
127. Ibid., 94–96.
128. McGrath, *Making of Modern German Christology*, 18–19.
129. See ibid., 19.

"that the controversy concentrated on *Christ* and that the *Life of Christ* by Strauß became, within the exceedingly vast Hegelian literature, one of the most famous and effective books."[130] To be fair, Schlatter acknowledges that

> Many Enlightenment philosophers [*Aufklärer*] had a high esteem for Jesus, notably those of German origin, and for Christianity they showed veneration. They gladly agreed that Jesus was surely sensible and that the religion of the New Testament was the best.[131]

Be that as it may, Schlatter comes to the conclusion that the Enlightenment Jesus who appeared on the Age of Reason's stage was a caricature of the New Testament's Jesus. In his philosophical studies, the student Schlatter had primarily engaged with Kant, Hegel and Schelling, and here, he encountered different Christologies—different "Christs," as he later put it. There is, for one, the moral Christ of Kant. With Kant, notes Schlatter, arose a "new Christology" (*neue Christologie*) that was contrary to the Christology of the New Testament and of the church.[132] For Schlatter, Kant's picture of Christ as the personified idea of the good principle was untenable because it clearly contradicted the findings of his own seeing-act, of his observations of the New Testament documents. Of course, Schlatter was happy to agree with Kant that Jesus was morally perfect, but then again, he was more than that, more than just the incarnation of Kant's categorical imperative. In fact, for Kant, Stephen R. Holmes remarks, and Schlatter would presumably agree, Jesus "is not what is important; the ideal to which he witnessed is."[133] Hence, one had from Schlatter's perspective, "two Christologies, [namely] one of Kantianism and one of the New Testament."[134] After Kant's Christ followed the Christ of Hegelian idealism, still in opposition to the Christ of the New Testament and thus to the Christ of the church (whose doctrine needs to be rooted in the biblical facts, Schlatter feels). "The two kind of theologies that stood against each other," he writes, "were distinctly separated . . . they had a different Christology: in Hegel the Christ as the enunciator of an idea that goes beyond him and makes him expendable,—in the church the Christ as the sole and eternal causer of God's gracious will."[135] This last comment, or

---

130. Schlatter, *Philosophische Arbeit*, 183 (emphasis original).
131. Ibid., 88.
132. Ibid., 143.
133. Holmes, *Quest for the Trinity*, 180.
134. Schlatter, *Philosophische Arbeit*, 145.
135. Ibid., 179.

rather, the last word, is significant as it directs our attention again to Schlatter's volitional and soteriological angle.

Thirdly, then, the notable absence of the gracious will of God is a crucial reason for Schlatter's dissatisfaction with the idealist versions of Jesus which oscillate between a rational or moral principle of the universe and the spirit coming to self-consciousness, without taking seriously Jesus' soteriological impact on humanity. Throughout his works, Schlatter highlights the organic connection between Jesus Christ's will and work. The Christ Schlatter encounters in the New Testament possesses a concrete volition which finds expression in the actual salvific deed. In regard to idealist Christologies, Schlatter complains:

> An individual like Jesus comes into consideration only as an example of a general truth. His being [*Dasein*] and his works [*Wirken*] count for nothing; it is merely a question of his thoughts, his "doctrines." The uniqueness of Christ, and his powerful efficacy [*Wirkungsmacht*] towards God as redeemer and towards humans as creator of the community are eliminated. The only title he can assume is that he is the best teacher of morals.[136]

This quote is central for our understanding of Schlatter's objection to idealist Christologies. Jesus is merely presented as a teacher of morals, Schlatter claims, while the intricacy of his being and his works are neglected. What is missing in the idealist portrayals of Jesus, then, in Schlatter's view, is the powerful efficacy of his salvific double-movement, both towards God as redeemer and towards humans as creator of the community. This aspect of Jesus' double-movement is central to Schlatter's relational Christology and will be addressed at the appropriate place (in chapters 4 and 5 on the thinking-act). By way of contrast, Schlatter laments, idealism ignored the doctrine of sin, and it thus did not need to ask for a redeemer or for any soteriological connection with him.[137] The Jesus who is, in Schlatter's eyes, the redeemer from sin and the creator of the new community was not the Jesus of the Enlightenment thinkers. He writes:

> The synoptic Jesus, who issues the call to repentance to the holy and righteous community and who dies in the completion of this mission and thereby creates the new community,

---

136. Ibid., 92.

137. Schlatter writes: "The Enlightenment did not work with ethical categories and did not preach a penitential sermon [*Bußpredigt*]. How one had to think, how to consider what is reasonable, the temperature of this question differed considerably from that of what one has to will and what sin was." Ibid., 88.

was completely veiled for the Kantians. The terms repentance, guilt, judgment, [and] community remained incomprehensible to them.[138]

In light of this serious neglect of hamartiology and soteriology, Schlatter opposed any proclamation of "idealism from the pulpit," such that sin was tamed and Jesus was reduced to an example for appropriate ethical behavior.[139] The preaching of an idealist Jesus as moral teacher is absurd as ethics is here pursued without soteriology, an impossible shortcut in Schlatter's view. For Schlatter, the ethical deed can only be the consequence of a soteriologically relevant connection with Jesus Christ. The ethical imperative must be based on the indicative of our relation with God through Jesus Christ. Our existential point of contact with Jesus through faith, the *Anschluss an Jesus*, is not just the only way to our salvation but also the basis for our sanctification. Only in connection with Jesus Christ will one be able to join the holy and righteous community that he created by his death. These significant soteriological and also ethical aspects of Schlatter's relational Christology will be discussed in more detail in the second part of this work (see chapter 6).

Conclusion

In this section, we have explored the early stages of the genesis and the development of Adolf Schlatter's Christology. Schlatter's Christocentric upbringing, with a distinct emphasis on an existential relationship with Jesus Christ through faith, the volitional lived ethics of central role models in his family and in his revival background, and the consolidation of both his holistic and empirical-realist theology through Beck and Baader, all contributed to his distinct response to idealist approaches to Christology. From our observations emerge at least five essential pillars of Schlatter's Christology, namely, *unity, observation, history, volition*, and *relation*. These are the key concepts on which Schlatter erects and expands his alternative christological approach as an answer to idealist views of Jesus Christ. Schlatter *observes* in the New Testament a *unified* account of Jesus Christ who possesses a distinct *will* to perform the concrete *historical deed* of redemption on the cross in order to provide for us an existentially relevant *relation* with God. In the following section, we will continue to trace Schlatter's theological development as we analyze his responses to the christological concepts and challenges of his liberal and dialectical contemporaries in Bern, Greifswald,

138. Ibid., 145.
139. Schlatter, "Idealismus und Erweckung," 17.

Berlin, and Tübingen. Proceeding this way, we will be able to identify the development of the characteristic shape of Schlatter's Christology in more detail.

BETWEEN RITSCHL AND CONFESSIONALISM

What sets Schlatter apart from the christological developments taking place around the end of the nineteenth and the beginning of the early twentieth century? So far we have pointed to Schlatter's critical interaction with German idealist theology in the context of his pietist upbringing. In this section we examine more closely how Schlatter interacted with theologians he considered to be influenced by idealist ideas and concepts. As mentioned in the introduction, one is at this stage faced with a distinct challenge regarding theological terminology. Terms such as liberal theology, Ritschlianism, mediating theology, and positive theology must be handled with care as we seek to identify Schlatter's position in relation to Ritschl and the Ritschlians, who more or less eschewed any theological labelling.[140] As already pointed out, the focus of this study is more on the characteristic profile of individual theologians, which makes the use of labels more or less dispensable. Hence, one is not interested in answering the general question of whether Schlatter was perhaps less liberal than Ritschl, but instead the goal is to identify precisely where Schlatter positioned himself in relation to Ritschl and the Ritschlians in matters of Christology. Where exactly did he agree? Where did he disagree, and why? By answering these questions one is adding crucial pieces to the mosaic that makes up Schlatter's christological development.

With regards to structure, this part is, like the previous one, closely tied to the chronology of Adolf Schlatter's life and work. We will, first, by way of introduction, set the scene by tracing Schlatter's professional development from his first post in Bern to his call to Greifswald, where he worked alongside Hermann Cremer from 1888 to 1893, and where he joined him in his rejection of Ritschl's influential theological agenda. We shall, secondly, take a closer look at the specific differences between the Christologies of Adolf Schlatter and Albrecht Ritschl. This paves the way, thirdly, for an analysis of Schlatter's interaction with the Christologies of Ritschl's followers and pupils, in particular with Wilhelm Herrmann and Adolf von Harnack. By

---

140. Joachim Weinhardt, for instance, disagrees with the common approach of labelling Ritschl a liberal theologian. According to Weinhardt, Ritschl himself rejected the label "liberal," as did Harnack. See Weinhardt, *Wilhelm Herrmanns Stellung*, 71. Weinhardt, along with Neugebauer, considers Ritschl a mediating theologian. See Weinhardt, *Wilhelm Herrmanns Stellung*, 17–8 and "Einleitung," 61; cf. Neugebauer, *Lotze und Ritschl*, 2.

carefully delineating the dynamic theological frictions between Schlatter and his contemporaries, one is able to determine how central characteristic features of his Christology crystallized during that time.

Christological Struggles: From Bern to Greifswald

Before he became a member of the Greifswald faculty, where he joined Hermann Cremer as one of the major representatives of the Greifswald school, Adolf Schlatter had to endure both personally and theologically a trying time in Bern. Having moved to Bern in 1880, Schlatter was introduced to a Protestant faculty which was dominated by critical rationalists. The considerably smaller positive group included, apart from Schlatter, Samuel Oettli, professor of Old Testament, and two honorary professors, Eduard Güder (1817–82) and Rudolf A. Rüetschie (1820–1903).[141] The Bern pietist circles had not only successfully arranged to call Oettli to the faculty, but were also responsible for Schlatter's appointment as an additional supporter for the positive camp.[142] As previously highlighted, Schlatter did not clearly belong to either the positives or the liberals and he thus became the pawn of two opposing powers, finding himself in a "double frontline position" in Bern, as Peter Stuhlmacher notes.[143] At that time, there was a deep-seated mistrust between the Bern pietists and the critical members of the faculty.[144] Church historian Friedrich Nippold (1838–1918),[145] a pupil of Richard Rothe (1799–1867), saw in Schlatter's call a conspiracy of the positive forces against the liberals.[146] Nippold complained about this publicly in the newspaper Berner Post, asking, "Who, in effect, is it that calls professors to the Bern Protestant faculty?"[147] As one might expect, Nippold did not welcome

141. See Neuer, *Adolf Schlatter*, 145.

142. Oettli had specifically asked for Schlatter as his future collaborator. See Schlatter, "Entstehung der Beiträge," 14–15.

143. Stuhlmacher, "Adolf Schlatter," 223.

144. Schlatter witnessed this theological tension between the ecclesiastical party and the university faculty not only in Bern. Later, in particular during his time in Berlin, he would be personally challenged to take a stand either for the church or the faculty. We will explore this in more detail below when we consider the so-called struggle over the Apostles' Creed of 1892.

145. For a brief summary of Nippold's theology, see Lessing, *Geschichte der deutschsprachigen evangelischen Theologie*, 1:211–12.

146. Neuer, *Adolf Schlatter*, 144. Up to Ritschl's break with the Tübingen school, Nippold was closely affiliated with Ritschl. Later, Nippold would heavily criticize Ritschl for not being 'liberal' enough. See Weinhardt, *Wilhelm Herrmanns Stellung*, 24.

147. "Wer beruft denn eigentlich die Professoren an der Berner evang.-theologischen Fakultaet?" See Neuer, *Adolf Schlatter*, 145.

Schlatter with open arms, to say the least. Nippold was certainly aware of the fact that Schlatter was influenced by Beck, whom he thought to be not scientific and not critical enough towards Scripture.[148] Schlatter thus comments on his first encounter with the Bern church historian:

> Its [the Bern faculty's] most influential man back then was the church historian Nippold, who announced his strong desire to lead Bern's church clergy and who was engaged in a passionate struggle with the city's pietists. Upon my request to sit the faculty's exam [*Fakultätsexamen*], he answered: "The only thing you have to do is to pack your suitcase immediately and leave."[149]

This Schlatter did not do. As a result, he was obviously more or less isolated at the outset of his academic career. Schlatter himself attributes the differences between him and the Bern faculty to a substantially different christological outlook. Schlatter writes:

> The battle for which I was recruited emerged from [the question of] the Christ, not from single dogmas, the doctrine of justification or pneumatology . . . but from the claims we were making about Jesus. The other theology tried to prove that Jesus was not the Christ and sought to call forth a religious movement that would carry us away from him and over and above him. I, on the other hand, stood near to those who saw God's grace in Jesus and had in him their Lord . . . [I was] coerced to live by faith, only by faith, but by faith I lived.[150]

Time and again conflicts between him and his colleagues would ignite due to different positions on Jesus Christ, as we shall see throughout this section.

Having completed his first major academic project, the 1885 "Faith in the New Testament" (*Glaube im Neuen Testament*), Schlatter was curious as to how his colleagues would receive it. However, they remained silent, much to Schlatter's disappointment.[151] While the Bern faculty rejected Schlatter's first major opus, it won the attention of the Greifswald professor, Hermann Cremer,[152] and "Faith in the New Testament" became Schlatter's passport

---

148. In one of his major works, Nippold complains about Beck, "whose warnings about the sinful flood of criticism [*Sündenflut des Kritizismus*] distracted him all too often from the ABC of the most essential criticism." Nippold, *Geschichte des Protestantismus*, 3:356.

149. Schlatter, "Entstehung der Beiträge," 17.

150. Schlatter, *Rückblick*, 92.

151. "The Bern faculty remarked not one syllable on my book," Schlatter complains. Schlatter, "Entstehung der Beiträge," 60.

152. Ibid., 61.

to the professorship in Greifswald.[153] In 1888, Schlatter thus followed "Cremer's call" (*Cremers Ruf*), as he himself says, and he became the successor of New Testament scholar Erich Haupt (1841–1910), who had relocated to Halle (Saale).[154] This was the beginning of a fruitful collaboration between Schlatter and Cremer, who was almost twenty years older than his Swiss colleague. In due course, Greifswald would become known as a center for theologians who critically engaged with Ritschl and his followers, and they attracted theology students from all over Europe. Together with Martin Kähler (1835–1912), professor of systematic theology and New Testament exegesis at the Martin-Luther University of Halle-Wittenberg,[155] only a few hours away by train from Greifswald, Schlatter and Cremer formed an influential theological triumvirate.[156] Hermann Cremer and Adolf Schlatter identified as their common goal a biblically founded critical interaction with both Ritschl's theology on the one hand and rigid pietist orthodoxy on the other.

In 1897, Schlatter and Cremer founded the journal "Essays for the Furtherance of Christian Theology" (*Beiträge zur Förderung christlicher Theologie*) as the leading organ of the Greifswald school. This was, in a way, an answer to the Ritschlian "Journal for Theology and the Church" (*Zeitschrift für Theologie und Kirche*). Schlatter and Cremer worked together despite a confessional divide as Schlatter came from the Reformed tradition and Cremer was a strict Lutheran. However, this was no barrier to a deep and fruitful collaboration. Schlatter clearly appreciated Cremer's Lutheranism,[157] though he did not feel compelled to convert to his confession.[158] What

153. Apparently, apart from Schlatter's monograph on "Faith in the New Testament," which was obviously a crucial stimulus, it was Schlatter's Bern lectures on prayer that tipped the scales for Cremer to "lobby vigorously for Schlatter's appointment," as Ernst Cremer notes, in his *Hermann Cremer*, 138. See also Neuer, *Adolf Schlatter*, 229.

154. Schlatter, *Rückblick*, 125.

155. Kähler taught in Halle-Wittenberg from 1867 until his death in 1912. Among Kähler's students were Julius Schniewind (1883–1948), Hans Emil Weber (1882–1950), and Karl Müller (1852–1940).

156. The basis for their theological agreement lies, to a great extent, in their similar educational background. Kähler and Cremer had both studied in Halle and were influenced by Julius Müller (1801–78) and the Schleiermacher-opponent and Strauss-critic August Tholuck (1799–1877). Both Kähler and Cremer were also influenced by the Erlangen theologian Johann Christian Konrad von Hofmann (1810–77). See Lessing, *Geschichte der deutschsprachigen evangelischen Theologie*, 1:44. In Tübingen, they sat, as Schlatter did later, under the teaching of Johann T. Beck. The three Beck students thus shared major theological common ground, such as their understanding of theology as science and, in particular, their strong christological emphasis.

157. See Schlatter, *Erlebtes*, 47–48, and also Neuer, *Adolf Schlatter*, 226.

158. Neuer, *Adolf Schlatter*, 237.

united the two Beck students was not so much a confessional connection as an affirmation of basic features of Beck's theology. Schlatter writes:

> We arrived at an agreement because we both desired a theology of faith, not an ignorant, unfounded faith, but a faith that is conscious of its truth and thereby able to point to its foundation; no more a godless theology that is driven by its fight against God and its struggle against Jesus, but such a science that finds in the faith that is given to us by Jesus its foundation and guidance... Cremer, too, was primarily a Christian... [he was] first of all connected with Christ and therefore a part of... the church. On this basis, the son of the Westphalian pietist shook hands with the son of the Swiss Baptist without any difficulty.[159]

This is clearly reminiscent of Beck: a biblically rooted theology of faith, where faith rests on the secure foundation of facts, together with an appreciation of well-founded scientific research which does not, however, forget the existential connection with Jesus Christ. It was through the Beckian heritage that Schlatter and Cremer sought to answer the claims of Ritschl and the Ritschlians. In general, Hermann Cremer was more engaged in the public debate with Ritschlian theology than Schlatter, especially in his spirited political struggle with Adolf von Harnack during the "struggle over the Apostles' Creed" (*Apostolikumsstreit*), which will be considered at the appropriate place later. Even so, Schlatter explicitly positioned himself theologically in relation to Ritschl and his followers, as he recognized the growing influence of their theological ideas in Protestant Germany. Schlatter might not have been as politically active as Cremer, yet he clearly addressed Ritschl's theology in his lectures, in his speeches and later in his *Dogma*.

In what follows, we enter uncharted theological territory. The theological, and in particular, christological differences between Schlatter and Ritschl have so far escaped scholarly attention. The following comparison of their views lays the foundation for our discussion of Schlatter's position in relation to Wilhelm Herrmann and Adolf von Harnack. A comprehensive assessment of the christological outlooks of Schlatter, Ritschl and the Ritschlians would easily fill a book on its own and thus lies beyond the scope of our study. The strategy, therefore, must be to provide a sufficiently concise comparison while doing justice to the inherent complexities of their theological programs, always with a view to chiseling out Schlatter's christological characteristics in the process.

---

159. Schlatter, *Rückblick*, 137–38; cf. "Entstehung der Beiträge," 72.

A Critique of Ritschl's Christology

It might be helpful in the first place to illustrate briefly some of Ritschl's main theological concepts, before we turn, secondly, to Schlatter's critique of the Göttingen professor's christological agenda, which will also reveal significant features of Schlatter's own view of Jesus Christ.

Key Aspects of Ritschl's Christology

Who, then, was Albrecht Ritschl and what were his central theological ideas?[160] In the 1840s, Ritschl had studied in Bonn, Tübingen and Halle, and he was strongly influenced by Schleiermacher, Kant, and his teacher Ferdinand Christian Baur (although he later dissociated himself from Baur and the Tübingen school).[161] After teaching for some time in Bonn, Ritschl lectured in Göttingen from 1864 until the end of his life. His most important contribution, which also marks the starting point for the so-called Ritschl school, is *The Christian Doctrine of Justification and Reconciliation* (*Die christliche Lehre von der Rechtfertigung und Versöhnung*).[162] It was published in three volumes between 1870 and 1874, just while Schlatter was studying in Basel and Tübingen, and, as Schlatter's discussion of Ritschl's work a few years later reveals, he must have read it very closely at the time.[163] Three features are central to Ritschl's theology: the kingdom of God (*Reich Gottes*), the person and work of Jesus Christ, and the value judgments (*Werturteile*) of the Christian community. Ritschl creatively combines these features like this: God's loving purpose[164] with this world is to build the kingdom of

---

160. For an introduction to Ritschl's theology, see Weinhardt, *Wilhelm Herrmanns Stellung*, 1–29, and also his "Einleitung," 1–113. See also Ritschl, *Unterricht in der christlichen Religion*, ix–xi. In addition, we have drawn upon Grenz and Olson's short summary in *Twentieth Century Theology*, 51–59, Richmond's work, *Ritschl: A Reappraisal*, 168–219, and Schäfer, *Ritschl*, 45–67.

161. At the outset, Ritschl followed his teacher Baur, who was based in Tübingen (where Ritschl studied from August 1845 to April 1846). Later, in the 1850s, however, Ritschl broke with Baur, as he could not support Baur's attempt to explain the origins of Christianity without miracles. See Weinhardt, "Einleitung," 29, 33.

162. Weinhardt, *Wilhelm Herrmanns Stellung*, 7.

163. While there are no explicit references to his Ritschl reading in Schlatter's personal records from his student time, one must assume that he studied Ritschl's works closely sometime between 1874 and 1880, as Schlatter refers to Ritschl in his 1881/82 lecture, "Geschichte der spekulativen Theologie seit Cartesius." I am grateful to Werner Neuer for clarification of this matter (e-mail message to author, December 18, 2013).

164. The notion of God's love is central to Ritschl's system. "The exhaustive Christian concept [*Begriff*] of God is love." Ritschl, *Unterricht in der christlichen Religion*, 9

God, which is the "universal ethical fellowship of humankind," and at the same time the fulfilment of humanity's highest good.[165] Human beings, says Ritschl, deliver value judgments on the kingdom of God, which is revealed in—and established by—Jesus Christ. Ritschl's value judgments are central in this context, as they point to his clear neo-Kantian trajectory. Value judgments, according to Ritschl, belong to the sphere of religious knowledge (or, in Kantian terminology, practical reason), which has to be distinguished from scientific knowledge, the neutral, disinterested observation of reality. Relevant for Ritschl, however, is the former, religious knowledge, where the Christian makes subjective value judgments on reality.[166]

This epistemological position has obvious implications for Christology. The divinity of Christ, for instance, is according to Ritschl an objective topic, which belongs to the scientific realm, rather than to the religious arena.[167] As a consequence, Ritschl excludes the Chalcedonian affirmation of Christ's divinity as idle; it is a scientific-objective assertion which has no theological, religious value.[168] Now if it is not Jesus' divinity, as traditionally understood, which makes Jesus unique, what is it then? This is where we must turn to Ritschl's notion of Jesus' unique role, his vocation (*Beruf*) in respect to the kingdom of God, given to him by the Father.[169] Jesus' vocation is unique since his own preaching, his volition, and his performance (all revolving around the kingdom of God) are uniquely directed to the moral good of humankind, which is, as noted earlier, at the same time also God's

---

(§ 11).

165. Ritschl, *Justification and Reconciliation*, 449 (§ 48). On the kingdom of God, see ibid., 334–35.

166. Grenz and Olson, *Twentieth Century Theology*, 54.

167. Ritschl contends: "But if Christ by what He has done and suffered for my salvation is my Lord, and if, by trusting for my salvation to the power of what He has done for me, I honour Him as my God, then that is a value-judgment of a direct kind. It is not a judgment which belongs to the sphere of disinterested scientific knowledge, like the formula of Chalcedon." Ritschl, *Justification and Reconciliation*, 398.

168. In his evaluation of Ritschl, Richmond explains that, "Ritschl and his nineteenth-century contemporaries did not understand Christ's deity in terms of *substance*, nor of *consubstantiality* with God, simply because such terms had become in post-Enlightenment Germany unintelligible, not to say meaningless." Richmond, *Ritschl: A Reappraisal*, 172 (emphasis original).

169. "His vocation, however," writes Ritschl, "is unique in its kind; for its special character is directed to the general moral task [*allgemeine sittliche Aufgabe*] as such, in other words to the founding of the Kingdom of God and the community destined for this task. . . . Therefore nobody can directly imitate Him; and an imitation which selects particular visible aspects of His life-course would still be no imitation of Christ." Ritschl, *Justification and Reconciliation*, 589 (emphasis mine).

highest goal.[170] In his morally perfect life on earth, in particular his patient sufferings, Jesus has demonstrated the unity of his will and work with God's purpose for humankind.[171] As a result, based on the value of Christ's life for God and the community, Christians address and confess him as God, ascribing to him divine status. Ritschl concludes that "we know the nature of God and Christ only in their worth for us."[172] Based on this brief overview of Ritschl's key concepts and thoughts, we are now in a position to turn to Schlatter's critical evaluation of the Göttingen professor's Christology.

Schlatter on Ritschl

Schlatter deals with Ritschl's theology to a great extent in his 1884 Bern lecture, "Christology and Soteriology." One also finds some critical interaction in his annotations in the *Dogma*, where Schlatter refers to Ritschl more than to any other theologian (a total of fourteen times, an unusual frequency for Schlatter, who, as noted earlier, generally hesitated to refer to secondary material in his works). These two sources are thus crucial references for our discussion in the following section. To begin with, one notices significant overlaps between Schlatter and Ritschl. Schlatter commends Ritschl for re-importing the lost notion of the *relational aspect of Christology*. In Schlatter's eyes, Ritschl rightly underlines the vital communion between Jesus and his disciples, between the community and its founder. Schlatter thus welcomes Ritschl's focus on the community of God's people; he appreciates that Ritschl "seriously considered afresh the church as the instrument of the divine dominion."[173] Moreover, Schlatter feels that Ritschl's notion of the value judgment is, in comparison to Schleiermacher's agenda, an improvement, as it complements Schleiermacher's emphasis on feeling with a "cognitive component" (*intellektuelle Moment*).[174] However, Schlatter is also keen to highlight where he parts with Ritschl. Three points deserve closer scrutiny. First, Schlatter feels that Ritschl ends up in subjective theological

170. Ritschl claims that "the vocational task of Jesus Christ [*Berufsaufgabe Jesu Christi*], or, the ultimate goal of his life, namely, the kingdom of God, is . . . God's ultimate goal in the world." Ritschl, *Unterricht in der christlichen Religion*, 20 (§ 23).

171. Ritschl, *Unterricht in der christlichen Religion*, 20 (§22). Ritschl somewhat avoids elaborating further on the nature of Christ's union with God. This sphere is, according to Ritschl, not accessible to the theologian: "One has to resist all attempts to go behind this fact: how it is brought to existence in detail, how it thus has become empirical." Ritschl, *Theologie und Metaphysik*, 29.

172. Ritschl, *Justification and Reconciliation*, 212.

173. Schlatter, *Dogma*, 603n289.

174. Schlatter, "Christologie und Soteriologie," 25.

speculation as he neglects empirical observation as the essential starting point for theology, with damaging implications for the notion of faith (one is reminded, here, of Schlatter's Kant-critique, introduced earlier). What is also missing in Ritschl's system, Schlatter claims, is secondly, a clear focus on Jesus' historical rootedness (a point of critique that Schlatter had also directed at idealist Christologies). He is, thirdly, unhappy with Ritschl's exclusive emphasis on Jesus' vocation (*Beruf*) without doing equal justice to his office (*Amt*), as this leads in his view to a downplaying of Jesus' divinity and of his soteriological impact upon humanity.

First of all then we turn to Schlatter's overall epistemological evaluation of Ritschl's approach. Having discussed Schlatter's critique of Kantian thought earlier, one will notice a similar pattern emerging here as Schlatter deals with Ritschl's neo-Kantian theology. Not a friend of dualisms, Schlatter disapproves of Ritschl's distinction between religious knowledge (through the value judgment) and objective scientific knowledge. While Schlatter agrees with Ritschl that the cognitive, judgment-forming dimension is central to dogmatics—one thinks of Schlatter's notion of the thinking-act—he laments that Ritschl relates the judgment to the subjective realm rather than the objective sphere. This is regrettable insofar as Ritschl's religious knowledge, Schlatter feels, is lacking any substance and universal validity. Ritschl's value judgments, Schlatter argues, do not "refer to the being of things," but instead express how one "wants to perceive things."[175] As Ritschl is critical of the empirical knowability of God's revelation in creation and history, the value judgment lacks any substantial foundation.[176] "It is indeed an essentially different form of logical reasoning," Schlatter writes, "whether we deal with the question 'What is?,' or [whether we] ask 'What is that which is being worth for us?' [*was ist das Seiende für uns wert?*]."[177] While neglecting the first question, Schlatter thinks, Ritschl deals predominantly with the second question, whereby he ends up in a kind of theological relativism. Schlatter explains:

> The task of determining the value of a fact is rendered possible only when the fact has become known to us. When one negates the knowability of a fact, the value judgment becomes worthless; it becomes the postulate of individual discretion. This is no longer a scientific mode of operation, for it is no longer a reasonable act.[178]

---

175. Ibid.
176. Cf. Weinhardt, "Einleitung," 50.
177. Schlatter, "Christologie und Soteriologie," 26.
178. Ibid., 27.

Hence, for Schlatter, the "basis" on which Ritschl builds his value judgment is simply "too narrow."[179] In contrast to Ritschl, the Swiss empirical realist is confident that our value judgment, or, our thinking-act, so to speak, must be based on an empirical seeing-act, where the theologian observes the objective facts, confident that he will gain reliable knowledge in the process. Only in this way, Schlatter claims, will theologians be able to make a case for universally valid truth statements.[180] As theology assesses and postulates propositional truth claims, through the close observation of the "objectively given fact" (*objektiv gegebene Thatbestand*), theology establishes itself as a rightful member of the academy.[181] Furthermore, Schlatter is convinced that Ritschl's approach has significant implications for faith. For faith to be a reliable faith it must be based on trustworthy, universally valid truth claims. Yet this is not the case with Ritschl's value judgments, as they do not meet the serious demands of the "truth claim" without which faith is denied "its sufficient base."[182] In Ritschl's system then, Schlatter feels, any certainty of faith does seem to lie outside the reach of the Christian. Faith, notes Schlatter, in order to be a confident faith in Jesus Christ, must be based on a "given reality" (*ein Gegebenes Reelles*), a concrete revelation in history.[183] This brings us to our second point.

From Schlatter's perspective, history in the general sense, and even more so history as the specific story of Christ, the history of the Christ, must be an essential element of Christology. It is the concrete historical setting which "sets the stage for Jesus' appearance . . . when the fullness of time had come, God sent forth his Son, Gal 4."[184] However, Ritschl's Christ is not sufficiently rooted in history, Schlatter complains. Jesus' historical context, with its significant impact on the community was in his view not adequately recognized by Ritschl and his colleagues.[185] More specifically, it seems to Schlatter that Jesus' actual words and deeds recede to the background, whereas the ideas the early community had of Jesus, the "representations of the original consciousness of the community," take center stage.[186] In con-

---

179. Schlatter, *Rückblick*, 158–59.
180. Schlatter, "Christologie und Soteriologie," 28.
181. Schlatter, "Religiöse Aufgabe der Universitäten," 72n1.
182. Schlatter, *Rückblick*, 158–59.
183. Schlatter, "Christologie und Soteriologie," 21.
184. Ibid., 38–39.
185. Ibid., 40.
186. Ritschl's understanding of traditional doctrines as "correlative representations of the original consciousness of the community," is surely different from Schlatter's view of the traditional doctrines' universal validity. Ritschl writes, "Thence follows for our present task, however, that the material of the theological doctrines of forgiveness,

trast, Schlatter underlines that the concrete history of the person and work of Jesus Christ was from the very beginning deeply intertwined with the history of the community. He continually points to the historical context-relatedness of Jesus' person and work.[187] Thus, Schlatter sees an objective historical contingency in Jesus Christ's being in action. There is a continuity which ranges from Jesus' own works via the deeds of the apostles down to the early Christian community (and even to our context today).[188] In fact, the titles of Schlatter's two-volume New Testament theology reflect his emphasis on this causal continuity: *The History of the Christ* (volume one) and *The Theology of the Apostles* (volume two). Schlatter fears that Ritschl overlooks this causal connection and substitutes for it a correlative relation, thus somewhat loosening the deep historical connection between Jesus, his apostles and the early community of faith.

With this we are moving, thirdly, closer to the core of Schlatter's critique. Perhaps Schlatter's main concern with Ritschl's Christology was his almost exclusive focus on Jesus' vocation (*Beruf*), paired with the neglect of his messianic office (*Amt*). In other words, for Schlatter, the main problem was that the divinity of Jesus Christ in Ritschl's account is reduced to the value it has for humankind. According to Schlatter's reading of Ritschl, Jesus' divinity is here limited to a subjective value judgment about Jesus' perfect performance in achieving God's and humanity's highest good as the "Founder of the Kingdom of God in the world."[189] Schlatter is convinced that the objective question of who Jesus is *in se* is intrinsically tied to the question of what value he has for us, *pro nobis*. Only when these questions are considered a unity, will the unity of Christology and soteriology make any sense. Thus, what Schlatter seems to miss in Ritschl's program is a clear commitment to the concept of Christ's office. "Ritschl only acknowledged the vocation [*Beruf*]," remarks Schlatter, "and rejected the office [*Amt*] . . . The consequences of this sentence are disadvantageous as the royal goal of Jesus . . . must now be reframed."[190] What Schlatter hints at here is that

---

justification, and reconciliation is to be sought not so much directly in the words of Christ, as in the correlative representations of the original consciousness of the community." Ritschl, *Justification and Reconciliation*, 3. David L. Mueller argues that for Ritschl the "apostolic circle of ideas" was even more significant than the New Testament. Mueller, *Introduction to the Theology of Albrecht Ritschl*, 45–47.

187. Jesus, writes Schlatter, "comes upon it [the messianic idea] as a product of the Old Testament history, as a firm possession of the community into whose midst he was born as their member." Schlatter, "Christologie und Soteriologie," 39.

188. Ibid., 10–12.

189. Ritschl, *Justification and Reconciliation*, 451.

190. Schlatter, *Dogma*, 564n54.

Ritschl's neglect of Christ's office leads, in his view, to a constrained soteriology, and in particular, to a fragmented *theologia crucis*. Schlatter complains that Ritschl merely speaks of Jesus' *Berufstreue*, his faithfulness to his vocation, whereas Schlatter rather intends to stress Jesus' *Pflichttreue*, namely his faithfulness to his duty as the bearer of the cross.[191] Jesus' faithfulness to his duty is made tangible in his concrete will to the cross (*Kreuzeswille*), which includes, Schlatter feels, more than Ritschl's term.[192] The following quote summarizes well Schlatter's Ritschl-critique:

> Jesus does not set himself up as an example that should remind [the Christian] of God, as the one who represents him, but God acts through him, precisely in that he dies. In this way God's lordship comes about, by reconciling us to himself. Neither does one find in Jesus the notion that he is supposed to represent humanity before God and remind him of it. In fact, just because God knows us and calls us to himself, that is, for the sake of the kingdom of God, does he unite himself with us, the sinful and dying, so that God's forgiveness might become ours. Substitution does not illustrate a thought, it does not symbolize an idea, but it is the creative deed of love. . . . This is why Christ's office [*Christusamt*] and his cross are in Jesus not two diverging goals, but, as he is the Lord of God's community, he becomes the crucified [One], and because he is the crucified [One], he becomes our Lord.[193]

Schlatter clearly feels that Ritschl, on his way to unfolding the paradigm of the kingdom of God, is taking a christological shortcut. Ritschl proceeds exclusively via Jesus' vocation in relation to humanity, while he fails to take into account the soteriological significance of Jesus' sacrificial and efficacious work in history, mutually directed towards the Father *and* towards us, in which he at the same time vindicates his divinity by becoming the Lord over the new community. Ritschl's position, as Schlatter reads it, is then a stark "reduction of [Jesus'] office, which not only displays but establishes the

---

191. Ibid., 291. See also his "Introduction" to "Christologie und Soteriologie."

192. He writes: "Defining Jesus' will to the cross [*Kreuzeswille*] only with the formula *Berufstreue* means that one identifies Jesus' work merely with the action that preceded his end, whereby death puts an end to it and becomes a disaster for him. . . . This does not only contradict the apostles' teaching of the cross but also Jesus' action; he did not see in his death a disaster against which he must protect himself and which he, after it became unavoidable, had to translate into a positive value by remaining true [*treu*] to himself." Schlatter, *Dogma*, 584n167.

193. Ibid., 585n173.

communion [between God and humanity]."[194] In other words, what Schlatter misses is a clear emphasis on the divine status of the Son of God, who is in perfect relation with the Father and with humanity, and who performed the historical deed on the cross, through which we are now invited to enjoy an existential connection with him as members of the new community of faith.

Having identified key christological differences between Albrecht Ritschl and Adolf Schlatter, one can now return to the broader question: Where was Adolf Schlatter relative to Ritschl? In general, one observes a significant overlap between the two theologians as they both put the person and work of Jesus Christ, and the concept of the community of faith back into the theological spotlight of their day. Looking at it more closely, though, significant differences emerge. Ritschl and Schlatter disagree on crucial epistemological prolegomena which has, as we have just seen, far-reaching consequences for their respective christological trajectories. Still, Joachim Weinhardt and Peter Stuhlmacher claim that both Ritschl and Schlatter occupy a "double frontline position" (*doppelte Frontstellung*), namely between liberalism and confessionalism.[195] Assuming that this might be a correct observation, one must clearly highlight that they aim their attacks at different directions. While Ritschl directed his critique also against the theological liberalism of his later followers, Wilhelm Herrmann and Adolf von Harnack,[196] his main criticism, it seems, aims at traditional orthodoxy (which explains why Karl Barth considered Ritschl a liberal—and this label had no positive connotation for Barth at all).[197] Adolf Schlatter, on the other hand, certainly criticized the rigid Protestant pietism of his days,[198] but Ritschl and his followers were obviously much more in the line of fire. That said, one needs to be very careful when using the label "mediating position," always defining precisely how one expects this to apply to Schlatter and Ritschl. In the course of Schlatter's career, Ritschl's influence somewhat diminished and Schlatter critically followed the growing influence of Ritschl's pupils, Wilhelm Herrmann and Adolf von Harnack.[199] In

---

194. Ibid.

195. Weinhardt, "Einleitung," 72; Stuhlmacher, "Adolf Schlatter," 223.

196. Weinhardt, "Einleitung," 71–72.

197. Barth, for example, writes to his friend Eduard Thurneysen, "He [Ritschl] is really a bad egg, in his way no less dire than Schleiermacher, if anything, worse." Barth to Thurneysen, 3 July 1928, in *Barth–Thurneysen: Briefwechsel*, 1:588. For a balanced evaluation of this critique see McCormack, *Barth's Critically Realistic Dialectical Theology*, 53n41, 299–300.

198. See my essay, "Good Will Hunting," 125–43.

199. This was not only because Ritschl died in 1889 and could no longer defend his

what follows, we will analyze Schlatter's critique of Herrmann and Harnack, always with a view to identifying the important building-blocks of Schlatter's own Christology.

Schlatter, the Ritschlians and the Question of the Christ

Adolf Schlatter very much enjoyed working in Greifswald among likeminded colleagues. Given that he was very happy with the Protestant faculty, which he called "one big family,"[200] he rejected several calls from notable universities during that time. In 1890, Schlatter was called to the University of Heidelberg (against the will of their faculty), and he was tempted to accept, as the Neckar town was much closer to his Swiss homeland than Prussian Greifswald.[201] Schlatter, however, declined, as his engagement in Greifswald was proving to be successful and fulfilling. Not much later, Schlatter was offered a chair at the University of Bonn, which he also declined.[202] Two years later, in June 1892, Schlatter received a call to Marburg—despite Ritschl-pupil Wilhelm Herrmann's "strong misgivings" (*schwere Bedenken*).[203] Systematician Wilhelm Herrmann (1846–1922), professor in Marburg since 1879, was aware of Schlatter's critical stance towards his theological approach and was, understandably, not enthusiastic about working alongside Schlatter.[204] Much to Herrmann's relief, Schlatter "quickly" and "without much consideration," declined the offer.[205] In what follows, we shall first turn to Schlatter's reaction to Herrmann's Christology before we deal, secondly, with the personal and, especially, theological relationship between Schlatter and Harnack.

---

position personally, but also because Ritschlianism separated into a left and right wing around the events of 1892, the struggle over the Apostles' Creed.

200. Neuer, *Adolf Schlatter*, 146.

201. Schlatter to his mother, 1 May 1890, in Neuer, *Adolf Schlatter*, 290.

202. See Neuer, *Adolf Schlatter*, 290.

203. Proceedings of the Marburg theological faculty, 4 May 1892, in Stupperich, "Adolf Schlatters Berufungen," 107, 114.

204. Wilhelm Herrmann was *the* major systematician of the Ritschl school. Weinhardt, *Wilhelm Herrmanns Stellung*, 2. Ritschl himself, as well as Martin Rade, even considered him the actual founder of the Ritschl school. Weinhardt, *Wilhelm Herrmanns Stellung*, 126. For a concise overview of Herrmann's life and work see McCormack, *Barth's Critically Realistic Dialectical Theology*, 49–66.

205. Schlatter to his mother, 16 June 1892, in Neuer, *Adolf Schlatter*, 291.

Part 1: The Genesis and Context of Schlatter's Christology

On Herrmann's *Communion of the Christian with God*

When Herrmann published his major work, the *Communion of the Christian with God* (*Verkehr des Christen mit Gott*, 1886), Schlatter responded in the same year with a lengthy, critical review, "From the inner life of the Ritschl school" ("Aus dem innern Leben der Schule Ritschls"). In many ways, Schlatter's treatment of Herrmann is reminiscent of his Ritschl-critique, although Schlatter clearly takes into account the specific aspects in which Herrmann further develops Ritschl's approach. We will highlight three major points of Schlatter's critique. In the first place, Schlatter expresses his approval of Herrmann's focus on the individual believer's relation with God through Jesus Christ. Still, Schlatter feels, secondly, that the basis for this relation too weak as it is not based on objective facts, which has, thirdly, damaging effects on the concept of faith and, of course, Christology.

To open then on a positive note, Schlatter is happy with Herrmann's focus on the Christian's communion with God. Perhaps more than Ritschl with his special interest in the community, Herrmann directed his attention to the individual Christian's relationship with God, between the soul and God,[206] which evokes in the believer a distinct religious experience. Schlatter not only appreciates Herrmann's emphasis on experience, the *Erlebnis* (a key term in Herrmann's work),[207] but he also applauds Herrmann's clear Christocentric orientation. He stresses positively that the Marburg theologian rightly reminds the Lutherans (in particular, as Schlatter perceives it, the Erlangen theologians)[208] of the fact (*Tathsache*) of God's actual revelation in Jesus Christ.[209] He writes:

> [T]he fact [*Tathsache*] that God seeks us and finds us consists in Jesus and his church. . . . This is God's revelation to us. In that we stand in Jesus before a man in whose presence we cannot deny the reality of God and [also cannot] doubt God's love, this is the experience [*Erlebniß*] which awakens in us the notion of God [*Gottesgedanken*] in such a way that it takes hold of us with the power of truth, creating faith. To this, I say, for my part: *macte! Sic itur ad astra* [Well done! Thus you shall go to the stars]. This

---

206. Timm, *Theorie und Praxis*, 101.

207. Schlatter, "Aus dem innern Leben der Schule Ritschls," 410.

208. Schlatter was generally critical of the Erlangen theologians' attempts to modify traditional orthodoxy (as he was equally critical towards those of the mediating theologians).

209. Schlatter would later also detect and appreciate this in Herrmann's student Karl Barth (see our discussion in the next section).

is the aspect of this [Herrmann's] theology that I would never renounce.[210]

Thus, Schlatter approves of what he considers Herrmann's return to the Reformation notion of the believer's experiential communion with Jesus Christ who reveals to us the reality of God.[211] However, although Schlatter might be pleased with Herrmann's experiential emphasis, he feels that Herrmann—much like Ritschl—commits what he considers the neo-Kantian fallacy of failing to ground the religious experience in its objective basis.

Secondly, then, from Schlatter's perspective the subjective *Erlebnis* lacks an objective foundation. Schlatter charged Herrmann (as he charged Ritschl) with a denial of an objective knowledge of God (*Gotteserkenntnis*), which belonged, in their view, to the inaccessible realm of objective knowledge, of science.[212] This has negative consequences, Schlatter remarks, for the Christian's communion with God which Herrmann wants to establish in the first place—an endeavor that is then doomed to fail. Directed at his Marburg contemporary, Schlatter writes: "In your opinion, however, the realm of knowledge [*Gebiet der Erkenntniß*] is possessed by 'science' which only deals with things of this world. . . . You thereby consider our communion [*Verkehr*] with God in tight, poor bounds, emptying it out."[213] At this point one wonders whether Schlatter's reading of Herrmann is entirely fair. According to Herrmann, the reality of God was in fact over and above every human scientific endeavor.[214] Herrmann clearly reacted—perhaps over-reacted, to Schlatter's mind—against the domestication of God by the proponents of the historical-critical method (like Ernst Troeltsch, for instance), emphasizing the transcendence of God and of our relation with him through faith. One wonders whether Schlatter could at this point have shown more appreciation for Herrmann, as the latter did not seem too far removed from his own agenda. Be that as it may, Schlatter is under the impression that Herrmann's focus on subjective experience somewhat eclipses the objective historical basis of faith, which is so important to Schlatter. And indeed, Herrmann claims that when we intend to talk about our communion with Jesus Christ, we are no longer to use the language of external historical facts; instead, we are to focus on Jesus' inner life (again, a key term in Herrmann's theological vocabulary to which Schlatter playfully refers in the title of his review, "innern Leben"). Thus in Herrmann's view, Jesus' re-

210. Schlatter, "Aus dem innern Leben der Schule Ritschls," 410.
211. Ibid., 411.
212. Schlatter, *Dogma*, 554n4.
213. Schlatter, "Aus dem innern Leben der Schule Ritschls," 413.
214. Herrmann, "Die Wirklichkeit Gottes," 292.

ligious importance for us consists in the inner life of his religious personality; the relation between Jesus and us is then defined by the way in which Jesus' inner life makes a definite impact on our inner life, independently of history. Still, Schlatter doubts that Herrmann has thereby managed to bridge Lessing's "ugly broad ditch" between historical and universal truths, between history and faith. "Herrmann's flight from history to a 'storm-free' inner reality"[215] is in Schlatter's eyes a pointless undertaking, for the believer might enjoy an experience (*Erlebnis*), which is, however, unrelated to objective knowledge (*Erkenntnis*). In Herrmann, Schlatter feels, Christology is reduced to a matter of inward experience without being grounded in objective facts. Instead of bridging the ditch, Herrmann is still left with an abyss, namely with the dualism of knowledge and experience. What the Beck-pupil misses is a distinct appreciation of God's revelation in creation as the basis for our subjective experience: the *Erlebnis* ought to be rooted in the *Erkenntnis*. "How dare we approach God inwardly," Schlatter asks the Marburg theologian, "when we disrupt his order in the natural realm?"[216] "Nothing," he writes, "that we find within ourselves can be the foundation of our confidence."[217]

As a result, and this is our third and final point, Schlatter feels that Herrmann has no solid basis for faith.[218] With a view to Herrmann's concept of the notions of faith (*Glaubensgedanken*),[219] Schlatter remarks that Herrmann detaches these from the universal natural realm, retreating somehow to a spiritual sphere where the *Glaubensgedanken* are valid only for the individual, without any reference to objective, universal truth. In Herrmann's direction, Schlatter writes that the notions of faith are "only valid for you as your own formation, possessing meaning only for you."[220] By contrast, Schlatter advances his own version of the notions of faith, which are "effective for you as the thoughts of *God*, which point to God's work, and which are God's gift to you, from the God who has also formed nature, whose word and will is the harmonious truth of all that exists."[221] Schlatter here clearly aims to advocate a broader and, in his view, more robust foundation for the Christian faith, where faith is rooted in the God who is not aloof from

215. McCormack, *Barth's Critically Realistic Dialectical Theology*, 63.
216. Schlatter, "Aus dem innern Leben der Schule Ritschls," 414.
217. Ibid., 413.
218. Ibid., 412.
219. Herrmann's concept of the *Glaubensgedanken* implies that faith reflects on its own genesis and thus becomes conscious of its relation to the world. See Weinhardt, *Wilhelm Herrmanns Stellung*, 227–28.
220. Schlatter, "Aus dem innern Leben der Schule Ritschls," 415 (emphasis original).
221. Ibid.

his creation but who grants faith to his creatures in a harmonious, organic way (we will return to this significant aspect in chapter 6). Overall then, Schlatter is convinced that his theology of objective facts provides a more sustainable christological account and a more solid foundation for faith. Herrmann, on the other hand, does not do justice to the New Testament facts as his theological foundation is simply too subjective and thus too unstable. Schlatter concludes:

> Here appears a young theology on the scene that again seeks and knows the ground, yet, it builds itself only a narrow, meagre little house, pleased when God and his goodness is not a doubtable factor. Surely, it renders to some a great service, as it points within all the theological and philosophical hurly-burly to Jesus as the solid, secure proof of God. Nonetheless, everyone who puts the New Testament next to Herrmann's *Communion with God* will develop the following wish: do not put the "master" [*Meister*] over the Scriptures. The Scriptures offer more than that.[222]

Taken together, we note a characteristic profile of Schlatter's critique in dealing with Ritschl and Herrmann. While he is in many ways appreciative of both the Göttingen and the Marburg theologian, he nonetheless identifies serious issues he feels obligated to address, such as a missing assertion of an objective knowledge of God as the basis for our experiential relation with God, and a retreat to inner, subjective states, which not only harms the notion of faith but also has damaging effects on Christology and soteriology. In his own major works, penned later in Tübingen, Schlatter would form his characteristic, critical-empirical realist approach to Christology (which we will discuss in the second part of this study). We now proceed by turning to Schlatter's fascinating encounter with the other major Ritschl-pupil, Adolf von Harnack. For a correct understanding of their theological differences it helps to consider first the concrete background of church politics, which brought the two theologians together, before examining the core of their christological dispute.

Schlatter, Harnack and the Struggle over the Apostles' Creed

Schlatter would have probably remained in Greifswald, had not the struggle over the Apostles' Creed (*Apostolikumsstreit*) ignited the Protestant scene

---

222. Ibid., 417.

in the late nineteenth century.[223] In the 1890s, the contrasting positions between Greifswald and the Ritschlians came plainly to the fore. In June 1892, Württemberg minister Christoph Schrempf was suspended for refusing to use the Apostles' Creed during a baptismal service. Displeased with Schrempf's removal, Berlin theology students intended to draw up a petition to be submitted to the senior consistory (*Oberkirchenrath*), demanding the abolition of the requirement to use the Apostles' Creed in the liturgy and as a compulsory formula in the ordination of ministers.[224] Before the students put their plan into action, they asked their teacher Adolf von Harnack[225] what he thought about the idea.[226] Harnack answered his students in a question and answer session during one of his lectures, fittingly on "Recent Church History," in which he advised them not to proceed with their petition. While explaining to them his own position, he also felt that he needed to give a more substantial account of his thoughts in written form.[227] No sooner said than done, Harnack published his opinion on the Apostles' Creed in the August 1892 edition of the Ritschlian journal, *Die Christliche Welt*, in a piece entitled "On the matter of the Apostles' Creed" ("In Sachen des Apostolikums"). In his short article, Harnack suggests either substituting or amending the Apostles' Creed in favor of a "short confession" that would "display the gospel as it was understood in the course of the Reformation" more clearly and that would avoid the current "wording that gives offence to many."[228] In contrast to his students, however, Harnack clearly does not want to "abolish the Apostles' Creed,"[229] though he proposes that churches

223. For a summary of the *Apostolikumsstreit* see Neufeld, *Adolf Harnacks Konflikt mit der Kirche*, 114–32. As to the original debate see Harnack, *Das Apostolische Glaubensbekenntnis. Ein geschichtlicher Bericht nebst einem Nachwort*, Cremer, *Zum Kampf um das Apostolikum*, and von Harnack's answer to Cremer, "Antwort auf die Streitschrift D. Cremers," 265–98.

224. Harnack, "In Sachen des Apostolikums," 768.

225. Harnack was clearly a follower of Ritschl, although, like many Ritschlians, he never actually sat in Ritschl's lecture hall as a student. Harnack was professor of church history at the University of Berlin from 1888 until 1921; he became a member of the Academy of Sciences, and later, from 1905 to 1921, he served as the general director of the Royal Library at Berlin. On Harnack's life and work see the compendium by Nowak et al., *Adolf von Harnack*. See also Osthövener, "Adolf von Harnack als Systematiker," 296–331, and by the same author the "Nachwort" to Harnack's *Wesen des Christentums*, 257–89.

226. Harnack, *Das Apostolische Glaubensbekenntnis*, 35–36.

227. Ibid., 36.

228. Harnack, "In Sachen des Apostolikums," 768.

229. Ibid.

could be given the right to decide for themselves whether they want to use it or would prefer to substitute it with another "formula of faith."[230]

Harnack's publication provoked a storm of protest, revealing clearly the frontlines between the Ritschlians on the one hand, and the Greifswald theologians, conservative Lutherans, and conservative pietists on the other hand. The *Deutsche Evangelische Kirchenzeitung* as well as the *Neue Lutherische Kirchenzeitung* criticized Harnack's statement as "destructive theology."[231] Thereupon Ritschlians, such as Wilhelm Herrmann, Julius Kaftan, Ferdinand Kattenbusch, Martin Rade, and others, drew up a declaration (*Eisenacher Erklärung*) in which they publicly supported Harnack's position.[232] Having provoked a lively debate, Harnack felt the need to clarify his position in more detail. His publication "drew heavy charges," Harnack admits, "and forced me to provide a short . . . historical report about the origin of the confession of faith."[233] A few weeks later, then, Harnack published a historical account of the Apostles' Creed from the early church to the Reformation (*Das Apostolische Glaubensbekenntnis: Ein geschichtlicher Bericht nebst einem Nachwort*). Again, Harnack's work triggered opposition. The most substantial critique came from the head of the Greifswald school, Hermann Cremer. Schlatter, although he had "a good mind" to take part in the public debate, left it to Cremer to frame a well-grounded answer.[234] According to Schlatter—and, it remains to be seen whether it is a correct self-assessment—

> [Cremer] possessed the courage for polemics that I lacked, plus he was involved in a lively war with the Erlangen [school] and even more so with the Ritschlian theologians. I immediately agreed with his opposition to the Ritschlian group's exclusive dominion over the church and the faculties.[235]

The Greifswald scholars apparently feared that the Ritschlians would be able to influence the church through their dominance over the Protestant faculties in Prussian Germany, a fear that was perhaps not unfounded. By 1892, thirteen Ritschlians had acquired theological chairs in Germany, and such

---

230. Ibid., 768–69. According to Harnack's view, the Apostles' Creed contained both too much and too little to be a satisfactory test for candidates for ordination; he thus preferred a briefer declaration of faith which could be rigorously applied across the board.

231. See Neufeld, *Adolf Harnacks Konflikt mit der Kirche*, 118.

232. See Weinhardt, *Wilhelm Herrmanns Stellung*, 68.

233. Harnack, "Das Apostolische Glaubensbekenntnis," 220.

234. Schlatter, "Entstehung der Beiträge," 73–75.

235. Ibid., 73.

chairs were, ultimately, responsible for the education of the future Protestant clergy.[236] Schlatter reflects on the lively character of the political-theological debate between Greifswald and the Ritschlians in his *Rückblick*:

> The glowing, manly rage [*glühender Manneszorn*] that Cremer carried with him commanded my ... cordial admiration; nothing connected me more closely with him than the manner in which he was able to be cross. Just as I agreed with his ambition to prevent the Ritschlian group from exclusively taking over the dominion over the church and the faculties, I admired the bravery he repeatedly demonstrated in this battle.[237]

With his critical stance towards the Apostles' Creed, Harnack had maneuvered himself into a precarious situation in that he now faced disciplinary action. This happened as a result of complaints from an Evangelical-Lutheran Conference on September 20, 1892, on the basis of which Emperor Wilhelm II asked for an immediate report (*Immediatbericht*) on Harnack.[238] Prussian Culture minister Julius R. Bosse (1832–1901) was able to aid Harnack in this predicament by suggesting—in order to appease the ecclesial camp— the founding of a chair of systematic theology at the University of Berlin that would support the church position. This proposal was endorsed by the Kaiser as the so-called punitive professorship (*Strafprofessur*) against von Harnack. The Prussian Ministry of Culture initially sought to call Martin Kähler, who was then professor in Halle and who received the Berlin faculty's unanimous support. Reinhold Seeberg (then in Erlangen) and Hermann Cremer were also short-listed. Kähler, however, declined as he did not want to leave Halle. The negotiations with Seeberg proved to be difficult, and the Berlin faculty categorically opposed issuing a call to Hermann Cremer. Adolf Schlatter was the last Greifswald theologian standing who could fulfil the requirements for the punitive professorship and appease the upset Lutherans. Schlatter himself, however, was certain that Cremer was the more suitable candidate. "If any one of us [the Greifswald school] must go, it has to be Cremer."[239] He was convinced that if the Prussian officials had been serious about finding an equal counterweight to Harnack, they would have called Cremer to the punitive professorship, yet the Berlin administration "feared his [Cremer's] potency [*Wirksamkeit*]," Schlatter thought.[240] Thus, Friedrich Althoff (1839–1908) approached Schlatter and repeatedly tried to

236. Weinhardt, *Wilhelm Herrmanns Stellung*, 124.
237. Schlatter, *Rückblick*, 140.
238. See Neufeld, *Adolf Harnacks Konflikt mit der Kirche*, 118.
239. Schlatter to his mother, 20 January 1893, in Neuer, *Adolf Schlatter*, 294.
240. Schlatter, "Entstehung der Beiträge," 84.

convince him to accept the call. Schlatter clearly knew that he was only the second, if not, third choice, which explains his hesitation. He notes that "the choice thus became, as I felt it, a dishonorable game and an empty pretense, as I was being pushed forward in his [Cremer's] place."[241]

Schlatter finally gave in and accepted the call, because, as he put it, "in such cases, personal desires have to remain silent . . . when it [the state] calls, Christianity has to be ready."[242] And in the end, interestingly, Schlatter felt that this call had also a spiritual dimension, as he suggests that through him the gospel of Jesus Christ, by God's grace, would be brought to the Berlin faculty. In a letter to his mother, Schlatter summarizes his thoughts as follows:

> I think, to tell the truth, the whole issue is about the gospel. It must also [be brought] to the University of Berlin. That I should take it there looks foolish; I would have preferred . . . somebody else to do it. Yet, no one else is available. The doors are closed for Cremer; and for me, they are not only opened but I am being forcefully pushed through. Well, then, I can do nothing else but look to God's grace.[243]

During the negotiations with Berlin, Schlatter insisted on receiving permission to teach (*Lehrerlaubnis*) not only systematic theology but also New Testament, for, as he continually reiterated, the historical New Testament discipline provides the basis for the dogmatic task, and the two organically belong together.[244] That Schlatter's theological chair was primarily designed for systematic theology irritated Julius Kaftan—he feared that Schlatter would draw students from his own lectures in systematics.[245] Be that as it may, in August 1893, Schlatter delivered his last lecture in Greifswald, and one month later he moved with his wife and by then five children to Berlin, where, many decades earlier, his uncle Gottlieb Schlatter (1809–87) had

---

241. Ibid.

242. Schlatter, *Erlebtes*, 14–15. See also Neuer, *Adolf Schlatter*, 293 and Stuhlmacher, "Adolf Schlatter," 225.

243. Schlatter to his mother, 6 March 1893, in Neuer, *Adolf Schlatter*, 296.

244. See for example his 1909 publication, "Die Theologie des Neuen Testaments und die Dogmatik," available in English as "The Theology of the New Testament and Dogmatics," 115–66. As a compromise, his teaching post was finally called "for systematic theology and the New Testament disciplines" (*für die systematische Theologie und die neutestamentlichen Disziplinen*). "This formula was not beautiful," says Schlatter in retrospect, "but I could live with it." *Rückblick*, 165; see also *Erlebtes*, 101–2, and "Selbstdarstellungen," 156, 158.

245. Schlatter, *Rückblick*, 181; cf. Weinhardt, *Wilhelm Herrmanns Stellung*, 125n940.

studied under Friedrich Schleiermacher,[246] and where he would now teach for the next five years.[247]

As Schlatter was awarded his chair as a penal professorship against Harnack, one would expect that a chilly reception awaited him in Berlin. Surprisingly, at least to Schlatter, Harnack had already written a welcoming letter a few months earlier, in March 1893, whose friendly tone would not only be reciprocated by Schlatter, but would also mark their positive future etiquette despite theological disagreement. Harnack writes:

> I assume you did not make this decision [to go to Berlin] a lightly, both with respect to your position in Greifswald and in face of the special circumstances here with us. I am still convinced that you will not come with hatchet [*Kriegsbeil*] to undertake a campaign [*Feldzug*], but rather in the manner of a professor, to speak what he has learned and what he cannot keep to himself. In any case I can assure you that I am happy that you are coming . . . I am not only glad that many a [professor]—who appeared on the horizon—did not come, but also—positively—that "you" decided to collaborate with us. I use the expression of "collaboration," although I know that nobody trusts us. Yet, I think . . . that the common ground of the work with the students is greater than what separates [us]. Please kindly accept these lines as a proof of this attitude; they should hearten you in your relocation to Berlin.[248]

These lines suggest that the first meeting between the professor occupying the penal professorship and the professor against whom this chair was directed would actually take place in a friendly atmosphere. In fact, this was then the case in autumn 1893 when the two theologians met for a long conversation. In a letter to his Greifswald friend Hermann Cremer, Schlatter reports the "lovely conversation" he enjoyed with Harnack:

> We pretty much talked about everything that affects our contemporary scientific world. We defined the religious difference to that effect: He reckoned the prophetic word: "Oh, that you

---

246. Schlatter, "Idealismus und Erweckung," 29.

247. Schlatter taught at the University of Berlin from October 1893 until March 1898.

248. Harnack to Schlatter, 9 March 1893. This wording is from an earlier draft by Harnack. The letter that reached Schlatter (same date) was slightly shorter and also differs somewhat in the wording. The welcoming tone, however, is the same. See for a comparison of both the draft and the original letter as it was sent, Adolf Schlatter archive, inventory no. 909 and no. 1306. For an extract of the draft, see Agnes von Zahn-Harnack, *Adolf von Harnack*, 209.

would rend the heavens" (Isa 64:1), is not realized and is unrealizable; we are limited to the psychological sphere, to "faith"; I replied that prior to faith comes a seeing that rests on certain testimonies of God, in which faith has its motive and its content. You see, it is the old polarity of the "facts"; but [we talked] openly and in a mutually measured way.[249]

This is relevant insofar as Schlatter, by pointing to the old polarity of the facts, touches here upon his central criticism of Ritschlian epistemology, namely its lacking an objective foundation for truth claims which harms the concept of faith. More precisely, in Schlatter's view, the main controversy between him and Harnack consisted in the fact that he rooted faith in the perceptible actuality of historical-*heilsgeschichtliche* facts, whereas Harnack, in his eyes, distinguished between objective knowledge (*Erkenntnis*) and existential experience (*Erlebnis*), in a way reminiscent of Herrmann. In what follows, we shall discuss this significant difference between the two eminent theologians in more detail.

History, Knowledge, and Experience

Evidently, Schlatter disagrees with Harnack on the extent to which objective facts, in this case, historical facts, can become the ground for subjective experience. Harnack, for one, argues that "Christ, as history introduces him," cannot become believable as Lord and savior through any historical knowledge (*Erkenntnis*);[250] this is only possible through religious experience (*Erfahrung*). Religious "experience," writes Harnack, "lies above the coercion that is exercised through historical knowledge."[251] He adds: "The question of who and what Jesus is can . . . only be ascertained by means of historical research; but the conviction that this historical Jesus is the redeemer [*Erlöser*] and Lord does not follow from the historical finding, but from awareness of sin and of God when Jesus Christ is proclaimed."[252] This seems to suggest that Harnack continues the tradition of his teacher Ritschl and his pupil Herrmann, as he separates in the neo-Kantian manner the religious question from the scientific question. In order to distil the religious essence, namely, the kernel (*Kern*) of who Jesus Christ was, Harnack has to

---

249. Schlatter to Cremer, 8 November 1893, in Stupperich, *Wort und Wahrnehmung*, 13.

250. Harnack, "Antwort auf die Streitschrift D. Cremers," 291.

251. Ibid.

252. Ibid., 293.

first peel away the historical husk (*Hülle/Schale*).²⁵³ From the Greifswald theologians' perspective, Harnack introduces here an extraneous dualism to christological method, namely a differentiation between the historical Jesus, who is accessible through critical-historical research (*geschichtliche Wissenschaft*), and the Christ of faith, who is solely accessible through experience.

On the one hand, Schlatter and Cremer agree with Harnack's endorsement of strenuous theological-historical research, and his sense of the importance of religious experience. They argue, however, that these processes are organically interrelated, whereas Harnack seems to tear them apart. Knowledge (*Erkenntnis*), according to the Greifswald scholars, is the basis for religious experience (*Erlebnis*); that is, critical-historical research is an essential basis (though not the only one) for faith. In Harnack, the two processes of *Erkenntnis* and *Erlebnis* seem to run in parallel, whereas Schlatter and Cremer stress that they are closely linked with each other. Apparently, Harnack was aware of creating an antagonism here, as he later admits in his *Wesen des Christentums*.²⁵⁴ This antagonism, however, can be "overcome within ourselves," as Harnack suggests.²⁵⁵ For Schlatter, of course, this dichotomy does not exist in the first place.²⁵⁶ The Swiss theologian categorically rejects any separation between knowledge and faith, science and religion. "This dilemma is misplaced," he argues, because "knowledge is intrinsic to faith and faith cannot be sustained without knowledge."²⁵⁷ This knowledge is obviously not perfect knowledge, but is knowledge nonetheless, knowledge which is indispensable for faith.²⁵⁸ Schlatter thus opts for a holistic theological approach which comprises both objective scientific research *and* a subjective exercise of faith, the former as the basis for the latter. Schlatter writes: "The historical task of the bible can be virtually nothing else than an intense listening to what the bible contains and renders visible; anything contrary to that is not *science*. There can therefore be no friction between historical scriptural research and faith."²⁵⁹ From the

---

253. See Harnack, *Wesen des Christentums*, 17–18, 39–40.

254. Harnack speaks of the "dualism" (*Zwiespalt*) between "God and the world, the Here and the Beyond [*Diesseits und Jenseits*], the visible and the invisible, matter and spirit . . . physics and ethics." Harnack, *Wesen des Christentums*, 88–89 [*What is Christianity*, 150].

255. Ibid., 89 [*What is Christianity*, 151].

256. Similarly to Schlatter, Weinhardt describes the conflict in Harnack's argument as the dualism of "objective doctrinal assertion" and "subjective inwardness." Weinhardt, "Einleitung," 105.

257. Schlatter, "Christologie und Soteriologie," 18.

258. Ibid., 18.

259. Schlatter, *Heilige Anliegen der Kirche*, 42 (emphasis original).

Greifswald perspective then, Harnack's approach is a continuation of the idealist heritage, where, according to Schlatter, "[w]e are not supposed to know, but we should have faith, and this faith is a substitute for the lack of knowledge."[260] To Schlatter's mind, however, "[t]he act of faith is an affirmation of the given [*des Gegebenen*]."[261] Again analogous to his Ritschl/Herrmann-critique, Schlatter considers the main difference between him and Harnack as one of theological method, which in turn leads to different christological outcomes. Schlatter writes:

> Whether or not Jesus was shown to us the way he is, whether we saw what he bestows upon us, or whether the New Testament disappeared behind our "science," this was the question that stood between me and the Liberals. Harnack's dogmatics required that he searched in Jesus for a "religion" that connected "the soul" with God. This entailed that history lost its power to transmit "religion" to us; the historical [*das Geschichtliche*] was in the past, and thereby individualized and consequently confined. . . . For that reason, Harnack instructs us to look behind Christianity for its "essence" [*Wesen*]. This "essence," however, did not possess a content defined by clear concepts. The goal to pursue was an internalization of the individual, who now, inevitably, had lost any relation to history and who perceived the church only as an oppressive burden. The *History of Dogma* [*Dogmengeschichte*] thereby became the proof that dogma had destroyed itself. Thus what stood between him and me was the question which had moved me from the very beginning of my theological work, namely, who Jesus was.[262]

Schlatter here illustrates how in his view, Harnack, with his critical-historical approach, disconnects Christology from history and, as a result, has to retreat to the inward subjective level.[263] Yet to base one's relation with Jesus Christ on subjective experience alone, Schlatter feels, means to paint a merely fragmentary picture of Jesus; the subjective experience must in his view grow out organically from an encounter with the objective, *heilsgeschichtliche* facts of the

---

260. Schlatter, "Christologie und Soteriologie," 20.

261. Ibid.

262. Schlatter, *Rückblick*, 160–61.

263. Schlatter would most likely echo Weinhardt's critique of Harnack: "In fact, the religious feeling, or religious experience, is in Harnack a foundational systematic-theological principle which secures numerous religious notions which otherwise rest on biblical transmission, which Harnack eliminates or relativizes with his historical-critical method." Weinhardt, "Einleitung," 107. Harnack's approach is then a fundamentally existentialist approach, as Kurt Nowak asserts, in Weinhardt, "Einleitung," 107.

New Testament. Despite these fundamental differences, Schlatter and Harnack enjoyed for the next five years, between 1893 and 1898, a close and friendly relationship. They chatted during lecture breaks, and sometimes in the tram, and they regularly visited each other's homes.[264] Positively impressed by this surprising development, Schlatter remarked: "I sincerely hope we can assist and serve each other."[265] Presumably, Schlatter would have never guessed that he would one day reflect on his time in Berlin as follows: "among the Berlin colleagues, I only had a connection with Harnack."[266] And Harnack perhaps felt very much the same. At one point he even let himself be so carried away as to exclaim, in the company of faculty members: "The only difference between me and my colleague Schlatter is the question of miracles!" whereupon Schlatter energetically interjected, "No, it is the question of God!"[267]

In February 1897, Tübingen systematician Theodor Haering (1848–1928) enquired whether Schlatter would be interested in taking over the newly founded sixth professorial chair of the theological faculty in Tübingen. Haering wrote enthusiastically to Schlatter that "this would mean for Württemberg [a] continuation of [the tradition of] Bengel and Beck under new circumstances."[268] The idea appealed to Schlatter and in September of the same year, Stuttgart prelate Carl von Burk (1827–1904) apparently sent Schlatter an official request.[269] Two months later, in November 1897, Schlatter accepted, as he anticipated more suitable conditions for teaching and research in Tübingen than in Berlin, even hoping for a "new version of Greifswald."[270] Schlatter agreed on the condition that he would also be entitled to teach systematic theology, for, as already pointed out, the two disciplines formed one organic entity in his view.[271] Schlatter's decision to leave Berlin came as a surprise to many. Robert Stupperich explains that "it caused a sensation that a Berlin professor would prefer another faculty

---

264. Neuer, *Adolf Schlatter*, 306.

265. Schlatter to his mother, 20 February 1894, in Neuer, *Adolf Schlatter*, 306.

266. Schlatter, *Rückblick*, 166.

267. Neuer, *Adolf Schlatter*, 307.

268. Haering to Schlatter, 15 February 1897, in Neuer, *Adolf Schlatter*, 359.

269. Neuer, *Adolf Schlatter*, 360.

270. As he expressed in a letter to Cremer, 4 November 1897, in Stupperich, *Wort und Wahrnehmung*, 41.

271. See Schlatter, *Rückblick*, 194. Adolf Schlatter named the newly established professorial chair New Testament professorate. He explains: "To secure the new professorate a proper status within the Tübingen faculty, I gave it the title 'New Testament professorate,' as the faculty did not have one yet and the dogmaticians and church historians had until now divided the New Testament teaching instruction between themselves. The Württemberg minister [of culture] secured my right to lecture also in dogmatics." Ibid.

to the one in Berlin."[272] Adolf von Harnack also regretted his colleague's decision, and once Schlatter had gone, he expressed his regret in a letter: "I am missing you in the consulting room and I feel the lack of a peer next to me, who with his opposition provokes my thoughts."[273] It is certainly an ironic historical episode that Schlatter's chair in Berlin, which was originally designed as a penal professorship against Harnack, resulted in one of the most fascinating theological interactions between two of the most influential theologians of the late nineteenth and early twentieth century. Over the following decades, they remained personally loyal to each other. In 1922, for example, Harnack contributed to the *Festschrift* in honor of Schlatter's seventieth birthday, *Aus Schrift und Geschichte*.[274] Their theological differences, however, remained.

Conclusion

In this second section of Where was Adolf Schlatter?, we focused on Schlatter's professional teaching career from around 1880 to the late 1890s, in which he found himself sitting between the two stools of Ritschlianism and Confessionalism. In Schlatter's view, Ritschl, Herrmann, and Harnack more or less adopt the Kantian suspicion of our ability to know objective facts and thus try to locate faith and religious experience in the subjective sphere. Whilst they might use different terminology and adopt different perspectives, they clearly share this epistemological premise, which leads in each case to a distorted Christology and a limited notion of faith. The faith of the believer who tries to connect with Jesus on the subjective level alone will shipwreck if the factual-historical foundation is missing. In contrast to Ritschl, Herrmann and Harnack, Schlatter affirms the possibility of a universal general knowledge of God, based on objective historical facts. To Schlatter's mind, then, Christology, if it indeed intends to capture the whole Jesus Christ, needs to focus on Jesus Christ's concrete volition that ushers in the historically effective, salvific deed on the cross. Only when our faith is based on the historical effectiveness of the person and work of Jesus Christ is our faith truly a faith in harmony with the New Testament. Our exploration into the genesis and the development of Adolf Schlatter's Christology would obviously remain incomplete without a consideration of his interaction with dialectical theology. By adding this perspective we shall complete

---

272. Stupperich, "Briefe Karl Holls an Schlatter," 174n5.
273. Harnack to Schlatter, 5 February 1899, in Neuer, *Adolf Schlatter*, 308.
274. Harnack, "Das Alter des Gliedes 'Heiliger Geist' im Symbol," 171–73.

our picture of Schlatter's christological development and thus open the door for our ensuing, more systematic-theological reflections.

SCHLATTER *ZWISCHEN DEN ZEITEN*

The theological encounter between Karl Barth and Adolf Schlatter has more or less been neglected by scholarship.[275] Although an exhaustive comparative study of these two fascinating figures might be both fruitful and stimulating, this is not the place to achieve this ambitious goal. For the present purpose, our analysis will be deemed successful if it provides a clear answer to the question: Where was Schlatter in relation to Barth? The intention is then to identify Schlatter's characteristic critique of Barth's theology, and in particular, his Christology, which will in turn add significant pieces to the overall picture of Schlatter's own christological approach. As in the previous two sections, we shall proceed chronologically, since their theological development is intrinsically tied to their personal histories.

This part is divided into four sections. We shall trace, first, the context of their early encounter at the beginning of the twentieth century, moving, secondly, to an exploration of Schlatter's fundamental critique of Barth's 1922 commentary on Romans, while looking, thirdly, at further developments and theological debates. Finally we deal more closely with Schlatter's critique of Barth's understanding of divine revelation, outlined in his discussion of Barth's *Prolegomena to Christian Dogmatics* (1927) and of the Barmen Declaration (1934).

Initial Difficulties

Twenty-five years after his first stay in Tübingen as a student, Schlatter returned in the spring of 1898 to the Swabian university town, where he would labor for the remaining four decades of his life. In a way, Schlatter would indeed continue in the tradition of his teacher Johann T. Beck, as Theodor Haering had expected and as Schlatter himself admits:

---

275. A rare exception is Werner Neuer's contribution. See particularly Neuer's analysis of the letter exchange between the two Swiss scholars, "Briefwechsel zwischen Karl Barth und Adolf Schlatter," 86–100, and the material in his Schlatter biography, *Adolf Schlatter*, 639–61, on which we heavily rely in this context. Peter Stuhlmacher and Udo Smid at least acknowledge theological parallels between Barth and Schlatter (the former in "Adolf Schlatter," 240, and the latter in "Natürliche Theologie: als Problem bei Adolf Schlatter," 106–16.

> I gladly became Beck's successor, not in his [manner], but in my own way, and I gladly continued the struggle where it has been fought with particular intensity, here, where D. Fr. Strauss had written his *Life of Jesus*, [where] F. Chr. Baur had claimed the fictitiousness for the most part of the New Testament and [where] Weizsäcker had contrasted Luke's story of the Apostles with his own. I expected that with Tübingen my years of pilgrimage would come to an end . . . and that it [Tübingen] would supply me with a lecture theatre in which a fruitful exchange with the students would become possible.[276]

Schlatter's expectations were largely fulfilled as he enjoyed his most fruitful and productive years, both as lecturer and as author, in Tübingen. Over the following decades many students sat in his lecture theatre who would later rise to prominence, among them a certain Karl Barth. In March 1906, Schlatter and the young Barth met for the first time, not in Tübingen, but in their native Switzerland. The then nineteen-year-old theological student Barth, who was at that time studying in Bern, participated in the Tenth Aarau Christian Student Conference, where Schlatter delivered a lecture about "Paul and Hellenism."[277] Barth prepared a report on the conference and published it (his first ever publication) in the *Berner Tagblatt*.[278] According to Barth, Schlatter's "penetrative" paper was the "highlight of the conference."[279] In the short article, Barth lists the key elements of Schlatter's presentation: his emphasis on the Apostle Paul's relational agenda ("no one lives from and for oneself"), and, what was most significant for Barth, Schlatter's moving from a (Hellenistic) human-centeredness towards a distinct God-centeredness.[280] As we shall see in due course, Schlatter recognized and appreciated in the later works of his former student Barth precisely this latter aspect of God-centeredness while continually complaining about the missing relational element in Barth's theology. While it is not clear whether there was a private meeting between the two at the conference, Schlatter was certainly aware of who Karl Barth was, as he was well acquainted with Barth's father, Johann Friedrich "Fritz" Barth (1856–1912), who established the student conference in the first place.[281] Fritz Barth succeeded Schlatter

---

276. Schlatter, *Rückblick*, 195.

277. Neuer, *Adolf Schlatter*, 424; cf. Busch, *Karl Barths Lebenslauf*, 49. Schlatter's lecture was published in *Gesunde Lehre*, 128–43, and also in Rengstorf and Luck, eds., *Paulusbild in der neueren deutschen Forschung*, 98–112.

278. Cf. Busch, *Karl Barth: His Life from Letters and Autobiographical Texts*, 37.

279. Barth, "X. christliche Studentenkonferenz in Aarau, 1906," 124.

280. Ibid., 124–25.

281. Busch, *Karl Barth: His Life from Letters and Autobiographical Texts* 37.

86   Part 1: The Genesis and Context of Schlatter's Christology

as professor of New Testament at the University of Bern in 1889 after Schlatter had accepted the call to the University of Greifswald.[282] Barth senior appreciated what he considered the positive theology of his fellow compatriot, the two enjoyed a letter exchange,[283] and Schlatter visited Barth occasionally in his Bern home.[284] With his clear preference for positive theology, Fritz Barth was obviously not fond of his son's flirting with the Ritschlians at that time. At the end of summer 1907, he encouraged his son Karl, who was then an enthusiastic Harnack student in Berlin,[285] to attend Schlatter's lectures in Tübingen. "He felt that it was time," Karl Barth reflects on his father's request, "that, with my liberal tendencies, I should hear some sound 'positive' theology . . . so he sent me off to Tübingen, to Adolf Schlatter."[286] Finally, in October 1907, Barth moved to Tübingen "at the bidding of my father," he remembers, "who was now much more insistent, and not according to my own inclination."[287] Barth thus attended Schlatter's New Testament lectures during the winter term 1907/8, and while it is again unclear whether a personal conversation took place, Schlatter obviously knew that Barth was among his hearers as Fritz Barth had told him.[288]

Overall, it seems, Barth senior's plan to win his son for positive theology was unsuccessful. His son was not only disappointed with Tübingen as a town, calling it "a wretched hole" (*ein miserables Nest*), but also with Schlatter's theological approach and the theological faculty as a whole, which he described as a "dive" (*Spelunke*).[289] "Only one thing never happened in Tübingen," Barth later explains, "I did not join the ranks of the 'positives.'"[290] In an autobiographical sketch, Barth reports that he heard Schlatter only "very irregularly, and then only with considerable resentment" (*mit heft-*

282. Busch, *Karl Barths Lebenslauf*, 21; cf. Neuer, *Adolf Schlatter*, 638. In Bern, Fritz Barth also worked at the same Christian private school, the Lerberschule, as Schlatter did earlier. Busch, *Karl Barths Lebenslauf*, 21; cf. Neuer, *Adolf Schlatter*, 136, 143, 152.

283. See Schlatter's letters to Fritz Barth (no. 1234, Adolf Schlatter archive, Stuttgart) and Barth's letters to Schlatter (no. 425, ibid.); cf. Neuer, *Adolf Schlatter*, 638.

284. Busch, *Karl Barths Lebenslauf*, 21; cf. Fritz Barth's letter to Schlatter, 4 March 1882, in Neuer, *Adolf Schlatter*, 638.

285. Busch, *Karl Barths Lebenslauf*, 50–55.

286. In a conversation with Tübingen students, 2 March 1964, in Busch, *Karl Barth: His Life from Letters and Autobiographical Texts*, 42.

287. Barth, *Autobiographical Sketch*, in Busch, *Karl Barth: His Life from Letters and Autobiographical Texts*, 43.

288. Fritz Barth to Schlatter, 14 November 1907, in Neuer, *Adolf Schlatter*, 638.

289. Barth to Wilhelm Spoendlin, 6 January 1908, in Busch, *Karl Barth: His Life from Letters and Autobiographical Texts* 43 [Busch, *Karl Barths Lebenslauf*, 55].

290. In a conversation with Tübingen students, 2 March 1964, in Busch, *Karl Barth: His Life from Letters and Autobiographical Texts* 43 [Busch, *Karl Barths Lebenslauf*, 55].

igster Renitenz).[291] Barth's description of Schlatter as "half-cannibal, half-primordial Christian" (*halb Menschenfresser, halb Urchrist*) perhaps dates from this time.[292] Barth sneered at "Schlatter's talent for moving difficulties elegantly out of the way without really tackling them."[293] He complains about Schlatter's "manner of reasoning," which was, in Barth's eyes, "unscientific, inaccurate and haphazard."[294] Looking back, Barth concisely sums up his early Schlatter-aversion thus: "I rejected that Schlatter" (*Also, ich habe den Schlatter abgelehnt*).[295] Apparently, Barth did not sit in Schlatter's dogmatic lectures during the semester; this obviously prevented him from getting to know Schlatter as a dogmatician at that stage of his education.[296]

Disappointed with both Tübingen and Schlatter, Barth moved to Marburg for the following semester, where he would encounter Wilhelm Herrmann, whose influence on Barth is well established.[297] Still, Schlatter undoubtedly had some residual impact on his student, as their ensuing dialogue and letter exchange suggest. Yet before there was room for greater appreciation, there was, first, further estrangement. Schlatter was once more a source of disappointment to Barth, for the following reason: Schlatter was, together with many of Barth's Ritschlian teachers, one of the ninety-three intellectuals who signed the petition "Aufruf an die Kulturwelt," published in major German newspapers on October 4, 1914.[298] Apart from Schlatter, other influential theologians who signed the appeal included Adolf von Harnack, Wilhelm Herrmann, Reinhold Seeberg, and Joseph Mausbach. With their signature, they expressed their support for Wilhelm II's decision to declare war. Judged from today's perspective one cannot but criticize Schlatter's "naïve gullibility towards the emperor's politics," as Werner Neuer termed it.[299] However, one must also point out that many of the signatories put their names to the petition without actually knowing the exact

---

291. Barth, *Autobiographical Sketch*, in Busch, *Karl Barth: His Life from Letters and Autobiographical Texts* 43 [Busch, *Karl Barths Lebenslauf*, 55]. Also in *Karl Barth–Rudolf Bultmann: Briefwechsel*, 294.

292. See Stuhlmacher, "Adolf Schlatter," 220.

293. Barth to Wilhelm Spoendlin, 4 November 1907, in Busch, *Karl Barth: His Life from Letters and Autobiographical Texts* 43 [Busch, *Karl Barths Lebenslauf*, 55].

294. Barth, "Interview von H.A. Fischer-Barnicol," 139.

295. Ibid.

296. B–Schl Br, 87.

297. See McCormack, *Barth's Critically Realistic Dialectical Theology*, 49–68.

298. See Jürgen von Ungern-Sternberg and Wolfgang von Ungern-Sternberg, *Der Aufruf 'An die Kulturwelt,'* 13.

299. Neuer, *Adolf Schlatter*, 564.

wording.[300] The "Manifesto of the Ninety-Three," as it was also called, was harshly criticized by Barth. He did not know what to make of "the teaching of all my theological masters in Germany. To me they seemed to have been hopelessly compromised by what I regarded as their failure in the face of the ideology of war."[301] The disappointment with his teachers' failures "sent him," as Bruce L. McCormack put it, "in search of a *new theology*."[302] Doing away with his bourgeois teachers' culturally overoptimistic theology, Barth re-introduced the lost notion of the transcendent God who reveals himself in Jesus Christ. Thus, Karl Barth appeared on the theological scene with the first edition of his *Römerbrief* in 1919, causing a stir in Germany.[303]

The "Shattered Thinking-Act"

By the early 1920s, Adolf Schlatter had entered his third decade of academic teaching in Tübingen and he certainly knew about Barth's 1919 *Romans*. It is unclear, though, whether he also studied it at that time.[304] Barth's thoroughly rewritten *Romans* edition of 1922 clearly stimulated Schlatter's interest, perhaps not least as Barth mentioned him in the preface. Barth names Schlatter—and this might have come as a surprise to him—as one of the few exegetes who shared his goal of theological exegesis.[305] From Schlatter's perspective, this comment was astonishing since he was, in fact, particularly unhappy with the hermeneutics of Barth's *Romans*, as we shall see in due course. In April 1922, Schlatter's friend, the church historian Karl Holl, asked him whether he would not want to write a Romans commentary himself in order to "muzzle" Barth's *Romans*:

> Do you not want to kill the book [*Wollen Sie nicht das Buch totmachen*] by writing your own commentary on Romans or Galatians? Do not tell me that you have already written one. This time I mean one that is seriously scientific yet one that at the same shows what *theological* science ought to look like. Even

---

300. See Härle, "Der Aufruf der 93 Intellektuellen," 211–12.

301. Barth, *Autobiographical Sketch* (Fakultätsalbum der Evangelisch-theologischen Fakultät Münster, 1927), in Busch, *Karl Barth: His Life from Letters and Autobiographical Texts* 81 [Busch, *Karl Barths Lebenslauf*, 93]. For Barth, the events of autumn 1914 were so radical that he was compelled to break with the liberal theology of his teachers. See Härle, "Aufruf der 93 Intellektuellen," 207–24.

302. McCormack, *Barth's Critically Realistic Dialectical Theology*, 79 (emphasis original).

303. Ibid., 162–65.

304. Neuer, *Adolf Schlatter*, 639.

305. Barth, *Epistle to the Romans*, 7.

though you might be a "seventy-year-old," you are still "bound" to [do] it.[306]

Schlatter, however, had neither the inclination to "kill" Barth's *Romans*, nor any intention of writing his own commentary on Romans any time soon; this project would have to wait for another thirteen years.[307] What he had done even before he received Holl's letter, though, was to write a review of Barth's *Romans*, published in the journal *Die Furche* in early May 1922.[308] Reading his former student's work, Schlatter easily finds words of praise. He appreciates in Barth's approach an "earnest, unbroken affirmation of God."[309] Compared to many of their contemporaries, Schlatter finds it remarkable that Barth, swimming against the liberal current of his Ritschlian teachers, returns to a full assurance of the reality of God. However, Schlatter also raises some points of critique. We shall briefly mention three significant issues: First, Schlatter claims that Barth overemphasizes the transcendence of God at the expense of the context of his revelation in history, creation and humanity. This results, secondly, in an idiosyncratic interpretation of Romans, which neglects its communal dimension. Thirdly, Schlatter feels that Barth's exegesis "smashes the thinking-act," which has negative effects on the concept of faith and our experiential connection with Jesus Christ.

First of all then, Barth's concept of God as the transcendent other, the "wholly other" (*der ganz Andere*) rankled with Schlatter.[310] Schlatter, though speaking in exactly the same terms of God as "wholly other,"[311] feels that his Swiss colleague's emphasis on the otherness of God is too strong, culminating in a neglect of the world and of humanity. Barth contrasts God and the world too sharply, and this is foreign to the Apostle Paul's intention. "Barth's God is 'the Other,'" Schlatter claims, "who is other than we are and other

---

306. Holl to Schlatter, 24 April 1922, in Stupperich, "Briefe Karl Holls an Schlatter," 235 (emphasis original).

307. Schlatter published a commentary on Romans as early as 1887, *Der Römerbrief: Ein Hilfsbüchlein für Bibelleser*. This commentary, however, was aimed at the theological layperson. His scholarly commentary was published in 1935, *Gottes Gerechtigkeit: ein Kommentar zum Römerbrief* (also available in English translation, *Romans: The Righteousness of God*).

308. Schlatter, "Karl Barths 'Römerbrief,'" published in *Die Furche* 12 (1922). I am indebted to Annemarie Kaindl of the Bayerische Staatsbibliothek München who was able to identify May 5, 1922 as the publication date of Schlatter's review (e-mail message to author, February 28, 2012). Schlatter's review has been translated into English by Keith R. Crim as "Karl Barth's *Epistle to the Romans*," 121–5.

309. Schlatter, "Barth's *Epistle to the Romans*," 121.

310. Barth, *Der Römerbrief (Zweite Fassung)*, 47, 59, 66, 76, 223, 435, 498, 522.

311. Schlatter, "Wert und Unwert unseres Wissens," 263.

than the world is."[312] In that Barth almost exclusively conceptualizes God over against humanity, Schlatter fears he renders theology absurd. As God is "the unattainably distant, the 'Other,'" he notes, "every thought directed to God breaks down; every religious statement, every theology, becomes basically folly, for it can speak only in perpetual self-contradictions."[313] Thus the Tübingen professor complains that in Barth's *Romans* "[a]ll that is human, all that is historical, sinks away. What is Rome, what is the early Roman Christian community, what is Paul?"[314] In rescuing the Word of God from the hands of his anthropocentric Ritschlian teachers, Barth has gone too far in the other, transcendent, direction that neglects the concrete historical context: "Are we still hearing Paul," asks Schlatter, "when the Greek and the Jew have disappeared from the Letter to the Romans?"[315] Of course, Schlatter does not object to Barth's emphasis on the pre-eminence of God's revelatory presence over any human authority and autonomy,[316] yet one must not completely neglect, as Schlatter fears Barth does, the creaturely context of that revelation.

Second, the result of Barth's one-sided theocentric agenda is that Barth's exegesis, according to Schlatter's assessment, fails to give an account of the Apostle Paul's original message. Barth's interpretation thus becomes isolated and idiosyncratic: "Since the exegete does not wish to say anything to us about the history of Roman Christendom, of Israel, of Paul and Jesus, what is he then going to talk to us about? He becomes the exegete of his own life and the interpreter of his own heart."[317] More specifically, Barth neglects, in Schlatter's view, the communal context of Romans. He writes:

> "The author to the readers." These are the words which Barth placed over Romans 1:1–7. These words repulse anyone who has learned to know Paul. Paul an "author" who had nothing but "readers" in mind—but how were things done in those days? After his letter arrived in Rome, it was read aloud to the Christian community there. Paul is here giving instruction to hearers, and these hearers were not sitting isolated, each in his study busily reading; they were a congregation gathered with one accord before God, and they then and subsequently carried out their

---

312. Schlatter, "Barth's *Epistle to the Romans*," 123.

313. Ibid., 124.

314. Ibid., 121.

315. Ibid., 123.

316. The human desire for autonomy was in fact, as Bruce McCormack highlights, for Barth synonymous with original sin. McCormack, *Barth's Critically Realistic Dialectical Theology*, 167.

317. Schlatter, "Barth's *Epistle to the Romans*," 122.

common worship by letting Paul speak to them. Does it have no consequences for the reproduction of the letter if the apostle is turned into an "author" and the community that listens to him into "readers"?[318]

Schlatter is clearly unhappy about Barth's reduction of Paul the apostle to an author and of the recipients to readers, as this camouflages the significant communal context of God's revelatory presence expressed in Romans. This leads to a discrepancy between the biblical text and Barth's commentary, to a "quarrel between the exegete and the apostle."[319] "In the hands of the exegete," laments Schlatter, "the Letter to the Romans ceases to be a letter to the Romans."[320] This criticism is also expressed by Schlatter's chosen review title in the genitive case, "Karl Barth's *Epistle to the Romans*" ("Karl Barths 'Römerbrief'"), indicating that Paul's epistle had morphed somewhat into Barth's epistle.

Thirdly, from Schlatter's perspective, Barth's exegesis has negative effects on our faith and thereby on our experiential connection with Jesus Christ. In Schlatter's system, the empirical-critical reading of the New Testament in the seeing-act is intrinsically connected with its interpretation in the thinking-act. Only via this route does faith become possible as a real faith since it is deeply rooted in the historical facts. According to Schlatter, Barth has omitted the step of critical observation, and he has thereby pulled the rug out from under the thinking-act, making a substantial grounding of faith impossible. "The 'No' which Barth places on our entire life situation," writes Schlatter, "falls with devastating force on the act of thinking [*trifft mit verheerender Wucht den Denkakt*]."[321] And once the thinking-act is impaired, faith is affected as well, Schlatter claims:

> If the act of thinking is shattered [*Wird der Denkakt zerschmettert*], faith does not remain untouched, since it needs a content that is accessible to our perception and can be appropriated by us by means of solid judgment. It gets this content through Christ. That is the statement that comes from Paul.[322]

According to Schlatter's reading, Barth's notion of faith is flawed, having serious consequences for our connection with Jesus Christ. "[F]or Barth faith remains a 'leap into the void,'" notes Schlatter, "and in this a deep

318. Ibid., 121.
319. Ibid., 123.
320. Ibid.
321. Schlatter, "Barth's *Epistle to the Romans*," 124 ["Karl Barths 'Römerbrief,'" 231].
322. Ibid. ["Karl Barths 'Römerbrief,'" 230].

gap between his exposition and the Letter to the Romans opens up. Paul did not leap into the void, but joined himself to Jesus."[323] This experiential *Anschluss an den Christus* is, as already mentioned, a crucial factor for the Tübingen scholar, and Eberhard Busch claims that this issue is perhaps the most significant point of Schlatter's critique. Busch observes in Schlatter a "distant echo of the Pietistic objection to Barth that the divine reality must be 'experienced.'"[324] In this way, Busch argues, Schlatter's "argument also touches a sore spot in the theology of the Epistle to the Romans. It was perhaps even one of the most weighty arguments that Barth had to listen to then, and he certainly did listen to it."[325] Indeed, Barth acknowledged Schlatter's criticism; in the preface to the subsequent, third edition of his Romans commentary, Barth writes:

> The strangest episode in the history of the book since the appearance of the second edition has been its friendly reception by Bultmann and its equally friendly rejection by Schlatter.... For the present I have simply noted carefully and gratefully the criticisms and questions put to me by Bultmann and Schlatter.[326]

Barth, at that time honorary professor of Reformed theology in Göttingen, penned these lines in July 1922. By then his initial frustration with Schlatter's critique seems to have ebbed away somewhat. A few months earlier, in late March—or early April—1922, Barth received an advance copy of Schlatter's review, and he was certainly not blasé about his former teacher's critique.[327] In a *Rundbrief* to his friends, of April 2, 1922, Barth notes:

> Furthermore I can report that a high-caliber missile has touched down in the form of a Romans review by Schlatter in the "Furche."... The punch-line is that I am accused of not taking part in the work of the "church," in the historical development of what Paul has said back then, my notion of God [*Gottesgedanke*] being different from the one of Paul, [so that] with me, "the thinking-act [*Denkakt*] is smashed" (!!).[328]

---

323. Ibid., 124–25.
324. Busch, *Barth and the Pietists*, 189.
325. Ibid., 189–90.
326. Barth, *The Epistle to the Romans*, 16.

327. The editors of the *Furche* had sent Barth an advance copy of Schlatter's review, inquiring whether Barth would want to reply to Schlatter's article. "Those ... fools," writes Barth to his friends: "[it] would really suit the *Furche* to become the stage for such a scuffle [*Handgemenge*]. Quod non! my father used to say." Barth's *Rundbrief* of 2 April 1922, in *Karl Barth–Eduard Thurneysen*, 1:66.

328. Ibid.

While Barth here alludes to some of the aspects of Schlatter's criticism (God as "wholly other," the missing emphasis on actual history and the Christian community), he does not seem to take up Schlatter's experiential critique. Apparently, what bothered Barth most was Schlatter's claim that he had "destroyed the thinking-act." He picks it up some two weeks later in a letter to Rudolf Bultmann, dated April 14, 1922: "In the upcoming issue of the *Furche* none other than *Schlatter* proceeds against me with a mildly appreciative rejection or mildly appreciative approval. . . . The worst he charges me with is: 'Barth smashes the thinking-act.'"[329]

At this point one could assume that this was the end of a theological debate that had not even properly begun. Schlatter's language, such as the "smashed thinking-act," certainly did not inspire hope for further personal theological exchange. However, Schlatter's "high-caliber missile" did not destroy future opportunities for dialogue. Barth most likely knew how to take his former teacher's criticism. Having experienced Schlatter in the Tübingen lecture hall, he knew about his compatriot's temperament, his liability to polemics and sarcasm.[330] Barth, then, presumably knew how to look behind Schlatter's rough façade, as he was, after all, at that time not very different from Schlatter himself with his animated style of debating theology.[331] Schlatter, for one, had clearly a realistic picture of his own lack of diplomatic finesse when it came to scholarly argument. In a letter to his parents, he writes that the success of a theological debate depends first and foremost on the "power of the lungs, for I have never been able to conduct a theological dispute in *piano*."[332] The *fortissimo* of Schlatter's critique, however, would soon give way to an ensuing correspondence in *piano* and a growing appreciation over the following years—on both sides.

Two years after Schlatter's *Furche* critique, in early 1924, Samuel Jäger, then director of Bethel Theological Seminary, suggested that Karl Barth be invited as a speaker for the biannual Bethel Theological Week in the autumn. Schlatter, who had set up the conference in the first place together with his friend Friedrich von Bodelschwingh ("der Ältere," 1831–1910),[333] was immediately open to this proposal and expressed his support.[334] In a let-

---

329. Barth to Bultmann, 14 April 1922, in *Karl Barth–Rudolf Bultmann*, 9 (emphasis original).

330. See Neuer, *Adolf Schlatter*, 377–78, 610, 614.

331. The earlier Barth, at least, is often described as an "*enfant terrible*," as "a theological dissident whose natural genre is the polemical essay or highly charged address." Webster, *Barth's Earlier Theology*, 3.

332. Schlatter to his parents, 6 February 1873, in Neuer, *Adolf Schlatter*, 61.

333. See Neuer, *Adolf Schlatter*, 355.

334. Ibid., 642.

ter to his son Theodor, Schlatter admits that he is "confident that I can team up with him [Barth] without any harsh collisions."[335] Schlatter subsequently wrote to his former student, "[I]t would give me great pleasure if you could take over a major part of the work this autumn."[336] With a view to Barth's lectures, Schlatter even issued him with a *carte blanche*: "You see," Schlatter assures him, "that we do not work under the burden of any law, but in total freedom, according to the New Testament conviction that our unity does not come about through harmonization [*Gleichmachung*]."[337] In his reply to Schlatter, Barth accepts the invitation and appreciates it as "proof of great trust."[338] He adds that "the happiness about it and everything that I could learn from it outweighs my concern that I could disappoint you."[339] Perhaps referring to Schlatter's earlier critique of his emphasis on God as wholly other, Barth explicitly states that one of his "main concerns" is still to point to the "distance that separates human beings and the world from God."[340] All the same, Schlatter was happy about Barth's acceptance. Full of optimistic anticipation, Schlatter looked forward to the conference, expressing his "personal delight . . . in watching a colleague at work."[341] Rudolf Bultmann, too, whom Barth had informed about his invitation to Bethel, was excited about the public rendezvous of the two Swiss theologians in Bethel: "That you will appear with Schlatter in Bethel could become interesting," he writes to Barth.[342] Unexpectedly though, and "with great disconcertedness," Barth decided not to join the conference after all. He argued that it "did not fit into the economy of my work . . . to express myself in this forum and to proclaim my doctrine of God openly to a large audience."[343] Barth, it seems, primarily wanted to steer clear of any criticism of his notion of God as wholly other at that point. Yet he assured his colleague that he would join the conference another time in the future.[344] Barth's withdrawal was very disappointing for Schlatter.[345] Still, one ought to recall the extent to which Barth's dialectical

---

335. Schlatter to his son Theodor, 9 February 1924, in *B–Schl Br*, 89.

336. Schlatter to Barth, 16 March 1924, in ibid., 96.

337. Ibid.

338. Barth to Schlatter, 25 March 1924, in ibid., 97.

339. Ibid.

340. Ibid.

341. Schlatter to Barth, 5 April 1924, in ibid.

342. Bultmann to Barth, 18 April 1924, in *Karl Barth–Rudolf Bultmann: Briefwechsel*, 34.

343. As quoted in Theodor Schlatter's letter to his father, 23 June 1924, in Neuer, *Adolf Schlatter*, 644.

344. As quoted in ibid.

345. In a letter to his son, Schlatter writes, "Barth's cancellation is painful. . . . I

theology polarized the theological landscape at that time. Schlatter's friend, Karl Holl, for example, was not willing to lecture alongside Barth at the Bethel Theological Week;[346] Friedrich von Bodelschwingh junior ("der Jüngere," 1877–1946) also had reservations,[347] and Barth perhaps felt that he would not be entirely welcome after all. Nevertheless, one observes a growing appreciation between the two scholars in 1924, notwithstanding their remaining theological differences. Although the time was not yet ripe for their public collaboration, their ensuing discussion bears witness to a sincere attempt towards understanding one another. Schlatter, professor emeritus from 1922, continued to teach in Tübingen until 1930,[348] and remained generally open to dialectical theology. He recommended, for instance, that the pietistic evangelical circles digest "a good portion of Barthian theology."[349] His son Theodor took him at his word: Theodor Schlatter, born in 1885, and thus just one year older than Barth, followed in his father's footsteps as a pastor and theologian and offered his own critical evaluation of Barth's theology.[350]

Further Developments and Debates

As the influence and fame of dialectical theology grew in the 1920s, so did Schlatter's curiosity about the movement. In early 1925, Schlatter had an

---

would have considered it as something new and great.... We must be satisfied with the fact that he was, initially, seriously prepared to shake hands with us." Schlatter to his son Theodor, 26 June 1924, in Neuer, *Adolf Schlatter*, 644.

346. Neuer, *Adolf Schlatter*, 643.
347. Ibid., 642.
348. Ibid., 592.
349. Schlatter to his son Theodor, 10 November 1924, in Neuer, *Adolf Schlatter*, 645.
350. In 1925, Theodor Schlatter published a review of Barth's "Resurrection of the Dead" (*Die Auferstehung der Toten*), a summary of the latter's Göttingen lectures on 1 Corinthians 15. Schlatter senior welcomed his son's critical essay. In a way reminiscent of his own praise for Barth's *Romans* earlier, Schlatter junior endorses Barth's work as a "liberating word, as he bears powerful witness to the greatness of God as the sole reality, the almighty Lord, creator and judge." Theodor Schlatter, "Vom Glauben an Gottes Offenbarung," 4. Much like his father, Theodor Schlatter appreciates that Barth "argues with holy gravity for the majesty of God" (ibid., 6), and he commends Barth's theology as it "deals seriously with the word of Scripture that becomes alive as the Word of God." (ibid., 5). The young academic, however, also echoes some of his father's critical remarks. Theodor Schlatter argues that the otherness of God takes in Barth center-stage whereas his concrete revelation in creation and history recedes to the background; this neglect of the creaturely and historical facts implies that our faith does not find its proper foundation which weakens the experience of our connection with Jesus Christ. (ibid., 8, 10).

opportunity to get a first-hand impression of some prominent advocates of dialectical theology. He attended lectures by Friedrich Gogarten (1887–1967) and his former student Rudolf Bultmann (1884–1976), and he also met Karl Barth personally in Basel.[351] Schlatter continued to be particularly interested in Barth, who from late 1925 had served as professor of dogmatics and New Testament exegesis in Münster.[352] This is reflected in Schlatter's 1925 and 1926 public speeches, lectures and seminars on Barth's theology.[353] Schlatter also revisited Barth's *Romans* when he delivered a speech in Halle on "The Theology of Karl Barth and the Ministry of the Pastor" ("Die Theologie Karl Barths und der Dienst des Pfarrers").[354] In a way reminiscent of his *Furche*-review three years earlier, Schlatter criticizes Barth's narrow rendering of God's revelation in creation and his lack of existential emphasis. Schlatter claims that, for Barth, "Wherever the Word seeks me out, with an impact like a bomb, there the revelation of God is [present], yet sure enough only as a tangent, not touching the arc of human life, therefore not aiming at the center—not yet."[355] According to Schlatter's reading of Barth, revelation seems to occur almost out of the blue, bypassing, as it were, the creaturely realm, the "arc of human life." This radically actualist understanding of revelation is too restrictive, Schlatter opines, as it excludes the significant aspect of God's revelation through the various media of creation, history, and anthropology.

Schlatter's critique, however, was accompanied by a notable respect for Barth's theology, and in the spring of 1926 the Tübingen professor emeritus supported Bethel Seminary's attempt to invite Barth again as a speaker for the Bethel Theological Week.[356] While Schlatter underlines in this context that he does not wish "that the pastors . . . or the [Bethel] theological school . . . speculate or preach in a Barthian way," still for him "personally," he notes, "it would be a joy to collaborate with Barth."[357] Barth agreed and informed Bethel of his chosen subject, namely, the sacraments. Based on Barth's choice, Schlatter decided that his contribution would consist in a public

---

351. After Schlatter had lectured about the "Deviation of the Church from the New Testament Ethics," they had a short meeting (see Neuer, *Adolf Schlatter*, 648).

352. See Busch, *Karl Barth: His Life from Letters and Autobiographical Texts* 164–72.

353. See Neuer, *Adolf Schlatter*, 649 for details.

354. For a short summary of Schlatter's 1925 lecture in Halle, see "Die Theologie Karl Barths," 116. In this lecture, Schlatter focuses on Barth's exegesis of Romans 1:18, 3:23, and chapter 12.

355. Schlatter, "Die Theologie Karl Barths," 116.

356. Neuer, *Adolf Schlatter*, 649.

357. Schlatter to his son Theodor, 10 March 1926, in Neuer, *Adolf Schlatter*, 649.

reply to Barth.[358] Unfortunately, however, their collaboration was again prevented as Barth suffered a riding accident.[359] Even so, Schlatter adopted Barth's original theme of the sacraments and subsequently produced four lectures on "God's well-pleasing Sacrifice" (*Das Gott wohlgefällige Opfer*) for the Bethel Theological Week. A close reading of these lectures reveals a subtle yet noticeable critical interaction with Barth's theology. Reading between the lines, one notices that Schlatter clearly composed these lectures aiming to continue his debate with Barth. Hence, Schlatter takes up significant theological issues he misses in Barth without directly referring to him on any page (which was not unusual, for, as mentioned earlier, it was Schlatter's habit to refrain, to a great extent, from alluding to other scholars' works). As Schlatter highlights the concrete factual-historical character of Christ's sacrifice,[360] the natural-creaturely realm as the context of God's revelation (such as the significance of Jesus' body in the sacraments),[361] and its implication for faith,[362] the communal aspect of the sacraments,[363] and our existential union with Christ,[364] one is clearly reminded of the contours of his overall Barth-critique discussed so far. Although Barth was not personally present at Bethel, Schlatter evidently intended to keep up the theological conversation with him throughout the lectures. Thus, later that year, towards the end of 1926, Schlatter sent Barth his Bethel lectures, which by then had been published (*Das Gott wohlgefällige Opfer. Vier Reden von Prof. D. Ad. Schlatter in Tübingen*). Having received Schlatter's work, Barth read it in a single sitting, clearly aware that these lectures were designed as an invitation for ongoing dialogue. Shortly before Christmas, Barth replied to Schlatter in a heartfelt letter, expressing his appreciation for his work.[365] Schlatter valued

358. Schlatter to his son Theodor, 13 May 1926, in ibid., 650.

359. Ibid.; cf. Busch, *Karl Barth: His Life from Letters and Autobiographical Texts* 171.

360. Schlatter, *Das Gott wohlgefällige Opfer*, 11, 20.

361. Ibid., 24–25.

362. "Once we assume a fighting position against nature [*Kampfesstellung gegen die Natur*]," Schlatter writes, "our remembrance of the creator becomes a burden and faith in him [becomes] difficult." Ibid., 31.

363. Ibid., 13–14, 18–19.

364. Ibid., 22.

365. Barth writes: "I . . . have to confess that I cannot remember much from your pen that has left such a deep impression on me. I very much notice to what extent you have . . . tailored your [contribution] to my collaboration at the conference; I specifically want to thank you for the ethos it reflects. In fact—I feel almost relieved that due to my accident it did not come to me having to display the little streamlet of my insights next to the large stream of knowledge that is given to you. . . . Let me sincerely thank you in my own name for the good message you conveyed to us all. One badly needs,

Barth's warm response, pointing out that they had been—finally—able to establish something like a "companionship" (*Gemeinschaft*).[366]

The German Protestant scene in the late 1920s was very much aware of the overshadowing presence of Schlatter and Barth. In 1927, Karl Barth was invited to speak at the Second Theological Week of the Reformed Union (*Reformierter Bund*) in Elberfeld, running from 18 to 21 October 1927. The conference's theme was the "Problem of the Word" (*Das Problem des Wortes*). Though Schlatter was, in all likelihood, not personally present at the conference,[367] his students and adherents clearly were, and they firmly voiced their theological concerns, so much so that the conference leader, Schlatter student Hermann Albert Hesse (1877–1957), summarized the gathering as "a conversation between Karl Barth and Adolf Schlatter."[368] Apparently not amused by the large number of Schlatterians at the conference, Barth notes that some "querulous persons [*Querulanten*] wanted to hear from me, too, at all costs, what Schlatter had said so beautifully."[369] This conference reflects the dominating influence of the two theologians on German Protestant Reformed theology and church life at the time. Hesse remarks that though they were different in their theological outlook, the church needed to listen to both of them as they complemented each other. Whereas Barth, Hesse claims, points to the "prophetic power" of the Word of God, Schlatter accentuates its concrete dependence on the historical context (*Kontextgebundenheit*).[370] "We are convinced that both men are given to us by God," he writes, "and that their dual service [*Doppeldienst*] can further help us to tackle the problem of the Word as required."[371]

On the Question of God's Revelation

In the same year, 1927, Barth published his first major dogmatic opus, *Die Lehre vom Worte Gottes: Prolegomena zur christlichen Dogmatik*. Schlatter studied Barth's *Prolegomena* in the spring of 1928 and was clearly impressed.

---

from time to time, to *hear* something like that, as if one were a young student." Barth to Schlatter, 18 December 1926, in *B–Schl Br*, 98 (emphasis original).

366. Schlatter to his son Theodor, 23 December 1926, in Neuer, *Adolf Schlatter*, 651.

367. This is, according to Schlatter biographer Werner Neuer (e-mail message to author, March 27, 2012).

368. Hesse, "Was war der Sinn unserer Theologischen Woche?," 346; cf. Barth's own remarks about the conference in "Das Wort in der Theologie von Schleiermacher bis Ritschl," 183–86.

369. Barth, "Das Wort in der Theologie von Schleiermacher bis Ritschl," 185.

370. Hesse, "Was war der Sinn unserer Theologischen Woche?," 346.

371. Ibid.

It is "a masterpiece," Schlatter admitted to his students during one of the open evenings at his home.[372] Nonetheless, it was challenging for Schlatter to evaluate Barth's work in detail. It cost him, he admits, "quite some time and effort" to clarify his "position towards Barth's *Dogmatik*."[373] Still ambivalent towards Barth, he again expressed both approval and criticism: "There is power and weakness in his position; since it [Barth's work] is closely connected with his own, individual life history, it endows his *Dogma* with both momentum [*Stoßkraft*] and constriction [*Enge*] at the same time."[374] Barth's major strength, in Schlatter's view, is his ability to root his dogmatics in God and God's Word:

> What do I preach and why do I preach? This is in Barth the root of dogmatics. An answer to this embarrassing agony is given in that God becomes for him the one who has spoken to us. *Deus dixit*. Thereby, the *Dogma* is not left in mid-air as speculation, but has a factual foundation and becomes the interpretation of what has happened and happens.[375]

Although Schlatter applauds Barth's focus on the God "who has spoken to us," he feels that Barth is too restrictive when it comes to the ways in which God has done so. Again, the question of the locus and the extent of divine revelation emerges. Schlatter clearly remains critical of Barth's neglect of nature and history as the context of divine self-disclosure:

> My topic is God's work; his topic is God's Word. Work and Word are not at odds, but one. The Word is the creative [Word] and the work the visualized Word. . . . His position connects him with Calvin, mine connects me with the New Testament. His position separates him from nature and history; mine puts me directly in it.[376]

Schlatter still misses in Barth a clear affirmation of the reality of God's (general) revelation in the context of creation, referring to Barth's aversion to nature and history as "Barth's *Katzenjammer*."[377]

---

372. Martin Tarnow to Peter Stuhlmacher, 30 May 1988, in Neuer, *Adolf Schlatter*, 652.
373. Schlatter to his son Theodor, 15 April 1928, in Neuer, *Adolf Schlatter*, 652.
374. Ibid.
375. Ibid.
376. Ibid.
377. Schlatter to his son Theodor, 16 January 1929, in ibid., 653. *Katzenjammer* means literally cat's wail and is in German used to describe an overall state of despair and bewilderment.

During the rise of National Socialism in Germany, Barth and Schlatter were like-minded in their support for the independence of the church from any interference by the state, and both proclaimed the primacy of the Word of God as the sole criterion for theology. Barth, who had been professor of systematic theology in Bonn since 1930, and Schlatter had both been very suspicious of Hitler and the *Deutsche Christen* from the very beginning.[378] Whereas many of Schlatter's former colleagues at the Tübingen faculty joined the *Deutsche Christen*, Schlatter was principally opposed to a movement that, he feared, would jeopardize the impartiality and independence of theology and the church.[379] In April 1934, a few weeks before the Barmen Confessional Synod, Schlatter, by now in his early eighties, sent Barth his recently published commentary on Paul's Letter to the Corinthians, *Der Bote Jesu*. In an accompanying letter, Schlatter underlines his moral support for Barth who was at the time working on his draft for the Barmen Theological Declaration:

> I send you the book . . . in order to express my conviction which unites me with you, [namely] that the church needs, in order to secure its existence and efficacy, essentially the collaboration of those who interpret for her the divine Word. May God use both our words subservient to his grace.[380]

Barth was "deeply moved" when he received Schlatter's post and he replied with a cordial letter. "It goes without saying," writes Barth, "that I will always remain, in relation to you, a beginner and a student."[381]

While Schlatter welcomed the establishment of the *Bekennende Kirche*—he recommended that his son Theodor show solidarity with the movement—he could not offer it his full support.[382] This was first and foremost due to theological concerns. Schlatter felt that the Barmen Declaration had too strong a dialectical flavor. It was in particular the strong Christocentric character of the Barmen Declaration's first thesis[383] which prevented

---

378. Neuer, *Adolf Schlatter*, 737.

379. See ibid., 739.

380. Schlatter to Barth, 28 April 1934, in *B–Schl Br*, 99.

381. Barth to Schlatter, 2 May 1934, in ibid.

382. Neuer, *Adolf Schlatter*, 768.

383. "Jesus Christ, as he is attested for us in Holy Scripture, is the one Word of God which we have to hear and which we have to trust and obey in life and in death. We reject the false doctrine, as though the church could and would have to acknowledge as a source of its proclamation, apart from and besides this one Word of God, still other events and powers, figures and truths, as God's revelation." On this first thesis of the declaration, see Busch, *Die Barmer Thesen*, 24–37.

Schlatter (as well as his students Wilhelm Lütgert and Paul Althaus) from subscribing to it.[384] In contrast to Barth, Schlatter maintains that God makes himself not only known "in Jesus Christ, as he is attested for us in Holy Scripture," but also in creation, through his works. For Schlatter, as noted above, the Word *and* the work of Christ (which can never be separated) are revelatory of God. Schlatter thus complains that "Barth's exegesis" in the Barmen Declaration was in "a strange way limited."[385] Contrary to Barth, Schlatter is again keen to emphasize the broader context of divine self-revelation, namely also in the realm of creation and history. In his 1935 commentary on Romans, Schlatter writes:

> God's incomparable power and glory are perceived. This occurs via God's *poiēmata* [things that are made, Rom 1:20], as a result of God's action, by what God's actions cause to be. Nature is something God has made. But the *poiēmata* of God consist not merely of those things and processes that fill the universe, for divine works also occur in the course of human history. . . . Just as the human being encounters what God does, so the perception of God [*Wahrnehmung Gottes*] is brought about because the work sets forth the one who made it.[386]

By affirming the possibility of a perception of God through his works, Schlatter's empirical-realist trajectory comes again to the fore. Yet one must clearly point out that Schlatter does not pursue a classic natural theology where the individual comes to know God automatically or autonomously. On the contrary, "[t]he knowledge of God that is present in humanity everywhere is God's gift and not human gain," writes Schlatter. "The individual knows God because God causes him to know."[387] In a way then, for Schlatter all revelation is special revelation as it ultimately depends on God's initiative. Revelation is, above all, special, in that it represents an encounter between the almighty Creator and his creatures. This aspect of *revelation as relation* is particularly important to Schlatter.

True divine self-disclosure in Schlatter's view occurs when the human being is put in a relation with God. "God's act of revelation . . ." Schlatter claims, "consists in setting human personalities in a specific relationship

---

384. See Neuer, *Adolf Schlatter*, 765.

385. Schlatter to his son Theodor, 1 July 1934, in Neuer, *Adolf Schlatter*, 766. He writes: "In my view we argue with irrefutable truth that the Bible consistently says that what is experienced is arranged by God, thus that God works effectively [*wirksam*] in history. I would have to close my Bible and [renounce] my faith in what I actually am and do if I had to abandon this [conviction]." Ibid.

386. Schlatter, *Romans*, 36 [*Gottes Gerechtigkeit*, 57].

387. Ibid., 34.

to himself by indwelling them."[388] Schlatter time and again underlines in his works the necessity of an existential connection with Jesus Christ, the *Anschluss an den Christus*, through which we not only receive knowledge of the reality of God, but also of the world, and of ourselves.[389] In Schlatter's view, the knowledge of God, of the world, and of the self, are intricately connected as they depend on our relationship with Jesus Christ. Whilst Schlatter affirms that it is only by empirical seeing that we perceive God's self-disclosure in the realm of creation, in Scripture, and in our consciousness, he highlights that in order to become clear, true seeing, it must be informed by our relation to Jesus Christ. Only through an existential relation with Jesus Christ does divine revelation become meaningful:

> The one who reveals God is his Son; this leads to the personal notion of God [*Gottesbegriff*]. With the Son, one has the Father. This, then, validates the notion of personality for ourselves. We as individuals are those whom God affirms, seeks, and cherishes, and those with whom he establishes his communion. What is real before God is the I [*Ich*] whose existence is unfolded in its consciousness and its will. Now we are being formed, within our personality, by grace, as the light that puts truth in our consciousness, as love that makes us alive. Now, the I [*Ich*] has found its "Thou" [*Du*] and in that it has gained itself.[390]

Divine self-disclosure for Schlatter always involves a personal encounter, where the human "I" encounters the divine "Thou." Through an existential encounter with Jesus Christ, we gain special knowledge of God, of the world, and of ourselves.[391] Schlatter's student Otto Weber (1902–66) describes, similarly, our "knowledge of God as an act of encounter, of fellowship."[392]

Given that they belonged to different generational cohorts, the debate between Schlatter and Barth found its inevitable end in Schlatter's demise in 1938. Hence, Schlatter would, unfortunately, not encounter the mature Barth of the later volumes of the *Church Dogmatics*. Their last recorded

---

388. Schlatter, "Wesen und Quellen der Gotteserkenntnis," 172. I owe this quotation to Loos, "Divine action, Christ and the doctrine of God," 173.

389. In his *Metaphysik*, Schlatter argues that through "our *Anschluß an den Christus*, we recognize him as the One who is set above all of us and who, with his works, embraces and unites us all." *Metaphysik*, 39.

390. Schlatter, "Christus und Christentum, Person und Prinzip," 17.

391. This explains why, for Schlatter, anthropology and Christology are inseparable. Schlatter underlines that "[we] do not achieve self-awareness without Jesus." *Dogma*, 277. Udo Smid thus rightly argues that Schlatter's "anthropology presupposes and processes a Christocentric interpretation." Smid, "Natürliche Theologie," 119.

392. Weber, *Foundations of Dogmatics*, 1:199.

conversation is a letter exchange in 1936. Barth was by then in Basel as he had had to leave Germany as a result of his opposition to National Socialism. The then eighty-four year old Schlatter sent a final letter to Barth, inquiring whether he would publish an essay of his, either in the *Theologische Existenz* or the *Evangelische Theologie*, a request to which Barth gladly agreed.[393] About two years later, on 18 May 1938, Schlatter died peacefully in his home in Tübingen. He clearly left an impression on Barth as on the dialectical theologians in general. In the journal *Zwischen den Zeiten* one of its co-founders, Georg Merz (1892–1959), writes about Schlatter: "Almost alone among academic theologians of the past generation, he asked questions and sought solutions that arose from an endeavor that must also be ours . . . his questions are ours, his doing is our example."[394]

Conclusion

Reflecting on Schlatter's Barth-critique, one notices a characteristic pattern recurring over the years. While Schlatter certainly welcomed Barth's emphasis on God's transcendence, he felt that Barth went too far, losing sight of the important context of God's revelation in creation, in history, and humanity. In Schlatter's approach, observation of divine revelation in the New Testament, in creation, and history through the seeing-act, its cognitive exploration in the thinking-act, and the appropriation of the divine truth in the life-act, are inseparably linked. In Barth's theology, Schlatter claims, the seeing-act is impaired through an idiosyncratic hermeneutics and an exaggerated focus on the wholly other God. As a consequence, the thinking-act is "shattered," that is, theology remains abstract and remote from the creaturely context of God's revelation. Although Schlatter affirms, to a greater extent than Barth, the possibility of human knowledge of God through the created order, this does not lead him to develop a classic natural theology as he is always keen to tie all human knowledge to its divine author, insisting on our total dependence upon him. Whilst human beings indeed do have a natural knowledge of God, this knowledge is only partial (and not saving) knowledge—who God is (*quis sit Deus*) remains hidden—and even this imperfect knowledge is always bound up with the divine revelatory initiative.[395] A theology proper is then always a supernatu-

---

393. See Schlatter to Barth, 25 September 1936, in *B–Schl Br*, 100. Schlatter's essay, "Allegorien-klingende Schellen, tönendes Erz," was published in the same year. See ibid., 95.

394. Merz, "Adolf Schlatter," 523–25.

395. Schlatter, *Gründe der christlichen Gewißheit*, 100.

ral, a revealed theology. "We know God only through God himself," writes Schlatter, "in that he grants us knowledge of himself, as far as he pleases."[396] Schlatter also highlights, perhaps more than the early Barth, our experiential viewpoint as he stresses the *relational* aspect of revelation. Schlatter feels that this perspective is foundational both for faith to become real and for our individual and communal *Anschluss an Jesus* to work. It is in particular this latter existential, relational aspect of revelation which seems to find a stronger expression in Schlatter than in the early writings of Barth. What emerges from Schlatter's interaction with his Swiss colleague is a picture of Schlatter's Christology that can be described not only as empirical-realist, but also as existential and communal. The following chapters explore this in more detail as we shall unfold Schlatter's relational Christology by looking at it through the lens of the seeing-act, the thinking-act, and, finally, the life-act.

---

396. Schlatter, *Dogma*, 11.

PART 2

The Shape of Schlatter's Christology

THIS SECTION REPRESENTS THE second major pillar of this thesis, looking more closely at the dogmatic shape of Schlatter's Christology. In the first part we presented a short introduction to Schlatter's life and theology (chapter 1), followed by an examination of the theological-historical context of his biography (chapter 2). In what follows we shall explore the characteristic features of Schlatter's christological agenda identified so far in more detail. While the first part of this work was more in the form of a theological narrative, it is the goal of this second part to move towards a systematic-theological discussion. The overarching aim is to portray the dogmatic shape of Schlatter's Christology in a holistic, and thereby very Schlatterian way, doing justice to Schlatter's unique linking of theological method, dogmatics and ethics. A professor of both New Testament and systematic theology, and an author of New Testament commentaries, as well as of works in dogmatics and in ethics, Schlatter unfolds a paradigm of Christocentric seeing, thinking and living. The advantage of presenting Adolf Schlatter's Christology in this way is that this threefold distinction mirrors Schlatter's own theological approach. True theology, according to Schlatter's theological triad, consists in the unity of exegetical seeing in the seeing-act, dogmatic thinking in the thinking-act, and ethical living in the life-act. The empirical analysis of the theological facts in the seeing-act, the cognitive evaluation in the thinking-act, and the existential appropriation in the life-act are organically united. Applied to Christology, this means that the act of seeing Jesus Christ as he is displayed in the New Testament ought to be closely related to the dogmatic thinking-act in which the dogmatician composes a systematic picture of Christ. The theological task, however, remains incomplete without the volitional-ethical stage of one's individual union with Christ (*Anschluss an Christus*) through faith. In proceeding as just outlined, we arrive at a threefold structure for this second part, moving, first, from the seeing-act (*Sehakt*), which correlates with theological method, through secondly, the thinking-act (*Denkakt*), which is more concerned with the dogmatic christological picture, to, thirdly, the life-act (*Lebensakt*), where we shall explore the existential, ethical ramifications.

Before we proceed according to this roadmap, one ought to mention two crucial points. It is, first, essential to point out that a study in Christology, on account of its very subject matter, will never arrive at a finished state. Certain questions will remain unanswered. How could one possibly fully comprehend Jesus' being as fully divine yet fully human? Or how could we ever completely understand his pre-existence or the wonder of his incarnation? Adolf Schlatter does not claim that he has a solution for these conundrums. On the contrary, more than once he confesses that what he is dealing with in his theological research contains a great element of mystery. Our knowledge of Christ, underlines Schlatter, will remain partial. A complete, finished Christology is thus out of reach: "This goal is not achievable in its entirety because Christ is the concealed one, and there exists no direct, apparent fellowship between him and us. We do not see face to face, 1 Cor 13."[1] However, what Schlatter does offer is a fresh and proficient approach to exploring this mystery as far as possible. In combining an empirical-realist method with a relational-volitional and experiential trajectory, Schlatter not only expands on traditional accounts of Christology, but also offers a unique approach that establishes him in the vanguard of today's relational christological accounts. There are, secondly, certain criteria we are going to use in order to test the validity of Schlatter's Christology.[2] That is, the questions we shall put to Schlatter are as follows: Does his christological account adequately integrate the person and work of Jesus Christ? Does it adequately describe the relation between the humanity and the divinity in Jesus Christ? Is Schlatter able to offer a coherent explanation of Jesus' cry of dereliction? And finally, does the account have a clear Trinitarian outlook? Having circumscribed our project, we turn next to the seeing-act, where we explore Schlatter's empirical-critical realist method (chapter 3), moving then to the thinking-act (chapters 4 and 5), and finally the life-act (chapter 6).

---

1. Schlatter, "Christologie und Soteriologie," 16–17.

2. In the compilation of these criteria I greatly benefited from Bruce L. McCormack's 2011 Croall Lectures, delivered at New College, Edinburgh.

3

The *Sehakt*
Empirical-Critical Realism
and the Unified Christ

ADOLF SCHLATTER IS A theologian of unity.[1] Schlatter's pursuit of a coherent theological framework with an impetus towards the whole might well be termed one of his major methodological priorities. The careful reader of Schlatter's works soon realizes how Schlatter aims to overcome any tendencies towards segmentation and compartmentalization in theology.[2] Schlatter's affinity for unity, linked with his aversion to dualisms, has major implications for his Christology, as will be explored in this chapter. In short, he develops a unified account of Jesus Christ and rejects any theological attempts to differentiate, for example, between a historical Jesus and a Christ of faith, or between Jesus' actions and his convictions. Schlatter arrives at his portrayal of a holistic Jesus Christ through his empirical-realist reading of the New Testament. In what follows we shall, first, look at the empirical basis of Schlatter's theological method, before we move, secondly, to its implications for his New Testament studies, and the resultant picture of a unified Jesus Christ.

---

1. Irmgardt Kindt was certainly right when she identified "the notion of unity" as a central theme in Schlatter; see her *Gedanke der Einheit*, 13–28. In addition to Kindt's monograph, see Egg, *Schlatters Kritische Position*, 22, 33, 73–76, 83; Walldorf, *Realistische Philosophie*, 78–79, 111; Lessing, *Geschichte der Deutschsprachigen Evangelischen Theologie*, 1:121; Neuer, *Adolf Schlatter*, 493; see also von Lüpke, *Wahrnehmung der Gotteswirklichkeit*, 43–47.

2. See Schlatter, "Selbstdarstellungen," 157–58; cf. *Dogma*, 44, 370.

A THEOLOGY OF SEEING

Adolf Schlatter was from an early age encouraged to relate very closely to nature—what he calls his "connection with nature" (*Anschluß an die Natur*).[3] Schlatter remembers that his interest in fauna and flora kept him from becoming a Kantian,[4] and throughout his works he calls attention to reality as the source for human knowledge of God. "God does not become credible to us if we do not have a great work before us that comes from him," he insists, "and the first work of God we have to see is nature."[5] (Reading assertions such as these, one must bear in mind that Schlatter did not pursue a natural *theology* as some have suggested,[6] rather, he intended to underline the reality of natural *revelation*.[7]) As mentioned earlier, Schlatter's realistic tendency was consolidated through his encounters with the Aristotelian Rudolf Eucken in Basel,[8] and with Johann T. Beck during his studies in Tübingen. In Aristotelian fashion, Schlatter thus advocates the "affirmation of that which is perceived" (*Bejahung des Wahrgenommenen*), which enables our human "consciousness to grasp the attributes of all being" (*die Merkmale alles Seins*).[9] The close perception of reality became thus an integral element of Schlatter's theological method. Schlatter writes: "I, for my part, consider the formula 'perception' [*Wahrnehmung*] as appropriate for my method and my goal; it characterizes what I have in mind ... I would ... not reject the label *empirical theology*."[10] For Schlatter, observation is key

---

3. Schlatter, "Selbstdarstellungen," 155.

4. "I guess that my familiarity with the plant," writes Schlatter, "childlike as it was, had the effect that it saved me from any inclination towards Kantianism." *Erlebtes*, 125.

5. Schlatter, *Erlebtes*, 126. "The certainty of God [*Gewißheit Gottes*]," Schlatter notes, "and the certainty of the world are presented to us conjointly." Schlatter, "Idealismus und Erweckung," 14.

6. See Bailer's summary in *Das systematische Prinzip*, 50–54.

7. As mentioned earlier in our discussion on Schlatter's evaluation of Barth's theology, Schlatter clearly highlights the significance of Scripture, history and creation as the media of God's revelation, without succumbing to a full-blown natural theology.

8. Eucken points out that "[w]hat we are offered by our senses, are, according to Aristotle, the real things [*wirklichen Dinge*], and that gives his epistemology a completely objective character." Eucken, *Methode der aristotelischen Forschung*, 21. "Thus," continues Eucken, Aristotle's "whole philosophy is pervaded by the conviction of the reality and objectivity of observation." Ibid., 24.

9. Schlatter, *Metaphysik*, 26. Werner Neuer concludes that for Schlatter metaphysics is therefore "an ontology of created reality which tries to identify the immovable and unchangeable basic structures of nature, humanity, and history." Neuer, "Einführung," 5.

10. Schlatter, "Briefe über das Dogma," 85, 11 (emphasis original).

as only through empirical observation do we gather relevant knowledge.[11] "There is no deduction," Schlatter claims, "that can work with any other material than that which is perceived; even the most audacious aprioician [*Aprioriker*] has never merely skimmed through his material and the most assiduous spurner of seeing [*eifrigste Verächter des Sehens*] has never produced a thought other than by means of seeing."[12]

In explanatory remarks on his systematic theology, the "Letters on Christian Dogmatics," Schlatter asserts that it is only through objective observation that the theologian arrives at a suitable framework for theology.[13] Thus, Schlatter feels that he needs no elaborate epistemology as such; we "need neither a theory of seeing, in order to see," he claims, "nor a theory of epistemology, in order to know."[14] In this sense, then, Schlatter basically argues for a common-sense approach to theology (not to be confused with Scottish common sense realism). He writes:

> The suspicion that theology needs a specific preparation in order to arrive at an understanding and proof of its positions is destructive. The theologian proves the accuracy of his intellectual work in that he does not insist on a special logic, but instead thinks according to the same logical laws as everyone else.[15]

For Schlatter, then, clearly echoing his teacher Beck, "every true theologian is first and foremost an observer."[16] It is exactly such an empirical-realist act of seeing that renders theology a science, a *Wissenschaft*,[17] and

---

11. See Schlatter, *Ethik*, 252; cf. *Metaphysik*, 18–25; "Selbstdarstellungen," 164. On Schlatter's empirical-realist framework, see Walldorf, *Realistische Philosophie*, 51–146. Herman Bavinck pursues a similar empirical-realist trajectory; he writes that "the starting point of all human knowledge is sense perception. . . . Truth must not be drawn from books but from the real world. Observation is the source of all real science." *Reformed Dogmatics*, 1:226. Bavinck also asserts, much like Schlatter, that "[n]atural certainty is the indispensable foundation of science. . . . Prior to all reflection and reasoning, everyone is in fact fully assured of the real existence of the world. This certainty is not born out of a syllogism, nor is it supported by proof; it is immediate, originating spontaneously within us along with perception itself." Ibid., 223.

12. Schlatter, *Jesu Gottheit und das Kreuz*, 37.

13. Schlatter, "Briefe über das Dogma," 17.

14. Schlatter, *Dogma*, 42.

15. Ibid., 558n15.

16. Schlatter, *Philosophische Arbeit*, 12.

17. We here use the term "science" in the broad sense of *Wissenschaft*, as Schlatter understood it (i.e., as also including the so-called *Geisteswissenschaften*, the humanities). Wilfried Härle notes that "*Wissenschaft*'s function is to expand knowledge in a revisable manner." Härle, *Dogmatik*, 4. In this sense, Schlatter argues that theology can indeed count itself among the sciences. See in particular Schlatter's "Atheistische

which at the same time justifies theology's rightful place among the other sciences within the academic setting.[18] When, at the celebrations on his seventy-fifth birthday, a colleague described him as a "religious genius [but] scientific nobody" (*religiöses Genie, eine wissenschaftliche Null*), Schlatter retorted, "There is no religious genius in this room, such a person does not exist!—A scientific nil, well, we will have to see about that."[19] Schlatter was emphatic that virtually all areas of science use the same empirical method of observation; this applies to both the natural sciences (*Naturwissenschaften*) and to the humanities (*Geisteswissenschaften*), and thus also to theology. "The first and foremost task of the dogmatician," writes Schlatter, "as in every scientific profession, is observation, which shows him on the basis of reality the processes that bring us into relation with God and mediate the divine work through which God reveals himself to us."[20] This statement is significant insofar as it points to Schlatter's fundamental conviction that observation—whether it be observation of plants, animals, or the New Testament—always brings us in "relation with God," as it is God's own work that we observe. The process of observing God's work in creation, in history, and in the Scriptures Schlatter calls the seeing-act (*Sehakt*).[21] To Schlatter's mind, this empirical-realist approach of seeing rendered his theological method unique among other contemporary approaches.[22] We shall next take a closer look at how the theologian conducts this seeing-act when it comes to the observation of the New Testament documents.

NEW TESTAMENT RESEARCH

In terms of New Testament research, Schlatter distinguishes between two different tasks that are closely related: the historical task of New Testament *history* and the dogmatic task of New Testament *theology*.[23] New Testament

---

Methoden," 228–50.

18. This view was, and still is, subject to controversy. I have dealt with this problem in more detail elsewhere, see my "Seeing, Thinking, and Living," 177–88, and, in collaboration with James Eglinton, "Scientific Theology?" 27–50.

19. Kittel, "Adolf Schlatter: Gedenkrede," 8.

20. Schlatter, *Dogma*, 12.

21. Ibid., 23; see also *Rückblick*, 208; *Erlebtes*, 102; *Philosophische Arbeit*, 12; cf. Walldorf, *Realistische Philosophie*, 51–73.

22. See Schlatter, *Rückblick*, 159.

23. William Baird presents a succinct overview of Schlatter's approach to New Testament research; see Baird, *History of New Testament Research*, 2:373–83. Whilst one must certainly applaud Baird for his attempt to relate Schlatter to historical-critical research, his treatment is at times in need of further refinement. Schlatter, for instance,

The *Sehakt* 111

history deals with the events through which Christianity developed in the first place, and New Testament *theology* examines the convictions presented to us in the New Testament documents.[24] While both tasks are significant in and of themselves, they are closely related, since on the one hand, the New Testament does not know of any "timeless concepts," and, on the other hand, convictions of the New Testament people undoubtedly influenced the course of history "with causal power."[25] In the following sections, we shall look at each of these tasks in more detail.

The Historical Task

Schlatter's strong emphasis on history and historical research has already surfaced in our earlier discussion. The study of the New Testament is first and foremost "a historical task."[26] Since "we receive God's revelation in history... there is no knowledge that is independent from the observation of history."[27] The context-relatedness of the New Testament documents is for Schlatter particularly important. In the historical task of the seeing-act, the theologian works as observing historian, who carefully explores the New Testament's cultural and linguistic background.[28] Consequently, Schlatter ventured into in-depth studies of the historical setting of the New Testament, pioneering in first-century Judaism and linguistic studies.[29] Through historical and linguistic research, Schlatter intends to sharpen

---

was probably not as committed to the historical-critical method as defined by Schlatter's peers (and by Baird) as Baird seems to suggest (ibid., 2:393).

24. Schlatter, "Theologie des NT und Dogmatik," 67. By assuming a close link between historical research and theology, Schlatter distances himself from William Wrede who rejected the title "New Testament theology." According to Wrede, "[t]he appropriate name for the subject-matter is: early Christian history of religion, or rather: the history of early Christian religion and theology." Wrede, "The Task and Methods of 'New Testament Theology,'" 116.

25. Schlatter, "Theologie des NT und Dogmatik," 67.

26. Schlatter, *History of the Christ*, 17.

27. Schlatter, "Theologie des NT und Dogmatik," 61; see also *Erlebtes*, 59; "Selbstdarstellungen," 162. Martin Heidegger actually supports this position when he notes that "[t]he more historical theology is, the more immediately it captures the historicity [*Geschichtlichkeit*] of faith in word and concept, [and therefore] the more 'systematic' it is." Heidegger, *Phänomenologie und Theologie*, 24. Interestingly, after witnessing Schlatter in the lecture hall, Martin Heidegger is said to have exclaimed, "Now that is theology!" Neuer, *Adolf Schlatter*, 607.

28. Schlatter, "Selbstdarstellungen," 164–65. See also "Entstehung der Beiträge," 76, and "Theologie des NT und Dogmatik," 71–73.

29. See Schlatter, "Selbstdarstellungen," 162.

his view of the New Testament, in order to figure out "what was true for them [the New Testament people]."[30] In his view, the theologian's agenda must be to expose what the text itself says, in order to find out what "actually happened."[31] Proceeding in this way, Schlatter feels, underwrites the scientific character of the seeing-act, mentioned earlier. "The historical task of the Bible," Schlatter claims, "can by no means be anything other than an intense hearing of what the Bible contains and what it renders visible; anything contrary to that is not 'science.'"[32] Thus in order to grasp correctly the facts (*Erfassung des Tatbestands*),[33] Schlatter calls for serious, "prejudice-free" observation,[34] where one observes the historical facts with objectivity and an "impartial eye."[35]

Up to this point, Schlatter's method certainly corresponds with central elements of the historical criticism of many of his contemporaries. In our earlier comparison of the Greifswald school with the Ritschlians, it was pointed out that both schools clearly emphasize the importance of a scientific, critical-historical study of the New Testament. However, a closer look reveals that Schlatter's understanding of critical-historical research differs considerably from that of his contemporaries. While Schlatter was obviously not opposed to rigorous *kritisch-historischen* New Testament research, he reacted strongly against what he considered an *exclusively* critical-historical method. He opposed any historicizing approach that was, in his view, detached from the New Testament content and which conducted its research independently, as it were, of the New Testament data, thus from a neutral or even critical atheist point of view.[36] It seems that objectivity, in Schlat-

30. Schlatter, "Theologie des NT und Dogmatik," 9–10; cf. "Bedeutung der Methode," 7.

31. Schlatter, *History of the Christ*, 17.

32. Schlatter, *Heilige Anliegen der Kirche*, 42; see also "Theologie des NT und Dogmatik," 56–57. When Schlatter stresses the hearing or the rendering visible of the Bible's content, he is, beside historical studies, concerned with linguistics, with the relationship between language and cognition ("Selbstdarstellungen," 164). "History means linguistics," says Schlatter ("Erfolg und Mißerfolg," 261). For a detailed discussion of Schlatter's emphasis on language see Joachim Ringleben's essay, "Exegese und Dogmatik bei Adolf Schlatter," 350–85.

33. Schlatter, *Dogma*, 19, see also "Theologie des NT und Dogmatik," 35, 40.

34. Schlatter, "Selbstdarstellungen," 159.

35. Schlatter, "Briefe über das Dogma," 16. By the same token, Joachim Ringleben, who exhibits a clear Schlatter-affinity, argues, "Impartiality in observation and conceptual flexibility are indispensable in order to understand this human being Jesus." Ringleben, *Jesus*, 7.

36. Cf. Köstenberger, "Translator's Preface," 13–14. Schlatter complains of what he labelled the "opulent overgrowing of historicism" (*üppig überwuchernde Historisieren*) of some of his contemporaries (perhaps he has F. C. Baur in mind, here. Schlatter,

ter's view, is not synonymous with neutrality—a position that, obviously, deserves closer scrutiny. Schlatter's plea for objectivity does not imply a neutral, "thoughtless empiricism,"[37] as some of his contemporaries demand. A closer reading of Schlatter suggests that he certainly does not require the exegete to suppress any subjective involvement. On the contrary: The seeing-act is, as the term indicates, still an *act* of a unique individual. And as such, subjective involvement is inevitable, for the exegete is never, and should never be, a "lifeless mirror,"[38] or an "observing machine."[39] Rather, the material is observed and processed by an individual who always possesses preconceived notions that are active during perception (what Schlatter calls *Vorstellungsmassen*).[40] In fact, Schlatter actually seems to allow for the infiltration of the seeing-process by the theologian's idiosyncrasies.[41] Yet how, one asks, can Schlatter then still pursue "prejudice-free" objectivity? How can he still call his empirical method "pure"? Schlatter claims that the purity of the seeing-act is not jeopardized if, and only if, the exegete is, as far as possible,[42] aware of his own presuppositions,[43] while also performing

---

"Christologie und Soteriologie," viii. This approach, he claims, clouds the view of the New Testament history of Christ and results in a distorted picture of him. See Schlatter, *Glaube im Neuen Testament*, 286n1.

37. Schlatter, "Selbstdarstellungen," 9; *Dogma*, 91.

38. Schlatter, "Bedeutung der Methode," 8; see also "Erfolg und Mißerfolg," 268; "Theologie des NT und Dogmatik," 19; "Briefe über das Dogma," 19.

39. Schlatter, "Theologie des NT und Dogmatik," 20. Similarly to Schlatter, Herman Bavinck underscores that the theologian "is not only an intellectual but also a willing and feeling being; he is not a thinking machine but in addition to his head also has a heart, an [inner] world of feelings and passions. He brings these with him in his scientific research." Bavinck, *Reformed Dogmatics*, 1:222.

40. Schlatter, "Selbstdarstellungen," 15; "Bedeutung der Methode," 6; "Theologie des NT und Dogmatik," 20, 25.

41. One observes here a fascinating parallel between Schlatter's hermeneutical realism and the creative expressionism of his Dutch contemporary, the painter Vincent van Gogh (1853–90). Both employ, in their own field, a quasi-objective critical realism combined with an idiosyncratic expressionism. "I am still living off the real world," writes van Gogh in a letter in 1888, "I don't invent the whole of the painting; on the contrary, I find it ready-made—but to be untangled—in the real world." Van Gogh to Emile Bernard, Arles, on or about Friday, 5 October 1888. Schlatter's seeing-act could thus be described as an exegetical expressionist form of hermeneutics. Bruce L. McCormack also detects characteristic parallels between the expressionist art movement and theology at that time, in *Karl Barth's Critically Realistic Dialectical Theology*, 33–34.

42. Schlatter acknowledges that there are many implicit influences that are not consciously accessible to the individual and therefore cannot be excluded from the judgment process. Schlatter, "Briefe über das Dogma," 29.

43. Schlatter, "Theologie des NT und Dogmatik," 20–21; see also "Atheistische Methoden," 247; *Jesu Gottheit und das Kreuz*, 20.

the hermeneutical task devotedly, with "objective faithfulness."[44] Objective faithfulness basically means that the exegete works a) with scientific objectivity, while being b) faithful to his subject matter as he attempts to approach it on its own terms. This brings us to the second aspect of Schlatter's method of New Testament research, the dogmatic task of New Testament theology.

The Dogmatic Task

Regarding the dogmatic task of New Testament theology, the theologian deals with the convictions that are presented in the documents. These convictions, and this is crucial for our understanding of Schlatter's position, have a clear impact on the theologian, in that they determine the attitude in which he is to approach the text. For Schlatter, the single valid criterion for New Testament theology was *not* the allegedly neutral "scientific" viewpoint of the critical-historical method, but the "content" of the New Testament, namely "of what it is in itself" (*was es in sich selber ist*)."[45] According to this agenda, the receptive theologian lets the text speak to himself and meets the New Testament on its own ground.[46] Theologians who interact with the New Testament documents in such a way "unite the content of their own consciousness with the assertions of the New Testament."[47] Its subject matter requires the scientific theologian to approach it not only empirically but also from a faith perspective. Schlatter, then, clearly has a presupposition—his empirical method is not "objective," "pure," or "prejudice-free" in the strict sense of the word. Schlatter was clearly realist enough to acknowledge that there could be no such thing as a "presuppositionless exegesis," an insight which his student Rudolf Bultmann picked up later.[48] Yet if presupposition was unavoidable, Schlatter clearly preferred it to be theistic rather than atheistic, since he considered only the former to be congruent with the material he observed. Gösta Lundström comments:

> Schlatter by no means abandoned this believing attitude in his critical researches, but considered on the contrary that it provided a better and clearer insight into the deeper meaning of the problems than is ever achieved by scholars who

44. Schlatter, "Theologie des NT und Dogmatik," 54, 20–21; "Briefe über das Dogma," 21; *Dogma*, 94; *Metaphysik*, 76.
45. Schlatter, "Theologie des NT und Dogmatik," 25.
46. Ibid.
47. Ibid., 28.
48. See Bultmann's essay, "Ist voraussetzungslose Exegese möglich?," 409–17.

believe themselves unprejudiced but are actually entirely bound by (to them) self-evident theological and philosophical preconceptions.[49]

New Testament theology is then always an existential task, Schlatter claims, as it confronts us with the question: "How does that which is written relate to our own, spiritual possession?"[50] Ideally, the past tense of New Testament history becomes the foundation of our own vitality in the present tense.[51] The New Testament itself exerts a significant impact on us as it introduces us to an "image of God that sets in motion our whole spiritual possession," and which can either lead to a relation (*Anschluss*) with Jesus or a rejection of him.[52] Schlatter thus connects hermeneutics with an ethical imperative of faithful New Testament interpretation. Only the faithful exegete, who performs the seeing-act from a position of faith, is a truthful observer who listens to the text carefully and thereby secures the accurate reading of Scripture which is Schlatter's ultimate goal.

However, the Swiss critical-empirical realist is eager to note that this almost paradoxical "subjective objectivity," as Walldorf puts it, is not a stumbling-block in the way of proper science.[53] It is not subjectivity per se which can harm the purity of the seeing-act, but only a profane, a selfish intention,[54] which is inimical to the subject matter.[55] Schlatter counters objections that this importing of faith into the theological task might obstruct his objective of scientific work (*scientifische Arbeit*).[56] In agreeing with Anselm's dictum that theology is "faith seeking understanding" (*fides quaerens intellectum*), he points out that faith is actually instrumental for accurate execution of theology, as only in the mode of faith does one achieve an elementary congruence between the God-given observed object (such as the Scriptures) and the God-made observing subject, the theologian.[57]

---

49. Lundström, *Kingdom of God*, 127.

50. Schlatter, "Theologie des NT und Dogmatik," 29.

51. Ibid., 30.

52. Ibid., 64.

53. Walldorf, *Realistische Philosophie*, 70. In this context, see also Walldorf's essay, "Aspekte einer realistischen Philosophie," 62–85.

54. Schlatter, "Theologie des NT und Dogmatik," 22–24.

55. Schlatter, *Metaphysik*, 25.

56. Schlatter to Hermann Cremer, 29 December 1894, in Stupperich, *Wort und Wahrnehmung*, 18.

57. See Schlatter, "Selbstdarstellungen," 15 and *Glaube im Neuen Testament*, xxii–xxiii. This congruence is, for example, absent in the atheistic method, which renders theology absurd and harms the church. Schlatter, "Atheistische Methoden," 235.

"Our object," Schlatter writes, "desires that we think of God."[58] Thus only as a coherent individual, with one's life-act intact, can the theologian, like the natural scientist, work properly and accurately.[59] Intellectual capacity and strenuous observation is obviously a precondition for adequate seeing, but the theologian is at the same time required to possess a pious connection with his subject. "Sure enough, the theologian must be a thinker," writes Schlatter, "someone who appreciates his knowledge [*Erkennen*] as a gift of God; however . . . it is equally essential for him to be pious."[60] Schlatter calls this mode of thinking faith-appropriate thinking (*glaubensgemäß denken*).[61] As a matter of fact, Schlatter goes so far as to say that the theologian's thinking is, through faith, in harmony with the "mind of Christ" (according to 1 Cor 2:16). Theology in conformity with God's will is possible as the theologian enjoys a spiritual fellowship (*Geistesgemeinschaft*) with Jesus Christ, "so that we might be able to say with Paul, it is no longer I who live, but Christ who lives in me! And it is no longer I who thinks but Christ who thinks in me."[62] Theology, from Schlatter's perspective, is therefore a deeply spiritual task.

In a way, then, Schlatter seems to suggest even stricter criteria for the science of theology than for any other science. One could obviously not expect an ornithologist to be transformed into a bird in order that he might be able to perform proper ornithology. Yet for theology, Schlatter claims, this metaphysical congruence between observer and the observed Word of God is not optional, but vital. Christian theology cannot be properly studied from a neutral point of view. The New Testament historian who inquires about Jesus Christ is not and must never become a *tabula rasa*. Rather, this task requires also the whole dogmatician, the whole person of faith with his own personality and his own life-story.[63] From this perspective then, it is evident that, for Schlatter, the historical task and the dogmatic task of New Testament research are not in a competitive relation but in fact complement each other, provided that there exists an analogy between the content of the New Testament and the "inner life" of the theologian. New Testament theology, in Schlatter's view, is thus not simply an intellectual exercise of objective observation, but primarily an "ethical struggle" about God and Christ.[64]

58. Ibid., 248.
59. See Schlatter, "Selbstdarstellungen," 15 and *Glaube im Neuen Testament*, xxii.
60. Schlatter, *Dogma*, 22.
61. Schlatter, "Unterwerfung unter die Gotteswirklichkeit," 11, 47–48.
62. Schlatter, "Christologie und Soteriologie," xii–xiii.
63. Schlatter, "Atheistische Methoden," 234–35; cf. *Dogma*, 5–6.
64. Schlatter, "Theologie des NT und Dogmatik," 62.

Any historian who abandons the notion of God—either in general or only in the field of scientific thinking—fails to recognize the central assertion of the New Testament.[65] Bearing in mind Schlatter's particular approach of subjective objectivity and faith-appropriate thinking, we now turn to analyze more closely how Schlatter develops on this basis his Christology.[66]

THE UNIFIED JESUS CHRIST

Jesus Christ, his person and work is for Schlatter the focal point of the seeing-act. "In my view," writes Schlatter, "there is no higher calling for the human eye than perception which apprehends what Jesus desires and claims."[67] "Theology," he contends, "remains forever Christology, perception [*Erfassung*] of Christ's image, insight into his history."[68] Perceiving Jesus' words and works within the context of human history is for Schlatter the ultimate purpose of the seeing-act, since the appearance of Jesus Christ constitutes for Schlatter the goal of history.[69] From Schlatter's study of the *History of the Christ* emerges, most notably, the notion of *unity*, a feature that surfaced in our earlier discussions and which deserves some closer exploration at this stage.

In Schlatter's view, the New Testament exhibits a clear theological unity. According to Heikki Räisänen, Schlatter's "insistence on the theological unity of the New Testament" mark him "unmistakably as a figure from a bygone era."[70] Of course, Schlatter continued in the tradition of Baader and Beck, who, as we have seen earlier, emphasized the theological unity of the New Testament. In contrast to Räisänen, however, whose term "bygone era" suggests a negative connotation, we hold the view that it is sometimes worthwhile to go back to bygone eras in order to make progress in our theological questions today. Schlatter portrays a unified picture of Jesus Christ, who reveals himself as the God-human within the context of a concrete and coherent history, and whose being is in harmony with his actions.[71] The reason for Schlatter's unified account lies, as already outlined, in his assumption of a close relationship between events and convictions, between

---

65. Ibid.
66. See Schlatter, *Dogma*, 369, 372.
67. Schlatter in his "Foreword" to *Das Wort Jesu* (in *History of the Christ*, 17).
68. Schlatter, *Gründe der christlichen Gewißheit*, 102–3.
69. As Peter Stuhlmacher correctly observes, in "Adolf Schlatter," 233.
70. Räisänen, *Beyond New Testament Theology*, 25.
71. See Schlatter's "Der Zweifel an der Messianität Jesu," and his New Testament theology, *History of the Christ* and *Theology of the Apostles*.

history and dogmatics. This has special implications for Christology: in the person and work of Jesus Christ, the fields of history and dogmatics converge. Schlatter writes:

> No division between history and doctrine does justice to Jesus' work and death. The events of his life do not simply get a particular colour from the ideas he wove with them. Their entire source and origin is to be found in his convictions. He acted on the basis of his mission in the certainty of being the Son and the Christ. So discussions of what happened through him which ignore his inner life are worthless.[72]

Jesus Christ is the prime example where history and *Dogma* meet, Schlatter argues, since the events of his life originate in his convictions. Jesus acted based on his convictions, namely that he was the Son who was sent by his Father and who appointed him to be the Christ.[73] To make a case for this account of a unified Jesus Christ was the purpose of Schlatter's two main New Testament works, *The History of the Christ* and *The Theology of the Apostles*. In these works, Schlatter argues for the unity of Jesus' life-act, carefully highlighting the harmony of his calling, his convictions, and his being in action, while also pointing to his continuing activity in the world through his presence in the apostles and in the early church. To Schlatter's mind, many of his contemporaries did not sufficiently emphasize the harmonious life-act of Jesus Christ. Schlatter is thus critical of approaches that assume a linear-chronological development both of Jesus' own convictions and of Christianity as a movement. In *The History of the Christ*, Schlatter lays out how Jesus Christ was from the very beginning of his earthly life convinced and assured of his messianic calling, having both perfect God-consciousness and perfect messianic self-consciousness.[74] Jesus neither gradually grew in his messianic self-awareness (as Heinrich Holtzmann, for instance, suggests),[75] nor was his messianic office ascribed to him by the early community of faith in

---

72. Schlatter, "Theology of the NT and Dogmatics," 156–57. Ward Gasque thus describes Schlatter's approach as follows: "[T]he focal point of his theology was simply the conviction that Jesus was 'the Christ of God' . . . and that Christ himself is the heart of the New Testament, indeed, of the Bible. . . . He was committed to the belief that Jesus was already in his earthly life Son of God and Messiah. . . . The Jesus of the New Testament was not the product of the church's faith but, rather, a historical given. To put it in other words, the church's faith was the product of Jesus, who himself was the Christ of God." Gasque, "Promise of Adolf Schlatter," 29.

73. Schlatter, "Theologie des NT und Dogmatik," 68.

74. See Schlatter, *History of the Christ*, 284.

75. See Holtzmann, *Die synoptischen Evangelien*, 484–85.

retrospect (as Hermann S. Reimarus believed).[76] Jesus, according to Schlatter, was from the outset assured of his mission, and, being convinced of his mission, he acted. Schlatter also rejected claims which argued for a chronological development from Jesus Christ to the Apostle Paul, and finally to the Apostle John, who is considered by some to be the "greatest representative" of early Christian history.[77] In Schlatter's view, such approaches—and he has most likely Bernhard Weiss in mind here—were influenced by Hegelian dialectic and by the assumption of dogmatizing tendencies, which he considered implausible.[78] Schlatter also disagrees with Wrede's and Bultmann's position, which suggest a discord between the teachings of Jesus and of Paul the apostle.[79]

What Schlatter notices as he pursues his seeing-act is the remarkable "uniformity" of Jesus' inner convictions and the "apostles' inner life."[80] Schlatter's emphasis on Jesus' "inner convictions" (*inwendiger Besitz*),[81] in this regard, shows distinct affinities with Wilhelm Herrmann's focus on Jesus' "inner life," mentioned earlier. Still, while Schlatter welcomes Herrmann's particular emphasis, he argues that his own approach offers more in that it establishes a vital link between Jesus' inner convictions and concrete history, something that Herrmann, as he feels, neglects. In Schlatter's view, Jesus' convictions, his teachings, his word, and his creative deeds are closely united. "I hope," writes Schlatter in the 1920 preface to *The History of the Christ*, "that the reader will succeed more readily in perceiving the unity binding everything that Jesus says and does when he pictures the interdependent activities of Jesus."[82] Moreover, Schlatter's method of New Testament research does not allow him to use critical-historical research as a means to go "behind" the New Testament sources in order to uncover some

76. See Spence, *Christology*, 90–93; cf. McGrath, *Making of Modern German Christology*, 34–35.

77. Schlatter, "Theologie des NT und Dogmatik," 43.

78. According to Weiss, Johannean theology represents the "final result of Biblical theology in the deepest conception and the highest glory." *Biblical Theology of the New Testament*, 2:315.

79. See Schlatter's work, *Jesus und Paulus*. For Wrede, the Apostle Paul is the "second founder of Christianity," who developed a Hellenistic theology that was very different from Jesus' own teaching. In Wrede's view, this "second founder of Christianity has even, compared with the first, exercised beyond all doubt the stronger—not the better—influence." Wrede, *Paul*, 179–80. Bultmann even goes so far as to stress that "Jesus' teaching is—to all its intents and purposes—irrelevant for Paul." Bultmann, "Significance of the Historical Jesus," 223.

80. Schlatter, "Theologie des NT und Dogmatik," 37.

81. Ibid.

82. Schlatter, *History of the Christ*, 21–22.

form of "hidden" information. Schlatter could thus not "demythologize" the New Testament data in order to rediscover the *kerygma* according to the method of his student Rudolf Bultmann, or isolate the christological kernel from the historical husk as his friend Adolf von Harnack envisioned.[83]

Instead of going *behind* the New Testament, it is Schlatter's declared intention to go *into* the New Testament and to discover "what is there." And what he discovers is a harmony between Jesus' person and his work in history. According to Schlatter, it is thus impossible to drive a wedge between the different gospel accounts; it is always the same Jesus Christ in his organic life-act to whom the evangelists bear witness. Schlatter could therefore not scrutinize the gospel accounts expecting to extract an underlying Christ-principle (*Christusprinzip*),[84] or a certain "messianic secret," as William Wrede attempted.[85] Schlatter could also not subtract alleged myths from the gospel story on the basis of an anti-supernatural presupposition in the manner of D. F. Strauss. For Schlatter, the miracles recorded in the New Testament are not products of the evangelists' imagination but are key elements of Jesus' mission and vocation. "The more we reinterpret the miracle record or seek to distance it from the course of history," Schlatter writes, "the farther we distance ourselves from the real events."[86] There was and is only this one history of Christ, only this one message, only this one person of Jesus Christ who displays an organic union of being and action, of his "inner life" and his creative action in concrete history. Schlatter explains:

> My attempt to concretize my theology for the church was based on the fact that I saw the history of Christ as a unity before me. I did not have next to a synoptic Christ a Johannine Christ, or next to a prophet who preached the Sermon on the Mount a Christ who carried the cross . . . I saw him before me pursuing *one* goal and *one* mission [*Sendung*] that generated the whole abundance of his word and work . . . I had the impression that I was entitled to this attempt, to show him to others like this as well.[87]

83. See Schlatter's criticism of Harnack in "Christus und Christentum, Person und Prinzip," 9.

84. See Schlatter, "Princip des Protestantismus," 241–47. Schlatter has in mind presumably here his Swiss contemporary Alois E. Biedermann (1819–85), who differentiated between a "religious principle" and the person of Christ. See Biedermann, *Christliche Dogmatik*, 1:331.

85. See Wrede, *Das Messiasgeheimnis in den Evangelien*.

86. Schlatter, *History of the Christ*, 191. For further reading on Schlatter's view on miracles see his lexicon entry on "Wunder," and his essay on "Die Wunder der Bibel," in *Hülfe in Bibelnot*, 63–69.

87. Schlatter, *Rückblick*, 233 (emphasis original).

According to his reading of the New Testament, Schlatter concludes that it nowhere forces its readers to distinguish between a historical Jesus and a Christ of faith.[88] This distinction, Schlatter thinks, is an artificial and unhealthy dualism that is foreign to the biblical text. Rather, the New Testament describes in a coherent manner the words, the convictions and the acts of the one person of Jesus Christ, who, as the Son of God, calls sinners to repentance, dies on the cross and thereby creates the possibility for the new community of faith. Hence, Schlatter is convinced that Jesus' self-consciousness did not shift from optimism to a later pessimistic outlook. Jesus, he clarifies, was never unsure of his assignment and never deviated from his goal, the cross.[89] Death came not as a surprise to Jesus but was the consciously willed apex of his kingly office, the culmination of the revelation of his divinity.[90] According to Schlatter, and this will take center stage in the next chapters, Jesus' kingly will (*königlicher Wille*), his divine sonship, his call to repentance, his will to the cross (*Kreuzeswille*), his fellowship with the disciples, and his creation of the new community of believers are all significantly inter-related and dependent upon each other, forming one harmonious unity:

> His sovereign will, his divine sonship, his witness to God's sovereignty, his call to repentance, his willing the cross [*Kreuzeswille*], his fellowship with the disciples—in short the whole sequence of his acts—are not just one item after another. We fail to do them justice if we simply note each one separately. His knowledge of himself as Lord of the community is grounded in his filial relationship to God, in his knowing himself empowered to call sinners and in his authority to bear his cross. Jesus will be comprehensible to us in proportion as these connections are perceived.[91]

When one understands the unity of Jesus' being in action in this way, Schlatter claims, it is impossible "to separate a 'message' from his actions, since, in

---

88. He writes: "The failure to believe that Jesus confirmed himself as the Christ can only be maintained with the destruction of his whole word and at best proceeds immediately to the negation of Jesus' existence. This is blatant rationalism, an inference from the alleged 'impossibility' to the destruction of the ability to see [*Sehfähigkeit*]." Schlatter, *Dogma*, 282.

89. See Schlatter, *History of the Christ*, 266.

90. Schlatter writes: "A Christ on whom the imminent catastrophe began to dawn only gradually is not the Christ of the Sermon on the Mount." Schlatter, "Christologie der Bergpredigt," 323. We will return to this important aspect in the following chapter.

91. Schlatter, "Theology of the NT and Dogmatics," 138 ["Theologie des NT und Dogmatik," 38].

his case, the word and the work, the assurance and the will, form a closely connected unity."[92] The Jesus who appears before Schlatter's eyes is the subject of a holistic life-act. Schlatter writes:

> According to my view, it is one unified goal that determines the whole path of Jesus, his earthly work, its completion, his heavenly efficacy through the Spirit. During his earthly work he draws from his kingly mission his word of repentance, his proclamation of the divine kingdom, his signs, [and] his cross. The same mission makes his goal unique and empowers him to establish his fellowship with the disciples anew, now as the one who lives eternally. The same mission he accomplished by granting those who are now connected with him through faith, justification, redemption and sanctification, and the same mission bestows on his community what it is hoping for.[93]

CONCLUSION

Schlatter's contribution to New Testament studies is timeless. In light of the current doubts regarding Jesus' self-understanding—as recently expressed by Bart D. Ehrman, for instance, who claims that Jesus did not refer to himself as the "Son of Man"[94]—Schlatter's theology of the seeing-act, with its two-pronged strategy of combining the historical task and the dogmatic task, offer crucial assistance to those who engage with the F. C. Baurs of today. Key to a correct reading of the New Testament text is first of all an in-depth knowledge of its historical-cultural context, of its language and particular setting. For the historical task, rigorous empirical observation is paramount. In this respect, Schlatter shares common ground with many of his contemporaries who promoted the critical-historical study of the New Testament. However, for Schlatter, the historical task of New Testament history is closely linked with the dogmatic task of New Testament theology. The latter requires the theologian to evaluate carefully and faithfully the convictions of the New Testament people. We noted that for Schlatter, the *content* of the New Testament convictions present a crucial challenge to the researcher in that it calls him to assimilate it and to pursue an existential connection (what Schlatter calls *Anschluss*) with it. New Testament research is thus a dual task that requires the exegete to explore the facts empirically

---

92. Schlatter, *History of the Christ*, 21.
93. Schlatter, "Briefe über das Dogma," 57.
94. See Ehrman, *How Jesus Became God*, 106–9, 121.

and the content faithfully. If the seeing-act is executed in this way, Schlatter claims, a unified picture of Jesus Christ emerges. Schlatter's New Testament picture of Christ differs considerably from that of many of his contemporaries. According to Schlatter, Jesus is more than a "religious genius"[95] who proclaims the universal kingdom of ethical performance and heartfelt religious experience. Jesus, in Schlatter's view, is the one with perfect messianic self-consciousness, who issues his authoritative call to repentance and his invitation to sinners. At the same time, he is the Christ who embraces the cross upon which he performs the kingly deed of reconciliation and through which he creates the new community of faith. These are the major building-blocks of Schlatter's holistic account of Jesus Christ and they shall next be examined in more detail as we turn to the thinking-act (*Denkakt*), moving thus to a more systematic-theological treatment of Schlatter's thought.

---

95. See Holtzmann, *Lehrbuch der Neutestamentlichen Theologie*, 1:173–75.

4

The *Denkakt* (I)
Jesus in Relation to God

HAVING SO FAR EXAMINED what Schlatter "sees" in the New Testament through the lens of his seeing-act, we will now consider how he processes the material perceived in the thinking-act. In Schlatter's words: "The religious question is never settled by simply handing on what Scripture says. The question is always: what does Scripture mean for us? This 'us,' with all it involves, takes us into the realm of dogmatics."[1] Or, in more conventional theological language, we are moving from Schlatter's exegetical approach to his dogmatics, and in particular, his christological framework. This is certainly an ambitious goal, which explains why the treatment extends over two separate chapters, *Denkakt* I and II. Our aim, however, is *not* to provide a detailed account of every minute aspect of Schlatter's christological approach (although this might be a promising task for a future project); rather, our research question is, as indicated earlier: What is Schlatter's specific contribution to Christology, and how viable is it? The move from exegesis to dogmatics is intrinsically Schlatterian, as for Schlatter, the empirical-historical seeing-act is fundamentally related to the theological thinking-act in the same way that New Testament research is vitally connected with dogmatics.[2] "Theology," he contends, "should therefore never be just exegesis

---

1. Schlatter, "Theology of the NT and Dogmatics," 133 (emphasis original); see also "Bedeutung der Methode," 7–8, and "Briefe über das Dogma," 50, 57.

2. See Schlatter, "Entstehung der Beiträge," 58; "Theologie des NT und Dogmatik," 21; *Rückblick*, 102.

... but the church needs continually ... the dogmatician."[3] While this might be a truism, one wonders whether today, in times of increasing segmentation and specialization in the theological ivory tower, Schlatter's reminder of the unity of these disciplines—also by way of his personal example as professor of systematics *and* New Testament theology—is a much-needed encouragement for positive interaction between the (unfortunately) often estranged departments of biblical studies and systematics.

In Schlatter's view, the findings of New Testament research in the seeing-act are organized and processed in the dogmatic thinking-act, through which the dogmatician delivers a judgment (*Urteil*).[4] Similar to the exegetical process, this task requires the "whole dogmatician," involving his own personality and the context of his life-story.[5] The systematic theologian (much like the biblical studies scholar), Schlatter points out, never works in isolation but always in dependence upon history, culture and tradition: "We receive the thought that we think," he writes, "through what has been thought before us;"[6] thus, the "manner in which he [the dogmatician] participates with his observation and experience in the experience of Christendom shapes his dogmatic judgment."[7] From this follows that the systematic theologian needs to be aware of his own particular presuppositions, his personality and his individual history, while pursuing dogmatic judgments in the thinking-act. This idiosyncratic aspect of the dogmatic task though is not a disadvantage and thus need not be suppressed. Parallel to the seeing-act, Schlatter insists on subjective objectivity, which is not a stumbling-block on the way to accurate dogmatic work, since for Schlatter, the faith-based imperative is effective at this stage as well, guaranteeing the congruence between the interpreting subject and the interpreted material. The dogmatic task is therefore intricately connected with the life-act (*Lebensakt*) of the dogmatician who enjoys an existential union with Christ (*Anschluss an Christus*). We now turn to some key aspects of Schlatter's christological *Denkakt*.

---

3. Schlatter, "Selbstdarstellungen," 156; see also *Dogma*, 556. On the one hand, Helmut Thielicke is right when he describes Schlatter's methodological intention thus: "one has to put it this simply: he only wanted to be a listening human being [*ein hörender Mensch*]." Thielicke is on the other hand, however, mistaken when he concludes that this empirical agenda prevented Schlatter from becoming a thorough systematician. See Thielicke, "Zum Geleit," 10–11. It is exactly through empirical-realist New Testament observation that Schlatter arrives at a theological system.

4. See Schlatter, *Dogma*, 373–74; "Briefe über das Dogma," 33.

5. Schlatter, "Atheistische Methoden," 234–35; *Dogma*, 5–6.

6. Schlatter, "Der Glaube und die Geschichte," 343.

7. Schlatter, *Dogma*, 5.

KEY FEATURES OF SCHLATTER'S RELATIONAL CHRISTOLOGY

For Schlatter, the notions of *relation* and *volition* are intrinsic to his christological project. Schlatter sees Jesus in a twofold relationship, what he calls a double communion (*doppelte Gemeinschaft*),[8] namely in relation to God and to humankind.[9] In relation to God, Jesus is the Son of God who enjoys the full love of the Father and who obeys him completely by uniting his will with the Father's will, thereby proving his own love for him in return.[10] In relation to humankind, Jesus is the Christ, the Son of Man, who shares in our human nature, who possesses the will to the cross (*Kreuzeswillen*) and who, through what he accomplished on this very cross, unites us with himself and establishes the new community of God.[11] In Schlatter's words:

> Jesus knew himself to be linked with God and with humanity through his origin so that this dual connection gave him the measure of his life and the goal of his work. By "Son of God" he said that he had his life from and for God. When he simultaneously called himself the Son of Man, he said that he had and wanted to have his life from and for man. While the one name expressed his closeness to God, the other expressed his closeness to man. This double communion [*doppelte Gemeinschaft*] determined what he was and did.[12]

This brief quote illustrates neatly Schlatter's preferred christological approach: his is obviously not a rationalistic approach in the Hegelian

---

8. Schlatter, *History of the Christ*, 135 [*Geschichte des Christus*, 166].

9. Hesitant to speculate about the inner life of the immanent Trinity (as we shall explore in more detail below), Schlatter's christological conversation focuses on the incarnate second person of the Godhead, while avoiding any speculations about the *Logos asarkos*. In Schlatter's view, it is thus not helpful to venture into in-depth speculations of the *Logos*' pre-existence, for it will, on this side of the *eschaton*, remain a mystery—in his eternal pre-existence, Jesus remains for us "incomprehensible" (*unfaßlich*), Schlatter notes. *Dogma*, 334; cf. *Theology of the Apostles*, 256. Schlatter argues that the church fathers did a disservice to Christianity in that they focused their attention too keenly on a miracle that must remain mysterious per se. *Dogma*, 334. However, Schlatter clearly affirmed the eternality of the *Logos*: "the thought of the creative process that gave him [Jesus] the beginning of his earthly life did not contradict his concept of eternity." *History of the Christ*, 33. On Jesus' pre-existence see also his *Theology of the Apostles*, 132–35, 254–55; *Dogma*, 333–41; *Johannes der Täufer*, 121–32; *History of the Christ*, 307.

10. Schlatter, *History of the Christ*, 27 [*Geschichte des Christus*, 11].

11. Ibid.

12. Ibid., 134–35 [*Geschichte des Christus*, 166].

tradition, nor does he move from religious experience to doctrinal assertions. His is rather a Christology based on the New Testament narrative and language (as one would expect from the New Testament seeing-act), which, and this is important, allows us to infer from Jesus in relation to Jesus' essence. This is basically his claim in the above quote, when he writes that Jesus' "double communion determined what he was and did." This is, evidently, a bold statement and it will keep us busy for most of our discussion in this and the following chapter. In this first part of the *Denkakt*, we focus predominantly on the relation between the Son and his Father (and the Spirit), whereas the following chapter broadens our discussion to Jesus in relation to humankind. Let us then turn, first, to explore Schlatter's view of Jesus in relation to God.

In terms of Jesus' relation to God, the concept of sonship is paramount for Schlatter. Sonship is *the* crucial New Testament description of who Jesus Christ is. According to Schlatter's reading, the Apostle John "proclaims Jesus in the conviction that the gospel is completely expressed by the statement 'Jesus is the Son.'"[13] "All John needed for his teaching regarding the Christ," Schlatter notes, "were the terms 'Father' and 'Son.'"[14] Now this Father-Son relationship is characterized by the Father's giving and the Son's receiving. "He knows himself as the Son," Schlatter writes, "and he describes thereby the whole content of his life as effected [*gewirkt*] and received from God."[15] Receptivity and dependency are thus the key marks of Jesus' divine sonship. Whilst this might well be a coherent display of the biblical witness, Schlatter's statements so far raise some serious questions, such as: Does Jesus' dependency upon the Father imply (ontological) inferiority? Does Schlatter represent a subordinationist, or a kenoticist viewpoint? Before we return to these pressing issues, let us for now continue with our journey through Schlatter's notion of divine sonship.

Jesus' sonship, Schlatter explains, is a very special sonship. Jesus is not only *a* Son, but he is *the* Son *par excellence*, the one and only, unique Son of God. Jesus is thus not just a *primus inter pares*, and it is not a special messianic awareness, a unique moral aptitude or a particular capacity for teaching that renders Jesus unique, as some of Schlatter's contemporaries suggested (see our observations in part 1). Rather, what describes Jesus

---

13. Schlatter, *Theology of the Apostles*, 132.

14. Ibid., 150.

15. Schlatter, *Dogma*, 311. Note a similar statement in his New Testament work on the *History of the Christ*: "By 'Son' he referred not to what he had made himself to be, but to what God had made him. By calling himself the Son of God, he derived, with complete assurance, his existence and will, his vocation and his success, from God." Schlatter, *History of the Christ*, 30.

more adequately is the "uniqueness of his sonship."[16] Jesus, Schlatter posits, is Son in a wholly different way than we are as God's human sons and daughters.[17] "By refusing to ascribe to God the same fatherly relationship to himself as obtains with us," Schlatter maintains, "he [Jesus] sanctified God's Law and preserved the boundary between sinners and the only one who is truly righteous."[18] In this sense then, Schlatter concludes, Jesus is the "[o]nly One with the Father;" he is "in the strict sense 'the only Son.'"[19] This is important to note because it distinguishes Schlatter from many of his contemporaries as discussed earlier. Reacting against any anthropological domestication of Christology, any reduction of Christ to a moral example, Schlatter underlines the "otherness" of Christ, making a strong case for Jesus' divinity. Schlatter's most significant christological works, such as his "Jesus' Divinity and the Cross" (*Jesu Gottheit und das Kreuz*), stress especially Jesus' divinity, in particular as it is revealed in and through his relation with the Father. This was Schlatter's creative way of offering a corrective of what he regarded as the "reduced" developments in recent Christology.

Schlatter suggests an alternative way for doing Christology. Initially, he argues, the theologian is *not* to look at Jesus through the ontological lens. This will only lead to philosophical speculation and produce a distorted picture of Jesus in isolation. If, instead, one focuses first on Jesus through relational spectacles, one sees a Son in relation to his Father, and from this one might certainly draw inferences to ontology.[20] We shall now explore

16. Schlatter, *History of the Christ*, 77. Kathryn Tanner points out, much like Schlatter, that "the uniqueness of Jesus is not to be sought in particular features of Jesus' life that one could identify as divine—for example, his unusual self-consciousness or psychology as a man with a perfect God-consciousness or his omniscient knowledge or even moral holiness. What is unusual about Jesus—what sets him off from other people—is his relationship to God (his relationship to the Word who assumes his humanity as its own), the shape of his way of life (as the exhibition of the triune life on a human level), and his effects on others (his saving significance)." Tanner, *Jesus, Humanity and the Trinity*, 20.

17. Schlatter clarifies that "Jesus distinguished his relationship with God consistently and clearly from that enjoyed by others, including the sonship of God he gave to his disciples." Schlatter, *History of the Christ*, 75; cf. *Glaube im Neuen Testament*, 233–34.

18. Schlatter, *History of the Christ*, 76.

19. Schlatter, *Theology of the Apostles*, 158.

20. Christoph Schwöbel argues along the same lines: "christological reflection tends to get lost in the intricacies of the relations of the two natures of Christ if the framework of the relations between the Father, the Son and the Spirit is no longer seen as that which defines the hypostatic identity and communal essence of God." Schwöbel, "Christ for Us," 186. "[T]he question of the divinity of Christ should not be interpreted in terms of his possession of a divine nature, but should primarily be seen in terms of his relationship as the Son to the Father as it is mediated through the Spirit." Schwöbel,

this significant aspect of Schlatter's Christology in more detail. In a first step, we consider Jesus' relational (and volitional) union with the Father, through the Holy Spirit, and how it relates to his essential union with God. Secondly, the focus shifts to the ethical aspect of this volitional union, namely, Jesus' concrete display of obedience and submission to the Father, again, mediated by the Holy Spirit. The adjacent question, then, is whether Schlatter is able to offer a balanced account of the Son's submission and the Father's *monarchia* without succumbing to the problematic position of subordinationism, or some of the other "isms" mentioned earlier; this shall be in the focus of our concluding, third, section.

VOLITIONAL UNION AND ESSENTIAL UNION

Relational Terminology

At the outset, one must acknowledge that Schlatter clearly approves of the patristic formula that Jesus is of one substance (*homoousios*) with the Father and he certainly agrees with the Symbol of Chalcedon, which regards Jesus as having two natures, one divine and one human.[21] Schlatter uses the concept of person regarding Jesus Christ, clearly aware of the term's problematic Greek baggage; but Schlatter stresses that in his view, person means always person in volitional relation with another person, which excludes any individualistic connotations.[22] Schlatter feels that it is difficult, perhaps even inadequate, to examine Jesus Christ in ontological terms like "nature" or "being" alone, since our knowledge of this aspect of reality will remain partial and thus lead to mere speculation.[23] Aiming to establish coherence

---

"Christology and Trinitarian Thought," 139.

21. Leontius of Byzantium (485–543) developed the concept of *enhypostasis*, where the human nature of Christ is not considered to exist in its own *hypostasis* but to subsist enhypostatically in the *hypostasis* of the *Logos*. Schlatter, though hesitant to use this vocabulary, would be happy with this affirmation, while pointing to the central aspect of Jesus in relation to the Father and the Spirit. See Loos, "Divine Action, Christ," 216–17.

22. In his treatment of "God's Will" in his "Christian Dogmatics," Schlatter claims that the volitional bond between the members of the Trinity is key to our understanding of their unity. See Schlatter, *Dogma*, 179–80, 573n108, 589n206.

23. If one considers Jesus' earthly life, Schlatter contends, one encounters someone who was clearly opposed to "theological intellectualism" (*theologisierenden Intellektualismus*). Jesus was, he adds, the "perfect anti-gnostic" (*der vollendete Antignostiker*). Schlatter, *Dogma*, 318. That is, Jesus neither "taught the presence of a divine power or substance in him nor the fusing [*Verschmelzung*] of his consciousness with the consciousness of God." Schlatter, *Glaube im Neuen Testament*, 231. Schlatter's aversion to gnostic speculations might actually have been one of the theological overlaps between him and his Berlin colleague Adolf von Harnack. Harnack complains about the

within his own framework, Schlatter intends to use the relational language of the New Testament seeing-act as a basis for his considerations in the dogmatic thinking-act. He thus intends to use "conceptions of God" that are "taken from personal life," as he finds them in the New Testament narrative, such as Son, Father, will, obedience, and the like.[24] Again, whilst this does not imply that Schlatter is blind to any ontological language in the New Testament, it reflects his theological carefulness as he seeks to speak of the God who is wholly other (*der ganz andere*).[25] Demonstrating a high doctrine of divine incomprehensibility,[26] Schlatter is hesitant to use "material formulas, forces, substances or the like to describe Christ."[27] Since we have no unmediated perception of the divine essence (*ousia*), the ideal starting-point is the divine relation and action described in the New Testament.[28] Only in this way, and from this angle—and this is Schlatter's important argument—can we infer any claims in respect of ontology. Of course, one could argue at this point whether Schlatter might have overlooked Jesus' crucial self-testimonies in the gospels, such as his statement in John, for instance: "I and the Father are one" (John 10:30). Schlatter would obviously agree that this is a statement that refers to Jesus' claim of his divinity; still, Schlatter feels that our language soon reaches its limits when we intend to penetrate the question of essence. Instead, he is interested in exploring the concrete ways in which this essence, in this case, Jesus' divine essence, finds

---

intrusion of foreign (Gnostic) concepts like substance, essence, and being into theological language and debate. See Harnack, *Wesen des Christentums*, 115–20. In rejecting any "philosophical volatilisation of our saviour" (*alle philosophische Verflüchtigung unseres Heilandes*), Harnack would surely have found Schlatter's support. Harnack in Agnes von Zahn-Harnack, *Adolf von Harnack*, 67. However, as noted earlier, Schlatter was not able to agree with Harnack's radical program of rediscovering Jesus' original message by separating the historical husk from the essential kernel of Christianity.

24. Schlatter, *Theology of the Apostles*, 254. "[The Apostle] John's concept of God," for example, Schlatter notes, "takes on a Trinitarian form without reflecting a formulaic use of the three divine names." Ibid., 144.

25. Schlatter, "Wert und Unwert," 263.

26. "For us," writes Schlatter, "he [God] retains the impenetrability of the one who is absolutely superior" (*Er behält für uns die Undurchdringlichkeit des uns schlechthin Überlegenen*). Schlatter, "Unterwerfung unter die Gotteswirklichkeit," 10. Schlatter's language is clearly reminiscent of Schleiermacher; we will highlight some fascinating parallels between the two theologians throughout this discussion.

27. Schlatter, *Theology of the Apostles*, 254.

28. With respect to the being of Jesus Christ, Schlatter prefers the term "form" over the term "nature," since the latter is foreign, he feels, to the New Testament language. That "Paul avoided this term," Schlatter writes, "shows how little he was concerned to accommodate his thought to Greek conceptualities." Schlatter, *Theology of the Apostles*, 259.

its concrete, tangible expression in real life, against the backdrop of concrete history, and, particularly, as it is revealed in his relation to God (Schlatter makes this case explicitly in the chapter on "Jesus' Statements Regarding Himself," in the *History of the Christ*).[29] Let us consider Schlatter's line of reasoning at this point in more detail.

From Relation to Essence

Schlatter desires to direct the theological conversation away from the—transcendent—being of the second person of the Trinity towards the phenomenological reality of Jesus Christ's relational-volitional union with the Father. Still, this does not mean that Schlatter disregards their essential union. On the contrary, in Schlatter's view, unity of will (*Willenseinheit*) and unity of essence (*Wesenseinheit*) are inseparable. He writes:

> The completeness of his divine sonship meant for Jesus that he was given unity of will with God so that he knew himself to be the one who did the entire will of God with complete obedience. This perfect communion of will [*Willensgemeinschaft*], however, was for him one with the perfect communion in essence [*Wesensgemeinschaft*]. This explains why he described himself as eternal. Jesus did not distinguish between unity of will and unity of essence but rather considered God's will and being as inseparable.[30]

While Schlatter regards volition and essence as inseparable, he argues that the unity of will should be the starting-point for our theological conversation, as it elucidates the unity in essence. And, following Schlatter, there is much to discover here. The volitional union between Jesus and the Father allows us to gain deeper insight into their essential union.

Schlatter claims that from our human point of view, the real christological miracle is Jesus' ability to enjoy a volitional union with God (and also with us). The "real miracle in Jesus," Schlatter notes, "lies in his volition, [namely] how he could love God wholeheartedly and at the same time could and can love the world."[31] "In my view," he contends, "the miracle in Jesus' being seems to be a miracle of union, of volitional [union] and thereby an essential [*wesentlichen*] union, not a transformation of nature."[32]

---

29. Schlatter, *History of the Christ*, 125–36.
30. Schlatter, *Geschichte des Christus*, 16; cf. *Der Evangelist Johannes*, 322.
31. Schlatter, "Christi Versöhnen und Christi Vergeben," 163.
32. Schlatter, "Bekenntnis zur Gottheit Jesu," 46–47. In that respect one must

Schlatter explains that he reached this conclusion through his reading of the New Testament. Jesus, he claims, did not explain the nature of his being, his communion in essence with God or his pre-existence in ontological terms; instead, Jesus revealed himself as the obedient Son who acts against the backdrop of concrete history in communion of will with the Father, and thereby reveals his union of essence with him.[33] The keyword here is *reveals*, that is, Schlatter seems to regard the relational-volitional union as a *manifestation*, or *demonstration* of the essential union.[34] Hence, the volitional union between the Father and the Son, what he calls their communion of will, is key to understanding their communion in essence—and not the other way round. In Schlatter's own words, and it is particularly the last sentence which is relevant here:

> Jesus' way leads him into the massive contrast of humiliation and exaltation; the New Testament's gaze on God, however, remains consistent in spite of this powerful tension and [it]

---

mention Schlatter's critical view of the concept of the communication of attributes. Schlatter fears that the doctrine of the *communicatio idiomatum* could jeopardize the humanity of Jesus Christ. "Luther's formula was," Schlatter echoes the Reformed critique, "insufficient due to its scholastic terminology. It gives rise to an obscure thought when one holds that the properties become separated from their substance and through their transfer do not change the other substance. The criticism, namely that the humanity of Jesus disappears when it is endowed with the attributes of the divinity, was justified." Schlatter, *Dogma*, 339. In Schlatter's view, a narrative approach to understanding the person of Jesus Christ, using notions of relation and volition, seems more helpful than speculation about a communication of attributes. Schlatter would have thus undoubtedly subscribed to Christoph Schwöbel's criticism in that context: "The way in which the *communicatio idiomatum* is conventionally defined sees it as the communication of attributes of one of the two 'natures' of Christ, the divine and the human, in the unity of the one person of Christ. This, however, presupposes that we know what the divine nature and what the human nature are so that we can specify which attributes can legitimately be communicated from one to the other. This presupposition is by no means unproblematical." Schwöbel, "Christ for Us," 193.

33. Schlatter writes: "Jesus' message did not consist in a description of heaven or of God's nature or of the glory of his pre-existence but rather in the claim that he had been sent to mankind and was calling it to himself. Accordingly, he did not point to what he had once been in unity with God but to what he now was for humanity by virtue of that unity. Therefore he never made his eternity the topic of instruction, with the theoretical purpose of fleshing out christological doctrine as fully as possible." Schlatter, *History of the Christ*, 128.

34. This is reminiscent of Gregory of Nyssa's credo that unity of potency implies unity of nature. Gregory writes: "For the community of nature gives us warrant that the will of the Father, of the Son, and of the Holy Ghost is one, and thus, if the Holy Spirit wills that which seems good to the Son, the community of will clearly points to unity of essence." Gregory of Nyssa, *Against Eunomius*, II, §15, in *Nicene and Post-Nicene Fathers*, 5:132.

regards Jesus, in whatever position [he might be], in unbroken union of will [*Willenseinheit*] with the Father. How could one still believe in their union of essence [*Homousie*] if the union of will were questionable! Unity of essence manifests itself in the unanimity of the wills [*In der Einstimmigkeit der Willen hat die Wesenseinheit ihre Manifestation*].[35]

To sum up our considerations so far, Schlatter encounters in the New Testament the Son of God who lives and acts in complete union of will and of love with the Father, which reflects his essential union with him. From Jesus' perfect volitional union with God, Schlatter infers his essential union with him, making the case for Jesus' divinity. Moving ahead in our discussion, we now look more closely at how Schlatter conceptualizes volitional union in detail. Especially the following questions demand careful scrutiny: How exactly *does* Schlatter conceive of Jesus' volitional union with the Father? And what is the Holy Spirit's role in this volitional union?

JESUS' WILL, HIS OBEDIENCE, AND THE HOLY SPIRIT

Following Schlatter, the union between Jesus and his Father is revealed most clearly in their *volitional-ethical union*. It is primarily through his actual obedience and his humble submission to the Father through love, Schlatter claims, that Jesus demonstrates the reality of his divine sonship and thus his essential union with God. In what follows we shall unpack the ethical dimension of divine sonship as Schlatter understands it.

Filial obedience is *the* hallmark of Jesus' divine sonship. Jesus' sonship, Schlatter underlines, "consisted in the exercise of obedience;"[36] "the Father counts on the will of the Son and the Son gives him the same [will]."[37] Jesus' obedience is thus the factual proof of his volitional union with God and, as such, also the sign of his essential union with the Father.[38] As the obedient Son, Jesus unites his will with the Father's will and thereby reveals his

---

35. Schlatter, *Jesu Gottheit und das Kreuz*, 9. Moltmann's vocabulary is strongly reminiscent of Schlatter's when he asserts the "conformity of will" (*Willenskonformität*) between Father and Son. Moltmann, *Der gekreuzigte Gott*, 230 [*Crucified God*, 252]. Much like Schlatter, Moltmann argues for a relational-volitional union between Father and Son on the cross as evidence for their essential union. With a view to the "volitional union [*Willensgemeinschaft*] between the Father and the Son on the cross," Moltmann writes, one can speak "also of an essential union [*Wesensgemeinschaft*], of a *homoousion*." Moltmann, *Crucified God*, 252 [*Der gekreuzigte Gott*, 231].

36. Schlatter, *History of the Christ*, 44–45.

37. Schlatter, *Glaube im Neuen Testament*, 233–34.

38. Schlatter, "Jesu Demut," 65, 85.

divinity. Through his New Testament seeing-act, Schlatter encounters the obedient Son, who says: "My food is to do the will of him who sent me and to accomplish his work" (John 4:34; cf. 5:30, 6:38).[39] Obedience is therefore not a theoretical concept, or an attribute that is supernaturally bestowed upon the Son by his Father; rather, what we have here in the biblical data is, in Schlatter's view, practical obedience, lived out in actual history and in response to God. "Jesus always linked the assurance of God," Schlatter writes, "with obedience, not with theory."[40] The obvious question at this point is: Which will is it that Jesus unites with the Father's will? Is it his human will, or his divine will, or both?

Jesus' Volitional Union with the Father

From what has been said so far, one might imagine that Schlatter, with his emphasis on the unified Jesus Christ, with one mission and one goal, would perhaps also prefer to speak of only one will in Jesus Christ. Schlatter, never a friend of dualisms, is in fact hesitant to elaborate on this issue; concrete references to Jesus' human will or his divine will are sparse. This obviously begs the question whether Schlatter was a monothelitist. However, this does not seem to be the case. A close reading of his works suggests that Schlatter agrees with Maximus the Confessor (c. 580–662), who claimed, against the Patriarch of Constantinople, that there are in Jesus two wills, a human will and a divine will. These two wills, however are not at odds, but harmoniously united in the one person of Jesus Christ (which is basically the dyothelitist position).[41] This finds Schlatter's support: In Jesus we observe, he writes, the "unity of willing and working of the deity and humanity."[42] Schlatter thus clearly acknowledges that there are two wills in Jesus Christ, a human

---

39. Commenting on this particular verse, Schlatter writes: "This [Jesus'] oneness with the divine will, which renders him subservient to the divine work, is the foundation of his life and the source of his power." Schlatter, *Der Evangelist Johannes*, 130.

40. Schlatter, *History of the Christ*, 92–93.

41. Pyrrhus I of Constantinople (d. 654) argued that Jesus Christ had only one will (monothelitism). Maximus the Confessor objected, claiming that volition is an intrinsic component of being human. Being able to choose, freely, is a central characteristic of humankind. From the assertion that Jesus is truly a human being thus follows that he must also possess a truly human will. Additionally, as he is God, he must also have a divine will. The two wills in Jesus are, according to Maximus, united in the one person of Jesus Christ; that is, the human will is in voluntary conformity with the divine will. The Sixth Ecumenical Council (Constantinople III) recognized in 681 Maximus' dyotheletic view as orthodox. See Menke, *Jesus ist Gott der Sohn Sohn*, 270–73; cf. Hoping, *Einführung in die Christologie*, 118–22.

42. Schlatter, *Jesu Gottheit und das Kreuz*, 28.

and a divine volition. However, in accordance with the empirical-realist principles of his seeing-act, he does not elaborate on the rather theoretical question of the two wills (and their unification) in Jesus, but focuses on the New Testament narrative where he sees *one* person with *one* will, leading to concrete action in history. Since Schlatter does not read of an internal volitional struggle within Jesus, that is, as he does not encounter in his New Testament observation any volitional confusion or competition between the two wills in Jesus, he thus focuses on the dynamic inner volitional union (*Willensverband*) of Jesus Christ.[43] One might wonder at this point whether Schlatter has perhaps overlooked Jesus' obvious volitional conflict in the garden of Gethsemane or his experience of temptation. We shall discuss the former at a later stage, and with a view to the latter, Schlatter apparently acknowledges some form of an internal volitional challenge in Jesus. In Schlatter's view, the role of the Holy Spirit is crucial in this context and one must therefore add the ministry of the Holy Spirit in the life and work of Jesus Christ to the overall picture.

The Ministry of the Holy Spirit

The involvement of the Holy Spirit is vital for Schlatter, both with a view to Jesus' internal volitional experience and his volitional union with the Father. First of all, Schlatter explains that God created Jesus' humanity, and therefore also his (human) volition, "through the Spirit and the Word."[44] For this reason, there can be no internal conflict between the human and the divine willing in Jesus Christ.[45] Through the Spirit, Schlatter contends, the

43. Schlatter, *Dogma*, 338; cf. "Bekenntnis zur Gottheit Jesu," 44.

44. Schlatter writes: "God's action directed to Jesus' humanity works through both the Spirit and the Word. In this way, Jesus' humanity receives its existence and history through God. As Jesus was begotten by the Spirit, he received his being [*Wesen*], his will and his power from the Spirit. Moreover, in that the Word brings forth flesh, that is, a human life together with its natural substrate, Jesus is, from the very beginning of his life, made through God's action." Schlatter, *Dogma*, 336; see also ibid., 340; *Theology of the Apostles*, 78. Whilst it is the Father "who had given him life through his creative activity" (Schlatter, *History of the Christ*, 29; cf. *Dogma*, 337; "Bekenntnis zur Gottheit Jesu," 33; "Furcht vor dem Denken," 12–13), one must not forget the "powerful-creative Spirit" (*schöpfermächtigen Geist*; Schlatter, *Marien-Reden*, 8), who "conceives [*erzeugt*] Jesus together with his bodily form [*Leiblichkeit*]." Schlatter, *Dogma*, 340.

45. In terms of Jesus' human will, one wonders whether Schlatter considers Jesus assuming a perfect human will or a fallen will? Subscribing to Gregory of Nazianzus' axiom, the "unassumed is the unhealed," Schlatter draws our attention to Jesus as "someone who carried a measure of fallen-ness in himself." Schlatter, "Bekenntnis zur Gottheit Jesu," 45. In so doing, he affirms the reality of Jesus' experience of temptation. On the other hand, while Schlatter clearly portrays Jesus as the one who has his

136 Part 2: The Shape of Schlatter's Christology

two wills in Jesus are organically united.[46] The ministry of the Holy Spirit has thus clear implications for Jesus' being in action, and in particular for the way in which he deals with temptations. "[T]hrough the power of the Spirit," Schlatter claims, Jesus did "not know sin even though [being] in the flesh."[47] Jesus is able to "to subdue the carnal and worldly stimuli through the power of the Spirit,"[48] and he finally embraced the cross as he put his confidence in the Holy Spirit.[49] Two aspects are noteworthy in this context: Schlatter's clear stress on the Holy Spirit in Jesus' life, and his emphasis on the historical reality of Jesus' volitional union with God through the Spirit. It is clearly important for Schlatter to recognize that Jesus' will was *actually* tempted, as only in this way would it become evident that Jesus' will was a real (and also human) will.[50] Resistance to temptation was no theoretical question for Jesus, rather, it was a matter of active and concrete obedience in real life, through the Holy Spirit.[51] "In temptation," Schlatter writes, "he

"sonship in the same flesh that mediates to us our sinful passion and weakness," he is eager to note that Jesus possesses at the same time a certain volitional "pre-eminence" which is, again, indicative of his "regal status." The complete section reads: "Paul portrayed Jesus' equality with us in stark terms when he attributed to him the 'likeness of sinful flesh' (Rom 8:3). Paul did not doubt Jesus' purity, his will and ability to bear the flesh in such a way that it did not become an occasion for sin for him, already because of the outcome of Jesus' life. But he considers it to be an essential characteristic of Jesus that he had his divine sonship in the same flesh that mediates to us our sinful passion and weakness and that he hung this same flesh on the cross, raising it to eternal glory at the resurrection. The fact, however, that he has the flesh not by natural compulsion but according to the power of his own will ensures that he possesses not merely equality with men but also that pre-eminence over them by which his regal status is established. Because through his will he possessed human likeness, he maintained over it an even loftier possession: he existed in the form of God." Schlatter, *Theology of the Apostles*, 257. Apparently, Schlatter does not intend to solve the dilemma for us. His strategy, it seems, is to present the reader with the complex polarities he discovers through his New Testament seeing-act, hesitant to offer quick and easy solutions.

46. See Schlatter, "Bekenntnis zur Gottheit Jesu," 48.

47. Schlatter, *Erläuterungen zum Neuen Testament*, 5:124. Loos's point to some parallels between Schlatter and Irving in this respect. See Loos, "Divine action, Christ and the Doctrine of God," 185n51; 189n68; 215n184.

48. Schlatter, *Dogma*, 320.

49. "The decisiveness that made Jesus the bearer of the cross," Schlatter writes, "was confidence in the Spirit. He dies because he honors the Spirit and trusts that he is the power that creates life." Schlatter, *Do We Know Jesus*, 428; cf. *Theology of the Apostles*, 144.

50. For Schlatter, the reality of Jesus' temptations is another reason why he thinks his narrative-volitional account of Christology is closer to the New Testament data than any exclusively ontological discussion. "Only will is tempted," he insists, "not powers." Schlatter, *History of the Christ*, 132.

51. See Schlatter, *History of the Christ*, 59, 83; cf. "Bekenntnis zur Gottheit," 48.

had to prove how he conceived of his divine sonship and how he used it."[52] Here, Jesus' actual will is challenged, that is, Jesus actively needed to distinguish between the "good will" and the "depraved will" (*verwerfliche Wille*).[53] Still, through the Holy Spirit, Jesus resisted temptations, thereby proving his concrete obedience to the Father and demonstrating his union of will and of essence with him.

Once could thus summarize Schlatter's position as follows: First, Schlatter is always keen to speak of the unified person of Jesus Christ, considering it idle to ask whether Jesus was tempted in his divine or human nature; this would in his view lead to a division in Jesus and Schlatter is not happy to go down that road.[54] Whilst Jesus was truly tempted, the volitional tension, so to speak, is balanced and mediated through the Holy Spirit. Secondly, and for Schlatter more importantly: Jesus' volitional union with the Father finds its concrete expression in his lived obedience. This is where the influence of the Holy Spirit in Jesus' life and work becomes tangible for Schlatter. Against the backdrop of concrete history, Jesus acted "according to the will of the Spirit" and "in the power of the Spirit."[55] Through the Spirit's ministry, Jesus' will and the Father's will are united, so that Jesus' "will was accomplished when God's will came to pass."[56] This volitional union reveals at the same time Jesus' divine sonship, his unity of essence with the Father. "Here is communion revealed," Schlatter insists, "not simply communion of nature and of power but something greater: communion which pervades the personal life, that communion which consists in the union of will."[57] This statement reflects Schlatter's core conviction, namely that a conversation about divine volitional union, as it finds concrete expression in real life, in time and in history, is more promising than any ontological speculation

---

52. Schlatter, *History of the Christ*, 88.

53. Ibid. [*Geschichte des Christus*, 99].

54. Schlatter asserts: "The apostle Paul did not distinguish between a cleansed and a corrupt part of his [Jesus'] soul. It is the same self which the body subjects to its commandment and to which the law comes and in which the Spirit makes effective the will of Christ. That which transpires in him has differing origins and is of various levels of worth, yet it does not take place in different parts of the soul but in the one, undivided self." Schlatter, *Romans*, 14.

55. Schlatter, "Jesus und wir heutigen Menschen," in *Hülfe in Bibelnot*, 177; cf. *History of the Christ*, 185.

56. Schlatter, *History of the Christ*, 127. In this sense then, Schlatter would certainly have approved of Bernard of Clairvaux's comment, that between the Father and the Son, there is "not a unity of wills but a unity of will." I owe this reference to Kathryn Tanner, *Jesus, Humanity and the Trinity*, 41.

57. Schlatter, "Jesu Verhalten gegen Gott," in *Hülfe in Bibelnot*, 105.

about a communion of nature. In Schlatter's view, the communion of will shows us the reality of Jesus' being in action.

Some Open Questions

Having introduced some foundational arguments of Schlatter's relational-volitional Christology, it might be best to pause and consider some unanswered questions. These questions fall into two categories: one has to do with *Jesus' divinity* and the other with *Jesus' personhood*. First, one wonders whether Schlatter is not getting close to a particular form of kenotic Christology.[58] Whilst his version might not be the radical form of kenoticism in the tradition of Gottfried Thomasius (1802–75), where Jesus is considered to be emptying himself of some of his divine attributes in the incarnation, one might still ask whether Schlatter's emphasis on the life of the humble, obedient, and dependent Son does not show at least some characteristic features of a kenotic Christology that tends toward subordinationism and could put Jesus' divinity at risk (something he obviously would have wanted to avoid as his whole intention is to make a strong case for Jesus' divinity). Secondly, the question arises whether Schlatter does not overemphasize Jesus' volitional union with the Father and his dependence upon the Holy Spirit to the extent that Jesus' own identity as a particular person of the Trinity is at risk of receding into the background. Is the person of Christ, in Schlatter's framework, not in danger of being conflated with the Father (and possibly the Spirit)? The dilemma seems to be that the distinctive character of Jesus' personhood almost dissolves in relational-volitional union, the hazard being that Jesus *becomes* the Father's (and the Spirit's) action? In other words, does it not seem that Schlatter's Christology navigates towards some form of modalism? These challenging questions call for a closer analysis.

JESUS' DIVINITY, HIS PERSONHOOD, AND INTRA-TRINITARIAN LOVE

Adolf Schlatter's proposal is to call upon the notion of love in order to meet the above-mentioned challenges.[59] Love is according to Schlatter funda-

---

58. Modern German kenoticism originated at the University of Erlangen and the movement was en vogue during Schlatter's lifetime—its proponents were almost entirely Schlatter's contemporaries. For an overview see Law, "Kenotic Christology," 251–79.

59. Andreas Loos is certainly right when he claims that "the notion of love constitutes the basis for Schlatter's doctrine of the Trinity." Loos, "Divine Action and the Trinity," 270.

mental to our understanding of Jesus' volitional union with the Father and the Holy Spirit. Since it is through love, Schlatter claims, that Jesus submits and humbles himself, he neither jeopardizes his divinity nor loses his distinct personhood in the process. The following section analyses Schlatter's line of reasoning in more detail.

Kenosis and Volition

First, responding to the challenge of subordinationism and the possibility of compromising Jesus' divinity, Schlatter underlines that Jesus' obedient volitional union with God does not lead to a kind of inferiority or a loss of divine identity. On the contrary, Schlatter is convinced—and this may come as a surprise—that submission in love is in fact central to Jesus' divine sonship: it does not so much emphasize his humanity as his *divinity*. Jesus actually demonstrates his essential equality with God through his loving submission. Schlatter explains: "That Jesus' unlimited coordination with God not only finds its ground in total subordination to him, but also renders him, in relation to human beings and nature, consistently as servant and puts him into equality [*Gleichheit*] with us, constitutes the seal of its [his divinity's] authenticity."[60] In other words, Schlatter somewhat turns the tables by arguing that Jesus' capability for subordination and his sharing in our humanity is truly a manifestation of his divinity.[61] As a matter of fact, Jesus' "majestic dignity" (*Hoheit*) arises from "his subordination under the Father."[62] Schlatter substantiates this basic proposition as follows: The crucial argument, in his view, is that the obedient and submissive Son's love is reciprocated by God. That is, the Son who submits himself in love and who unites his will with the Father's will through the Holy Spirit is also the recipient of God's perfect love in return, which represents the authentic seal of Jesus' divinity.[63] "That the Son is the beloved [Son]," Schlatter writes, "excludes all diminutions and demotions in his relation to the Father and

---

60. Schlatter, "Bekenntnis zur Gottheit Jesu," 46.

61. C. F. D. Moule (1908–2007), although not referring to Schlatter, developed a similar argument. Moule argues that "Jesus saw God-likeness essentially as giving and spending oneself out . . . precisely *because* he was in the form of God he recognized equality with God as a matter not of getting but of giving." Moule, "The Manhood of Jesus," 97 (emphasis original). I am grateful to Donald Macleod for pointing me to this parallel.

62. Schlatter, *Dogma*, 356.

63. "As the Son," Schlatter writes, "he knew that the Father gave him his complete love, and this love was perfected by his work in him so that his work was accomplished through the Son." *History of the Christ*, 126.

grants him the full unity which bestows 'the sameness of being' [*die Selbigkeit des Wesens*] with the Father upon him."[64] Schlatter thus avoids the fallacy of classic subordinationism (which involves an inferiority of being), and tends more towards the less problematic position of relational (or soteriological) subordination.

The adjacent question is whether Schlatter's concept of love could also help him to avoid the charge of buying into certain problems associated with classic kenotic Christology, which tends to emphasize Jesus' humanity at the expense of his divinity. The already mentioned Gottfried Thomasius, for example, introduced a distinction between *essential attributes* (which are essential for God to be God, such as absolute power, holiness, truth, and love), and *relative attributes* (such as omnipotence, omniscience, and omnipresence) in order to do justice to the unity of Jesus' humanity and divinity.[65] In Thomasius' view, the incarnate *Logos* divested himself (temporarily) of the relative attributes while retaining the essential attributes in and through his human existence. Still, Thomasius then went one step further in his attempt to do justice to the humanity of Christ, as he argued that the *Logos* also surrendered his "divine self-consciousness" (*göttliches Bewußtseyn*).[66] This is clearly problematic, since Thomasius is thereby giving up on his distinction between the attributes (one would think that divine self-consciousness should be an essential attribute), while he is also at risk of leaving behind divine immutability, moving towards a kind of christological theophany.[67] It seems that Schlatter is able to put forward a more balanced christological account, which does justice both to the humanity and the divinity of Christ. Taking into account our earlier observations, we conclude that Schlatter understands *kenosis* first and foremost as referring to Jesus' humble *role* and *status* as God's servant. It does not, Schlatter is keen to add, involve a diminution or weakening of Jesus' divine *nature*.[68] *Kenosis*, for Schlatter—again, a typically Schlatterian move—is not so much about what Jesus laid aside, such as his divine attributes, rather it is more about what Jesus freely assumed, namely the form of a slave. Schlatter explains, in characteristic volitional language:

> Corresponding to the divine will is the will of Christ, who,
> in unity with God's will, was intent not on equality with God

---

64. Schlatter, *Dogma*, 198 (emphasis original).
65. Thomasius, *Christi Person und Werk*," 241–42.
66. Thomasius, *Beiträge zur kirchlichen Christologie*, 94–95.
67. See McCormack, "Person of Christ," 165.
68. See his comments on Phil 2:7 in the *Erläuterungen zum Neuen Testament*, 8:65–66.

but on human existence: he emptied himself (Phil 2:6–8). Paul derived the origin of Christ and his taking on human likeness not from a natural destiny or compulsion, to which God was subjected or to which he subjected Christ, but conceived of it in terms of a free act that occurs because Christ wills to be what we are, desiring human likeness and the position of slave as they characterize us.[69]

Along these lines, Schlatter seems to suggest some form of divine volitional self-actualization as way towards exploring the mystery of *kenosis*, that is, the Son freely wills—in volitional union with the Father—his humanity.[70] In 1896, thus perhaps as an answer to contemporary kenotic approaches, Schlatter penned these lines: "This is the 'relinquishing' (*kenosis*)," he explains, "insofar as the Godhead carries it out, in that it wills the human being Jesus [*den Menschen Jesus*] and unites it with himself, and this is a constant will, both in the moment of the conception and no less in the event of the cross, and also on God's throne in eternal firmness."[71] Schlatter's model of divine volitional actualization offers a fresh perspective for our conversation today. With his focus on the divine willing (in freedom) of the humanity of Christ as interpretation of the *kenosis*, Schlatter is able to avoid Thomasius' problems while at the same time doing justice to the humanity and divinity of Christ. Next, we turn to the question raised earlier, namely whether Schlatter is able to affirm Jesus' distinct personhood.

Individuality and Unity

Given Schlatter's strong emphasis on the volitional union between Father and Son, one wonders whether this could somewhat veil the distinctiveness of the person of Jesus Christ and thus possibly invite a modalistic reading. Schlatter seems to have acknowledged that his agenda might be interpreted in this way, and he thus unmistakably highlights that Jesus at no point loses his own individuality (*Eigenständigkeit*) as a person. As Jesus was "neither

---

69. Schlatter, *Theology of the Apostles*, 257.

70. Schlatter writes: "Both the words of Jesus and the words of the apostles do not place the divinity and the humanity [of Jesus Christ] next to each other as two static entities, but they speak of a volitional union (*Willensverband*). The humanity of Jesus is willed by the divinity, thereby also generated, 'assumed' . . . yet not in such a way that we might understand this assumption passively, for Jesus' humanity enjoys the full Yes of the divinity and it is Christ's condition [*Zustand des Christus*] which is given by God and through which God reveals himself." *Dogma*, 338; cf. "Bekenntnis zur Gottheit Jesu," 44.

71. Schlatter, "Bekenntnis zur Gottheit Jesu," 44.

a gnostic nor a mystic," Schlatter writes, he did not teach "the presence of a divine power or substance in him," nor did he "pursue the conflation of his consciousness with the consciousness of God;" what he did though was that he "stood as the I before the Thou, as person before the person of the Father, as a Son stood before the Father."[72] Whilst Schlatter thus strongly affirms Jesus' personal idiosyncrasy, he makes clear that it must not be pitted against his intrinsic unity with the Father and the Spirit. Always keen to stress divine simplicity, Schlatter insists on the intrinsic harmony of the Godhead. In his view, one could approach this complex scenario, that is, the tension between idiosyncrasy and unity, as follows: Unity and differentiation are not two opposite poles but they embrace each other through love. Schlatter writes, and it is helpful quoting him at length in this context:

> In order to be the Son of God, Jesus did not lead a struggle of annihilation [*Vernichtungskampf*] against himself, for he possesses his communion with God not above or below his personal life, but in it. He is thus, as Son, sovereign over his own life, as is the Father. Yet, this distinctiveness from God does not involve separation from him. It is rather the precondition as well as the outcome of his communion with him. What he wants and possesses is communion, not conflation with God. This means: Jesus' relation to God was love. To love's essence belongs that it knows and wants simultaneously both: differentiation and fellowship [*Unterschiedenheit und Verbundenheit*]. This has nothing in common with tendencies of conflation or absorption.[73]

The key seems to be intra-Trinitarian love through which both sovereign differentiation and perfect communion are harmoniously balanced within the Godhead.[74] Avoiding both the pitfalls of (chronological) modalism and tritheism, Schlatter suggests that Jesus does not lose his idiosyncrasy as the second person of the Trinity, since love's essence consists of both clear distinction and perfect communion.[75] Analogous to his loving relationship with the Father, Jesus' relationship with the Holy Spirit is characterized by love. For this reason, Jesus gladly receives the ministry of the Spirit; yet, again, as Schlatter underlines, not at the expense of giving up the distinctiveness of his own personhood. That is, Jesus does not render himself fully passive, so that it would be exclusively the Holy Spirit working in and through him. "The differentiation between the Spirit and his [Jesus'] own life, however,"

72. Schlatter, *Glaube im Neuen Testament*, 231.
73. Schlatter, "Jesu Demut," 80–81.
74. See Schlatter, *Dogma*, 34; cf. 179–80.
75. This is clearly reminiscent of Augustine. See Augustine, *On the Trinity*, 25–26.

Schlatter writes, "did not result in Jesus sensing a contrast between them and in seeking to suppress his personal life [*persönlichen Lebensakt*] in order to sense and enhance the Spirit within himself."[76]

The relationship between the Son and the Father, and the Son and the Spirit, is thus a harmonious, organic relationship, since it is a relationship of love; and as such it is free from any traces of conflation or competition.[77] Love is the key factor that guarantees both Jesus' idiosyncrasy and his unity in harmony with the Father and the Spirit. "Within the loving relations of Father, Son and Holy Spirit," Andreas Loos comments on Schlatter's proposal, "each actively seeks the other and in and through this the particular identity of each is mutually secured."[78] With a view to the immanent Trinity, then, the persons of the Godhead indwell each other whilst their distinctiveness remains intact.[79] This applies, similarly, to the economic Trinity, where the divine action *ad extra* works in harmonious unity although the members of the Godhead perform different roles. Schlatter's language here reflects an intention to strike a balance between divine unity and distinction, aiming to avoid both the pitfalls of modalism on the one hand and tritheism on the other hand.[80] Schlatter was obviously aware of the challenges involved here,[81] and, although this might sound theologically unsatisfying, it seems that for Schlatter—and his language somewhat reflects this—oscillation, or polarity as we have called it earlier, comes perhaps closest to the divine mystery.

---

76. Schlatter, *History of the Christ*, 133 [*Geschichte des Christus*, 164].

77. See Schlatter, "Jesu Demut," 37.

78. Loos, "Divine Action and the Trinity," 273.

79. Schlatter writes: "The formula 'unity in distinction' [*Einheit in der Verschiedenheit*] possesses an actual foundation [*realen Grund*]. It is based on the fact that the one God actively indwells [*innewirkt*] a plurality of personalities, each of which has, and should have, its own life [*eigenes Leben*]." *Glaube im Neuen Testament*, xvii–xviii. Schlatter emphatically distinguishes distinct persons within the Trinity (*Dogma*, 179–80, 589n206), and posits that the concept of person remains essential for our concept of God (*Gottesgedanken*). *Dogma*, 573n108.

80. Schlatter, *Dogma*, 573n108.

81. This is evident from his assertions in *Dogma*, 573n108. Schlatter would presumably have agreed with Schleiermacher's lament that one either overemphasizes the unity of the Trinity at the expense of the "distinctiveness of the persons" (*Geschiedenheit der Personen*), or one does emphasize the "Triunity" (*Dreiheit*) and at the same time renders the unity abstract. Schleiermacher, *Glaubenslehre*, §171, 2:523–24. Schleiermacher is sceptical that a real balance could be achieved, as he fears that we continually "remain oscillating between the two" (*bleiben unstätt zwischen ihnen schwanken*). Ibid.

CONCLUSION

Schlatter suggests a harmonious unity of will and love between the Son and the Father (and the Holy Spirit), while affirming Jesus' distinct personhood. According to Schlatter, the Son submits himself and obeys in and through love and thereby not only reveals his humanity but, most importantly, demonstrates his divine status as the beloved Son who is equal to God. The Holy Spirit is involved in Jesus' union of will with the Father, which is reflected in Jesus' actual ministry, without causing Jesus' idiosyncrasy to diminish or to recede into the background. One could certainly challenge Schlatter, questioning whether his notion of love is not made to carry more weight than seems reasonable; that is, one might query whether love has indeed enough explanatory power to solve the conundrum of discreteness in unity. Still, Schlatter is apparently not alone in suggesting the notion of love as the way forward in our understanding the complexity (and the mystery) of the relationship between the persons of the Trinity, as the work of John D. Zizioulas (1931–)[82] and Christoph Schwöbel (1955–) shows.[83] If this is the right path to pursue, it would indeed be promising to develop further Schlatter's proposal in conversation with these recent contributions.

At the outset, we introduced Schlatter's view of Jesus in double communion, that is, in relation to God and to humankind. Up until now we have primarily focused on the former, namely Jesus' relation to God. It is now time to turn to the other aspect of Jesus in relation: his relation to human beings. In doing so, however, one must not ignore our previous findings on Jesus' communion with God, for, according to Schlatter's dictum, Jesus' communion with God is the foundation for his communion with humanity. Bearing this in mind, we shall now turn to the second part of the thinking-act.

---

82. According to John D. Zizioulas, for example, love is indeed the central constituent of the distinctiveness of divine personhood. See Zizioulas, "The Doctrine of the Holy Trinity," 57–59. Zizioulas' relational trajectory in fact reveals interesting parallels to Schlatter, and future research, exploring the two relational approaches, is certainly to be recommended.

83. Christoph Schwöbel suggests that we conceive of love not as an attribute of God in the traditional sense but in fact as an ontological statement. See Schwöbel, "Christology and Trinitarian Thought," 132. It remains to be seen whether Schwöbel's "ontology of love as relation" is a helpful approach to explain discreteness in unity within the Godhead.

5

The *Denkakt* (II)
Jesus in Relation to God and Humanity

HAVING EXPLORED SCHLATTER'S VIEW of Jesus Christ in relation to the Father and the Holy Spirit, we now expand our conversation by including more explicitly Jesus' relation with humanity. In so doing, we are instantly faced with questions of soteriology and ecclesiology, for, as Schlatter insists, the apex of Jesus' work consists in the salvation of humanity and the creation of the new community. However, this does not mean that we limit our focus exclusively to Jesus' relation to humanity; rather, our discussion in this chapter is closely related to the findings of the previous one, simply because we could never have a meaningful conversation about Jesus' relationship with humanity without referencing his intra-Trinitarian fellowship. In fact, Jesus' relationship with the Father and the Spirit is the prerequisite for a correct understanding of his salvific work with a view to humanity. In Schlatter's words, Jesus' service to God (*Gottesdienst*) is the basis for his service to humanity (*Menschendienst*).

Taking this into account, we arrive at the following structure for this second part of the thinking-act: First, we offer a brief outline of Schlatter's view of the fundamental relation between Christology and soteriology, setting out how Jesus' service to God represents the basis for his service to humanity. Secondly, we turn to what Schlatter considers Jesus' service to God; in this regard we explore Schlatter's theology of the cross in more detail, considering in particular how Jesus is able to sustain his union with God even in the midst of God-forsakenness. Thirdly, we move to Jesus' service to humanity, which encapsulates for Schlatter the establishment of the new community of faith.

JESUS' DOUBLE-COMMUNION

We continue our exploration into Schlatter's Christology by way of the significant notions of relation and volition. As we shall see in due course, Schlatter considers Jesus to be in volitional union both with God through his "will to the cross," and with us through his "will to salvation." Before we turn to these concepts in greater depth, some aspects of Schlatter's thinking on the relation between Christology and soteriology demand our attention.

Theocentric Christology and Soteriology

As already noted in our discussion of the seeing-act, Schlatter claims that Jesus' person and work are closely "interrelated" and, in fact, "inseparable."[1] For Schlatter, there exists an organic union between ontological Christology and functional Christology. "What Christ is," Schlatter writes, "is demonstrated by the benefits he brings,"[2] and he thereby reiterates Philipp Melanchthon's dictum: "To know Christ is to know his benefits."[3] In order to understand who Jesus is, then, it is important that one integrates the salvific aspects of his being in action and in relation.[4] "There are, therefore, not two questions: [one] of Jesus' divinity and [one] of our redemption through him," Schlatter claims, "but the two questions are one."[5] Jesus' being (the Son) and his office (as the Christ) are in fact identical: they "penetrate each other completely."[6] Whilst Schlatter underscores the close unity of Christology and soteriology, there is, however, a clear direction in Schlatter's theological method that moves from Christology to soteriology. For Schlatter,

1. Schlatter, "Christologie und Soteriologie," 4.
2. Ibid.
3. Melanchthon, *Loci communes*, 63.
4. Schlatter, *Jesu Gottheit und das Kreuz*, 18.
5. Ibid., 24.
6. Schlatter writes: "Sonship and the office of the Christ penetrate each other completely in Jesus' word. What the Father is for him establishes his vocation [*Beruf*] and determines his work. His relation to the Father does not end in his person but includes and determines his relation to the world, as in turn this completely establishes what the Father is for him. He receives in order to give, is loved in order to love, is exalted in order to reign. Sonship is given to him as the root of action." *Glaube im Neuen Testament*, 232. "In Christ," notes Schlatter, "office and person are one; as the office is given to him by God so also is the person made by God." *Dogma*, 332.

Christology is not a "function of soteriology,"[7] but rather vice versa. Schlatter in fact raises concerns about what he considers the unruly treatment of Christology through a soteriological lens which necessarily carries with it a subjective, anthropocentric bias and thus results in a lopsided Christology. According to Schlatter's reading, theological scholarship (and it seems likely that Schlatter here has the neo-Kantian Christology of Ritschl and his followers in mind, as discussed earlier) has extensively focused on soteriology, that is, on the question of who Jesus Christ is in relation *to us* (as king, savior, redeemer, role model, etc.) and what he has purchased *for us* (forgiveness, justification, adoption, eternal life, etc.).

While these aspects might all well be true, too strong an emphasis on these issues reflects, to Schlatter's mind, a "subjective," "eudemonistic" bias, as one overlooks that it is actually Jesus' relation to God that is constitutive for his salvific activity in relation to humanity.[8] Although Schlatter agrees with Anselm that an emphasis on the substitutionary and satisfactory aspect of the cross is certainly biblical, he adds that this does not display "the whole picture of the New Testament" (*nicht die ganze Aussage des Neuen Testaments*).[9] What is missing in Anselm, Schlatter argues, is the foundational theocentric perspective of the cross, namely, Jesus' action in relation to the Father, through which he reveals his divinity. Only from this theocentric angle can one understand Jesus' concrete salvific action towards humanity in its fullest sense.[10] Schlatter's student Paul Althaus echoes his teacher's critique of the anthropocentric perspective in theology and clearly adopts Schlatter's theocentric vision of Christology:

> Jesus died for God before he died for us. It was a severe deficit of the old Protestant theology not to understand the cross inherently based on the Son's relation to the Father, but unswervingly to refer to it as *obedientia passiva* with a view to humanity's sin ... This treatment is not theocentric enough. In this respect, it was only Schlatter's *Dogmatik* that struck the right note.[11]

---

7. As Paul Tillich suggested, see his *Systematic Theology*, 2:150.

8. Schlatter, "Christi Versöhnen und Christi Vergeben," 162.

9. Schlatter, *Dogma*, 303.

10. See Schlatter, *Jesu Gottheit und das Kreuz*, 14, 27, 37–38, 42, 45n1, 46–48, 56, 75–76, 79, 86. Schlatter would have thus agreed with Wolfhart Pannenberg who warned, against Tillich's direction, that "[s]oteriology must follow from Christology, not vice versa. Otherwise, faith in salvation itself loses any real foundation." Pannenberg, *Jesus: God and Man*, 48.

11. Althaus, *Theologische Aufsätze*, 23–24.

Althaus is certainly right. Schlatter clearly stresses the theocentricity of Jesus' death on the cross, through which he somewhat anticipated Moltmann's later statement that "the cross was an event between God and God."[12]

Gottesdienst and *Menschendienst*

In terms of the cross—and our reflections in this chapter focus particularly on Schlatter's *theologia crucis*—Adolf Schlatter uses two terms to describe Jesus' action in relation to God and to humanity. On the cross, as introduced earlier, Jesus performs both a service to God (*Gottesdienst*) and a service to humanity (*Menschendienst*).[13] These two movements form one holistic, organic activity. In Schlatter's words: "He [Jesus] gave himself as a sacrifice to the Father and [he] pardons us with the selfsame deed. The wrath yields and guilt passes by and faith arises. This is a holistic, merciful work of God."[14] It is exactly in this double-communion that Schlatter sees "the real miracle of Christology," as Hans-Martin Rieger remarks.[15] Schlatter, whom we have introduced as a theologian of unity, thus emphatically underlines the close bond between Jesus' service to God and his service to humanity. He writes:

> For whom did he die, for God or for us? I am not supposed to ask in this way. I would thereby divide what he has united. He honors the Father, he strives for his glory and remains adamantly separated from those who rob God of what is his and refuse to be obedient. He, in contrast, glorifies the Father, since he professes him as the almighty and alone righteous merciful forgiver. At the same time, however, he honors human beings, preserves community with them and takes the blemish of their sin away.[16]

Still, in Schlatter's view—and this is obviously a corollary of his theocentric perspective—Jesus' service to God enjoys conceptual priority over his service to humanity. From Schlatter's theocentric viewpoint, Jesus' love for humanity is clearly rooted in his love for God.[17] Schlatter notes: "Jesus' service to God [*Gottesdienst*] determines and forms his service to humanity [*Menschendienst*]. The latter has its base and its power in Jesus' service

---

12. Moltmann, *Der gekreuzigte Gott*, 231.
13. Schlatter, *Sprechstunde*, 29–30.
14. Schlatter, *Andachten*, 111.
15. Rieger, *Schlatters Rechtfertigungslehre*, 312.
16. Schlatter, *Andachten*, 111.
17. See Schlatter, "Die letzte Bitte Jesu," in *Gesunde Lehre*, 328–29.

to God."[18] With his account of Jesus in double-communion with God and humanity, Schlatter attempts to explain two crucial facets of Jesus' being in action. Referring to Jesus' service to God, Schlatter maintains that Jesus vindicates his divinity by demonstrating volitional union and fellowship with God in spite of God-forsakenness on the cross. Jesus' service to humanity, on the other hand, consists in his creation of the new community of faith, making our volitional union with him possible. We shall look at each of these aspects in turn.

JESUS' *GOTTESDIENST*: FELLOWSHIP IN FORSAKENNESS

The cross is of vital significance for Christology, since on the cross, Schlatter contends, Jesus reveals his divinity by demonstrating communion with God through volitional union with him, even in the midst of God-forsakenness. In the following, we shall, first, elucidate Schlatter's position more fully, and secondly, critically evaluate his view.

Jesus' Will to the Cross

First of all, the cross represents for Schlatter the ultimate proof of Jesus' obedience as the divine Son of God. By going to the cross, Jesus obediently fulfils his vocation (*Beruf*),[19] his messianic-kingly duty as the Christ.[20] Schlatter calls Jesus' determined volition to embrace the cross his "will to the cross" (*Kreuzeswille*).[21] This is the "rock-hard [*stahlharte*] will that did not collapse even under the load of his cross."[22] Jesus' will to the cross, Schlatter adds, was not a stoic or a sterile will, but a joyful will that was born out of love for God. Possibly with Anselm in mind, Schlatter insists that the divine will that Jesus grasps is primarily associated with God as the Father and not as the judge: "[I]t is the Father whose will is done here, not only the judge's."[23] Jesus' view was plainly directed to the Father and his

18. Schlatter, "Christi Versöhnen und Christi Vergeben," 161.

19. Schlatter, "Christologie und Soteriologie," 5. Schlatter's notion here comprises more than Ritschl's concept of Jesus' *Berufstreue* (see Schlatter, *Dogma*, 584n167, and our discussion in chapter 2; cf. Rieger, *Schlatters Rechtfertigungslehre*, 314n58; Schmid, *Erkenntnis des Geschichtlichen Christus*, 297–99).

20. Schlatter, *Dogma*, 290, 430.

21. See Schlatter, "Jesu Verhalten gegen Gott," in *Hülfe in Bibelnot*, 103.

22. Schlatter, *Do We Know Jesus*, 429 [*Kennen wir Jesus*, 399].

23. Schlatter, *Jesus und Paulus*, 55.

150   Part 2: The Shape of Schlatter's Christology

glory as he embraced the will to the cross. And here, again, we come across the notion of love as the means by which volitional union is made possible. "Jesus' will to the cross," Schlatter explains, "revealed love for God that was intent on the revelation of God's greatness, the execution of God's justice, and the operation of God's grace."[24] Through his unwavering commitment to carry his cross, and, indeed his actual suffering on the cross, Jesus thus fully revealed "what genuine love and complete obedience" are.[25] Jesus' will to the cross is the ultimate litmus test for his volitional union with the Father. He denies his own will and is prepared to unite his will with God's "will to salvation" (*Heilandswille*), that is, God's will to save the world from sin and judgment.[26] Parallel to our earlier observations, we note here, too, that Jesus' volitional union with the Father does not jeopardize his idiosyncrasy, since he unites himself with the Father through love.[27]

So much for the theory; yet where does Schlatter see volitional union as it plays out in the concrete context of Jesus' life and work? The New Testament episode of Jesus' struggle in the garden of Gethsemane comes to mind, where Jesus prays, "'My Father, if it be possible, let this cup pass from me; nevertheless, not as I will, but as you will'" (Matt 26:39). In his annotations to this verse, Schlatter states:

> Jesus' prayer shows how he placed himself, in dying, in relation to God. What he did before God was *the obedient unification of his will with the divine will*. In nothing else did Matthew recognize the glory of Jesus' death and his victorious power more than in his complete obedience.[28]

This illustrates that Schlatter interprets this occasion not so much as a volitional struggle between the divine and the human will in Jesus, but as an inter-volitional challenge that requires him to unite his will with the Father's

---

24. Schlatter, *History of the Christ*, 291.

25. Ibid., 292; cf. *Dogma*, 293–94.

26. See Schlatter, *Jesu Gottheit und das Kreuz*, 50–52; *Dogma*, 291; "Der Ausgang Jesu," 145; see also Rieger, *Schlatters Rechtfertigungslehre*, 315–16.

27. Schlatter makes clear that Jesus' will to the cross is not a form of "self-destruction" (*Selbstvernichtung*) but a free "denial of his will" (*Entselbstigung*), because he knows "to whom and why he gives himself." *Jesu Gottheit und das Kreuz*, 100. This will to the cross is not an empty will, but a will with a "certain content," as Jesus is focused on the Father's righteousness, and his people, whom he is about to free from sin, death and judgment. In dying, Jesus possesses his will to salvation (*Heilandswillen*) together with the will to the cross (*Kreuzeswillen*), and he is thereby obedient as the "performer of God's will" (*Gotteswillen*). Ibid.

28. Schlatter, *Der Evangelist Matthäus*, 751 (emphasis added); cf. "Jesus und wir heutigen Menschen," in *Hülfe in Bibelnot*, 175.

will. According to Schlatter, the serious volitional challenge presents itself to Jesus as follows: Jesus' own will, obviously, involves a natural aversion to pain and a strong (and legitimate) desire for life, victory and glory.[29] This is at odds with the task and the will that confront him in Gethsemane, and one thus one observes here a very real and painful struggle. Yet even in this most difficult situation, Jesus continues to act "as the Son, who even now remained in fellowship with the Father."[30] Interestingly, one observes here a quasi-Hegelian dialectic in Schlatter's thinking.[31] Discussing Jesus' "prayerful interchange with God" in Gethsemane, Schlatter seems to argue for a movement of Jesus choosing what is not his will and thereby gaining a "greater will."[32] That is, Schlatter claims that Jesus "confronted his initial desire with an opposite desire, one gained through a new and higher will by which he agreed unconditionally with the will of God."[33] One wonders whether Schlatter would here allow for some form of divine self-actualization within history; that is, through the stages of affirmation (of God's will), and negation (of his own will), Jesus' gains a "new and higher will." Schlatter himself, however, hesitates to offer any specific comments in this context, which is regrettable. It remains to be seen whether one detects here at least a slight inconsistency in Schlatter, who was, as previously noted, usually very critical towards (especially Hegelian) speculation, who, however, seems to exhibit speculative tendencies here himself.[34] We shall return to the difficulties of interpreting this dialectical aspect of Schlatter's Christology at a later stage.

The main aspect for Schlatter, it seems, and this he highlights emphatically, is that Jesus' prayer does not suggest uncertainty about the Father's will; he neither questions the Father's will nor ponders the purpose of his impending suffering. Instead, what Jesus expresses in this prayer is his need for fatherly reassurance. And it is only intimate, prayerful exchange with

29. Schlatter, *History of the Christ*, 365.

30. Schlatter, *Do We Know Jesus*, 430. In his *History of the Christ*, Schlatter offers a careful treatment of this struggle in chapter 19, entitled "The Decision in Gethsemane." Schlatter, *History of the Christ*, 363–67.

31. We have noted earlier that Schlatter sat for six years in the classroom of the Hegelian Johann Jakob Alder (see Neuer, *Adolf Schlatter*, 42–43); it should therefore not surprise us to detect some Hegelian influence in Schlatter.

32. Schlatter, *History of the Christ*, 365.

33. Ibid.

34. William Baird has a similar view: "Schlatter, who claims to be concerned with facts, sometimes veers into speculation.... Although he scorns intellectualism, his own work is highly theological and speculative." *History of New Testament Research*, 2:380, 383.

the Father that can yield the desired confirmation.[35] Having received this fatherly assurance through prayer, Jesus is thus prepared to unite his will with the Father's will. In this volitional union, Schlatter sees, as noted earlier, true evidence for Jesus' glory and victorious power. Having focused on the aspect of volitional union in preparation for the cross, we now move to the core of Schlatter's argument. For it is on the cross, according to Schlatter's line of reasoning, that Jesus actually reveals his divinity by maintaining fellowship with his Father in the face of God-forsakenness.

Jesus' Divinity and Fellowship in Forsakenness

It is Schlatter's intention to move the aspect of Jesus' God-forsakenness on the cross to the center of the christological stage.[36] From Schlatter's point of view, Jesus experienced real forsakenness on the cross as he endured the consequences of human sin and rebellion against God. Since Jesus was identified as closely as possible with human sin (he was made "to be sin," 2 Cor 5:21), he had to accept that his relationship with the Father, who "cannot look at wrong" (Hab 1:13), was challenged, to say the least. As Jesus bore the horrendous consequences of human sin on the cross, he undoubtedly experienced God-forsakenness, allowing for the "disruption of communion with God" (*Störung der Gottesgemeinschaft*).[37] Thus, Jesus' cry of derelication, "My God, my God, why have you forsaken me?" (Mark 15:34; cf. Matt 27:46, Ps 22:1), was not only a genuine psychological experience but also a reflection of what actually happened to him. In Schlatter's own words:

> What rendered his [Jesus'] suffering difficult was that God had forsaken him, and this happened not only through the helplessness into which he had been thrown by his circumstances but also in his internal existence. Dying is not merely an external

---

35. Schlatter, *History of the Christ*, 365. In one of his devotional works, Schlatter writes: "As he now, enchained, professes God's omnipotence, and [as he] must say as the crucified one: 'I am Lord,' and as the one who dies, testify: 'I am the life,' this [affirmation] transcended, with august novelty, everything that was his vocation [*Beruf*] to date [*das ging in erhabener Neuheit über alles hinaus, was bisher sein Beruf gewesen war*]. For this he needs the assurance that tells him that he will now through his action accomplish the Father's will. . . . He does not discuss the purpose of his suffering with his Father. . . . Obedience does not ask: 'Why do you do this?' Only one thing must he know, namely that it is God's will, and this he comes to know through prayer." Schlatter, *Andachten*, 135.

36. Jürgen Moltmann's proposal, of course, reveals a similar focus and we shall point to significant parallels throughout this section.

37. Schlatter, *Jesu Gottheit und das Kreuz*, 53; see also ibid., 3.

change; it also affects the person. God had taken his hand away from him. . . . God's protection and gift were no longer with him.[38]

Now if Schlatter were to affirm, as this quote suggests, that there was indeed a time on the cross when Jesus was actually forsaken by the Father, he would create serious problems for his own christological position. As highlighted in the previous chapter, sonship is for Schlatter the incarnate Christ's very *raison d'être*; it defines who he is in relation to the Father. Would not a severing of the filial relationship imply that the (now) fatherless Son would have no basis left for his own existence?[39] How can he still be the Son without the Father? Within his own framework Schlatter is thus faced with significant difficulties.

A close observation of Schlatter's language reveals, as suggested earlier, an underlying dialectic, or polarity. Given that Wilfried Härle considers Schlatter's "thinking in polarities [*Denken in Polaritäten*] stimulating and trendsetting,"[40] one wonders whether recognizing this feature of his thought might be a step towards solving the apparent dilemma. Looking at things more closely, then, one notes that Schlatter is generally hesitant to speak of God-forsakenness without including at the same time the notion of God-fellowship on the cross. Schlatter thus pictures Jesus as the one, who, "in the perfection of his whole obedience, possessed and acquired, *within* complete forsakenness, communion with God."[41] Schlatter's basic claim could thus be

---

38. Schlatter, *History of the Christ*, 373; cf. *Do We Know Jesus*, 446–47.

39. See McCall's discussion in *Forsaken*, 34–35.

40. Härle, "Vorwort," 5.

41. Schlatter, *Das Gott wohlgefällige Opfer*, 48 (emphasis added). "On the cross," Schlatter claims elsewhere, "died the one who did not allow himself to be separated from the Father by anything." "Das Kreuz Jesu unsere Versöhnung mit Gott," 13. Interestingly, Moltmann echoes Schlatter in this respect as he develops, likewise, a dialectic of God-forsakenness in God-fellowship on the cross. Even using similar relational-volitional vocabulary to Schlatter, Moltmann writes: "This deep community of will [*Willensgemeinschaft*] between Jesus and his God and Father is now expressed precisely at the point of their deepest separation, in the godforsaken and accursed death of Jesus on the cross." Moltmann, *Crucified God*, 252 [*Der gekreuzigte Gott*, 230]. While Moltmann thus seems to side with Schlatter in arguing for the continuation of God-fellowship in the midst of God-forsakenness, Schlatter draws different inferences from this dialectic as we shall see in due course. Moltmann writes: "If one sees in the death on the cross both historical God-forsakenness and eschatological devotion [*Hingabe*], then this event between Jesus and his Father contains communion in separation and separation in communion [*Gemeinschaft im Getrenntsein und Getrenntsein in Gemeinschaft*]. . . . In the cross, Father and Son are most deeply separated in forsakenness and yet at the same time most intimately united in their devotion." Moltmann, *Crucified God*, 252 [*Der gekreuzigte Gott*, 230–31].

described as follows: Jesus is able to remain in communion with God even in face of God-forsakenness, and in this manner he demonstrates his divinity, since only God can maintain union with God.[42] The "elevation of the dying one into communion with God"[43] on the cross is thus a manifestation of his divinity. Jesus reveals his divinity on the cross, Schlatter writes, in that for him, "God-forsakenness passes away" (*daß für ihn die Gottverlassenheit vergeht*).[44] The advantage of this suggestion is obvious: By avoiding a sequential move from God-forsakenness "back" into God-fellowship, as it were, Schlatter steers clear of the christological dilemma mentioned above. However, this position is still perplexing on several grounds. For one, Schlatter would have to provide some evidence for his claim that Jesus is simultaneously in God-abandonment and in God-fellowship. Moreover, Schlatter would need to show more clearly how he considers Jesus revealing his divinity in this context. Once more, the question of whether Schlatter allows for some form of divine self-actualization emerges. That is, does the "elevation of the dying one into communion" with God imply certain ontological changes in the second person of the Trinity? Or does this point to some new level of relationship between the Father and the Son? This demands a closer scrutiny.

Mutual Giving in Love and the Holy Spirit

Earlier, we pointed to the centrality of love for Schlatter's view of the Godhead. It is thus not surprising to note that Schlatter emphasizes the significance of love in the context of what happens on the cross between the Son and his Father, too. In short, Schlatter observes on the cross *a divine exchange in love*, which in fact constitutes the intimate communion between the Son and the Father over against the threat of forsakenness, and which clearly reveals Jesus' divinity. Particularly relevant for our understanding of Schlatter's model of divine exchange in love on the cross is the aspect of Jesus actually giving himself as *gift* to the Father. What Schlatter offers here is nothing less than a highly creative theocentric interpretation of the penal substitution model, which was, in his view, too often approached merely from a (limited) anthropocentric perspective. Divine fellowship on the cross, he argues, is "only completely and truly established when the gift returns to the giver."[45] Now how does Schlatter conceive of this mutual giv-

---

42. Schlatter, *Jesu Gottheit und das Kreuz*, 6.
43. Ibid.
44. Ibid., 27.
45. Ibid., 52.

ing in love on the cross in detail, and how does it relate to Jesus' divinity and his communion with the Father?

We shall explore these questions by, first, considering Jesus' involvement in this exchange, then, secondly, looking at the Father's and the Holy Spirit's part in this exchange, and on this basis, we consider, thirdly, more closely the question of self-actualization, namely whether Jesus is, in and through forsakenness, somewhat elevated to a new level of relationship with God.

The Gift returns to the Giver

First, then, in terms of Jesus' involvement in the divine exchange on the cross, Schlatter regards Jesus as giving himself as the "effective sacrifice" for human sin to God.[46] Jesus is the faultless "Lamb of God that takes away the sin of the world;"[47] he is the one, who, as the perfect substitute,[48] atones for the sin of humanity by giving himself completely to the Father. Jesus basically dedicates himself, through the Holy Spirit, as a gift to the Father.[49] Schlatter writes:

> He [Jesus] entered into total self-denial [*Entselbstigung*] with his eyes raised toward the Father, and he then praised him as his God, even when and because it was finished [*hat ihn als seinen Gott gepriesen dann, als, und deshalb, weil es mit ihm zu Ende war*]. When he ceased to be Lord over his spirit, letting it go, "handing it over to the Father," he gave everything to God; he gave himself fully to God.[50]

By giving himself to the Father, Jesus returns the gift of life he has received through the incarnation back to the giver of life. In Schlatter's words: "Now his [Jesus'] service to God [*Gottesdienst*] was carried out according to the formula 'Not as I will, but as you will.' . . . It is likewise evident that he, even as he went into death, embraced God as the giver of life. . . . Since his life was God's gift he could die. . . . Since it is God's gift, he gives it to God."[51] This devotional act of self-sacrifice lies at the heart of Jesus' loving and obedient

---

46. See Schlatter, *History of the Christ*, 97; cf. *Dogma*, 300.

47. See Schlatter, *History of the Christ*, 94–97.

48. On Schlatter's broad affirmation of substitutionary atonement, see *Dogma*, 295–96; cf. *Erlebtes*, 73–77; "Der Ausgang Jesu," 119; "Christologie und Soteriologie," 10–11.

49. Schlatter, *Jesu Gottheit und das Kreuz*, 34–35.

50. Ibid., 63.

51. Schlatter, "Der Ausgang Jesu," 118.

service to God (*Gottesdienst*). Schlatter, as noted earlier, is keen to point to the conceptual pre-eminence of Jesus' *Gottesdienst* over his *Menschendienst*. "Jesus' dying is on its own, irrespective of its fruit, purely and completely service to God [*Gottesdienst*] and not service to humanity [*Menschendienst*]."[52] Since Jesus is wholly God-oriented in his action on the cross, Jesus makes his "walk to the cross his walk towards the Father" (*aus dem Gang zum Kreuz den Gang zum Vater gemacht*).[53] Jesus' last words on the cross offer in Schlatter's view a helpful clue here. Commenting on Jesus' cry, "Father, into your hands I commit my spirit!" (Luke 23:46), Schlatter observes that this points on the one hand to the fact of "how piercingly his God-forsakenness has been felt by him;"[54] yet on the other hand, and Schlatter most likely refers here to Jesus' invocation of God as Father, it shows how he "unabatedly carried his certain rest in God even on the cross."[55] Schlatter sees here clear Scriptural warrant for his position of polarity. On this basis, he can say that "Jesus went with God into death;" "[h]is cross was his service to God [*Gottesdienst*] through which he fulfilled the divine will and revealed God's greatness."[56] The ultimate end, then, of Jesus' work is to glorify the Father through the perfect *Gottesdienst*.[57] Schlatter argues:

> Do I still have to ask? Do I not see that here [on the cross], only here, yet certainly here, God is fully conceived as God? Here, God is given his whole glory. When Jesus took the cross from God's hand it was said as never before in truth: your will be done.... Without grumbling and reluctance, not only with words but through deed there was testified: you are righteous in judging; and with equally unconditional assurance the deed was put into practice: you are the one who forgives. When was it ever considered that all things are possible for God? Back when Jesus made himself the dying one.... There is no other service to God [*Gottesdienst*] in which God has been praised more perfectly than in that hour.[58]

52. Schlatter, *Jesu Gottheit und das Kreuz*, 77.
53. Schlatter, *Das Gott wohlgefällige Opfer*, 13.
54. Schlatter, *Erläuterungen zum Neuen Testament*, 2:330.
55. Ibid., 2:330–31.
56. Schlatter, "Der Ausgang Jesu," 112.
57. In his *Dogma*, Schlatter claims: "The necessity of the cross results from theology, from what God is... 'I have glorified you'; this was in fact the goal of the Crucified. His dying is the act of love, a cultic act that glorifies God, and this was not only one goal for Jesus among others, but we describe with this formula his whole will. It is not wrong to name God's honour the goal for whose completion Jesus died." *Dogma*, 304.
58. Schlatter, *Andachten*, 132, 117.

The glorification of his Father is thus the grand objective of the Son's being in action on the cross, as the gift returns to the giver.

The Father's Gift in Return and the Holy Spirit

Secondly, moving to the Father, Schlatter notes that the Father answers to the devout service of his Son by gladly receiving his gift. In that the Father replies to the Son, he establishes dialogue and communication. In short, we have here some form of God-fellowship in spite of forsakenness. Schlatter writes:

> The statement has to be followed by the answer, in order that each of the parties [*Verbundenen*] speaks, each listens, and both give and receive; now is communion established. The notion of "divine fellowship" [*Gottesgemeinschaft*] thus remains empty and rhetorical until his [Jesus'] service to God [*Gottesdienst*] is understood.[59]

This is then how communion in the midst of forsakenness is possible: The Son gives himself as a gift to the Father and the Father, correspondingly, receives the gift of his Son. Still, the Father does much more than simply passively receive the sacrificial gift of his Son. The receiving Father, and this is an important Schlatterian idea, acts also as giver, namely in that he hands Jesus the new community as a gift. In so doing, the Father closes the circle of divine giving on the cross and appoints Jesus as the Lord of the new community, who has the authority to forgive his people. Schlatter sees Scriptural evidence for his position in John 6:38, where Jesus says that it was his Father's will that he "should lose nothing of all that he has given me." Commenting on this verse, Schlatter notes: "The gift that the Father's love makes him consists in the human beings who come to him."[60] Schlatter describes the Father's gift in return as follows:

> In the Son's relation to the Father the gift [*Gabe*] constitutes the gift in return [*Gegengabe*], love [constitutes] love in return [*Gegenliebe*]. The Father's gift to his Son consists in those whom he may forgive; the Son's gift to the Father is [the Son] himself. He renders himself the lamb offered to God; this is how he is set over the world so that he might take away its sin.[61]

---

59. Schlatter, *Jesu Gottheit und das Kreuz*, 52.
60. Schlatter, *Erläuterungen zum Neuen Testament*, 3:96.
61. Schlatter, "Christi Versöhnen und Christi Vergeben," 165.

This illustrates that for Schlatter, love is the underlying motif of the divine mutual giving and receiving: The Son loves and is loved in return. Their intimate interaction in love obviously points to the involvement of the Holy Spirit. In the previous chapter, we highlighted the Spirit's ministry in Jesus' volitional union with the Father. Now, in the context of Jesus offering himself as a gift to the Father, the Holy Spirit plays an equally significant role. Key to Schlatter's argument here is Hebrews 9:14: "How much more will the blood of Christ, *who through the eternal Spirit offered himself without blemish to God*, purify our conscience from dead works to serve the living God" (emphasis added). In his "Annotations to the New Testament," Schlatter comments on this verse as follows: "The move, by which the Son is drawn towards the Father, in that he offered himself up and sacrificed himself, [the move] which unites him with the Father . . . is the Spirit, the eternal Spirit, because it is God's Spirit who unites the Son with his Father in eternal fellowship."[62] It is only through the Holy Spirit, then, that the divine mutual transaction on the cross, as well as fellowship in forsakenness is conceivable in the first place.

> From where does his sense of sacrifice and the will to salvation that drove him to his priestly work come? From the Spirit. And from where does the power that allowed him to carry the cross and to shed his blood and to honor God until his last gasp come? From the Spirit. And from where does his power, so that death could not hold him captive, but rather so that he would be exalted through death, come . . . ? From the Spirit. The Spirit is the eternal and living bond which unites Jesus inwardly with the Father.[63]

The love between the Father and the Son, expressed in their divine exchange on the cross, is clearly sustained and mediated by the Holy Spirit, the "living bond which unites Jesus inwardly with the Father." Only in this sense is fellowship in forsakenness imaginable and, indeed, possible.[64] Mutual love through the Holy Spirit implies mutual glorification: In their divine interaction on the cross, the Son glorifies the Father and the Father glorifies the Son in return, thereby confirming the latter's divine status.[65]

62. Schlatter, *Erläuterungen zum Neuen Testament*, 9:298.

63. Ibid., 9:297.

64. Schlatter writes: "The cross of Jesus is not only the measure for the Father's love to the world . . . but also the reason why Jesus himself possesses the Father's love. This takes away the horror of the cross. Jesus suffers for the sake of love through which the Father unites him with himself." *Der Evangelist Johannes*, 238–39.

65. Schlatter writes, "Jesus would have not desired the cross had he not, through his cross, achieved the glorification of God. The Son loves the Father and he thus goes to

Based on what has been said so far we can summarize Jesus' service to God on the cross as follows: Jesus gladly gives himself as a gift to God and he remains, in spite of God-forsakenness, in divine fellowship, since a) the volitional union remains intact (Jesus consistently wants and indeed performs the Father's will), and b) we witness on the cross the divine exchange in love (the Son giving himself to the Father and the Father, receiving the Son's gift, giving to the Son the community of faith in return), and mutual glorification (demonstrating at the same time Jesus' divinity).

For now, we note that Schlatter's proposal reveals a highly creative attempt to approach the mysteries of the cross, as he seeks to combine complex elements, such as forsakenness and fellowship, and Jesus' sacrificial death and the revelation of his divinity. Especially Schlatter's emphasis on love seems an adequate tool to approach these conundrums. The question remains, however, whether Schlatter considers Jesus to move in and through this divine mutual exchange in love to a new ontological status, or a new level of relationship with the Father? Schlatter's language at times seems to point in such a direction.

Suffering and the Completed God-human

It is important to consider in this context Schlatter's notion of Jesus Christ as the "completed" God-human. He writes: "The necessity and the salvific power of the cross consists in the fact that Jesus, for himself, entered by means of the cross into communion with God. He revealed his divinity on the cross as it was there that the God-human was prepared, sustained and completed [*vollendet*]."[66] This raises the intriguing question of what Schlatter means by prepared, sustained, and, particularly, completed? Does it involve any (ontological) change in Jesus? Or, with a view to his relational union with the Father, is there now, with the Son's mission complete, a new level of relationship between the Father and the (now completed) Son? This calls for closer exploration.

First of all, one is well advised to recall Schlatter's basic principle of the seeing-act, namely, of simply acknowledging "what is there" in the New Testament. This seems to be Schlatter's underlying strategy here, as his language reveals clear affinities with the New Testament vocabulary. Evidently, his description of the "completion" (*Vollendung*) of Jesus' work on the cross echoes Jesus' cry, "It is finished" (*Es ist vollbracht*, John 19:30). Or, even

---

the cross since through it he glorifies God; and the Father loves the Son and sends him to the cross because he thereby glorifies the Son." *Andachten*, 131–32, see also 110–11.

66. Schlatter, *Jesu Gottheit und das Kreuz*, 94.

more obvious, one observes a distinct parallel between Schlatter's completion of the God-human and Hebrews 2:10, which reads: "For it was fitting that he, for whom and by whom all things exist, in bringing many sons to glory, should make the founder of their salvation *perfect* through suffering" (like Luther, Schlatter translates *teleio* as to complete, "vollenden"). Now, with a view to our question, it seems unlikely that, for Schlatter, completion here implies any change in the being of Jesus Christ; rather, it seems to mean that in suffering on the cross, Jesus reveals his perfection (*Vollkommenheit*) as the promised Messiah. "The letter [to the Hebrews] is happy to use the word 'completing' [*vollenden*] in order to display Jesus' work and gift," Schlatter writes, "for it thereby points to the expectation with which Israel viewed the promised [One]."[67] In Schlatter's view, the completion of the God-human thus displays the messianic fulfilment of the Christ in time and history, his public demonstration of a perfection he always possessed. It is unlikely, then, that Schlatter assumes here any ontological changes in the being of Christ.

Moreover, Schlatter applies this trope of perfection (*Vollendung*) in suffering not only to the person of Christ but also to his relationship with the Father. In his "Christian Dogmatics," Schlatter describes Jesus as the one who "had in suffering the reason for complete joy, since suffering did not loosen his communion with God but completed [*vollendete*] it."[68] Again, one is faced with the question of how to interpret the notion of completion. Does it point to a new level of relationship between the Father and the Son? Based on our considerations so far, it seems possible but not probable. It is difficult to imagine Schlatter signing up to Moltmann's statement that "[t]he pain of the cross determines the inner life of the triune God from eternity to eternity."[69] In fact, rather than focusing on the aspect of suffering, on divine passibility, as Moltmann does, Schlatter draws our attention to the aspect of divine communion, to the significant fact that it is precisely *through* the pain that Jesus establishes communion with God on the cross; this is perhaps how one should read Schlatter's above comment.[70] Thus, in

---

67. Schlatter, *Erläuterungen zum Neuen Testament*, 9:211–12.
68. Schlatter, *Dogma*, 132.
69. Moltmann, *Trinity and the Kingdom*, 161; see also *Crucified God*, 151–53.

70. Namely in the sense that "suffering did not loosen his communion with God but completed it." Moltmann would most certainly complain that Schlatter does not take seriously enough Jesus' pain of forsakenness, a charge that seems to have some validity. Although Schlatter clearly speaks of the Father as offering his Son, as regarding him as an object of his divine displeasure (Schlatter clearly states that the one who handed Jesus over and who, ultimately, proclaimed the death sentence over him was "none other than God," *Evangelium des Lukas*, 445; cf. *Jesu Gottheit und das Kreuz*, 35), one still wonders whether Schlatter truly does justice to the horror and the intensity of

contrast to Moltmann, who risks reading the pain of the cross back into the immanent Trinity (and thus losing divine immutability on the way), Schlatter seems more careful. In our view, it is more plausible to interpret Schlatter's notion of completing communion here also in terms of a *demonstrating* and *displaying* of a communion which does not break apart in suffering but transcends suffering. This does not involve any ontological change, or any new (essential) level of intra-Trinitarian relationship.

Ultimately, Schlatter admits that what happened on the cross is beyond our human cognitive and linguistic capacities. Schlatter's approach of speaking and thinking in polarities, it seems, is an attempt to reflect our limited capabilities, while at the same time trying to get as close as possible to the truth of the mystery of the cross. This might explain why he speaks of non-fellowship and fellowship, suffering as completing communion, de-glorification and glorification, taking and giving:

> In that he [Jesus] is excluded from communion with God, and as he goes without it, he establishes it, since indeed his 'I' becomes nothing, yet God does not become nothing to him. As he is negated by God whilst not negating him, forsaken by God whilst not forsaking him, his God-forsakenness becomes the basis for communion with God, his abandoning of the spirit [*Entgeistigung*] and his de-glorification [*Entherrlichung*] become the condition for his inspiration [*Vergeistigung*] and glorification [*Verherrlichung*].... What God took from him he gave willingly and freely to God, and thus, as he turns divine taking into his free giving, it becomes the basis for God's gift in return that brings him into complete communion.[71]

Schlatter's language of polarities is in our view a creative and satisfactory way of approaching the profound intra-Trinitarian action on the cross. In his own, unique way, Schlatter takes seriously the New Testament narrative, which, in and of itself, leaves many a question unanswered and certain tensions unresolved. Schlatter's careful attempt to strike a balance between seemingly antagonistic poles is certainly an adequate way of approaching the mysteries of the cross, offering much by way of promise for our christological discussion today. Based on our considerations of Schlatter's view of Jesus' service to God (*Gottesdienst*) we are now in a position to turn to the second aspect of Jesus' double-service (*Doppeldienst*), namely his service to humanity (*Menschendienst*).

God-forsakenness that Jesus experienced. See for example Macleod, *Person of Christ*, 174–77.

71. Schlatter, *Jesu Gottheit und das Kreuz*, 65.

JESUS' *MENSCHENDIENST* AND THE NEW COMMUNITY

Jesus' vertical move towards the Father in his *Gottesdienst* is at the same time a horizontal move towards humanity in his *Menschendienst*.[72] It is in Jesus' "upward gaze to God that his whole love for humanity is alive," Schlatter states.[73] This reminds us again of how closely Schlatter relates the divine action *ad intra* (Jesus' service to God) to the divine action *ad extra* (Jesus' service to humanity). According to Schlatter, Jesus' service to humanity consists most fundamentally in the establishment of the new community (*neue Gemeinde*) over which Christ himself is Lord.[74] As we have seen earlier, Schlatter considers the establishment of the community to be the result of the mutual divine exchange on the cross. The obedient Son gives himself as a gift to the Father and the Father returns the community as a gift to the Son, while the Holy Spirit is the bond of love in the process of divine giving and receiving. It is remarkable that Schlatter doctrinally places the establishment of the community precisely here, on the cross. Obviously, the Schlatterian seeing-act would require clear Scriptural evidence for this position. One could think, for example, of the imagery of the bride given to the bridegroom (Rev 19:7, 21:2), or of Jesus' interaction with his Father regarding the new community in John 17 (verses 9 and 24 in particular). Whilst it would certainly be possible exegetically to relate these passages to the events of the cross, one wonders whether Schlatter does not overemphasize the

---

72. Schlatter writes: "His oneness with the Father accounts for his dying, because out of it emerges the struggle of the world against him; it is therefore impossible that the world should keep him for himself and that he could have his place anywhere else than with the Father. His oneness with believers accounts for his dying, because it places him into the world, thus allowing the assault on him. The same makes it impossible for him to abandon his own people and he establishes [*begründet*] through his death his bond with them and brings it to perfection. From this double-movement [*Doppelzug*] of his love results his destiny: both upward towards the Father and towards human beings; that he does not arrive earlier or differently at the Father than by his death brings forth this twofold, yet in and by itself completely uniform love, as its necessary outcome." *Jesu Gottheit und das Kreuz*, 30–31.

73. Schlatter, *Jesu Gottheit und das Kreuz*, 77. "The immediate success of the cross," Schlatter concludes, "can only lie in the upward [move], in the relation to the Father, and everything it [the cross] means for us is based on what happened with it before and for God." Ibid.

74. Schlatter uses the different German denotations, such as *Kirche* (church), *Gemeinde* (this term can refer to the local community or council as well as to a local congregation/church) or *Gemeinschaft der Glaubenden/der Liebe* (communion/fellowship of believers, of love) interchangeably. See Rieger, *Schlatters Rechtfertigungslehre*, 367–70.

divine action on the cross at the expense of Pentecost and the eschatological realization of the community still to come.

On the one hand, this placement of Jesus' service to humanity is certainly a rather idiosyncratic Schlatterian move; it perhaps reflects, with its clear focus on the cross, the Lutheran influence of his friend Hermann Cremer.[75] On the other hand, however, a careful reading of Schlatter shows that he incorporates some of the aforementioned points in his model of Jesus' service to humanity. For one, Schlatter clearly admits that the full completion of the new community lies from Jesus' perspective still in the future. Schlatter argues: "[Jesus] waits for the Spirit, in agreement with the fact that the gathering of the new community likewise remains to be accomplished in the future. For 'the Spirit' and 'the community' are concepts that are firmly connected with one another."[76] Schlatter is clearly aware of the already-but-not-yet tension expressed in the New Testament, hence, he presents Jesus as the "custodian of a now," as the one who "sets the present in a strong causal relation to the final end."[77] One could summarize as follows: Schlatter regards the cross as the central, inaugural moment of the new community which is to be realized through the Spirit at Pentecost, and which still awaits its full completion in the *eschaton*. For our purposes we shall focus then on what is for Schlatter the significant inaugural moment of the new community on the cross.

We proceed as follows: First, Schlatter's distinct communal perspective is particularly conspicuous and we begin our discussion with this crucial feature. Secondly, we turn our attention to the divine Trinitarian action in respect of the establishment of the community, while thirdly, and finally, the conversation focuses on Schlatter's distinct emphasis on the community's relational oneness, both on a vertical level (with God) and on a horizontal level, with one another.

Relational Beings in Communion

We have already alluded to Schlatter's strong communal focus at several stages in this study (such as in the context of his Barth-critique), and we have also pointed to Schlatter's autobiographical work, *Erlebtes* (which

---

75. More research is needed to better understand the Lutheran influence on Schlatter's theological project. Future studies could build on the work by Althaus, "Adolf Schlatters Verhältnis zur Theologie Luthers," 245–56, and Dreher, "Luther als Paulus-Interpret bei Adolf Schlatter," 109–25.

76. Schlatter, *History of the Christ*, 335.

77. Ibid., 122.

translates as "experiences"), where he describes his own life as intertwined with relational networks. In the preface to the first edition of that work, he writes: "I was a part of the state, a member of the church, a listener of the bible, a guest at Jesus' table, a comrade in the band of teaching and researching workers, and . . . I was a creation of nature."[78] By describing his relational rootedness, he underlines at the same time what he was not, namely, an individualist. Schlatter identified individualism as one of the main obstacles facing contemporary theology and church life. He was concerned about what he considered the subjectivism and individualism of the Swabian pietism he encountered in Tübingen.[79] In his "Christian Dogmatics," Schlatter criticizes "[a]scetics, who, in order to secure their sinlessness, separate themselves from others,"[80] and he issues the warning that the Christian, who is "led away from his human relationships becomes a hermit."[81] Schlatter speaks of the "total guilt which rests on German theology," on account of its blindness for its own individualism which "taught us merely to nurture our own consciousness."[82] With his characteristic communal trajectory, then, Schlatter intends to put forward a corrective of what he considered individualistic tendencies in contemporary theology. Schlatter's contribution has much to offer even today. In face of today's postmodern Western individualism, Schlatter's critique is an enduring voice of correction.[83]

Throughout his œuvre, Schlatter time and again indicates that Jesus did not come to create redeemed eremites, but relational beings who enjoy an inseparable link with God and with each other.[84] Now this does not mean that Schlatter neglects the existential aspect of soteriology. On the contrary: As we shall see in the next chapter, Schlatter has a keen interest in applying soteriology to the individual believer's life-act (*Lebensakt*). Yet for Schlatter this existential salvific connection with Jesus must never be considered in isolation from the context of the community.[85] (This was one of the main aspects of his Barth-critique discussed earlier, see chapter 2).

---

78. Schlatter, *Erlebtes*, 5.
79. Neuer, *Adolf Schlatter*, 395.
80. Schlatter, *Dogma*, 474.
81. Ibid., 473.
82. Schlatter, *Rückblick*, 70.
83. Miroslav Volf claimed recently that the task of today's theology is "to counter the tendencies toward individualism in Protestant ecclesiology and to suggest a viable understanding of the church in which both person and community are given their proper due." Volf, *After Our Likeness*, 2. Whilst Schlatter would perhaps not have subscribed to Volf's Trinitarian agenda, he could not have agreed more with this statement.
84. See, for instance, Schlatter, *Ethik*, 176–248; *Dogma*, 357–524.
85. Schlatter, *Dogma*, 20–21, 386–87.

The believer's faith is not a "private revelation" (*Privatoffenbarung*), and her life as a Christian is not an individualistic life, but a life of dialogue and interaction with other human beings and with the Triune God.[86] In soteriological language, this means for Schlatter that the fruit of Jesus' atoning work on the cross on behalf of human beings certainly includes the removal of God's wrath from the individual, the personal offer of forgiveness of sins, and justification by faith and adoption for the individual.[87] However, all these benefits are available only by being part of the community. He writes: "God's work does not consist in the completion of many or of a few human beings. It rather creates the abiding community, and individuals in it and for it."[88] There is then no individual experience of faith without the community of faith, Schlatter claims, as any act of faith presupposes the "affirmation of the community."[89] The community established by Jesus is in fact the "instrument through which union with him becomes possible for us" (*das Organ, durch das uns der Anschluß an ihn gewährt wird*).[90] It is on theological grounds then that Schlatter rules out any "tension between the community and one's personal state of life."[91] He explains:

> God's glory and God's grace can only appear among us as they bring us together. If we remain in lonely abandonment, we can neither be God's witnesses nor a witness to Jesus' government. We carry the image of the one who created the community by being within the community.[92]

In this way, Schlatter highlights his understanding of soteriology as both individual and communal. In fact, the heading under which Schlatter treats this whole section on soteriology in his *Dogma* affirms this characteristic angle: "Christendom as a community called towards God—soteriology" (*Die Christenheit als die zu Gott berufene Gemeinde—Soteriologie*).[93] Jesus' service to humanity, according to Schlatter, thus has a clear relational impetus as it ushers in the creation of the new community where a wholly new relation with God and with one another is made possible for humanity.[94] Keeping in mind these central remarks on Schlatter's communal perspec-

86. Ibid., 386.
87. See Rieger, *Schlatters Rechtfertigungslehre*, 327–64.
88. Schlatter, *History of the Christ*, 28.
89. Schlatter, *Dogma*, 497.
90. Ibid., 382.
91. Schlatter, *Glaube im Neuen Testament*, 537.
92. Schlatter, *Ethik*, 176.
93. Schlatter, *Dogma*, 357.
94. See ibid., 295.

tive, we shall next examine more closely how Schlatter weaves together the establishment of the community with the Trinitarian action on the cross.

The Trinity and the New Community

From Schlatter's perspective, "the establishment of the community" is *the* culmination of Jesus' earthly work; it represents the apex of his "kingly office."[95] Schlatter thus has a clear Christocentric angle when it comes to the formation of the new community. Still, as the following discourse will show, Schlatter underlines the involvement of each member of the Godhead in the divine action *ad extra*. So how does Schlatter then conceive of the divine action directed to the creation of the new community?

The events on the cross between the Father and the Son, through the Spirit, are central for our understanding of the creation of the new community. Schlatter writes that "the purpose for which God led him [Jesus] into death was that a community would be born through him, one free from guilt and death."[96] Through his accomplished work on the cross, Schlatter notes, Jesus gains "as his own possession the large community that possessed freedom from guilt and death as the fruit of his death."[97] This new community with Jesus Christ as Lord is unique, different from any other (natural) community, since it was established "through a divine creative deed" (*durch eine göttliche Schöpfertat*).[98] Note in this context again Schlatter's distinct notion of relational subordination: Jesus was led into death by the Father as the above quote indicates. Elsewhere, Schlatter writes: The Son does not "work for himself. . . . Only God could reveal him and make him the Lord of the community."[99] Hence, it is only "[i]n God" that Jesus "had authority, the authority of the one who gathered the eternal community."[100] As pointed out earlier, Schlatter subscribes to functional (or soteriological) subordinationism without subscribing to classic (ontological) subordinationism as Jesus submits himself in love. "Jesus' inaugural experience . . . ," Schlatter clarifies, "did not consist in a decision by which he offered himself to God and said, 'I am your Son.' It rather lay in his hearing of the declaration, 'You are my Son.'"[101] In a similar way, Schlatter argues, Jesus does not declare

---

95. Schlatter, *Dogma*, 280, 357.
96. Schlatter, *History of the Christ*, 315.
97. Ibid.; cf. "Die letzte Bitte Jesu," in *Gesunde Lehre*, 319.
98. Schlatter, *Dogma*, 246; cf. *Ethik*, 176.
99. Schlatter, *History of the Christ*, 93.
100. Ibid., 311.
101. Ibid., 48.

himself Lord over the community, rather, his Lordship over the community is declared for him by his Father. The Holy Spirit also plays a significant role in this context. It is the "word of Jesus Christ's grace and the love of God, the Father, and the communion of the Holy Spirit through which we are one church," Schlatter writes.[102] And it is "[b]y the Spirit of God that "Christ will fashion into a holy community those who were in danger of divine judgement."[103] Once again, the Spirit, in Schlatter's view, unites himself with the work of the Son—this echoes our earlier observations in the context of Jesus' volitional union with the Father through the Holy Spirit (see chapter 4). Schlatter writes:

> Through Jesus the community became in the highest sense the place where the Father was active. As he himself lived through the Father as the Son, the community was transferred into light and life by the Father. Likewise, the work of the Spirit formed a complete unity with that of the Christ. Both held possession of the called community and simultaneously performed a universal work upon humanity, and both effected righteousness and grace in complete unity.[104]

This illustrates Schlatter's motive of balancing distinctiveness within the Godhead and their harmonious divine action *ad extra*. The members of the Trinity have distinct roles—the Son giving himself as gift, the Father giving the community as a gift to the Son and the Holy Spirit as the bond of love between Father and Son—yet they work in perfect harmony. Divine action, for Schlatter, is "always Trinitarian action."[105] Hence, Schlatter can agree with Protestant scholastics that the external works of the Trinity are undivided (*opera trinitatis ad extra sunt indivisa*), but he would probably also add: "and distinct" (*et distincta*).[106] Schlatter infers the divine action *ad intra* from the divine action *ad extra*, for, according to Schlatter, the "revealed Trinity [*Offenbarungstrinität*] witnesses [to] the essential Trinity [*Wesenstrinität*]."[107] For Schlatter, the former is a manifestation or revelation, though not an exhaustive one, of the latter. While the Trinitarian relations *ad intra* constitute their action *ad extra*, Schlatter does not read the

---

102. Schlatter, *Die neue deutsche Art in der Kirche*, 22; cf. *Dogma*, 352, 344.
103. Schlatter, *History of the Christ*, 59.
104. Ibid., 389.
105. Loos, "Divine Action and the Trinity," 274.
106. Ibid.
107. Schlatter, "Wesen und Quellen der Gotteserkenntnis," 158. I owe this quotation to Loos, "Divine action, Christ," 137.

divine action *pro nobis* back into the immanent Trinity.[108] Schlatter applies this to Jesus' service to humanity as follows:

> The Father's gift establishes the giving of the Son, and this [establishes] the giving of the Spirit. In turn, the Spirit's work establishes the giving of the Son and this [establishes] the giving of the Father. The Father is both the foundation and the goal of all acts that reveal him and he is without division and rupture in everything that is Christ's and the Spirit's. What is different is only the manner of the divine action [*Weise des göttlichen Wirkens*].[109]

Through his service to humanity, then, Jesus establishes the new community of faith on the cross; this task, however, is not the sole work of the second person of the Godhead; rather, Schlatter involves the whole Trinity in the community's foundation and he offers here novel ways of thinking about it as the outcome of the divine interaction in love on the cross. The cross is central: "The cross of Christ is the revelatory act; here God's will is visible; the question: What is God? is answered here: he gave Christ into death; here, you recognize him."[110]

Here, on the cross, we encounter divine agency in action, harmonious activity in distinction, directed towards us. Although it is at times difficult to discern Schlatter's underlying Trinitarian structure, and his (sometimes) cryptic language does not make things easier, we can recognize his intention to strike a balance between the unity and distinction of the Trinitarian persons in action. Overall, it seems, Schlatter's model seeks to do justice to the inherent complexities of the Trinitarian relationship as displayed in the New Testament, where we read of unity, distinction, subordination, intimacy and forsakenness. To argue that Schlatter's creative way of relating the divine relations *ad intra* to their action *ad extra* proves stimulating for today's discussion of Trinitarian theology would certainly not be an overstatement. Having examined the Trinitarian foundations of the new community's creation, we now proceed to discuss the key characteristics of the new community.

---

108. See Loos, "Divine Action, Christ," 243.

109. Schlatter, *Dogma*, 352. Schlatter seems to affirm here Irenaeus's concept of the two hands of God.

110. Schlatter, *Jesus und Paulus*, 54.

Relational Oneness: Vertical and Horizontal

In Schlatter's view, the community's main feature is relational oneness; this does not come as a surprise by now, given the prominence of relationality and unity in Schlatter's opus. The ultimate goal of the harmonious Trinitarian action concerning the community is to establish relational unity, both vertically, between the community and God, and horizontally, between the members of the community. In our concluding considerations, we shall discuss first Schlatter's Christocentric perspective on our (vertical) relational union with God, and secondly, trace how Schlatter roots (horizontal) ecclesial unity in Trinitarian oneness.

First of all, Schlatter argues that the community's new, vertical, fellowship with God is shaped by Jesus Christ. The new community enjoys an essentially new kind of relationship with God through its union with Christ. Through his sacrifice on the cross, Jesus Christ has not only established the new community, but has also connected the community with himself, and thus thereby demonstrated his divinity: "When Jesus is, on the cross, the creator of communion with God [*Gottesgemeinschaft*] for us, then certainly he possesses, as the crucified one, divinity, because no one grants communion with God but God."[111] Hence, the community's "whole possession consists in its connection with Jesus and the value of this connection is defined by its share in Jesus [*was sie an Jesus hat*]."[112] According to Schlatter's view, Christ, as the head of the body, not only unites the community under his Lordship, but is also the one who sustains and indwells the new community. Schlatter thus speaks of Christ's "being-with-us" (*bei-uns-sein*) and our "being in him" (*in-ihm-sein*).[113] In this sense, Schlatter is even prepared to speak of the church as being "perfect" (*vollkommen*) since "Christ unites himself with us and us with one another in perfect grace."[114] And through Christ, we participate in the Trinitarian fellowship, as the community's oneness with Christ rests on Christ's oneness with the Father. "The one who, in his sovereign grace, made the man Jesus one with him," writes Schlatter, "is also willing to unify those who are with one another in him."[115] Schlatter also points to the involvement of the Holy Spirit in the establishment of relational unity; he writes:

---

111. Schlatter, *Jesu Gottheit und das Kreuz*, 13–14; cf. "Das Bekenntnis zur Gottheit Jesu," 37.
112. Schlatter, *Glaube im Neuen Testament*, 522.
113. Ibid., 536.
114. Schlatter, *Ethik*, 177.
115. Schlatter, *Do We Know Jesus*, 493.

By the giving of his blood, God's fellowship with humanity is revealed in a completely new way. This is a new will of God, a new grace, a new union of human beings with God, a life of humanity from God by the Spirit for the accomplishing of his will. Under the old covenant, God was not so close to the human being and humans were not so close with God. Now, because Jesus ended his life in free obedience, God has made new his relation to humanity.[116]

On this basis, then, Schlatter claims that the community of faith enjoys a new, unprecedented quality of fellowship with God. There is no higher status, no more elevated position than the one we enjoy through relational union with God in Christ as members of the community.[117]

From the community's new vertical connection with God follows its inherent horizontal unity, since the unity of the Trinity defines the horizontal unity of the community. As the Father is one with the Son (John 10:30), the community displays, within itself, this very same oneness. Commenting on the words of Jesus' high-priestly prayer, "I do not ask for these only, but also for those who will believe in me through their word, that they may all be one, just as you, Father, are in me, and I in you, that they also may be in us, so that the world may believe that you have sent me" (John 17:20–21), Schlatter remarks: "This is why here [John 17:21] the community's unity rests on Jesus' oneness with the Father. From Jesus' love arises for the church the source of its love; his connection with the Father is its foundation and rule for its own harmony [*Eintracht*]."[118] Furthermore, as the Godhead is characterized by the notion of unity in distinction, as discussed earlier, so too is the new community of faith. The inner unity and harmony of the new community of faith is thus rooted in the loving fellowship between the Father, the Son and the Holy Spirit—this is Schlatter's version of an *analogia relationis*.[119] Horizontal oneness, as it is rooted in the Trinitarian oneness, is in fact the key characteristic of Christianity. Again referring to the oneness of the church as expressed in John 17, Schlatter writes: "We know of no more complete, catholic [*umfassend*] and yet at the same time simple lesson of what 'Christianity' is than in what John has given us with Jesus' last prayer."[120]

---

116. Schlatter, *Kennen wir Jesus*, 396–97.

117. Schlatter, *Erläuterungen zum Neuen Testament*, 10:7.

118. Ibid., 3:226. The German noun *Eintracht*, what we have here translated as harmony, also denotes peaceful unity, or brotherly unanimity.

119. Loos, "Divine Action, Christ," 228.

120. Schlatter, *Erläuterungen zum Neuen Testament*, 3:228.

Now at this point one wonders if there might be a considerable discrepancy between theory and reality. For if one contemplates the present state of the church, one looks in vain for Schlatter's notion of oneness, as substantial ecclesiastical disagreement and disunity seem to prevail.[121] Does Schlatter's vision perhaps merely reflect wishful thinking? Several things might be said in answer to this challenge. In the first place, we have introduced Schlatter as an empirical *realist* (and not idealist); hence, one can rest assured that his assumption of ecclesial unity rooted in Triune unity is not a position of naivety. The notion of polarity, it seems, again sheds light on Schlatter's position as he clearly opts for an already-but-not-yet view of ecclesial reality. The new community, though in a sense already perfect, lives in hope, looking forward to its final completion (and thus perfect unification) upon Jesus' return.[122] Christian eschatological hope is thus central for Schlatter; it is, in fact a central function of the community.[123] "God has appointed him [Jesus] the completer [*Vollender*] of the community," Schlatter affirms, "and he will fulfil his calling by completing it."[124] This completion, however, Schlatter admits, has not yet been realized through his "work on earth . . . or by his veiled omnipresence, but this will happen through his new revelation. This is why Christianity's hope is as much set on him as its faith."[125] Moreover, if one reads Schlatter's agenda pragmatically, that is, as a goal to which to aspire, one can detect a distinct ecumenical impulse. This is not far-fetched, as Schlatter was throughout his life at pains to work towards ecumenical understanding. In various speeches and essays, Schlatter continually reminded his contemporaries of the inter-confessional precept of an ethics of love which must be the key element of the new community of faith.[126] Overall, Schlatter's emphasis on the oneness of the community of faith offers here much by way of ecumenical promise.[127] Schlatter's explorations of the Trinitarian basis of ecclesial unity can provide significant material for inter-denominational understanding.

---

121. See, for example, the recent contributions in Root and Buckley (eds.), *Morally Divided Body*.

122. Schlatter, *Dogma*, 533.

123. Ibid., 526.

124. Ibid., 533.

125. Ibid.

126. See for example his, "Der Dienst des Christen in der älteren Dogmatik," "Noch ein Wort über den christlichen Dienst," and "Die Dienstpflicht des Christen in der apostolischen Gemeinde" (in *Der Dienst des Christen*).

127. See Neuer, "Die ökumenische Bedeutung," 71–92, and Rieger, *Schlatters Rechtfertigungslehre*, 427–36.

CONCLUSION

In this chapter we continued our exploration of Schlatter's thinking-act. Focusing in particular on Jesus in relation to humanity, we established how in Schlatter's view, Jesus' service to God (*Gottesdienst*) forms the basis for his service to humanity (*Menschendienst*). Our observations in this context concentrated on the cross of Christ, as the cross is the cardinal point for his Christology. Schlatter undoubtedly offers a unique and highly creative *theologia crucis* with his relational-volitional trajectory. The cross, for Schlatter, is first and foremost a matter between the Father and the Son. At the heart of Schlatter's theology of the cross lies the divine exchange in love, mediated by the Holy Spirit, which unites Father and Son even in the most extreme moment of dereliction. The cross, in fact, is the quintessential litmus test for Schlatter's relational Christology. It constitutes the apex of Jesus' obedience to the Father, and at the same time it reveals the perfection of his communion of will and of essence with the Father in spite of forsakenness. Having presented himself as the perfect offering to his Father on the cross, the divine Son receives as a gift from his Father the new community of faith, over which he is declared Lord. The establishment of the new community is the key element of Jesus' service to humanity, and Schlatter thereby points to the communal aspect of his theology. In the same way as the Trinity does not consist of "individuals," but distinct persons in unity, so too does the community represent distinct members who live in harmony with God and with each other. Schlatter sees a relational analogy between Trinitarian oneness in distinction and the community's oneness in distinction.

In the following, final chapter, we move to the individual believer as she experiences union with Jesus Christ in her life-act (*Lebensakt*). In doing so, however, we do not leave the sphere of the community behind, since, as highlighted at the outset of this chapter, the life of the individual Christian is always intricately linked to the new community of faith.

6

The *Lebensakt*
Organic Volitional Union with Christ

ADOLF SCHLATTER'S VISION WAS to arrive at a holistic understanding of theology in general and Christology in particular. He sought to unite exegetical observation (biblical studies), theological examination (systematic theology) and theological application (ethics) under one single banner. So far, we have studied the first two elements of this method. We looked at the seeing-act (*Sehakt*), by which the theologian perceives the history of Jesus Christ, and the thinking-act (*Denkakt*), through which he is prompted to analyze his findings systematically in order to arrive at a Christology proper. Seeing and thinking however do not suffice. The exegetical seeing-act and the dogmatic thinking-act lead in an organic way to the existential life-act (*Lebensakt*), in which we assimilate the observed and processed material. For Schlatter, New Testament theology and dogmatics go hand in hand with ethics, the application of theology in real-life situations. As noted earlier, Schlatter not only produced a New Testament theology and a dogmatics, but also an ethics (*Die christliche Ethik*, 1914/1929).[1] Whilst Schlatter first hesitated to pen the *Ethik*, as he felt he had to "respect the boundaries of the disciplines,"[2] his friend Karl Holl finally succeeded in convincing Schlatter that he was the right candidate to do it.[3] In his third (and successful) attempt, Holl writes to Schlatter: "It is my firm conviction that Protestantism will perish if it does not renew itself based on ethics. If I could, I would tell

1. For the context see Neuer, *Adolf Schlatter*, 498–508.
2. Schlatter to Lütgert, 23 April 1913, in Neuer, *Adolf Schlatter*, 499.
3. See Neuer, *Adolf Schlatter*, 500.

you, like Farel told Calvin, that you will be guilty of a severe sin of negligence if you shirk your duties."[4] Schlatter evidently agreed with Holl that ethics was a sore point in contemporary Protestantism;[5] he articulated, like Holl, a serious need for improvement since the "Reformation doctrine did not bequeath us with an adequate ethics."[6]

In the previous chapter, we alluded to Schlatter's critique of individualistic tendencies in post-Reformation Protestantism and contemporary German pietism. He feared that what he considered the introspective and isolationist tendencies in pietism—he speaks of a "listless passivity" (*unbewegliche Ruhe*)[7]—would lead to an isolation of the believer and to a passive church.[8] Schlatter in fact caricatures the passive pietist as one who regards the Christian life as "a journey of tears until we reach a blessed death."[9] In the words of Stephen F. Dintaman, Schlatter "saw in Luther an emphasis on the totality of human sin . . . which had the effect of overemphasizing the passivity of the believer in faith and the Christian life. He saw a tendency in Luther toward an egoistic perversion of faith where the justification of the individual is made the center of personal and theological concern."[10] Whilst this language is perhaps slightly exaggerated, Dintaman certainly points to the crux of Schlatter's critique. Schlatter highlights the active human being who is equipped with a positive vocation (*positiven Beruf*),[11] and who serves as an active member of the new community of faith. Echoing his Tübingen teacher Johann T. Beck, Schlatter thus calls for a "completion of the Reformation" (*Vollendung der Reformation*),[12] in such a way that ethics becomes the completion of dogmatics. Beck's credo, "Go and do what

---

4. Holl to Schlatter, 17 August 1913, in Stupperich, "Briefe Karl Holls an Adolf Schlatter," 213.

5. Schlatter, "Selbstdarstellungen," 150; see also ibid., 165–66.

6. Schlatter, *Erlebtes*, 117.

7. Schlatter, "Noch ein Wort," 68.

8. Ibid., 69.

9. Quoted in Dintaman, *Creative Grace*, 163n5. Herman Bavinck's criticism of contemporary pietism in the Netherlands is reminiscent of Schlatter's; he writes of the pietists: "They spoke of earthly life as a life of trouble and grief. The world was to them nothing but a vale of tears, a desert, a Meshech. They would have preferred to withdraw from it completely and restrict themselves to the narrow circle of like-minded people. Family and society, science and art, state and church were given up to unbelief and revolution as wholly spoiled and unredeemable." Bavinck, *Certainty of Faith*, 44–45.

10. Dintaman, *Creative Grace*, 152.

11. Schlatter, "Noch ein Wort," 68.

12. Schlatter, "Becks theologische Arbeit," 34, 41–42; see also *Rückblick*, 67, 107; Riggenbach, *Johann Tobias Beck*, 18, 270.

you have heard," clearly resonates in Schlatter's works,[13] and he was committed to what he called Beck's goal of a "lived-out word of Scripture."[14] Beck indeed regards the "Christian teaching science as an organic union of dogmatics and ethics," with ethics as the goal of dogmatics.[15] In Beck's view, then, and Schlatter is happy to follow his former teacher here, it is "[n]ot the right knowledge but the right action [that] determines the relation to God and the condition of life [*Lebensstand*]."[16] For Schlatter, then, theology is a dead discipline if it is not applied to one's own life in the life-act.[17] "Theology," Schlatter contends, "that declines to create an ethic does not completely carry out its duty."[18] In his view, "dogmatics is given to us so that we would have an ethics."[19] In terms of Schlatter's threefold method of seeing-act, thinking-act, and life-act, one could put it like this: The theologian only takes his vocation seriously when he exhibits the threefold pursuit of seeing, thinking, *and living*. "To me," Schlatter writes, "observation was valid as the process that gave us the dogmatic knowledge and that created duty [*Pflicht*]."[20] Observation in the seeing-act, the analysis of dogmatic knowledge in the thinking-act, and the performance of duty in the life-act are inseparably united, in particular, as these acts converge in the person

13. Beck, *Christliche Liebeslehre*, 8. See also Neuer, "Das Verhältnis Adolf Schlatters zu Johann Tobias Beck," 85–95.

14. Schlatter, "Becks theologische Arbeit," 28.

15. Beck, *Einleitung in das System der Christlichen Lehre*, 45. See also Schlatter, "Becks theologische Arbeit," 40. Schlatter's Dutch contemporary, neo-Calvinist Abraham Kuyper (1837–1920), notes likewise: "The Calvinist . . . does not hold to religion, with its dogmatics, as a separate entity, and then place his moral life with its ethics as a second entity alongside of religion, but he holds to religion as placing him in the presence of God Himself, Who thereby embues him with His divine will." Kuyper, *Lectures on Calvinism*, 72. On significant theological overlaps between Schlatter and Kuyper see my essay, "Pilgrimage to Kuyper?," 32–50.

16. Schlatter, "Becks theologische Arbeit," 34.

17. See also my "Good Will Hunting," 125–43.

18. Schlatter, "Briefe über das Dogma," 45. "For this reason," Schlatter writes, "every dogmatics that does without ethics is an aberration [*Verirrung*] as it denies the will, duty before God and love for God." *Dogma*, 212. Elsewhere, Schlatter argues that "the New Testament does not know of a concern with the divine that would not create an ethics." "Theologie des NT und Dogmatik," 80. This ethical agenda was not simply a theoretical construct for Schlatter but had a concrete impact on his personal life-act. Schlatter was, for instance, closely connected with the Christian relief organisation Bethel, which was founded by his friend Friedrich von Bodelschwingh and offered care for the socially disadvantaged. See Neuer, *Adolf Schlatter*, 819–20.

19. Schlatter, "Entstehung der Beiträge," 78; cf. "Briefe über das Dogma," 41, 44.

20. Schlatter, "Entstehung der Beiträge," 44, 55; see also *Rückblick*, 102 on the unity of thinking-act and life-act.

and work of Jesus Christ.[21] For Schlatter, the New Testament question of the history of the Christ, the dogmatic question of Christology, and the existential question of what human beings become (and are called to do) through their union with him are one: "When we define our relation to Jesus," he writes, "we are faced with a new question, namely: what is he? and what becomes of us through our union with him [Anschluß an ihn]?"[22]

The christological task is thus not finished when one merely "sees" Christ in history and "thinks" him in dogmatic elaboration. Rather, the theologian's goal, as that of any individual, is to experience fundamental experiential and ethical change through the encounter with Jesus Christ. And this ethical change, in Schlatter's view, is confirmed by a substantial volitional change in us. We act differently because of a new will in us. How does this come about? How are we empowered to act with a new volition? And how does this volitional transformation tie in with his relational Christology? This is what we intend to explore in this chapter according to the following outline: First, we introduce briefly the basic elements of Schlatter's model of our volitional union with Christ, exploring the significance of volition, and its relation to cognition and history. We then turn, secondly, to the crucial question of how our volitional union with God comes about, and we discuss Schlatter's significant emphasis on the work of Christ and the Holy Spirit in this context. Thirdly, moving even deeper into the intricacies of volitional union with God, we clarify whether Schlatter is able to offer a balanced account of volitional union that takes our anthropology seriously while at the same time doing justice to the divine work in us. This will allow us, fourthly and finally, to weave the threads together, offering a full picture of Schlatter's understanding of our union with Christ (*Anschluss an Christus*).

HUMAN VOLITION, COGNITION, AND HISTORY

In the previous chapters on the seeing-act and the thinking-act we already considered the relevance of *volition* for Schlatter's Christology. We discussed the importance of Jesus' volitional union with the Father and through the Holy Spirit, in particular with a view to the cross. Now, with a view to our existential connection with God, volition seems equally significant. Human volition in general is central for Schlatter, who speaks of the "primacy of the

---

21. See Schlatter, "Entstehung der Beiträge," 8.
22. Schlatter, *Dogma*, 278.

will,"[23] and claims that the will is "the highest function of our life."[24] And in order to perform the right action the human being needs the right will, namely the good will, which is in harmony with God's will. "Not the extinction of our will," writes Schlatter, "but its creation arises through God's redeeming grace; not the absence of will, but a good will is its goal."[25] We receive this good will, this sanctified volition through volitional union with God. Through our volitional union (*Willenseinigung*),[26] or volitional communion (*Willensgemeinschaft*)[27] with God, Schlatter claims, we are enabled to perform the ethical deed within our life-act and thereby glorify God. In that volitional transformation allows us to glorify God, Schlatter contends, it is in fact one of the greatest gifts that God gives (we return to this important issue at a later stage).[28]

At this point one wonders whether Schlatter, in stressing the volitional aspect of our union with God, does not overlook the important cognitive component of this union, namely a transformation of our knowledge and understanding. According to the Apostle Paul, this cognitive transformation seems to be the prerequisite for any volitional transformation, as Romans 12:2 indicates: "Do not be conformed to this world, but be transformed by the renewal of your mind, that by testing you may discern what is the will of God, what is good and acceptable and perfect." While Schlatter would probably agree that only by having received "the mind of Christ" (1 Cor 2:16) is one able to distinguish the good will from the bad will, his focus is clearly more on the actual outworking of a transformed cognition as it plays out in a new volition. In fact, Schlatter warns of a dogmatism that reduces faith to its cognitive elements. Based on our earlier comments, it seems likely that Schlatter intended with his volitional emphasis to correct what he considered a pietistic overemphasis on cognitive introspection.

23. Schlatter, *Rückblick*, 93.

24. Schlatter, "Moral oder Evangelium," in *Gesunde Lehre*, 98; cf. *Rückblick*, 172–73; *Gründe der christlichen Gewißheit*, 59; see also Schlatter's dictionary entry on "Wille, Wollen" in the *Calwer Bibellexikon*, 1011–12.

25. Schlatter, *Dogma*, 456.

26. Schlatter, *Philosophische Arbeit*, 95; see also "Moral oder Evangelium," in *Gesunde Lehre*, 97–98; *Dogma*, 148–62; note also Schlatter's elaborate description in *Ethik*, 22–29, 34–49.

27. Schlatter, *Ethik*, 29.

28. See Schlatter, *Hülfe in Bibelnot*, 8; cf. *Ethik*, 33–45. Commenting on Jesus' saying, "Not everyone who says to me, 'Lord, Lord,' will enter the kingdom of heaven, but the one who does the will of my Father who is in heaven" (Matt 7:21), Schlatter notes: "He [Jesus] does not speak of a faith that consists in empty words, but rather talks about the highest gifts that a human being can receive through faith from above." *Erläuterungen zum Neuen Testament*, 1:98.

For Schlatter, the Christian faith comprised more than that. Obviously, in order to believe "we also need a brain."[29] "Faith needs cognition," he admits, "but is not identical to it. It is a plus because it contains an energetic and comprehensive activation of the will."[30] That is, whilst Schlatter does not downplay the cognitive aspect of the renewal of our minds, he is keen to stress that cognitive renewal always goes hand in hand with a transformed volition that embraces the divine will as its own. "The renewal of our reason [*Vernunft*]," he writes, "means that it now asks for God's will and that it utilizes all its knowledge of the world and of human nature so that the healthy will of God might be done through us."[31] Of course, Schlatter admits, Jesus' disciples, then and now, "should learn from him [Jesus], but not merely [in terms of] insights. . . . His influence on them was directed toward the entire person, not merely toward their cognition but also toward their will."[32] The goal is then not only a renewed mind, but also ultimately a "new will that obeys God" and finds expression in concrete action to the glory of God in the context of concrete history.[33] This latter aspect of concrete history is, of course, of special significance to Schlatter.

Throughout his works, Schlatter is keen to emphasize our dependence on history, that is, both on history in general and, significantly, on the concrete history of the Christ in particular (as we have discussed in chapter 3 on the seeing-act).[34] Any connection with Jesus (*Anschluss an Jesus*) is in Schlatter's view only achievable in conjunction with a connection with history (*Anschluss an die Geschichte*).[35] "Our participation in God [*Anteil an Gott*]," notes Schlatter, "is not established through theories, through abstract, timeless concepts, but through history."[36] As laid out previously, for Schlatter there is no ugly broad ditch between historical and universal truths, between history and faith, or between *Historie* and *Geschichte*.[37] The history of the Son of God, who became flesh and lived on this earth in a distinct period in time, is existentially relevant for the believer in his or her concrete historical context. It is precisely in our specific historical setting

29. Schlatter, *Das Gott wohlgefällige Opfer*, 47.

30. Schlatter, "Christologie und Soteriologie," 23.

31. Schlatter, *Das Gott wohlgefällige Opfer*, 27.

32. Schlatter, *History of the Christ*, 240.

33. Ibid., 245.

34. For a discussion of the existentially relevant factor of history in Schlatter's *Dogma*, see Bockmühl, "Wahrnehmung der Geschichte," 93–112.

35. Schlatter, "Selbstdarstellungen," 162–63; see also *Dogma*, 300.

36. Schlatter, *Dogma*, 300.

37. Schlatter, "Briefe über das Dogma," 18–19.

that we encounter God's revelation in Jesus Christ. Hence, our point of contact (*Anknüpfungspunkt*) with Jesus Christ, to borrow Brunner's language, lies within concrete history, and volitional union, which can be considered the key element of our *Anschluss an Jesus*, similarly works against the backdrop of concrete history.

Emerging from our observations thus far is Schlatter's clear focus on ethics as the goal of dogmatics and his emphasis on volitional renewal working through our volitional union with God in history. In what follows, we shall take a closer look at the nature of this volitional union with God, considering in the first place Schlatter's distinct emphasis on Christ and the Spirit, and secondly the organic nature of volitional union.

CHRIST, THE SPIRIT, AND VOLITIONAL UNION

How does Schlatter conceive of volitional union with God in detail? That is, how exactly is our will united with God's will? According to Schlatter, both the work of Jesus Christ and the involvement of the Holy Spirit are central: we unite our will with God's will on the basis of Christ's work and through the Holy Spirit. It is in particular Schlatter's strong emphasis on the Holy Spirit that deserves closer scrutiny in our following discussion. In times when pneumatology has tended to be sidelined in the theological debate, Schlatter directs our attention to the significant contribution of the Holy Spirit in our volitional union with God. Of course, much has been said about the neglect of the doctrine of the Holy Spirit in theology and church life.[38] And Schlatter clearly noticed a similar disregard for pneumatology in his own day and age. Instead of assimilating the "concept of the Spirit" (*Geistgedanken*), Schlatter laments, the church has "anxiously rejected it again and again."[39] By giving due prominence to the Holy Spirit, Schlatter seeks to fulfil his goal of ameliorating the shortcomings of contemporary Protestantism as mentioned earlier. Even today, it seems, Schlatter's distinct reference to the Holy Spirit has much to offer for today's theological debate.

What then are the concrete pneumatological implications for our volitional union with God? As previously indicated, Schlatter puts forward a model of union in distinction when it comes to the divine action *ad extra*. Hence, the whole Godhead is, in his view, harmoniously united yet distinctively involved in bringing our human will into harmony with the divine will.[40] Schlatter suggests that the Father works through his "two hands,"

---

38. See, for instance, Migliore, *Faith seeking Understanding*, 224–26.
39. Schlatter, *Dogma*, 346.
40. Ibid., 466.

namely Christ and the Spirit, in order to bring about a deep volitional change in us. The Holy Spirit, as the Spirit of Jesus Christ, works in close coordination with Christ. "Paul," Schlatter writes, and he is referring here to Philippians 2:13, "expresses the unity between Christ and the Spirit by linking their ministries through a complete and thus dual causal relationship."[41] Schlatter underlines that "liberation from our evil will" is equally rooted "in our portion *in Christ and in the Spirit.*"[42] There is then close economic cooperation as Jesus and the Spirit perform their work in us, and Schlatter sees clear evidence for this in the New Testament. "[T]he New Testament directs our view to God's Spirit," Schlatter posits, "so that we would know God's gift and Christ's work, and thereby grasp what our union with God comprises and what determines our relation with him."[43] Now what exactly is "Christ's work" in this context? Primarily, the work of Christ consists in the way he enables volitional union with God. The offer of volitional union with God is in fact the significant result of Jesus' efficacious work on the cross. Jesus Christ has come, Schlatter writes, so that "we want what God wants."[44] This is the Christocentric basis for our volitional union with God. Furthermore, Schlatter holds the view that Christ makes the Spirit the foundation of our cognition and volition. "[T]he dominion of Christ," Schlatter writes, "manifests itself in us as he grants us in a certain situation the good will. We thereby experience that we are surrounded by his presence and that *he makes his Spirit the foundation of our thinking and willing.*"[45] Hence, Schlatter speaks of the Spirit as the "architect of the good will" in us.[46] In this way, as the Spirit works within us, we experience a fundamental inner volitional change. Schlatter writes: "Jesus' gift comprises not only the attempt to shape the human being from the outside, but—and this is why Jesus spoke of the Spirit—[also] that human beings are gripped at the core of their personal life, at the core of their willing and thinking and thereby united with the divine thinking and willing."[47] Schlatter is eager to note that this volitional change empowers us to perform the ethical deed. He writes:

> When we really have been given the Spirit of God, it means possession, not merely poverty; this is power . . . freedom and life . . . As God's Spirit is the founder and mover of our inner life,

---

41. Schlatter, *Theology of the Apostles*, 268.
42. Schlatter, *Dogma*, 452 (emphasis added).
43. Schlatter, "Noch ein Wort," 49–50.
44. Schlatter, "Dienst des Christen," 25.
45. Schlatter, *Dogma*, 467 (emphasis mine).
46. Ibid., 452.
47. Schlatter, *Hülfe in Bibelnot*, 12.

so there arises through him faith, but also love, assurance, and deed, happiness in God, but also duty and vocation.[48]

We return to this significant aspect of ethical empowerment later. For now, we note that the Father grants volitional union through the work of Christ and the Spirit, and in such way that we are empowered from within "to will and to work for his good pleasure" (Phil 2:13).

Having established the Trinitarian basis for volitional union, some further questions demand answers, such as: How exactly does Schlatter conceive of the interplay between Trinitarian action and our human standpoint with a view to our volitional union with God? That is, in what way does the divine unifying action affect anthropology? Do we experience a foundational change in our human nature in the process? The next section deals with these significant issues.

ORGANIC VOLITIONAL UNION

Put briefly, Schlatter presents a model of organic volitional union where divine action and human response work in harmony. To explore this idea in more detail, first, we attend to Schlatter's general assumption of a polarity of passivity and activity on our side as we receive God's grace of volitional union with him. Secondly, we address Schlatter's view of *unified grace*, which entails that God's grace is not bestowed on us in successive portions, as it were, but in a holistic way. This brings us thirdly, to a closer examination of how volitional union relates to our human psychology, and fourthly, of how it ties in with our service to God (*Gottesdienst*).

Grace works Calming and Moving

To begin with, Adolf Schlatter is convinced that our volitional union with God works in an organic, harmonious way. Schlatter clearly rejects any modes of volitional union with God where the Triune action is everything and the human being, as he put it, "disappears."[49] Schlatter complains that it was the Reformers in particular who focused primarily on God as the giver of grace while its recipients remained passive supporting actors on the stage of the theatre of God.[50] In this framework, he argues, "[t]he divine action is

48. Schlatter, "Noch ein Wort," 49.
49. Schlatter, "Dienst des Christen," 65.
50. Ibid., 5. He laments that "their gaze is fixed on God as the giver of grace, on Christ, on God, on what he does for us; the picture of the recipient remains rather

presented as the annihilation of the human action. . . . God does everything by himself and the glory of his revelation is supposed to consist in the fact that the human being dissolves through it to nothing."[51] One ought to point out in this context that Schlatter's train of thought does not lead to semi-Pelagianism. In regards to union with Christ, the question is not whether we, in any way, *contribute* to God's gracious work—we clearly do not—instead, the question is how we *respond* to the grace we receive. And here, we respond with what one could call passive activity, since God's grace works in us both calming and moving.[52] Benjamin Schliesser observes that for Schlatter, "the receptive nature of faith . . . is not to be equated with quietism or tranquility. . . . Here Schlatter seeks to correct a misunderstanding of Reformation theology that originated—in Schlatter's perception—already in Luther's own faith: the one-sided emphasis on the calming, salvation-giving function of faith, which does not release adequately its active component."[53]

Schlatter thus proposes a dialectical understanding of passivity *and* activity in the believer, who not only receives passively but also acts according to the grace given to her. In his "Dienst des Christen," Schlatter explains:

> The gaze upon God and his grace works in our volition both calming and moving; calming, as it satisfies our quest, for in God's grace, gift and deed lies everything that we need . . . yet, at the same time also moving, arousing our aspiration, because God's grace, gift and deed grants our will the goal and the power . . . and enables us to [accomplish] the deed. In that faith works both in equal measure calming and moving . . . lies the health of our Christian life.[54]

Faith, obviously, is central to volitional union and we will come back to this in due course. God's grace, then, always has both a passive (calming) and active (moving) impact on the Christian. To use a New Testament picture, and most fittingly a truly organic one, the branches in John 15:1–5 rest passively (but not lifelessly) in the vine; the branches, as it were, actively abide in it, hanging through a "living bond" (*mit lebendigem Band*) on the vine, and only in this way producing much fruit.[55] Only when they "[t]ake from him [Jesus] their thinking and willing will their service to humanity and their

---

obscure."

51. Schlatter, "Dienst des Christen," 64–65.
52. Ibid., 4.
53. Schliesser, *Abraham's Faith in Romans 4*, 15.
54. Schlatter, "Dienst des Christen," 4.
55. Schlatter, *Erläuterungen zum Neuen Testament*, 3:203.

work in this world become a powerful blessing," Schlatter notes.[56] With his emphasis on the living and activating effect of divine grace, Schlatter supplements what he considers the Reformation emphasis on passive, quietistic grace.[57] The Christian is neither only passive nor only active, but lives in the simultaneity of passivity in the reception and activity in the consummation of divine grace.[58] Schlatter argues that there is "no work of God that would render us passive, as it would then cease to be a work of grace. With a view to God's work, as his grace enters us, we are volitionally and thus also effectively involved."[59] The recipients of God's grace are thus "seriously recipients" as they are moved towards vitality. In Schlatter's words:

> Grace seeks and creates the recipient and thereby puts us into passivity; yet, it makes us seriously recipients, so that it holds us, endues us and moves us into vitality. There is therefore no reception of the divine gift where this gift has not previously caused its activity within us, nor is there an activity that has not before itself as its foundation, and behind itself as its fruit and its goal, the reception of the divine gift.[60]

In Schlatter's view, contemporary theology and church were weakened by the latent dualism of passive faith and active works. In contrast, Schlatter suggests a balanced view of our Christian life that displays a simultaneity of passive reception of faith *and* active performance of the concrete volitional act.[61] Hence, it is "impossible," writes Schlatter, "that one could regard oneself only as the recipient of grace but not at the same time as its instrument."[62]

---

56. Ibid.
57. Schlatter, "Dienst des Christen," 65.
58. Schlatter, "Noch ein Wort," 54.
59. Schlatter, *Rückblick*, 109.
60. Schlatter, "Noch ein Wort," 55.
61. Schlatter refers to the "indissoluble relation between reception and action, between faith and work." Schlatter, "Noch ein Wort," 57. One observes a significant parallel to Schleiermacher here, who writes: "The activity of the self [*Selbstthätigkeit*] in [one's] communion of life with Christ thus begins immediately, and without interval, when one is received into it; thus one could say that conversion is nothing other than the evocation of the self's activity which is united with Christ, that is, lively receptivity gives way to lively self-activity [*die lebendige Empfänglichkeit geht über in belebte Selbstthätigkeit*]." Schleiermacher, *Glaubenslehre*, §108, 2:190.
62. Schlatter, "Dienst des Christen," 58–59.

Unified Grace: Justification and Sanctification

At this point one wonders whether Schlatter's reading does justice to the theological tradition. It is questionable whether he was entirely correct in his judgment that the human being was in danger of "dissolving" into passivity in the Reformers. By contrast, Schlatter's proposal of grace as "calming" *and* "moving" in fact reveals significant parallels to John Calvin's account of the *duplex gratia* (twofold grace) of justification and sanctification.[63] Calvin, for instance, understands sanctification as a "grateful fulfilment of the law of love, empowered by the life-giving Spirit."[64] According to Calvin, writes Julie Canlis, "God's life is not just passively received but brings with it an active, wholly pneumatological 'capacity.'"[65] At least in Calvin's framework of union with Christ, it seems, the human being is depicted less passively than Schlatter perhaps assumed. Be that as it may, one observes in Schlatter the clear intention to highlight the wholeness of God's grace. This reflects again Schlatter's overall motif of unity and his aversion to anything remotely associated with dualisms. Regarding the traditional distinction between justification and sanctification, then, Schlatter remarks that "[t]he dissection of grace into two succeeding gifts is not Pauline."[66] Referring to the Apostle Paul's remarks in 1 Corinthians 1:30, "He [God] is the source of your life in Christ Jesus, whom God made our wisdom and our righteousness and sanctification and redemption," Schlatter writes: "The liberation from guilt, which arose from the reprehensibility of our desires, through the granting of righteousness [*Rechtbeschaffenheit*] . . . and the removal of our separation from God through the bestowal of fellowship with him . . . are both received through the same experience."[67]

The nub of the issue for Schlatter was to steer clear of a "lifeless," artificial understanding of justification, and instead relate it closely to sanctification, as the two form one experiential entity of grace. While justification certainly includes a forensic aspect (as Schlatter claims against his teacher Beck, see chapter 2), Schlatter argues that the whole point of justification is *relation*, namely reconciliation with the divine judge. For Schlatter, then, justification aims at our communion with God.[68] In fact, "connectedness with God" (*Verbundenheit mit Gott*) is according to Schlatter the greatest

---

63. See Calvin, *Institutes*, 3.11.1.
64. Billings, *Calvin, Participation, and the Gift*, 15–16.
65. Canlis, *Calvin's Ladder*, 228.
66. Schlatter, *Gottes Gerechtigkeit*, 221–22.
67. Schlatter, *Paulus der Bote Jesu*, 97.
68. See Rieger, *Schlatters Rechtfertigungslehre*, 412.

gift brought about by justification.[69] He explains: "Since God unites himself completely with the one he declares to be righteous, the human being receives, together with the justification awarded him by God's affirmation of his conduct, the full communion with God, his entire love and gift."[70]

While this might be a creative recasting of the classic doctrines, Schlatter, and this is noteworthy, is in fact consistent within his own paradigm. As discussed in our previous section on the thinking-act (chapter 5), Schlatter sees a close unity between the person and work of Jesus Christ, from which follows that there is, likewise, an inseparable bond between our participation in Christ's own righteousness by faith in justification and in his righteousness present within us through his Spirit in sanctification. Sanctification is not an artificial *plus* but already enveloped, as it were, in the gift of justification. "A saint is nothing else than a justified [person]" (*Ein Heiliger ist nicht mehr als ein Gerechter*), Schlatter insists.[71] From this perspective, it is comprehensible that Schlatter does not find the idea of an *ordo salutis* very helpful. However, space does not allow us to offer a more detailed account of Schlatter's highly creative understanding of justification and sanctification.[72] Suffice to note Schlatter's distinct emphasis on relationality and unity when it comes to the grace which works both calming and moving. Yet how exactly does Schlatter apply the calming and moving effects of grace to our volitional union with God? We shall next discuss Schlatter's suggestion of the organic, harmonious way in which God's grace transforms us as human beings in volitional union.

Human Psychology, the Spirit, and Organic Union

Having already pointed to the crucial involvement of the Holy Spirit in our volitional union with God in Schlatter's framework, we now return to pneumatology. Given the special way the Spirit acts within us, Schlatter's argument goes, our human will is neither destroyed nor neglected, but organically united with God's will, through faith. How exactly does Schlatter

---

69. Schlatter, *Theologie der Apostel*, 301, 313.

70. Ibid., 300. Consider also the following quote: "Paul's juxtaposition of justification and reconciliation with God's sanctifying work does not suggest that he conceived of the divine gift as divided in parts, such as that justification made help possible without actually granting it, so that it required sanctification as the second exercise of divine grace in order to make that grace effective. Paul sees in God's justifying verdict that divine will that removes everything that separates us from God and grants as our aim everything that is assigned to us." *Theology of the Apostles*, 248.

71. Schlatter, *Theologie der Apostel*, 328.

72. We refer to Rieger's treatment in *Schlatters Rechtfertigungslehre*, 150–74.

develop this thought in detail? First of all, Schlatter is keen to take our human nature seriously, because he feels that God takes it seriously.[73] In agreement with Aquinas and Calvin, Schlatter is convinced that God's grace does not destroy but fulfils our human nature, and on this basis he suggests an organic understanding of our volitional union with God.[74] He is keen to stress that "this new *life*" is not simply "*planted in us* apart from our will."[75] God does not perform his good work in us artificially, miraculously bypassing our human volition, which would necessarily lead to a "life without a subject."[76] Such a view, says Schlatter, neither takes our natural condition of life seriously nor displays the biblical data correctly.[77]

By contrast, Schlatter assumes that volitional union happens in such a way that God does not annihilate but rather sanctifies what he has created. That means, God neither overpowers nor replaces the human will. Rather, God puts his gift "into our thinking and willing" in such a way that it does not violate our human psychology.[78] With "gift," Schlatter is here obviously referring to the Holy Spirit's involvement in our union of will with God as introduced earlier. Schlatter affirms that the Apostle Paul "does not conceive of the Spirit as a power that substitutes, overcomes, or makes the will of human beings superfluous by force. The Spirit does not assault the individual."[79] Instead, the Holy Spirit establishes our responsibility in making the conscious volitional decision possible.[80] "The activity of the Spirit engages our personal life in its unity; thus it does not suppress or substitute our natural capacities, but the Spirit preserves, wills and uses the whole range of our natural vitality."[81] Volitional union, then, does not happen automatically (*wie von selbst*),[82] without or even against our human will. Schlatter is

73. Schlatter, *Gründe der christlichen Gewißheit*, 127.

74. According to J. Todd Billings, Calvin thus holds the view that "grace fulfils rather than destroys human nature." Billings, *Calvin, Participation, and the Gift*, 17. Calvin seems to have adopted this dictum from Thomas Aquinas, see his *Summa Theologica* I, Q. 1, Art. 8.

75. Schlatter, "Noch ein Wort," 67 (emphasis original).

76. Ibid.

77. Ibid., 80.

78. Schlatter, *Glaube im Neuen Testament*, 191. It seems that Schlatter has Calvin on his side here, for Calvin writes: "I say the will is abolished, but not in so far as it is will, for in conversion everything essential to our original nature remains: I also say, that it is created anew, not because the will then begins to exist, but because it is turned from evil to good." Calvin, *Institutes*, 3.3.6.

79. Schlatter, *Jesus und Paulus*, 78.

80. Ibid., 78–79.

81. Schlatter, *Dogma*, 348.

82. Schlatter, "Noch ein Wort," 64.

emphatic that volitional union with God is not about the passive acknowledgement of a foreign, divine will working through us, but, on the contrary, about an existential affirmation, a positive embrace of God's will through faith. Faith, as indicated earlier, is central in volitional union with God, for we unite our will with God's will *through faith in Jesus Christ*. Here, Schlatter's dialectic of passivity and activity also applies. That is, whilst Schlatter affirms that faith is truly "an act of the subject,"[83] it is also—as faith is a gift of God—a "receptive act" (*rezeptives Verhalten*).[84] The Father in granting faith draws us to his Son, and the Son brings us to the Father, through the Holy Spirit.[85] "God's pulling, which creates faith," Schlatter clarifies, "must not be considered a physical process but a spiritual act whereby the conscious, free movements of [our] will are not repressed but created."[86]

One notices again Schlatter's eagerness to bring out the harmonious Trinitarian divine activity in respect of our organic volitional union with God. The Father draws, the Son mediates and the Spirit forms the new person with a view to "cognition, volition and action" (*im Erkennen, im Wollen, im Wirken*).[87] Again, note that this divine activity does not meet the believer's resistance. Instead, the Spirit's work is a welcome divine activity due to the Father's preparatory work of drawing the believer to himself through his Son. In an organic, harmonious way, then, the Spirit "works in the human being in that he creates the good volition, [yet] not by breaking the psychological principles; the whole human organization of our inner life remains [intact]."[88] The believer thus unites her will with the divine will, precisely in such a way that the divine will is organically assimilated as her own.[89] Schlatter explains:

> [T]he purpose of grace were not fully recognized when its recipient remains insignificant in the shadow, as if grace did not elevate us into the individual, free vitality, as if it not wanted, elected, loved and grasped by us. Our volition is given to us in a manner such that it is *our* volition; this volition is therefore established in our consciousness as the one to be contemplated

---

83. Ibid., 57.
84. Schlatter, *Glaube im Neuen Testament*, 218.
85. Ibid, 207; see also *Ruf Jesu*, 25–27.
86. Schlatter, *Glaube im Neuen Testament*, 207.
87. Schlatter, *Jesus und Paulus*, 77.
88. Ibid., 78.
89. See ibid., 44; "Noch ein Wort," 55–57.

and chosen as the one with which we can, may and should unite ourselves, with our own being and possession.[90]

Schlatter is keen to point out that our human psychology is not undermined by our volitional union with God. He writes: "We think, feel and want formally in the same manner as in every other aspect of life. Through the working of the Holy Spirit there does not arise a special psychology, but with the same cognitive and volitional capacities we now think and will another content; now, we think of God and we desire not egoistically, but [we desire to] love him."[91] Understood in this way, Schlatter argues, we do not have to fear a loss of control, as if our volitional capacity is delegated to a higher authority and then out of our reach. This is a dualistic misunderstanding that does not represent the teaching of the New Testament. The Apostle Paul's exhortation, "work out your own salvation with fear and trembling, for it is God who works in you, both to will and to work for his good pleasure" (Phil 2:12–13), has thus often been misunderstood, Schlatter claims. It is a sentence that has been regarded as if the Apostle "is speaking rubbish here," that is, as if this divine volitional activity in us were "self-destructive."[92] On the contrary, Schlatter clarifies:

> But when it is granted to us to believe in God, we no longer see in God the destroyer of our lives, and we no longer see in his creative power the defiler of our wills. Through faith in God we have recognized in Christ the love of God. Love gives not just things, not just fate, not just assistance that helps us from the outside, but much more: love gives his Spirit, the one who awakens our thinking and willing, the one through whom his love is poured out into our hearts. In this way we remain in fellowship with God, a fellowship through which God will be the "Savior"—the one who works the salvation he calls us to work out.[93]

Overall, then, through our organic volitional union with God there are no qualitative features added to our humanity (*Menschsein*), rather we are being transformed as God's own creatures.[94] "The Spirit effectively grasps our

90. Schlatter, "Dienst des Christen," 28 (emphasis original).
91. Schlatter, "Noch ein Wort," 80; see also *Jesus und Paulus*, 78; "Dienst des Christen," 27–28.
92. Schlatter, *Do We Know Jesus*, 511.
93. Ibid., 512.
94. Schlatter writes: "What Jesus grants us causes the unity, which is implanted as a law in our personal life-act [*Lebensakt*], to persist.... What Jesus grants us is not an addition to our being human [*menschlichen Wesen*] and does not lie alongside our

personal life in its unity; therefore, it neither inhibits our natural functions nor becomes a substitute for it, rather the Spirit sustains, wills and uses the whole scope of our natural vitality."[95] Hence, Schlatter claims, "Someone who is led by the Spirit thinks differently, but not with a different logic, or with a different mental mechanism."[96]

Evidently, Schlatter is eager to put forward a model of volitional union with God that shows a distinct appreciation of creatureliness (*Geschöpftsein*).[97] As God's creation, fallen humans still image God, and his divine action in volitional union seems, from Schlatter's perspective, to work towards a healing transformation (instead of a total re-creation) of our natural capacities. In this regard, Schlatter feels, the Reformers perhaps introduced too broad an understanding of total depravity. Of course, with a view to salvation, we owe everything to God: "Our repentance is God's victory over our antipathy against him," Schlatter admits.[98] Still, all is not lost, the human being has not lost its ontology, but it remains God's image and instrument. For Schlatter, volitional union with God is thus not an elimination of human life but the realization of true human life within our redeemed personhood. "Jesus," Schlatter concludes, "addresses the human being, he mobilizes the capacities that are available to him; it is with human thinking that we ought to think God's will; it is with the human will that we ought to obey; we do not arrive at a superanatural religion, but at a religion that puts the human being into God's service [*Dienst Gottes*]."[99] This leads us our fourth point, namely to the ultimate goal of organic volitional union with God: service to God (*Gottes-Dienst*).[100]

Organic Union and *Gottesdienst*

As already mentioned, Schlatter sees in our service to God the natural outworking of our volitional union with Christ; those who have united their wills with God's will live to his glory. "Our role" as human beings, Schlatter claims, "is the service of God" (*Unsere Funktion ist Dienst Gottes*).[101] This service of God, however, is not a "lazy piety" but an energetic volitional

---

human capacity and calling." "Briefe über das Dogma," 41–42.
95. Schlatter, *Dogma*, 348.
96. Ibid., 350.
97. See Bailer, *Das systematische Prinzip*, 142–46.
98. Schlatter, "Dienst des Christen," 22.
99. Schlatter, *Jesus und Paulus*, 76.
100. Schlatter, "Dienst des Christen," 3.
101. Schlatter, *Ethik*, 124; see also *Dogma*, 519.

activity which finds expression in active love of God and neighbor.[102] "This is why God's work has only happened in us," writes Schlatter, "when we are moved to perform the deed; God's love has not reached its goal until we are enabled to love."[103] For those who enjoy volitional union with God the following applies: "[E]very act is worked by the Spirit, who turns us with our consciousness and our volition towards God, and with this insight we walk on the same path as the Apostle, who described love as spiritual in the highest possible sense, precisely because with love, everything that is in us thinking, willing, acting receives its determination from God."[104]

In the end, love of God is according to Schlatter the apex of our volitional union with him. It is the result of the Triune action in us. We are invited through our union with God into the Triune mutual love and glorification. More precisely, we mirror to an extent Jesus Christ, who has gone before us in his service of God and service to humanity, as we have seen earlier in the chapter on the thinking-act. Hence, through our union with Christ, who loved the Father as the obedient Son (Jesus' *Gottesdienst*) and who also loved humanity as the Christ (Jesus' *Menschendienst*), we are likewise enabled to love God and neighbor. Only in this way will we fulfil the highest command, namely living to the glory of God and thus performing true *Gottesdienst*. This happens organically and practically, Schlatter is eager to add, with our own sanctified will, in concrete history and in the concrete situations and relations in which we find ourselves in our life-act. "God's grace sustains us at our place in history; it does not give us any perfections according to our wishful thinking, but the ability to perform, at the place where we are, what is now good and right before God."[105] Schlatter thus speaks of "the glory of divine grace that makes us an instrument of God with a free movement of our knowledge and love at the place that is assigned to us."[106] Schlatter's model of organic volitional union culminates in the assumption that we actively participate in God's creative action. Through our union with Christ we organically share in the divine creative activity and we are thereby elevated to a new degree of fruitfulness. "[T]he one who has become obedient to God by faith," writes Schlatter, "and for whom Christ has become Lord, produces works in a new dimension; and, compared with the natural condition, he does so to an incomparably greater degree because

---

102. Schlatter, *Dogma*, 468.
103. Schlatter, "Dienst des Christen," 56.
104. Schlatter, "Noch ein Wort," 81.
105. Schlatter, *Dogma*, 471, 473–74.
106. Schlatter, *Erlebtes*, 117–18; see also *Ethik*, 87.

he now shares in the divine activity."[107] Schlatter's version of participation, then, has a clear practical, ethical impetus.

In terms of the question of *theosis* (deification), Schlatter thus argues that attempts that focus on our volitional-ethical union with God are more promising than those which involve speculations about our essential union with him. The crucial factor is not a share in God's essence, but a participation in his action through volitional union. On the whole, then, Adolf Schlatter's perspective of organic volitional union with God is a blueprint for an active, relational Christian ethics of love of God and of neighbor that is free from any dualist notions but rather suggests a harmonious view of divine action and human response. Having said that, one must not forget Schlatter's communal emphasis highlighted earlier. As we are saved not as individuals but as members of the community, part of the body of Christ, so too we glorify God as members of the community. "The congregation was established as the cooperative [*Genossenschaft*] which performs, conjointly, the will of God."[108] The ethical imperative is rooted in "the being of the congregation" (*im Sein der Gemeinde*).[109] This, he remarks, is the "triumph of Paul's ethics."[110] United with God through volitional union with him, we glorify him by acting according to what he makes us to be as members of the new community of faith.

EXPRESSIVE REALISM AND UNION WITH CHRIST

It is now time to pause and consider Schlatter's overall picture of our union with Jesus Christ in the life-act. At the present stage, the picture might perhaps remind us more of an abstract painting than of an accurate drawing. Schlatter's sketch of our union with Christ in the life-act, it seems, conveys a complexity of different shapes, sizes and colors: there is Christology, pneumatology, and soteriology, not forgetting, a distinct appreciation of anthropology; we have also mentioned justification, sanctification, active volition and ethics. One wonders whether Schlatter is able to weave all these threads together to a "unified whole," as he time and again describes his intention. Does Schlatter actually arrive at a harmonious and holistic account of our union with Christ?

It might be promising in this regard to draw an analogy between the visual arts and Schlatter's theology. (We have mentioned earlier a similarity

107. Schlatter, *Romans*, 51.
108. Schlatter, *Hülfe in Bibelnot*, 13.
109. Schlatter, *Glaube im Neuen Testament*, 380.
110. Ibid.

between Vincent van Gogh's expressionist style and Schlatter's theological method). In fact, the modernist movement of expressionism serves particularly well as a comparison for Schlatter's theology of union with Christ. For one, there is a clear modernist streak in Schlatter's theology, mirrored in his effort to balance faithfulness to the theological tradition with the intention to correct what he considered the shortcomings of the same. Bruce L. McCormack describes modern theologians as those who tried to "defend and protect the received orthodoxies of the past against erosion and took up the more fundamental challenge of asking how the theological values resident in those orthodoxies might be given an altogether new expression, dressed out in new categories for reflection."[111] This clearly applies to Schlatter, who is particularly creative in dressing out "new categories for reflection." Yet how does his endeavor to offer a new expression of theological values, in particular with regard to union with Christ, look? In short, what would Schlatter's painting look like?

First of all, one has by now an inkling of how it would *not* look. Schlatter's is clearly not an impressionist work. His vision of our union with Christ is undoubtedly not tinted by a romantic, idealist notion of our mystical union with Christ.[112] While the union itself, of course, remains a mystery—Schlatter is happy to admit that—he feels that this has been sufficiently emphasized in the past. Thus, it is difficult to imagine the believer, in Schlatter's painting, standing at Monet's bridge of Giverny, gazing at the beautiful flowers, completely absorbed in the romantic, almost panentheistic experience of our union with Christ. One imagines Schlatter's technique involving swifter, more vivid brushstrokes, creating more movement in the whole scene. Hence, Schlatter's painting would perhaps be more at home in the exhibition hall of expressive realism, as his method represents a mixture of empirical observation and existential appropriation. Schlatter's work resembles a modern work of avant-garde, aiming to arrive at new forms of theological expression while staying true to the orthodox tradition. That is, Schlatter without doubt speaks, for instance, of the doctrines of justification and sanctification, yet he puts his own spin on these doctrines, emphasizing their unity and the activating aspect of God's creative grace. More specifically, in terms of our union with God, Schlatter puts into relief the work of Christ and of the Spirit, and he draws our attention to the organic way in which God unites us with himself. Through the Spirit's organic work in us

---

111. McCormack, "On 'Modernity,'" 3.

112. Schlatter writes: "Union with Jesus is not the result of a mystical experience; it is rather grounded in the outcome of Jesus' earthly life: his cross, resurrection, exaltation, and return. What the congregations possess, perform, and suffer is determined by Jesus' life and suffering." *Theology of the Apostles*, 53.

our human volition is not ruined but revitalized. We participate in God's divine agency as we are empowered with a new volitional ethical impetus to perform good deeds to the glory of God. Schlatter's picture then differs considerably from what Kant and neo-Kantian theology offers on its canvas. *Imitatio Christi* is not based on Kant's maxims or Christ's external moral example but on our experience of internal change through the Spirit. Schlatter writes:

> Because Jesus' commandments arise from what he is for us, they are not difficult. If they approach us solely from the outside, they are not merely difficult; they are impossible. For they run counter to our nature. Yet now they are commandments of the One who moves us from within by his Word and Spirit, and therefore they are easy.[113]

One would also, surely, recognize the human being in Schlatter's picture. Even though it might not be in the center, it would also not fall out of the canvas, or "dissolve to nothing." Schlatter would be keen to draw not just one individual, but to depict persons in communion, since salvific union with Christ works only by the individual being part of the new community of faith.

Finally, stepping even nearer to the painting, an even closer examination reveals also some surreal elements in Schlatter's *œuvre*. Schlatter clearly draws out eschatological elements in our union with Christ. The new community, he argues, lives in eschatological hope, trusting in the "New Testament promise that the perfection of divine grace grants us, even in death and after death, connectedness with Christ [*Verbundenheit mit Christus*]."[114] Still, Schlatter could have perhaps offered a more elaborate treatment of eschatology in his *Dogma*, in particular with regard to our union with Christ. It is plausible to assume that Schlatter was here somewhat limited by the empirical-realist presupposition of his seeing-act. Schlatter, it seems, was slightly uncomfortable in making eschatological statements in his dogmatics. "Thoughts, which describe future things," he writes, "inevitably contain uncertainty."[115] Based on this truism, Schlatter perhaps feared his realist expressionism might devolve into abstract expressionism or even outright surrealism and he somewhat decides to leave it at that, perhaps a regrettable decision. There are obviously other elements in Schlatter's picture of our union with Jesus which are worthy of contemplation, yet space does not allow us to go into more detail here. In focusing on Schlatter's key emphasis,

---

113. Schlatter, *Do We Know Jesus*, 145.
114. Schlatter, *Dogma*, 541.
115. Ibid., 525.

namely the relational-volitional aspect of our union with Christ, no space at all has been given, for example, to Schlatter's view of regeneration or election in respect of our union of Christ, although Schlatter has much to offer here.[116] Moreover, we could have explored to a greater extent the concrete ramifications of our volitional union with Christ in everyday life. Acknowledging that our observations focused more on Schlatter's meta-ethic, we must rest content in referring to his *Ethik*, where he in fact exhibits a clear vision of how volitional union with Christ plays out in everyday life.[117]

CONCLUSION

Adolf Schlatter presents a creative account of organic volitional union with Christ that takes both human psychology and Trinitarian action seriously. In so doing, Schlatter offers a kaleidoscope of inter-related features; he speaks of the dialectic of receptivity and activity, he sees the divine grace as calming and moving, and the divine economic action as indivisible yet distinct. The main thrust of Schlatter's argument, it seems, is that God's grace moves us into *action*. Through organic volitional union with God we participate in his divine action in the world. Here, Schlatter's work is particularly relevant for us today. Today, our problem is probably not the predominance of a German pietistic quietism or asceticism. What we observe today is rather a global postmodern individualistic passivism that challenges the fabric of the church. In times of declining church membership, Schlatter's passionate plea for active ethics through organic volitional union with God is a wake-up call for theology and the church. The church as Schlatter envisages it, with Christ as its head and Lord, is an active church as it consists of members who possess a new will through union with Christ and thus act to the glory of God. A completion of the Reformation as Schlatter pictured it, is thus only possible with an active church that enjoys volitional union with its Creator. Schlatter once said that "[t]he church is being assessed by those who do not attend it, not on the basis of what the church *says*, but according to what it *does*."[118] If we were to take this call seriously today, Schlatter would indeed have succeeded in making a valuable contribution towards what he

---

116. See ibid., 460–66, 474–79.

117. In his "Christian Ethics," Schlatter covers a whole range of possible applications, suggesting how volitional union applies to marriage, family and the workplace, for instance (*Ethik*, 393–422). Also contemplating issues such as alcoholism, compulsive gambling, and even legal protection of sex workers, Schlatter's ethics remains a fresh and timeless work today (ibid., 366–69).

118. Schlatter, "Dienstpflicht des Christen," 11 (emphasis added).

called a completion of the Reformation. With his own life, an active life dedicated to theology, the church and society, Adolf Schlatter exemplified how organic volitional union with Jesus Christ to the glory of God and the good of humanity can indeed, by God's grace, be realized in one's life.

Epilogue
Christology after Schlatter

THIS STUDY SET OUT to explore both the shape and the cogency of Adolf Schlatter's Christology. In so doing, we have also paid attention to the context of Schlatter's life, since we believe that theology and biography are intimately connected. In the work's first part, we thus traced the *Sitz im Leben* of Schlatter's relational motif while its distinct dogmatic impetus was examined in the second part.

Schlatter's characteristic life-long focus on Christology is certainly to a great degree rooted in his family's Christocentric piety. Given his grandmother Anna's heritage and his parents' example, it is certainly not surprising to encounter Schlatter as someone for whom personal union with Christ was pivotal, transcending confessional barriers. This Christocentric trajectory allowed Schlatter to adopt a rather independent, eclectic position that was somewhat in between, that is, neither explicitly positive-orthodox nor obviously liberal. At one point, we made the bold claim that Schlatter's relational Christology is seminal for our theological conversation today and it is now time to assess briefly whether this hypothesis is correct. Christoph Schwöbel recently expressed the following grievance:

> Modern Christology seems to be increasingly unable to conceive and to conceptualize the unity of the person of Christ and seems to be left with the fragments of the historical Jesus, the Christ of faith and the Son of God of christological Dogma. Therefore modern christological reflection seems mainly concerned with finding ways of integrating the fragments in a new synthesis, of joining together what has been put asunder.[1]

This study has presented Adolf Schlatter as a theologian who was strongly committed to joining together what has been put asunder. Schlatter's

1. Schwöbel, "Christology and Trinitarian Thought," 119.

Christology reveals a clear "impetus towards the whole" (*Richtung auf das Ganze*), as he seeks to offer a holistic representation of Jesus Christ based on the New Testament narrative. Returning to our test criteria outlined earlier, we conclude that Schlatter's christological account indeed adequately integrates the person and work of Jesus Christ, sufficiently describes the relation between the humanity and the divinity in him, offers a substantial explanation for the problem of God-forsakenness, and approaches these issues from a clear Trinitarian perspective. We arrive at this assessment by the following route: To begin with, the results of this investigation illustrate that Schlatter presents a unified picture of Jesus Christ where person and work are closely integrated. We have observed how Schlatter opposed any influx into theology of German idealism, which, in his view, resulted in a limited account of Jesus Christ, in which his humanity was stressed at the expense of his divinity. Over against any Ritschlian tendencies to separate Jesus' vocation (*Beruf*) from his duty (*Pflicht*), or any attempts to distinguish between a Jesus of history and a Christ of faith, Schlatter introduces a unified account of the Son of God who stands in perfect relation to God and to humanity. Proceeding in this way, this study has also found that Schlatter suggests a creative, yet robust account of the unity of Christ's divinity and humanity. Ascribing only limited explanatory power to the classic two-natures exposition, Schlatter moves—based on his New Testament seeing-act—towards a relational understanding of Jesus Christ which allows him to make inferences concerning Christ's essence from his relations. While subscribing to the Symbol of Chalcedon, Schlatter offers new avenues of thinking about the unity of the divine and the human in Jesus Christ. The unique feature of his account is the notion of Jesus in double communion, namely both with the Father and with us. Jesus' volitional union with the Father, through the Holy Spirit finds its expression in perfect obedience and submission against the backdrop of concrete history. While this clearly underlines Jesus' humanity, it does not jeopardize his divinity. On the contrary, and this is crucial for Schlatter, Jesus' submissive obedience actually reveals his divinity. Since the intra-Trinitarian relationship is characterized by love, there is no divine identity-loss on the part of the Son. The polarity of distinction in unity is not only tolerated, but, in fact, central to Jesus' being and status as the divine Son. Schlatter shows how it is possible to construct a coherent Christology based on a narrative empirical method that makes a strong case for Jesus' humanity, while safeguarding his divinity and the unity of both natures in the person of Jesus Christ.

The cross is for Schlatter the ultimate revelation of Jesus' divinity, for here Jesus demonstrates his divinity by remaining in fellowship with the Father, mediated by the Holy Spirit, even in the midst of God-forsakenness.

Schlatter carefully develops a model of fellowship in forsakenness by arguing that even in the depths of God-forsakenness on the cross there is still something like fellowship through the divine mutual exchange of gifts in love: The Son gives himself as a gift to the Father and the Father responds by handing the new community of faith to the Son. Schlatter's language of relation and volition is promising for future theological christological exploration of the person and work of Jesus Christ, and one must applaud his successful attempt to move beyond a simple two-natures approach towards a relational Trinitarian understanding of Jesus' being in action on the cross. It is specifically Schlatter's creative move to infer essence from relation that presents a significant addition to traditional, more substance-focused, accounts. This unique *modus operandi* allows him to open a new window into christological research. While suggesting novel ways of speaking about God creatively and intelligibly, Schlatter still remains faithful to the New Testament narrative. A group of feminist theologians recently encouraged the development of "relational theologies in the twenty-first century."[2] For a successful pursuit of this goal theological scholarship ought not to ignore Schlatter's profound contribution with a special focus on his relational motif. It is a particularly promising endeavor to bring Schlatter into conversation with the proponents of similar relational approaches, such as those of Christoph Schwöbel (*Gott in Beziehung*) and John Zizioulas (*Being as Communion*), for example. Future investigations could also pay attention to the intriguing parallels between Schlatter's program and Jürgen Moltmann's *theologia crucis*. It would be fruitful to assess more closely the ways in which Moltmann, while adopting the Schlatterian relational-volitional vocabulary, might in fact abandon central premises dear to the latter (such as the Son's filial obedience and subordination in love and the distinction between the immanent and the economic Trinity). In this respect, a closer comparison of their views on divine impassibility also seems promising.

However, as we have seen throughout this work, we would not do justice to Schlatter if we remembered him simply in terms of his contribution to our christological seeing-act or thinking-act. It thus seems appropriate to close this work on a Schlatterian note by pointing to the life-act (*Lebensakt*), which was so crucial for Schlatter. In our view, it is particularly noteworthy how Schlatter manages to arrive at both an existential and an ecclesial application of his Christology. That means, for Schlatter, that union with Christ is on the one hand obviously designed for us as individual persons. God grants us personally in our own life-act *Anschluss an Jesus* by faith. In this sense, Schlatter surely aims at the center of the whole plan of creation and

---

2. Isherwood and Bellchambers, eds., *Through Us, With Us, In Us*.

redemption, as we humans were made for a relationship with God, one that is consummated and perfected in Jesus Christ. Still, and this is Schlatter's important reminder for us today: God not only connects us with himself but also with *one another*. Horizontal oneness at the level of the community represents an analogue to the Trinitarian oneness. We enjoy harmonious oneness by participating in the Trinity's oneness. It is here that Schlatter's Christology reveals its powerful ecumenical potential, for Schlatter's Christology is certainly a Christology of and for the church.

Bibliography

Althaus, Paul. "Adolf Schlatters Gabe an die systematische Theologie." In *Adolf Schlatter: Gedächtnisheft der Deutschen Theologie*, 28–35. Stuttgart: W. Kohlhammer, 1938.
———. "Adolf Schlatters Verhältnis zur Theologie Luthers." *Zeitschrift für Systematische Theologie* 22.3 (1953) 245–56.
———. "Adolf Schlatters Wort an die heutige Theologie. Gedenkrede zur zehnten Wiederkehr seines Todestages gehalten in der Stiftskirche zu Tübingen am 9. Mai 1948." *Zeitschrift für Systematische Theologie* 21 (1950/52) 95–109.
———. *Theologische Aufsätze*. Vol. 1. Gütersloh: Bertelsmann, 1929.
Ameriks, Karl. "Introduction: Interpreting German Idealism." In *The Cambridge Companion to German Idealism*, edited by Karl Ameriks, 1–17. Cambridge: Cambridge University Press, 2000.
Augustine. *On the Trinity: Books 8–15*. Edited by Gareth B. Matthews, translated by Stephen McKenna. Cambridge: Cambridge University Press, 2002.
Axt-Piscalar, Christine. "Liberal Theology in Germany." In *The Blackwell Companion to Nineteenth-Century Theology*, edited by David Fergusson, 468–85. Chichester: Wiley-Blackwell, 2010.
Baader, Franz von. *Sämtliche Werke. Systematisch geordnete, durch reiche Erläuterungen von der Hand des Verfassers bedeutend vermehrte, vollständige Ausgabe der gedruckten Schriften samt Nachlaß, Biographie und Briefwechsel*, 16 vols., edited by F. Hoffmann et al. Leipzig: Verlag des literarischen Instituts, 1851–60.
Bailer, Albert. *Das systematische Prinzip in der Theologie Adolf Schlatters*. Stuttgart: Calwer, 1968.
Baird, William. *History of New Testament Research*. Vol. 2, *From Jonathan Edwards to Rudolf Bultmann*. Minneapolis: Fortress, 2003.
Barth, Karl. *Die Auferstehung der Toten: Eine akademische Vorlesung über 1. Korinther 15*. München: Christian Kaiser, 1924.
———. *The Epistle to the Romans*. Translated by Edwyn C. Hoskyns. London: Oxford University Press, 1933.
———. "Interview von H. A. Fischer-Barnicol, Südwestfunk (5.5.1964)." In *Karl Barth Gesamtausgabe 28 (Gespräche 1964–1968)*, edited by Eberhard Busch, 131–66. Zürich: Theologischer Verlag, 1997.
———. *Der Römerbrief (Zweite Fassung, 1922)*. In *Karl Barth Gesamtausgabe 47*, edited by Cornelis van der Kooi and Katja Tolstaja. Zürich: Theologischer Verlag, 2010.

Bibliography

———. "Das Wort in der Theologie von Schleiermacher bis Ritschl, 1927." In *Karl Barth Gesamtausgabe 24 (Vorträge und kleinere Arbeiten 1925-1930)*, edited by Hermann Schmidt, 183–214. Zürich: Theologischer Verlag, 1994.

———. "X. christliche Studentenkonferenz in Aarau, 1906." In Karl Barth Gesamtausgabe 21 (*Vorträge und kleinere Arbeiten 1905-1909*), edited by H. Helms, et al., 120–25. Zürich: Theologischer Verlag, 1992.

Barth, Karl, and Eduard Thurneysen. *Karl Barth-Eduard Thurneysen, Briefwechsel 1913–1921*. Vol. 1–2. Edited by Eduard Thurneysen. Zürich: Theologischer Verlag, 1973.

Barth, Karl, and Rudolf Bultmann. *Karl Barth-Rudolf Bultmann, Briefwechsel 1911–1966*. 2nd ed. Edited by Bernd Jaspert. Zürich: Theologischer Verlag, 1994.

Bauer, Walter. Review of *Die Geschichte des Christus*, by Adolf Schlatter. *Theologische Literaturzeitung* 48 (1923) 77–80.

Bavinck, Herman. *The Certainty of Faith*. Translated by Harry der Nederlanden. St. Catharines, Ontario: Paideia, 1980.

———. *The Philosophy of Revelation: The Stone Lectures for 1908-1909*. London: Longmans, Green and Co., 1909.

———. *Reformed Dogmatics*. Vol. 1, *Prolegomena*. Edited by John Bolt and translated by John Vriend. Grand Rapids: Baker Academic, 2003.

Bayly, Christopher Alan. *The Birth of the Modern World 1780–1914: Global Connections and Comparisons*. Oxford: Blackwell, 2004.

Beck, Johann Tobias. *Die christliche Liebeslehre. Erste Abtheilung*. Stuttgart: J. F. Steinkopf, 1872.

———. *Einleitung in das System der Christlichen Lehre, oder, propädeutische Entwicklung der christlichen Lehr-Wissenschaft: ein Versuch*. Stuttgart: C. Belser, 1838.

Beintker, Michael. "Johann Tobias Beck und die neuere evangelische Theologie." *Zeitschrift für Theologie und Kirche* 102 (2005) 226–45.

Bender, Julius, et al. *Vom Dienst an Theologie und Kirche: Festgabe für Adolf Schlatter zum 75. Geburtstag, 16. August 1927*. Berlin: Furche, 1927.

Benrath, Gustav Adolf. "Die Erweckung innerhalb der deutschen Landeskirchen 1815–1888: Ein Überblick." In *Der Pietismus im neunzehnten und zwanzigsten Jahrhundert*, edited by Ulrich Gäbler, 150–271. Vol. 3 of *Geschichte des Pietismus*, edited by Martin Brecht, et al. Göttingen: Vandenhoeck & Ruprecht, 2000.

Beyreuther, Erich. "Christentumsgesellschaft." In *Religion in Geschichte und Gegenwart*. 3rd ed., vol. 1, edited by Kurt Galling, 1729–30. Tübingen: Mohr (Paul Siebeck), 1957.

———. "Erweckung." In *Religion in Geschichte und Gegenwart*. 3rd ed., vol. 2, edited by Kurt Galling, 621–29. Tübingen: Mohr (Paul Siebeck), 1958.

Biedermann, Alois Emanuel. *Christliche Dogmatik*. Vol. 1. Reprint, 1869. Berlin: Reimer, 1884.

Billings, J. Todd. *Calvin, Participation, and the Gift: The Activity of Believers in Union with Christ*. Oxford: Oxford University Press, 2008.

Bock, Heike. Review of *Der frühe Zürcher Pietismus (1689-1721): Der soziale Hintergrund und die Denk- und Lebenswelten im Spiegel der Bibliothek Johann Heinrich Lochers (1648-1718)*, by Kaspar Bütikofer. *H-Soz-u-Kult*, October 22, 2010. http://hsozkult.geschichte.hu-berlin.de/rezensionen/2010-4-056.

Bockmühl, Klaus. "Die Wahrnehmung der Geschichte in der Dogmatik Adolf Schlatters." In *Die Aktualität der Theologie Adolf Schlatters*, edited by Klaus Bockmühl, 93–112. Gießen: Brunnen, 1988.

Bockmuehl, Markus. *Seeing the Word: Refocusing New Testament Study*. Grand Rapids: Baker Academic, 2006.

———. *This Jesus: Martyr, Lord, Messiah*. Downers Grove, IL: InterVarsity, 1994.

Bräutigam, Michael. "Adolf Schlatter on Scripture as Gnadenmittel: Remedy for a Hypertensive Debate?" *Scottish Journal of Theology*, forthcoming.

———. "Good Will Hunting: Adolf Schlatter on Organic Volitional Sanctification." *Journal of the Evangelical Theological Society*, 55.1 (2012) 125–43.

———. "The Pilgrimage to Kuyper? Adolf Schlatter and Abraham Kuyper on Theology, Culture and Art." In *The Kuyper Center Review*. Vol. 3, Calvinism and Culture. Edited by Gordon Graham, 32–50. Grand Rapids: Eerdmans, 2013.

———. "A Queen without a Throne? Harnack, Schlatter and Kuyper on Theology in the University," in *The Kuyper Center Review*. Vol. 5, Church and Academy. Edited by Gordon Graham, 104–18. Grand Rapids: Eerdmans, 2015.

———. "Seeing, Thinking, and Living: Adolf Schlatter on Theology at the University." *Scottish Bulletin of Evangelical Theology* 30.2 (2012) 177–88.

Bräutigam, Michael, and James Eglinton. "Scientific Theology? Herman Bavinck and Adolf Schlatter on the Place of Theology in the University." *Journal of Reformed Theology* 7 (2013) 27–50.

Bubser, Eberhard. "Spinoza." In *Religion in Geschichte und Gegenwart*. 3rd ed., vol. 6, edited by Kurt Galling, 250–51. Tübingen: Mohr (Paul Siebeck), 1962.

Bultmann, Rudolf. "Ist voraussetzungslose Exegese möglich?" *Theologische Zeitschrift* 13 (1957) 409–17.

———. "The Significance of the Historical Jesus for the Theology of Paul." In *Faith and Understanding: Collected Essays*, edited by Robert W. Funk, 220–46. London: SCM, 1969.

Burridge, Richard A. "From Titles to Stories: A Narrative Approach to the Dynamic Christologies of the New Testament." In *The Person of Christ*, edited by Stephen R. Holmes and Murray A. Rae, 37–60. London: T. & T. Clark, 2005.

Busch, Eberhard. *Die Barmer Thesen: 1934–2004*. Göttingen: Vandenhoeck & Ruprecht, 2004.

———. *Karl Barth: His Life from Letters and Autobiographical Texts*. Translated by John Bowden. Philadelphia: Fortress, 1976.

———. *Karl Barth and the Pietists: The Young Karl Barth's Critique of Pietism and its Response*. Translated by Daniel W. Bloesch. Downers Grove, IL: InterVarsity, 2004.

———. *Karl Barths Lebenslauf: Nach seinen Briefen und autobiographischen Texten*. München: Christian Kaiser, 1978.

Bütikofer, Kaspar. *Der frühe Zürcher Pietismus (1689–1721): Der soziale Hintergrund und die Denk- und Lebenswelten im Spiegel der Bibliothek Johann Heinrich Lochers (1648–1718)*. Göttingen: Vandenhoeck & Ruprecht, 2009.

Calvin, John. *Institutes of the Christian Religion*. Translated by Henry Beveridge. Grand Rapids: Eerdmans, 1983.

Canlis, Julie. *Calvin's Ladder: A Spiritual Theology of Ascent and Ascension*. Grand Rapids: Eerdmans, 2010.

Chadwick, Owen. *The Secularisation of the European Mind in the Nineteenth Century*. Cambridge: Cambridge University Press, 1975.

Bibliography

Chapman, Mark D. "History of Religion School." In *The Blackwell Companion to Nineteenth-Century Theology*, edited by David Fergusson, 434–54. Chichester: Wiley-Blackwell, 2010.

Cremer, Ernst. *Hermann Cremer: Ein Lebens und Charakterbild*. Gütersloh: Bertelsmann, 1912.

Cremer, Hermann. *Zum Kampf um das Apostolikum. Eine Streitschrift wider D. Harnack*. 6th ed. Berlin: Verlag von Wiegandt & Grieben, 1893.

Dintaman, Stephen F. *Creative Grace: Faith and History in the Theology of Adolf Schlatter*. New York: Peter Lang, 1993.

Donagan, Alan. "Spinoza's Theology." In *The Cambridge Companion to Spinoza*, edited by Don Garrett, 343–82. Cambridge: Cambridge University Press, 1996.

Dreher, Matthias. "Luther als Paulus-Interpret bei Adolf Schlatter und Wilhelm Heitmüller: Ein forschungsgeschichtlicher Beitrag zur 'New Perspective on Paul.'" *Luther* 79.2 (2008) 109–25.

Dymale, Herbert R. "The Theology of Adolf Schlatter with Special Reference to His Understanding of History: An Investigation into His Methodology." PhD diss., University of Iowa, 1966.

Egg, Gottfried. *Adolf Schlatters kritische Position: Gezeigt an seiner Matthäusinterpretation*. Stuttgart: Calwer, 1968.

Ehrman, Bart D. *How Jesus became God: The Exaltation of a Jewish Preacher from Galilee*. New York: HarperOne, 2014.

Eucken, Rudolf. *Die Methode der aristotelischen Forschung*. Berlin: Weidmannsche Buchhandlung, 1872.

Fergusson, David. "Preface." In *The Blackwell Companion to Nineteenth-Century Theology*, edited by David Fergusson, xi–xiii. Chichester: Wiley-Blackwell, 2010.

Ford, David, and Rachel Muers, eds. *The Modern Theologians: An Introduction to Christian Theology since 1918*. Oxford: Blackwell, 2005.

Fraas, Hans-Jürgen. "Die Bedeutung der Gotteslehre für die Dogmatik bei Adolf Schlatter und Reinhold Seeberg." PhD diss., University of Halle (Saale), 1960.

Gäbler, Ulrich. *Auferstehungszeit: Erweckungsprediger des 19. Jahrhunderts*. München: Beck, 1991.

———. "Erweckungsbewegung." In *Evangelisches Kirchenlexikon. Internationale Enzyklopädie*. Vol. 1, 3rd ed., 1081–88. Göttingen: Vandenhoeck & Ruprecht, 1986.

———. "Evangelikalismus und Réveil." In *Der Pietismus im neunzehnten und zwanzigsten Jahrhundert*, edited by Ulrich Gäbler, 27–86. Vol. 3 of *Geschichte des Pietismus*, edited by Martin Brecht, et al. Göttingen: Vandenhoeck & Ruprecht, 2000.

Gasque, Ward W. "The Promise of Adolf Schlatter." *Evangelical Review of Theology* 4 (1980) 20–30.

Gerdmar, Anders. *Roots of Theological Anti-Semitism: German Biblical Interpretation and the Jews, from Herder and Semler to Kittel and Bultmann*. Leiden: Brill, 2008.

Gockel, Matthias. "Mediating Theology in Germany." In *The Blackwell Companion to Nineteenth-Century Theology*, edited by David Fergusson, 301–18. Chichester: Wiley-Blackwell, 2010.

Gogh, Vincent van. "Letter to Emile Bernard." Arles, October 5, 1888. http://vangoghletters.org/vg/letters/let698/letter.html#translation.

Goppelt, Leonhard. *Theology of the New Testament*, Vol. 1. Translated by John E. Alsup. Edited by Jürgen Roloff. Grand Rapids: Eerdmans, 1981.
Grenz, Stanley J., and Roger E. Olson. *Twentieth Century Theology: God and the World in a Transitional Age.* Carlisle: Paternoster, 1992.
Hadorn, Walter. *Geschichte des Pietismus in den Schweizerischen Reformierten Kirchen.* Konstanz: Carl Kirsch, 1901.
Hägele, Clemens. *Die Schrift als Gnadenmittel: Adolf Schlatters Lehre von der Schrift in ihren Grundzügen.* Stuttgart: Calwer, 2007.
Härle, Wilfried. "Der Aufruf der 93 Intellektuellen und Karl Barths Bruch mit der liberalen Theologie." *Zeitschrift für Theologie und Kirche* 72 (1975) 207–24.
———. *Dogmatik.* 2nd ed. Berlin: de Gruyter, 2000.
———. "Vorwort." In *Realistische Philosophie: Der philosophische Entwurf Adolf Schlatters*, edited by Jochen Walldorf, 5–6. Göttingen: Vandenhoeck & Ruprecht, 1999.
Hake, Claudia. *Die Bedeutung der Theologie Johann Tobias Becks für die Entwicklung der Theologie Karl Barths.* Frankfurt am Main: Lang, 1999.
Hardy, Daniel W. "Karl Barth." In *The Modern Theologians: An Introduction to Christian Theology Since 1918*, edited by David F. Ford and Rachel Muers, 21–42. Oxford: Blackwell, 2005.
Harnack, Adolf von. "Das Alter des Gliedes 'Heiliger Geist' im Symbol." In *Aus Schrift und Geschichte: Theologische Abhandlungen Adolf Schlatter zu seinem 70. Geburtstage, dargebracht von Freunden und Schülern*, 171–73. Stuttgart: Calwer Vereinsbuchhandlung, 1922.
———. "Antwort auf die Streitschrift D. Cremers: Zum Kampf um das Apostolikum (1892)." In *Reden und Aufsätze*, vol. 1, 265–98. Gieszen: J. Riecker'sche Verlagsbuchhandlung, 1904.
———. *Das Apostolische Glaubensbekenntnis: Ein geschichtlicher Bericht nebst einem Nachwort.*" Berlin: A. Haack, 1892.
———. "Das Apostolische Glaubensbekenntnis. Ein geschichtlicher Bericht nebst einer Einleitung und einem Nachwort." In *Reden und Aufsätze*, vol. 1, 219–64. Gieszen: J. Riecker'sche Verlagsbuchhandlung, 1904.
———. "Die Aufgabe der theologischen Fakultäten und die allgemeine Religionsgeschichte nebst einem Nachwort." In *Reden und Aufsätze*, vol. 2/1, 159–87. Gießen: J. Ricker'sche Verlagsbuchhandlung, 1904.
———. "Letter" (draft) from Harnack to Schlatter [apparently not sent, 9 March 1893] Adolf Schlatter Archiv, Landeskirchliches Archiv Stuttgart, Bestand D 40 [No. 1306].
———. "In Sachen des Apostolikums." *Christliche Welt* 32 (1892) 768–70.
———. *Das Wesen des Christentums.* 3rd ed. Edited by Claus-Dieter Osthövener. Tübingen: Mohr Siebeck, 2012.
———. *What is Christianity?* Translated by Thomas Bailey Saunders. 1900. Reprint, Philadelphia: Fortress, 1986.
Harrisville, Roy A., and Walter Sundberg. *The Bible in Modern Culture: Baruch Spinoza to Brevard Childs.* Grand Rapids: Eerdmans, 2002.
Hegel, Georg Wilhelm Friedrich. *Werke in zwanzig Bänden.* Frankfurt: Suhrkamp, 1979.
Heidegger, Martin. *Phänomenologie und Theologie.* Frankfurt: Klostermann, 1970.

Herrmann, Wilhelm. "Ergebnisse des Streites um das Apostolikum." *Zeitschrift für Theologie und Kirche* 4 (1894) 251–305.

———. "Die Wirklichkeit Gottes." In *Schriften zur Grundlegung der Theologie*, edited by Peter Fischer-Appelt, 290–317. München: Chr. Kaiser, 1967.

Hesse, Hermann Albert. "Was war der Sinn unserer Theologischen Woche?" *Reformierte Kirchenzeitung* 77.44 (1927) 345–6.

Hoffmann, Willi. "Das Verständnis der Natur in der Theologie von J. T. Beck." Phd diss., Friedrich-Wilhelms-Universität Bonn, 1975.

Holmes, Stephen R. *The Quest for the Trinity: The Doctrine of God in Scripture, History and Modernity*. Downers Grove, IL: IVP Academic, 2012.

Holtzmann, Heinrich Julius. *Lehrbuch der Neutestamentlichen Theologie*. Vol. 1. Tübingen: Mohr, 1911.

———. Review of *Theologie des Neuen Testaments, Zwei Teile* (*Das Wort Jesu & Die Lehre der Apostel*), by Adolf Schlatter. *Theologische Literaturzeitung* 35 (1910) 299–303

———. *Die synoptischen Evangelien: Ihr Ursprung und geschichtlicher Charakter*. Leipzig: Wilhelm Engelmann, 1863.

Hoping, Helmut. *Einführung in die Christologie*. 2nd ed. Darmstadt: Wissenschaftliche Buchgesellschaft, 2010.

Isherwood, Lisa, and Elaine Bellchambers, eds. *Through Us, With Us, In Us: Relational Theologies in the Twenty-First Century*. London: SCM, 2010.

Israel, Jonathan Irvine. "Introduction." In *Theological-Political Treatise*, by Benedict de Spinoza, edited by Jonathan Israel, translated by Michael Silverthorne and Jonathan Israel, viii–xxxiv. Cambridge: Cambridge University Press, 2007.

———. *Radical Enlightenment: Philosophy and the Making of Modernity, 1650–1750*. Oxford: Oxford University Press, 2001.

Jaeger, Paul. "Das 'atheistische Denken' in der neueren Theologie. Zur Verständigung." *Christliche Welt* 25 (1905) 577–82.

Jehle-Wildberger, Marianne. *Anna Schlatter-Bernet, 1773–1826: Eine weltoffene St.Galler Christin*. Zürich: TVZ, 2003.

Kähler, Martin. *The Christ of Faith and the Jesus of History*. Philadelphia: Fortress, 1977.

Kant, Immanuel. *Critique of Pure Reason*. Translated and edited by Paul Guyer and Allen W. Wood. Cambridge: Cambridge University Press, 1998.

———. *Philosophical Correspondence: 1759–1799*. Edited and translated by Arnulf Zweig. Chicago: University of Chicago Press, 1967.

———. *Religion within the Boundaries of Mere Reason and other Writings*. Translated and edited by Allen Wood and George Di Giovanni. Cambridge: Cambridge University Press, 1998.

Kärkkäinen, Veli-Matti. *Christology: A Global Introduction*. Grand Rapids: Baker Academic, 2003.

Kindt, Irmgard. *Der Gedanke der Einheit: Adolf Schlatters Theologie und ihre historischen Voraussetzungen*. Stuttgart: Calwer, 1978.

Kittel, Gerhard. "Adolf Schlatter: Gedenkrede." In *Adolf Schlatter: Gedächtnisheft der Deutschen Theologie*, 6–17. Stuttgart: W. Kohlhammer, 1938.

Köberle, Adolf. "Beck." In *Religion in Geschichte und Gegenwart*. 3rd ed., vol. 1, edited by Kurt Galling, 953–54. Tübingen: Mohr (Paul Siebeck), 1957.

Köstenberger, Andreas J. "Preface: The Reception of Schlatter's New Testament Theology 1909–23." In *The Theology of the Apostles: The Development of New*

Testament Theology, by Adolf Schlatter, translated by Andreas J. Köstenberger, 9–22. Grand Rapids: Baker, 1999.

———. "Translator's Preface." In *The History of the Christ: The Foundation of New Testament Theology*, by Adolf Schlatter, translated by Andreas J. Köstenberger, 9–15. Grand Rapids: Baker, 1997.

Köstenberger, Andreas J., and Richard D. Patterson. *For the Love of God's Word: An Introduction to Biblical Interpretation*. Grand Rapids: Kregel, 2015.

———. *Invitation to Biblical Interpretation*. Grand Rapids: Kregel, 2011.

Kühn, Manfred. *Kant: Eine Biographie*. München: C. H. Beck, 2003.

Kuhn, Thomas K. *Religion und neuzeitliche Gesellschaft: Studien zum sozialen und diakonischen Handeln in Pietismus, Aufklärung und Erweckungsbewegung*. Tübingen: Mohr Siebeck, 2003.

Kupisch, Karl. *Die Deutschen Landeskirchen im 19. und 20. Jahrhundert*. Vol. 4 (Lieferung R, 2. Teil) of *Die Kirche in ihrer Geschichte*, edited by Kurt Dietrich Schmidt and Ernst Wolf. Göttingen: Vandenhoeck & Ruprecht, 1966.

Kuyper, Abraham. *Lectures on Calvinism*. Grand Rapids: Eerdmans, 1931.

Larsen, Timothy, ed. *Biographical Dictionary of Evangelicals*. Downers Grove, IL: InterVarsity, 2003.

Law, David R. "Kenotic Christology." In *The Blackwell Companion to Nineteenth-Century Theology*, edited by David Fergusson, 251–79. Chichester: Wiley-Blackwell, 2010.

Lehmann, Hartmut. "Die neue Lage." In *Der Pietismus im neunzehnten und zwanzigsten Jahrhundert*, edited by Ulrich Gäbler, vol. 3 of *Geschichte des Pietismus*, edited by Martin Brecht, et al., 1–26. Göttingen: Vandenhoeck & Ruprecht, 2000.

Lessing, Eckhard. *Geschichte der deutschsprachigen evangelischen Theologie von Albrecht Ritschl bis zur Gegenwart*. Vol. 1, *1870 bis 1918*. Göttingen: Vandenhoeck und Ruprecht, 2000.

Levertoff, Paul P. "Translator's Note." In *The Church in the New Testament Period*, edited by Adolf Schlatter, translated by Paul P. Levertoff, xii. London: SPCK, 1955.

Lister, Rob. *God is Impassible and Impassioned: Toward a Theology of Divine Emotion*. Nottingham: InterVarsity, 2012.

Loos, Andreas. "Divine Action and the Trinity: A brief exploration of the grounds of Trinitarian Speech about God in the theology of Adolf Schlatter." *International Journal of Systematic Theology* 4.3 (2002) 255–77.

———. "Divine Action, Christ and the Doctrine of God: the trinitarian grammar of Adolf Schlatter's theology." PhD diss., University of St. Andrews, Scotland, 2006.

Luck, Ulrich. *Kerygma und Tradition in der Hermeneutik Adolf Schlatters*. Köln: Westdeutscher Verlag, 1955.

Lütgert, Wilhelm. "Adolf Schlatter als Theologe innerhalb des geistigen Lebens seiner Zeit." *Beiträge zur Förderung Christlicher Theologie* 37.1 (1932) 1–52.

Lüpke von, Johannes. "Vorwort." In *Adolf Schlatter: Glaube und Gotteswirklichkeit, Beiträge zur Wahrnehmung Gottes*, edited by Johannes von Lüpke, 7–12. Stuttgart: Calwer, 2002.

———. "Wahrnehmung der Gotteswirklichkeit: Impulse der Theologie Adolf Schlatters." In *Realistische Theologie: Eine Hinführung zu Adolf Schlatter*, edited by Heinzpeter Hempelmann, et al., 43–66. Gießen: Brunnen, 2006.

Lundström, Gösta. *The Kingdom of God in the Teaching of Jesus: A History of Interpretation from the Last Decades of the Nineteenth Century to the Present Day*. Translated by Joan Bulman. Edinburgh: Oliver and Boyd, 1963.

Macleod, Donald. *Christ Crucified: Understanding the Atonement*. Nottingham: InterVarsity, 2014.

———. *The Person of Christ*. Downers Grove, IL: InterVarsity, 1998.

Maier, Gerhard. "Der anthropologische Ansatz der Gotteslehre Adolf Schlatters." In *Wer ist das—Gott? Christliche Gotteserkenntnis in den Herausforderungen der Gegenwart*, edited by Helmut Burkhardt, 142–55. Gießen: Brunnen, 1982.

McCall, Thomas H. *Forsaken: The Trinity and the Cross, and Why it Matters*. Downers Grove, IL: InterVarsity, 2012.

McClendon, James Wm. Jr. *Biography as Theology: How Life Stories Can Remake Today's Theology*. Philadelphia: Trinity, 1990.

McCormack, Bruce L. *Karl Barth's Critically Realistic Dialectical Theology: Its Genesis and Development 1909–1936*. Oxford: Clarendon, 1995.

———. "On 'Modernity' as a Theological Concept." In *Mapping Modern Theology: A Thematic and Historical Introduction*, edited by Kelly M. Kapic and Bruce L. McCormack, 1–19. Grand Rapids: Baker Academic, 2012.

———. "The Person of Christ." In *Mapping Modern Theology: A Thematic and Historical Introduction*, edited by Kelly M. Kapic and Bruce L. McCormack, 149–73. Grand Rapids: Baker Academic, 2012.

McGrath, Alister E. *The Making of Modern German Christology: 1750–1990*. Eugene, OR: Wipf & Stock, 1994.

McLeod, Hugh. *Secularisation in Western Europe 1848–1914*. London: Macmillan, 2000.

McNutt, James E. "Adolf Schlatter and the Jews." *German Studies Review* 26.2 (2003) 353–70.

———. "A Very Damning Truth: Walter Grundmann, Adolf Schlatter, and Susannah Heschel's *The Aryan Jesus*." *Harvard Theological Review* 105.3 (2012) 280–301.

———. "Vessels of Wrath, Prepared to Perish: Adolf Schlatter and the Spiritual Extermination of the Jews." *Theology Today* 63 (2006)176–90.

Melanchthon, Philipp. *The Loci communes of Philipp Melanchthon (1521)*. Translated by Charles Leander-Hill. Boston: Meador, 1944.

Menke, Karl-Heinz. *Jesus ist Gott der Sohn: Denkformen und Brennpunkte der Christologie*. 2nd ed. Regensburg: Friedrich Pustet, 2011.

Merz, Georg. "Adolf Schlatter." *Zwischen den Zeiten* 5 (1927) 523–29.

Metzger, Wolfgang. *Adolf Schlatter: Gedächtnisheft der Deutschen Theologie*. Stuttgart: W. Kohlhammer, 1938.

Meyer-Wieck, Karl. "Das Wirklichkeitsverständnis Adolf Schlatters." PhD diss., University of Münster, 1970.

Michaelis, Wilhelm. "Nachwort des Herausgebers." In *Johannes der Täufer*, by Adolf Schlatter, edited by Wilhelm Michaelis, 159–86. Basel: Friedrich Reinhardt, 1956.

Michel, Otto. "Adolf Schlatter als Ausleger der Heiligen Schrift." *Für Arbeit und Besinnung* 6 (1952) 227–38.

Migliore, Daniel L. *Faith Seeking Understanding: An Introduction to Christian Theology*. 2nd ed. Grand Rapids: Eerdmans, 2004.

Moltmann, Jürgen. *The Crucified God: The Cross of Christ as the Foundation and Criticism of Christian Theology*. Translated by R. A. Wilson and John Bowden. London: SCM, 1974.

———. *Der Gekreuzigte Gott: Das Kreuz Christi als Grund und Kritik christlicher Theologie*. München: Christian Kaiser, 1972.

Morgan, Robert. "Introduction: The Nature of New Testament Theology." In *The Nature of New Testament Theology: The Contribution of William Wrede and Adolf Schlatter*, edited by Robert Morgan, 1–67. Naperville, IL: Alex R. Allenson, 1973.

Moule, Charles F. D. "The Manhood of Jesus in the New Testament." In *Christ, Faith and History: Cambridge Studies in Christology*, edited by Stephen W. Sykes and John P. Clayton, 95–110. Cambridge: Cambridge University Press, 1972.

Mühlhaupt, Erwin. "Das reformierte Erbe in den Händen Adolf Schlatters." In *Adolf Schlatter: Gedächtnisheft der Deutschen Theologie*, 35–41. Stuttgart: Kohlhammer, 1938.

Mueller, David L. *An Introduction to the Theology of Albrecht Ritschl*. Philadelphia: Westminster, 1969.

Mussner, Franz. "Geleitwort." In *Der Brief des Jakobus*, edited by Adolf Schlatter, vi–xiv. Stuttgart: Calwer, 1985.

Neuer, Werner. *Adolf Schlatter*. Wuppertal: SCM R. Brockhaus, 1988.

———. *Adolf Schlatter: A Biography of Germany's Premier Biblical Theologian*. Translated by Robert W. Yarbrough. Grand Rapids: Baker, 1995.

———. *Adolf Schlatter: Ein Leben für Theologie und Kirche*. Stuttgart: Calwer, 1996.

———. "Adolf Schlatter: Leben, Werk, Wirkung." In *Realistische Theologie: Eine Hinführung zu Adolf Schlatter*, edited by Heinzpeter Hempelmann, et al., 9–41. Gießen: Brunnen, 2006.

———. "Der Briefwechsel zwischen Karl Barth und Adolf Schlatter: Ein Beitrag zum 100. Geburtstag Karl Barths." *Theologische Beiträge* 17 (1986) 86–100.

———. "Einführung." *Zeitschrift für Theologie und Kirche* Beiheft 7 (1987) 1–15.

———. "Der Idealismus und die Erweckung in Schlatters Jugend: Beobachtungen zu einem nichtedierten Manuskript aus Schlatters Nachlaß." *Zeitschrift für Kirchengeschichte* 96 (1985) 62–72.

———. "Die ökumenische Bedeutung der Theologie Adolf Schlatters." In *Die Aktualität der Theologie Adolf Schlatters*, edited by Klaus Bockmühl, 71–92. Gießen: Brunnen, 1988.

———. "Schlatters Theologie der Liebe und sein Dienst für die Kirche." In *Realistische Theologie: Eine Hinführung zu Adolf Schlatter*, edited by Heinzpeter Hempelmann, Johannes von Lüpke and Werner Neuer, 111–42. Gießen: Brunnen, 2006.

———. "Das Verhältnis Adolf Schlatters zu Johann Tobias Beck." *Jahrbuch für Evangelikale Theologie* 2 (1988) 85–95.

———. *Der Zusammenhang von Dogmatik und Ethik bei Adolf Schlatter: Eine Untersuchung zur Grundlegung christlicher Ethik*. Giessen: Brunnen, 1986.

Neufeld, Karl H. *Adolf Harnacks Konflikt mit der Kirche: Weg-Stationen zum 'Wesen des Christentums.'* Innsbruck: Tyrolia, 1979.

Neugebauer, Matthias. *Lotze und Ritschl: Reich-Gottes-Theologie zwischen nachidealistischer Philosophie und neuzeitlichem Positivismus*. Frankfurt/Main: Peter Lang, 2002.

Ninck, Johannes. *Anna Schlatter und ihre Kinder*. Leipzig: Schloeßmann, 1934.

Nippold, Friedrich. *Geschichte des Protestantismus seit dem deutschen Befreiungskriege—1. Buch: Geschichte der deutschen Theologie*. Handbuch der neuesten Kirchengeschichte 3. Berlin: Wiegandt & Schotte, 1890.

Noll, Mark A. "Evangelikalismus und Fundamentalismus in Nordamerika." In *Der Pietismus im neunzehnten und zwanzigsten Jahrhundert*, edited by Ulrich Gäbler, vol. 3 of *Geschichte des Pietismus*, edited by Martin Brecht, Klaus Deppermann,

Ulrich Gäbler, and Hartmut Lehmann, 465-531. Göttingen: Vandenhoeck & Ruprecht, 2000.

———. "Foreword." In *Adolf Schlatter: A Biography of Germany's Premier Biblical Theologian*, edited by Werner Neuer. Translated by Robert W. Yarbrough, 7-8. Grand Rapids: Baker, 1995.

Nowak, Kurt, Otto Gerhard Oexle, Trutz Rendtorff, and Kurt-Victor Selge, eds. *Adolf von Harnack: Christentum, Wissenschaft und Gesellschaft*. Göttingen: Vandenhoeck & Ruprecht, 2003.

Osterhammel, Jürgen. *Die Verwandlung der Welt: Eine Geschichte des 19. Jahrhunderts*. München: C. H. Beck, 2009.

Osthövener, Claus-Dieter. "Adolf von Harnack als Systematiker." *Zeitschrift für Theologie und Kirche* 99 (2002) 296-331.

———. "Nachwort." In *Das Wesen des Christentums*, edited by Adolf von Harnack, 257-89. Tübingen: Mohr Siebeck, 2007.

Pannenberg, Wolfhart. *Jesus—God and Man*. Translated by Lewis L. Wilkins and Duane A. Priebe. London: SCM, 1968.

Pfeifer, Hans. "Editor's Afterword to the German Edition." In *The Young Bonhoeffer: 1918-1927*. Dietrich Bonhoeffer Works 9, edited by Paul D. Matheny, Clifford J. Green, and Marshall D. Johnson, translated by Mary Nebelsick, 563-78. Minneapolis: Fortress, 2002.

Pfister, Rudolf. *Kirchengeschichte der Schweiz*. Vol. 3, *Von 1720 bis 1950*. Zürich: Theologischer Verlag, 1985.

Räisänen, Heikki. *Beyond New Testament Theology*. London: SCM, 1990.

Ratzinger, Joseph Cardinal. *Truth and Tolerance: Christian Belief and World Religions*. San Francisco: Ignatius, 2004.

Rengstorf, Karl Heinrich, and Ulrich Luck, eds. *Das Paulusbild in der neueren deutschen Forschung*. Darmstadt: Wissenschaftliche Buchgesellschaft, 1964.

Renkewitz, Heinz. "Erneuerte Brüderunität." In *Religion in Geschichte und Gegenwart*. 3rd ed., vol. 1, edited by Kurt Galling, 1439-43. Tübingen: Mohr (Paul Siebeck), 1957.

Richmond, James. *Ritschl: A Reappraisal*. London: Collins, 1978.

Rieger, Hans-Martin. *Adolf Schlatters Rechtfertigungslehre und die Möglichkeit ökumenischer Verständigung*. Stuttgart: Calwer, 2000.

———. "'Vollendung der Reformation': Adolf Schlatters Lutherkritik im Kontext seiner Gesamtperspektive." *Kerygma und Dogma* 46.4 (2000) 318-36.

Riggenbach, Bernhard. *Johann Tobias Beck. Ein Schriftgelehrter zum Himmelreich gelehrt*. Basel: C. Detloff's Buchhandlung, 1888.

Ringleben, Joachim. "Exegese und Dogmatik bei Adolf Schlatter." In *Arbeit am Gottesbegriff*, vol. 2, *Klassiker der Neuzeit*, 350-85. Tübingen: Mohr Siebeck, 2005.

———. *Jesus, ein Versuch zu Begreifen*. Tübingen: Mohr Siebeck, 2008.

Ritschl, Albrecht. *The Christian Doctrine of Justification and Reconciliation*. Translated by Hugh R. Mackintosh and A. B. Macaulay. Edinburgh: T. & T. Clark, 1900.

———. *Die christliche Lehre von der Rechtfertigung und Versöhnung*. 3 vols. Bonn: Adolph Marcus, 1870-74.

———. *Theologie und Metaphysik: Zur Verständigung und Abwehr*. Bonn: Adolph Marcus, 1881.

———. *Unterricht in der christlichen Religion*. 2nd ed. Bonn: Adolph Marcus, 1881.

Root, Michael, and James J. Buckley, eds. *The Morally Divided Body: Ethical Disagreement and the Disunity of the Church*. Eugene, OR: Wipf & Stock, 2012.

Rüegg, Daniel. *Der sich schenkende Christus: Adolf Schlatters Lehre von den Sakramenten*. Gießen: Brunnen, 2006.

Schäfer, Rolf. *Ritschl: Grundlinien eines fast verschollenen dogmatischen Systems*. Tübingen: Mohr (Paul Siebeck), 1968.

Schaff, Philip, and Henry Wace, eds. *Nicene and Post-Nicene Fathers*. Second series, vol. 5, *Gregory of Nyssa: Dogmatic Treatises, Select Writings and Letters etc*. Peabody, MA: Hendrickson, 1994.

Schlatter, Adolf. *Adolf Schlatter: Glaube und Gotteswirklichkeit: Beiträge zur Wahrnehmung Gottes*, edited by Johannes von Lüpke. Stuttgart: Calwer, 2002.

———. "Adolf Schlatter on Atheistic Methods in Theology." In *Adolf Schlatter: A Biography of Germany's Premier Biblical Theologian*, translated by Robert W. Yarbrough, 211–25. Grand Rapids: Baker, 1995.

———. "Adolf Schlatter on Prayer." In *Adolf Schlatter: A Biography of Germany's Premier Biblical Theologian*, translated by Robert W. Yarbrough, 159–67. Grand Rapids: Baker, 1995.

———. "Allegorien-klingende Schellen, tönendes Erz. Eine Fortsetzung zu Hellbardts Deutung der Lüge Abrahams." *Evangelische Theologie* 3 (1936) 422–29.

———. "Atheistische Methoden in der Theologie." *Beiträge zur Förderung Christlicher Theologie* 9.5 (1905) 228–50.

———. "Aus dem innern Leben der Schule Ritschls." *Der Kirchenfreund* 20.12 (1886) 409–17.

———. "Baaders Verhältnis zu den wissenschaftlichen Bestrebungen seiner Zeit." (unpublished) Adolf Schlatter Archiv, Landeskirchliches Archiv. Stuttgart, Bestand D 40 [No. 185].

———. "Die Bedeutung der Methode für die theologische Arbeit." *Theologischer Literaturbericht* 31.1 (1908) 5–8.

———. *Die Bibel verstehen: Aufsätze zur Biblischen Hermeneutik*. Edited by Werner Neuer. Giessen: Brunnen, 2002.

———. "Biblische, theologische und philosophische Begriffe bei Franz von Baader." (unpublished) Adolf Schlatter Archiv, Landeskirchliches Archiv. Stuttgart, Bestand D 40 [No. 184].

———. *Der Brief des Jakobus*. 3rd ed. Stuttgart: Calwer, 1985.

———. "Briefe über das Christliche Dogma." *Beiträge zur Förderung Christlicher Theologie* 5.5 (1912).

———. *The Church in the New Testament Period*. Translated by Paul P. Levertoff. London: SPCK, 1955.

———. "Die Christologie der Bergpredigt." *Der Kirchenfreund* 21 (1879) 321–8.

———. "Christi Versöhnen und Christi Vergeben." *Evangelisches Kirchenblatt für Württemberg* 59 (1898) 161–5.

———. *Das christliche Dogma*. 2nd ed. Stuttgart: Calwer Vereinsbuchhandlung, 1923.

———. *Die christliche Ethik*. 3rd ed. Stuttgart: Calwer Vereinsbuchhandlung, 1929.

———. "Christologie und Soteriologie." (unpublished) Bern: lecture, 1884. Adolf Schlatter Archiv, Landeskirchliches Archiv. Stuttgart, Bestand D 40 [No. 192].

———. "Christus und Christentum, Person und Prinzip." *Beiträge zur Förderung Christlicher Theologie* 8.4 (1904) 5–24.

———. *Daß meine Freude in euch sei: Andachten*. 3rd ed. Stuttgart: Calwer, 1957.

———. *Der Dienst des Christen: Beiträge zu einer Theologie der Liebe*. Edited by Werner Neuer. Giessen/Basel: Brunnen, 1991.

———. "Der Dienst des Christen in der älteren Dogmatik." *Beiträge zur Förderung Christlicher Theologie* 1.1 (1897).

———. "Die Dienstpflicht des Christen in der apostolischen Gemeinde." [Referat auf der Tagung der Südwestdeutschen Konferenz für Innere Mission. Tübingen, 07/10/1929] Stuttgart: Quell-Verlag der Ev. Gesellschaft, 1929.

———. *Do We Know Jesus? Daily Insights for the Mind and Soul*. Translated by Andreas J. Köstenberger and Robert W. Yarbrough. Grand Rapids: Kregel, 2005.

———. *Einführung in die Theologie*. Stuttgart: Calwer, 2013.

———. *Der Einzige und wir anderen*. Velbert: Freizeiten-Verlag, 1929.

———. "Die Entstehung der Beiträge zur Förderung christlicher Theologie und ihr Zusammenhang mit meiner theologischen Arbeit zum Beginn ihres fünfundzwanzigsten Bandes." *Beiträge zur Förderung Christlicher Theologie* 25.1 (1920).

———. *Der Evangelist Johannes. Wie er spricht, denkt und glaubt. Ein Kommentar zum vierten Evangelium*. 2nd ed. Stuttgart: Calwer, 1948.

———. *Das Evangelium des Lukas. Aus seinen Quellen erklärt*. Stuttgart: Calwer Vereinsbuchhandlung, 1931.

———. *Der Evangelist Matthäus: Seine Sprache, sein Ziel, seine Selbständigkeit. Ein Kommentar zum ersten Evangelium*. 7th ed. Stuttgart: Calwer, 1982.

———. "Erfolg und Mißerfolg im theologischen Studium. Eine Rede an die evangelisch-theologische Fachschaft in Tübingen." In *Zur Theologie des Neuen Testaments und zur Dogmatik. Kleine Schriften*, edited by Ulrich Luck, 256–72. München: Christian Kaiser, 1969.

———. *Erläuterungen zum Neuen Testament*, vol. 1–10. Berlin: Evangelische Verlagsanstalt, 1952–3.

———. *Erlebtes. Erzählt von D. Adolf Schlatter*. 5th ed. Berlin: Furche, 1929.

———. "Die Furcht vor dem Denken. Eine Zugabe zu Hiltys 'Glück' III." *Beiträge zur Förderung Christlicher Theologie* 4.1 (1900) 3–48.

———. *Die Gabe des Christus: Eine Auslegung der Bergpredigt*. Velbert: Freizeiten-Verlag, 1928.

———. *Die Geschichte des Christus*. [*Die Theologie des Neuen Testaments I. Das Wort Jesu*. Calw/Stuttgart, 1909] 2nd ed. Stuttgart: Calwer Vereinsbuchhandlung, 1923.

———. "Geschichte der speculativen Theologie seit Cartesius." (unpublished) Bern: lecture, winter semester 1881/82. Adolf Schlatter Archiv, Landeskirchliches Archiv. Stuttgart, Bestand D 40.

———. *Gesunde Lehre. Reden und Aufsätze*. Velbert: Freizeiten-Verlag, 1929.

———. *Der Glaube im Neuen Testament*. 6th ed. Stuttgart: Calwer, 1982.

———. *Gottes Gerechtigkeit: ein Kommentar zum Römerbrief*. 2nd ed. Stuttgart: Calwer, 1952.

———. *Das Gott wohlgefällige Opfer. Vier Reden von Prof. D. Ad. Schlatter in Tübingen*. Velbert: Freizeiten-Verlag, 1926.

———. "Die Grenzen der kirchlichen Gemeinschaft." In *Müssen wir heute lutherisch oder reformiert sein? Beiträge zur Frage einer neuen kirchlichen Einheit von D. Dr. Adolf Schlatter, D. Wilhelm Lütgert und D. Hermann Strathmann*, 3–20. Velbert: Freizeiten-Verlag, 1936.

———. *Die Gründe der christlichen Gewißheit, Das Gebet*. Stuttgart: Calwer Verlag, 1927.

———. *Heilige Anliegen der Kirche: Vier Reden*. Calw & Stuttgart: Verlag der Vereinsbuchhandlung, 1896.

———. *The History of the Christ: The Foundation of New Testament Theology*. Translated by Andreas J. Köstenberger. Grand Rapids: Baker, 1997.

———. *Hülfe in Bibelnot: Neues und Altes zur Schriftfrage*. 3rd ed. Gladbeck: Freizeiten-Verlag, 1953.

———. "Der Idealismus und die Erweckung in meiner Jugend" (n.d., probably 1926, unpublished) Adolf Schlatter Archiv, Landeskirchliches Archiv. Stuttgart, Bestand D 40.

———. "J. T. Becks theologische Arbeit." *Beiträge zur Förderung Christlicher Theologie* 8.4 (1904) 25–46.

———. "Jesu Demut, ihre Mißdeutungen, ihr Grund." *Beiträge zur Förderung Christlicher Theologie* 8.1 (1904) 33–93.

———. *Jesu Gottheit und das Kreuz*. 2nd ed. Gütersloh: Bertelsmann, 1913.

———. *Jesus und Paulus: Eine Vorlesung*. Edited by Theodor Schlatter. Stuttgart und Berlin: W. Kohlhammer, 1940.

———. *Johannes der Täufer*. Edited by Wilhelm Michaelis. Basel: Friedrich Reinhardt, 1956.

———. "Karl Barth's *Epistle to the Romans*." In *The Beginnings of Dialectic Theology*, edited by James M. Robinson, translated by Keith R. Crim, 121–5. Richmond, VA: John Knox, 1968.

———. "Karl Barths Römerbrief." *Die Furche* 12 (1922) 228–32.

———. *Kennen wir Jesus? Ein Gang durch ein Jahr im Gespräch mit ihm*. 3rd ed. Gladbeck: Freizeiten Verlag, 1952.

———. *Die Kirche der Griechen im Urteil des Paulus: Eine Auslegung seiner Briefe an Timotheus und Titus*. Stuttgart: Vereinsbuchhandlung, 1936.

———. *Marien-Reden*. Freizeit-Bücher Nr. 2. 3rd ed. Gladbeck: Freizeiten-Verlag, 1951.

———. *Markus. Der Evangelist für die Griechen*. Stuttgart: Calwer Vereinsbuchhandlung, 1935.

———. *Aus meiner Sprechstunde*. 3rd ed. Bethel: Verlagshandlung der Anstalt Bethel, 1952.

———. *Metaphysik*. Edited by Werner Neuer. Zeitschrift für Theologie und Kirche, Beiheft 7. Tübingen: J.C.B. Mohr (Paul Siebeck), 1987.

———. *Müssen wir heute lutherisch oder reformiert sein? Beiträge zur Frage einer neuen kirchlichen Einheit von D. Dr. Adolf Schlatter, D. Wilhelm Lütgert und D. Hermann Strathmann*. Velbert: Freizeiten-Verlag, 1936.

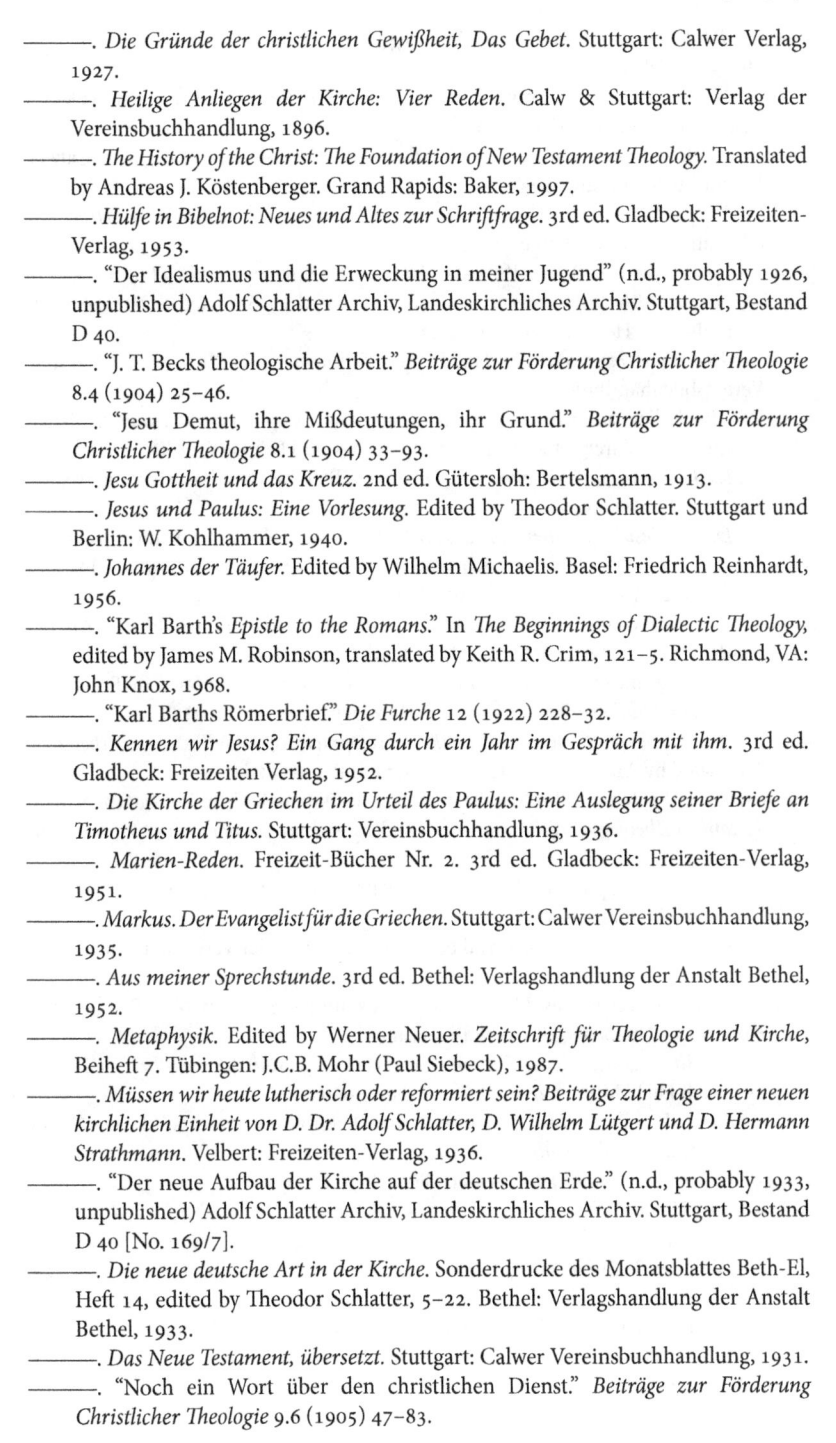

———. "Der neue Aufbau der Kirche auf der deutschen Erde." (n.d., probably 1933, unpublished) Adolf Schlatter Archiv, Landeskirchliches Archiv. Stuttgart, Bestand D 40 [No. 169/7].

———. *Die neue deutsche Art in der Kirche*. Sonderdrucke des Monatsblattes Beth-El, Heft 14, edited by Theodor Schlatter, 5–22. Bethel: Verlagshandlung der Anstalt Bethel, 1933.

———. *Das Neue Testament, übersetzt*. Stuttgart: Calwer Vereinsbuchhandlung, 1931.

———. "Noch ein Wort über den christlichen Dienst." *Beiträge zur Förderung Christlicher Theologie* 9.6 (1905) 47–83.

----. *Paulus, der Bote Jesu. Eine Deutung seiner Brief an die Korinther*. 2nd ed. Stuttgart: Calwer Verlag, 1956.

----. "Paulus und Griechentum." In *Gesunde Lehre. Reden und Aufsätze*, 128–43. Velbert: Freizeiten-Verlag, 1929.

----. *Petrus und Paulus. Nach dem 1. Petrusbrief*. Stuttgart: Calwer Vereinsbuchhandlung, 1937.

----. *Die philosophische Arbeit seit Descartes: Ihr ethischer und religiöser Ertrag*. 4th ed. Stuttgart: Calwer Verlag, 1959.

----. "Ueber das Princip des Protestantismus." *Der Kirchenfreund* 15 (1881) 241–7.

----. *Romans: The Righteousness of God*. Translated by Siegfried S. Schatzmann. Peabody, MA: Hendrickson, 1995.

----. *Der Römerbrief. Ein Hilfsbüchlein für Bibelleser*. Calw/Stuttgart: Verlag der Vereinsbuchhandlung, 1887.

----. "Rückblick auf meinen Entwicklungsgang" (unpublished) Adolf Schlatter Archiv, Landeskirchliches Archiv. Stuttgart, Bestand D 40 [SZAZ T30a 12].

----. *Rückblick auf meine [seine] Lebensarbeit*. Edited by Theodor Schlatter, 2nd ed. Stuttgart: Calwer, 1977.

----. *Der Ruf Jesu. Predigten von Adolf Schlatter*. 2nd ed. Stuttgart: Calwer, 1925.

----. "Adolf Schlatter." In *Die Religionswissenschaft in Selbstdarstellungen*, edited by Erich Stange, 145–71. Leipzig: Felix Meiner, 1925.

----. "Sentenzen aus Franz von Baader." (unpublished) Adolf Schlatter Archiv, Landeskirchliches Archiv Stuttgart, Bestand D 40 [No. 187].

----. "The Significance of Method for Theological Work." Translated by Robert W. Yarbrough. *Southern Baptist Journal of Theology* (Summer 1997) 64–76.

----. *The Theology of the Apostles: The Development of New Testament Theology*. Translated by Andreas J. Köstenberger. Grand Rapids: Baker, 1999.

----. "The Theology of the New Testament and Dogmatics." In *The Nature of New Testament Theology*, edited and translated by Robert Morgan, 115–66. London: SCM, 1973.

----. *Zur Topographie und Geschichte Palästinas*. Calw/Stuttgart: Verlag der Vereinsbuchhandlung, 1893.

----. *Die Theologie der Apostel*. 2nd ed. Stuttgart: Verlag der Vereinsbuchhandlung, 1922.

----. "Die Theologie des Neuen Testaments und die Dogmatik." *Beiträge zur Förderung Christlicher Theologie* 13.2 (1909) 7–82.

----. *Zur Theologie des Neuen Testaments und zur Dogmatik. Kleine Schriften*. Edited by Ulrich Luck. München: Christian Kaiser, 1969.

----. "Die Theologie Karl Barths und der Dienst des Pfarrers." *Evangelisches Kirchenblatt für Württemberg* 86 (1925) 116.

----. *Unsere Abendmahlsfeier*. Velbert: Freizeiten-Verlag, 1928.

----. "Die Unterwerfung unter die Gotteswirklichkeit." *Die Furche* (Oct–Nov 1911) 6–12, 47–53.

----. "Von der Rechtfertigung, Röm. 4,25." *Der Kirchenfreund* 17 (1883) 5–10, 22–23.

----. "Warum ich an der landeskirchlichen Versammlung teilnahm. Antwort auf die 'Nationalzeitung' vom 16.5.1895." *Deutsche Evangelische Kirchenzeitung* 9.3 (1897) 214–15.

———. "Was ist heute die religiöse Aufgabe der Universitäten?" *Beiträge zur Förderung Christlicher Theologie* 5.4 (1901) 61–79.

———. "Der Wert und Unwert unseres Wissens." *Monatsschrift für Pastoraltheologie* 28 (1932) 259–65.

———. "Wesen und Quellen der Gotteserkenntnis." Bern: lecture, summer semester 1883. Adolf Schlatter Archiv, Landeskirchliches Archiv. Stuttgart, Bestand D 40 [No. 191].

———. *Wird der Jude über uns siegen? Ein Wort für die Weihnachtszeit.* Freizeit-Blätter Nr. 8. Essen: Freizeiten-Verlag, 1935.

———. "Wille, Wollen." In *Biblisches Handwörterbuch—Calwer Bibellexikon.* Edited by Paul Zeller, 1011–12. Stuttgart: Verlag der Vereinsbuchhandlung, 1885.

———. *Wort und Wahrnehmung. Briefe Adolf Schlatters an Hermann Cremer und Friedrich von Bodelschwingh.* Edited by Robert Stupperich. *JVWKG*, Beiheft 7. Bethel: Verlagsbuchhandlung der Anstalt Bethel, 1963.

———. "Ein Wort zum Preise meines Amtes." *Evangelisches Kirchenblatt für Württemberg* 83 (1922) 97–98.

———. "Wunder." In *Biblisches Handwörterbuch—Calwer Bibellexikon*, edited by Hermann Zeller, 831–32. Stuttgart: Calwer Vereinsbuchhandlung, 1924.

———. "Der Zweifel an der Messianität Jesu." *Beiträge zur Förderung Christlicher Theologie* 11.4 (1907) 7–75.

Schlatter, Theodor. "Die Feier am Grabe Adolf Schlatters, gehalten am 23.5.1938 durch Prälat Lic. Theodor Schlatter, Stuttgart." In *Adolf Schlatter: Gedächtnisheft der Deutschen Theologie*, 1–6. Stuttgart: W. Kohlhammer, 1938.

———. "Vom Glauben an Gottes Offenbarung in der Geschichte. Einige Fragen zur Theologie Karl Barths." *Beth-El* 18 (1925) 4–12.

Schleiermacher, Friedrich D. E. *Der christliche Glaube nach den Grundsätzen der evangelischen Kirche im Zusammenhange dargestellt, 2. Auflage (1830/31), Erster und zweiter Band.* Edited by Rolf Schäfer. Berlin: Walter de Gruyter, 2008.

Schliesser, Benjamin. *Abraham's Faith in Romans 4: Paul's Concept of Faith in Light of the History of Reception of Genesis 15:6.* Tübingen: Mohr Siebeck, 2007.

Schmid, Johannes Heinrich. *Erkenntnis des Geschichtlichen Christus bei Martin Kähler und bei Adolf Schlatter.* Basel: Friedrich Reinhardt, 1978.

Schmidt, Kurt Dietrich. *Kirchengeschichte.* 9th ed. Göttingen: Vandenhoeck & Ruprecht, 1990.

Schreiner, Thomas R. *New Testament Theology: Magnifying God in Christ.* Grand Rapids: Baker Academic, 2008.

Schweitzer, Albert. *The Quest of the Historical Jesus.* Translated by Dennis Nineham. Minneapolis: Fortress, 2001.

Schwöbel, Christoph. "Christ for Us—Yesterday and Today: A Response to 'The Person of Christ.'" In *The Person of Christ*, edited by Stephen R. Holmes and Murray A. Rae, 182–201. London: T. & T. Clark, 2005.

———. "Christology and Trinitarian Thought." In *Trinitarian Theology Today*, edited by Christoph Schwöbel, 113–46. Edinburgh: T. & T. Clark, 1995.

———. *Gott in Beziehung: Studien zur Dogmatik.* Tübingen: J.C.B. Mohr (Paul Siebeck), 2002.

Smid, Udo. "Natürliche Theologie–als Problem bei Adolf Schlatter." *Evangelische Theologie* 3 (1952/3) 105–20.

Spence, Alan. *Christology: A Guide for the Perplexed.* London: T. & T. Clark, 2009.

Spinoza, Benedict de. *Spinoza: The Letters*. Translated by Samuel Shirley. Indianapolis, IN: Hackett, 1995.

———. *Theological-Political Treatise*. Edited by Jonathan Israel, and translated by Michael Silverthorne. Cambridge: Cambridge University Press, 2007.

Staehelin, Ernst. *Die Christentumsgesellschaft in der Zeit der Aufklärung und der beginnenden Erweckung*. Basel: Friedrich Reinhardt, 1970.

Strauss, David Friedrich. *The Life of Jesus Critically Examined*. Translated by Marian Evans. New York: Calvin Blanchard, 1860.

Stuhlmacher, Peter. "Adolf Schlatter als Bibelausleger." *Zeitschrift für Theologie und Kirche* (1978), Beiheft 4.

———. "Adolf Schlatter (1852–1938)." In *Theologen des Protestantismus im 19. und 20. Jahrhundert*, vol. 2, edited by Martin Greschat, 219–40. Stuttgart: Kohlhammer, 1978.

———. "Adolf Schlatter's Interpretation of Scripture." *New Testament Studies* 23 (1978) 433–46.

———. "Foreword." In *Romans: The Righteousness of God*, by Adolf Schlatter, translated by Siegfried S. Schatzmann, ix–xxiv. Peabody, MA: Hendrickson, 1995.

———. "Zum Neudruck von Adolf Schlatters 'Der Glaube im Neuen Testament.'" In *Der Glaube im Neuen Testament*, by Adolf Schlatter, v–xiii. Stuttgart: Calwer, 1982.

Stupperich, Robert. "Adolf Schlatters Berufungen." *Zeitschrift für Theologie und Kirche* 76.1 (1979) 100–17.

———, ed. "Briefe Karl Holls an Adolf Schlatter: 1897–1925." *Zeitschrift für Theologie und Kirche* 64.2 (1967) 169–240.

———, ed. *Wort und Wahrnehmung: Briefe Adolf Schlatters an Hermann Cremer und Friedrich von Bodelschwingh*. Bethel: Verlag der Anstalt Bethel, 1963.

Tanner, Kathryn E. *Jesus, Humanity and the Trinity: A Brief Systematic Theology*. Edinburgh: T. & T. Clark, 2001.

Tebbe, Walter. "Adolf Schlatter: Leben und Werk." *Monatsschrift für Pastoraltheologie* 4 (1952) 263–74.

Thielicke, Helmut. "Zum Geleit." In *Die Philosophische Arbeit seit Descartes*, by Adolf Schlatter, edited by Theodor Schlatter, 7–21. Stuttgart: Calwer, 1959.

Thomasius, Gottfried. *Beiträge zur kirchlichen Christologie*. Erlangen: Theodore Bläsing, 1845.

———. *Christi Person und Werk. Darstellung der evangelisch-lutherischen Dogmatik vom Mittelpunkte der Christologie aus*. Das Werk des Mittlers 2. Erlangen: Andreas Deichert, 1888.

Tillich, Paul. *Systematic Theology*. Vol. 2. Chicago: University of Chicago Press, 1957.

Timm, Hermann. *Theorie und Praxis in der Theologie Albrecht Ritschls und Wilhelm Herrmanns: Ein Beitrag zur Entwicklungsgeschichte des Kulturprotestantismus*. Gütersloh: Mohn, 1967.

Ungern-Sternberg, Jürgen von, and Wolfgang von Ungern-Sternberg. *Der Aufruf 'An die Kulturwelt.' Das Manifest der 93 und die Anfänge der Kriegspropaganda im Ersten Weltkrieg; mit einer Dokumentation*. Stuttgart: Franz Steiner, 1996.

Vieweger, Hans-Joachim. "Der protestantische Papst-Schüler." *Evangelisches Sonntagsblatt für Bayern* (8/2012) February 19, 2012, http://www.sonntagsblatt-bayern.de/news/aktuell/2012_08_11_01.htm.

Volf, Miroslav. *After Our Likeness: The Church as the Image of the Trinity*. Grand Rapids: Eerdmans, 1998.

Walldorf, Jochen. "Aspekte einer realistischen Philosophie: Einführung in das philosophische Denken Adolf Schlatters." *Theologische Beiträge* 33 (2002) 62–85.

———. *Realistische Philosophie: Der philosophische Entwurf Adolf Schlatters*. Göttingen: Vandenhoeck & Ruprecht, 1999.

Wallmann, Johannes. *Der Pietismus*. Vol. 4 (Lieferung O 1) of *Die Kirche in ihrer Geschichte*, edited by Bernd Moeller, founded by Kurt Dietrich Schmidt and Ernst Wolf. Göttingen: Vandenhoeck & Ruprecht, 1990.

Weber, Otto. *Foundations of Dogmatics*. Vol. 1, translated by Darrell L. Guder. Grand Rapids: Eerdmans, 1981.

———. *Grundlagen der Dogmatik*. Vol. 2. 3rd ed. Berlin: Evangelische Verlagsanstalt, 1977.

Webster, John. *Barth's Earlier Theology: Four Studies*. London: T. & T. Clark, 2005.

Weigelt, Horst. "Die Allgäuer katholische Erweckungsbewegung." In *Der Pietismus im neunzehnten und zwanzigsten Jahrhundert*, edited by Ulrich Gäbler, 87–111, vol. 3 of *Geschichte des Pietismus*, edited by Martin Brecht, et al. Göttingen: Vandenhoeck & Ruprecht, 2000.

———. "Die Diasporaarbeit der Herrnhuter Brüdergemeine und die Wirksamkeit der Deutschen Christentumsgesellschaft im 19. Jahrhundert." In *Der Pietismus im neunzehnten und zwanzigsten Jahrhundert*, edited by Ulrich Gäbler, 113–49, vol. 3 of *Geschichte des Pietismus*, edited by Martin Brecht, et al. Göttingen: Vandenhoeck & Ruprecht, 2000.

Weinhardt, Joachim. "Einleitung." In *Albrecht Ritschls Briefwechsel mit Adolf Harnack: 1875–1889*, edited by Joachim Weinhardt, 1–127. Tübingen: J.C.B. Mohr (Paul Siebeck), 2010.

———. *Wilhelm Herrmanns Stellung in der Rischlschen Schule*. Tübingen: J.C.B. Mohr (Paul Siebeck), 1996.

Weiss, Bernhard. *Biblical Theology of the New Testament*, vol. 2. Translated by James E. Duguid. Edinburgh: T. & T. Clark, 1883.

Wellenreuther, Hermann. "Pietismus und Mission: Vom 17. bis zum Beginn des 20. Jahrhunderts." In *Glaubenswelt und Lebenswelten*, edited by Hartmut Lehmann, 168–93, vol. 4 of *Geschichte des Pietismus*, edited by Martin Brecht, et al. Göttingen: Vandenhoeck & Ruprecht, 2004.

Wellhausen, Julius. *Einleitung in die ersten drei Evangelien*. Berlin: Georg Reimer, 1905.

Wilson, John E. *Introduction to Modern Theology: Trajectories in the German Tradition*. Louisville, KY: Westminster John Knox, 2007.

Wrede, William. *Das Messiasgeheimnis in den Evangelien. Zugleich ein Beitrag zum Verständnis des Markusevangeliums*. Göttingen: Vandenhoeck & Ruprecht, 1901.

———. *Paul*. Translated by Edward Lummis. London: Philip Green, 1907.

———. "The Task and Methods of 'New Testament Theology.'" In *The Nature of New Testament Theology: The Contribution of William Wrede and Adolf Schlatter*, edited by Robert Morgan, 68–116. Naperville, IL: Alex R. Allenson, 1973.

Wright, N. T. *The New Testament and the People of God*. Minneapolis: Fortress, 1992.

———. *Scripture and the Authority of God: How to Read the Bible Today*. New York: Harper Collins, 2011.

Wurster, Paul. *Aus Schrift und Geschichte: Theologische Abhandlungen Adolf Schlatter zu seinem 70. Geburtstage, dargebracht von Freunden und Schülern*. Stuttgart: Calwer Vereinsbuchhandlung, 1922.

Yarbrough, Robert W. "Adolf Schlatter." In *Dictionary of Historical Theology*, edited by Trevor Hart, 505–7. Grand Rapids: Eerdmans, 2000.

———. "Modern Reception of Schlatter's New Testament Theology." In *The Theology of the Apostles*, edited by Adolf Schlatter, translated by Robert W. Yarbrough, 417–31. Grand Rapids: Baker, 1998.

Zahn, Franz Michael. *Anna Schlatters Leben und Nachlass*. Vol. 1. Edited by Franz M. Zahn. Bremen: W. Valett, 1865.

Zahn-Harnack, Agnes von. *Adolf von Harnack*. 2nd ed. Berlin: Walter de Gruyter, 1951.

Zizioulas, John D. *Being as Communion: Studies in Personhood and the Church*. Crestwood, NY: St. Vladimir's Seminary, 1985.

———. "The Doctrine of the Holy Trinity: The Significance of the Cappadocian Contribution." In *Trinitarian Theology Today: Essays on Divine Being and Act*, edited by Christoph Schwöbel, 44–60. Edinburgh: T. & T. Clark, 1995.

Subject Index

A

abstract scholasticism, 51–52
academic studies, Schlatter's, 2, 19n10, 39, 57–60, 69, 81
"act of the will" (*Willensakt*), 48
activity, response to grace, 181–83
"Adolf Schlatter: A Life for Theology and the Church" (Neuer), 6
Allgäu Catholic revival movement, 36
"Annotations to the New Testament" (Schlatter), 26n49, 158
Anschluss (relation) with Jesus, ix, x, xn9, 14, 14n58, 18n3, 31, 55, 92, 102, 102n389, 104, 105–6, 115, 122, 125, 165, 176, 178, 179, 198
anthropocentric perspective, 102n277, 147, 154
apostles and Jesus, 119–20, 119n78–79
Apostles' Creed, 73–79
atheistic method, 115n57
attributes, of Jesus
 communication, 131–32n32
 essential, 140
 relative, 140
autonomy, 90, 90n316

B

Baader's theology, 4, 35, 42, 46–49, 47n96
Barmen Confessional Synod (1934), 100–101
Barmen Theological Declaration, 100–101
Basel Bible Society, 36
Basel Missionary Society, 36
Beck's theology, 42–46, 45–46nn83–87
Berlin, Germany, missionary societies, 34n7
Bern, Switzerland, 21–23, 57–60
Berner Tagblatt (journal), 85
Bethel, Christian relief organisation, 175n18
Bethel Theological Seminary, 26n52, 93
Bethel Theological Week
 1924 conference, 93–95
 1926 conference, 96–97, 97–98n365
 establishment of, 24
Beuggen Institution for the Education of Schoolteachers for the Poor, 36n21
Beuggen Social Welfare Institutes, 36n21
Biographical Dictionary of Evangelicals, 2

C

Calvinism, 175n15, 184, 186, 186n74, 186n78
career, Schlatter's
 Bern, Switzerland, 21–23, 57–60

Greifswald, Germany, 23–24, 57–60, 69
career, Schlatter's *(continued)*
  lectures, 2
  pastorate career, 20–21, 26
  punitive professorship, 76–79
  Tübingen University, 24–30, 82, 84–88
  University of Berlin, 24–25, 76
Catholic. *See* Roman Catholic Church
Chalcedon affirmation, 62, 62n167, 129, 197
The Christian Doctrine of Justification and Reconciliation (Ritschl), 61
"The Christian Dogma" (Schlatter), 11, 27, 48, 63
"Christologie und Soteriologie" (Schlatter), 11, 63
Christology
  academic disputes, 21–24
  after Schlatter, 196–99
  alternative way for doing, 128, 128n20
  anthropocentric perspective, 102n277, 147, 154
  apostles and Jesus, 119–20, 119nn78–79
  Apostles' Creed controversy, 73–79
  attributes, of Jesus, 131–32n32, 140
  Baader on, 46–49
  Beck on, 42–46
  cross. *See* the cross
  divine will of Jesus, 134–35
  divinity of Christ, 62, 62n168, 66, 128, 138–43
  double communion. *See* double communion of Jesus
  double-movement of Jesus, 54
  empirical-critical realism. *See* empirical-critical realism
  form (nature) of Jesus, 129, 129n21, 131–32n32
  general history as essential element, 65
  historical Jesus. *See* historical Jesus
  history, knowledge, and experience, 79–83
  history and dogmatics of Jesus, 118, 178–79
  human will of Jesus, 134–35, 135–36n45, 159–61
  idealism and. *See* idealism
  inner life of Jesus, 71–72, 119
  Kant and, 53
  kenotic, 138–41
  mission of Jesus, 121
  obedience, Jesus,' 133–38
  personhood of Jesus, 138–43
  relational aspect, 7–8, 63, 126–29
  revival movement and, 33–39
  Ritschl on, 61–69
  Schlatter's academic struggles, 57–60
  Schlatter's genesis and context of, 15–16
  Schlatter's pillars of, 55
  scholarly contribution, 5–8
  self-actualization, of Jesus, 141, 151, 154
  self-understanding of Jesus, 122
  sin, Jesus' atonement for, 152n35, 155
  Sonship. *See* Sonship of Christ
  soteriology and, 54–55, 66–67, 67n192, 146–49, 191
  Spinoza on, 39–42
  temptation, 136–37, 136n50
  union of Jesus and Father, 129–33
  unity of Jesus' will, 63, 63n171
  vocation of Jesus, 62–64, 63n170, 66–67
  will to the cross. *See* Kreuzeswille (will to the cross), 150n27, 160–61
classic subordinationism, 139–40
cognitive renewal, 177–78
communication of attributes concept, 131–32n32
communion
  of the Christian, 70–73
  double. *See* double communion of Jesus
  experiential, 71
  revealed, 137
  of will, 131–33

Subject Index   223

Communion of the Christian with God
  (Herrmann), 70
community
  context of in Romans, 90–91
  eschatological hope, 193
  Holy Spirit and, 167
  salvation as members of, 191
  value of, 61, 63, 65–66n186, 66n187
  See also new community
conceptions of God, 130
confession of faith, 75, 75n230
confessional/conservative theology, 8
contemporary theology, 164, 179, 183
convictions
  of Jesus, 118–19
  of NT content, 122–23
  presented in documents, 114
critical-historical research, 80
the cross
  Schlatter's theology of, 172
  suffering of Christ, 160–61,
    160–61n70
  will to. *See Kreuzeswille* (will to the cross)

D

Deaf-Mute Foundation, Riehen,
  36n21
death, of Adolf Schlatter, 30, 102–3
de-Christianization in Europe, 33
deification (*theosis*), 191
Denkakt (I)
  divinity of Jesus, 138–43, 152–54
  dogmatic task, 114–17, 124–25
  Holy Spirit, 135–38
  individuality and unity, 141–43
  intra-trinitarian love, 138–43,
    144n82–83, 150
  kenosis and volition, 139–41
  obedience, Jesus,' 133–38
  personhood of Jesus, 138–43
  from relation to essence, 131–33
  relational Christology, 126–29
  relational terminology, 129–31
  volitional union and essential
    union, 129–33

volitional union with the Father,
  134–35
will of Jesus, 121, 133–35
Denkakt (II)
  divinity and fellowship in forsaken-
    ness, 152–54
  gift returns to the giver, 155–57
  God's gift in return and Holy Spirit,
    157–59
  God's giving in love, 154–61,
    158n64
  Jesus and new community, 162–71
  overview, 145–46
  relation to God and humankind,
    126–27, 126n9
  relational beings in communion,
    163–66
  relational oneness, 169–71
  soteriology and, 146–49
  suffering and completed God-
    human, 159–61
  trinity and new community,
    166–68
  See also thinking-act (*Denkakt*)
depraved will, 137
Deutsche Christen movement, 100
dialectical theology, 8, 9–10n46,
  94–98
"Dienst des Christen" (Schlatter), 182
divine action, 167–68
divine self-revelation, 101–2, 104,
  129–30, 129–30n23
divine will of Jesus, 134–35
divinity of Christ, 62, 62n168, 66, 128,
  138–43, 152–54
Do We Know Jesus? (Schlatter), 11,
  29–30
doctoral dissertation, Schlatter's,
  22–23, 22nn29–30
dogmatic task of NT research,
  114–17, 124–25
dogmatician's judgement, 125
dogmatics
  ethics and, 175, 175n18
  history of Jesus and, 118
Dogmatik (Barth), 98–99
double communion of Jesus

divinity and fellowship forsaken-
    ness, 152–54
  gift returns to the giver, 155–57
double communion of Jesus
    (continued)
  God's gift in return and Holy Spirit,
    157–59
  God's giving in love, 154–61,
    158n64
  Jesus and new community, 162–71
  relation to God and humankind,
    126–27, 126n9
  relational beings in communion,
    163–66
  relational oneness, 169–71
  soteriology and, 146–49
  suffering and completed God-
    human, 159–61
  trinity and new community,
    166–68
double-movement of Jesus, 54
Dr. Kurt Hellmich Trust, 5n14

E

early life, of Adolf Schlatter, 17–20
ecclesial unity, hope for, 171
Ecumenical Council, Sixth, 134n41
ecumenical dialogue, 1, 4–5, 5n14
ecumenical perspective, 3–5
empirical-critical realism
  dogmatic task of NT research,
    114–17
  historical task of NT research,
    111–14
  New Testament research, 110–11
  overview, 107
  theology of seeing, 108–10
  unified Jesus Christ, 117–22
Enlightenment, Christology critique,
  52–53
Erkenntnis. See knowledge
Erlebtes (Schlatter), 163–64
Erweckung (revival), 34–39, 52
eschatology, 193
"Essays for the Furtherance of Chris-
    tian Theology" (journal), 59

essential attributes, of Jesus, 140
essential union, 129–33
ethics
  applications of, 194n117
  Christology and, 54–55
  social context, 38, 48–49
  struggle about God and Christ, 116
  volition union with Christ, 173–76
  of war, 28n56
  writings on, 27
evangelicalism, in Great Britain, 34
Evangelical-Lutheran Conference
    (1892), 76
exegesis
  to dogmatics, 124–25
  presuppositionless, 114
existential experience, 79
experience
  existential, 79
  religious, 80, 81n263, 83
  subjective, 71–73, 79–80, 83
experiential communion, 71
expressive realism, 191–94

F

faith
  Apostles' Creed controversy, 73–79
  Christ's sacrifice, 97
  knowledge and, 51–52, 80
  Luther's emphasis on passive aspect
    of, 182
  private revelation and, 165
  as a receptive act, 187
  Schlatter on, 79
  Schlatter's definition, 81
  science and, 44–45, 80–81
  subjectivity of, 72
  theology and, 115
  truth and, 65
  in volitional union with God, 187
"Faith in the New Testament" (Schlat-
    ter), 23, 58
faith-appropriate thinking, 116
family, Schlatter's
  ancestor, 34n8

Subject Index   225

children, 26, 26n49, 27, 29, 95, 95n350, 100–101
grandmother, 36–37
parents, 4, 17–18, 18nn2–3, 37–38
uncles, 38, 77–78
wife, 20, 26
Father (God). *See* God
female theology students, 14n57
form (nature) of Jesus, 129, 129n21, 131–32n32
forsakenness, of God, 152–54, 152n35
fragment controversy, 41n56
Free Evangelical Church, St. Gallen, Switzerland, 38
"From the inner life of the Ritschl school" (Schlatter), 70
Die Furche (journal), 89, 92n327, 93

G

general history
  as essential element of Christology, 65
  impact on theological thinking, 15, 46n87
German Christians movement, 100
German idealism. *See* idealism
German Protestant theology and theologians, 2, 15, 98, 164
German Society of Christianity, 36, 36n19
gifts of God, 177, 177n28
giving in love and Holy Spirit, 154–61, 158n64
Gnostic concepts, 129–30n23
God
  conceptions of, 130
  ethics struggle about, 116
  faith in volitional union with, 187
  forsakenness of, 152–54, 152n35
  gifts of, 177, 177n28
  horizontal unity with, 170
  individual's relation with, 70–71
  kingdom of, 62–63
  knowledge of, 101–4, 108
  receives gift from the Son, 157–59
  transcendence of, 88–90, 103

union with Son, 129–33, 134–35
vertical fellowship with, 169–70
wholly other concept of, 89–90, 93, 103, 128, 130
will of, 54, 63, 63n171
Word of, 99–101, 100n383
See also Christology; Holy Spirit; Trinity
God-human nature, 134–35, 135–36n45, 159–61
"God's well-pleasing Sacrifice" (Schlatter), 97
good will, 137, 177, 180
Gottesdienst (service to God)
  Jesus' divinity and fellowship in forsakenness, 152–54
  Jesus' will to the cross, 149–52
  mutual giving in love and Holy Spirit, 154–61, 158n64
  organic volition, 189–91
  overview, 148–49
grace, 181–84, 187, 190
Greek philosophy, 49–50
Greifswald, Germany, 23–24, 57–60, 69

H

Hegelian thought, 38, 53–54
Heidelberg Catechism, 21n19
Hellenistic theology, 119n79
Hellmich Trust, 5n14
historical Jesus
  Christ of faith and, 31, 121
  idealism and, 55
  knowledge of, 79–83
  quest for, 41, 52
  Ritschl and, 64–66
  Schlatter's publications, 27
  See also Christology
historical task of NT research, 111–14
history
  general, 15, 46n87, 65
  human connection with Jesus and, 178–79
  personal, 15–16, 45n87
  theological, 15, 45n87, 64, 79–83

Subject Index

The History of the Christ (Schlatter), 6, 11, 27, 117–18
Holy Spirit
  in community, 167
Holy Spirit *(continued)*
  God's gift in return, 157–59
  harmony of human will and divine will, 179–81
  human volitional union with God, 185–89
  ministry of, 135–38
  Protestantism and, 179
horizontal unity with God, 170
human psychology, 185–89
human volition, 176–79
human will of Jesus, 134–35, 135–36n45, 159–61

I

idealism
  Baader's theology, 46–49
  Beck's theology, 42–46
  defined, 33
  Erweckung and, 34–39, 52
  historical Jesus and, 55
  idealist Christologies, 49–55
  overview, 33–35
  sin and, 54–55
  Spinoza's theology, 39–42
individualism, 164–66, 174
individuality and unity, 141–43
individual's relation with God, 70–71
inner convictions of Jesus, 119
inner life of Jesus, 71–72, 119
inter-denominational understanding, 171
Introduction to Modern Theology: Trajectories in the German Tradition (Wilson), 2
"Introduction to the Bible" (Schlatter), 23

J

Jesus Christ. *See* Christology

"Jesus' Divinity and the Cross" (Schlatter), 7, 128
"Journal for Theology and the Church," 59, 74
judgements
  dogmatician's, 125
  value, 61–65, 62n167
justification, 45, 45n84, 174, 184–85

K

Kantianism
  Christology, 53
  moral power, 38–39
  participation in divine agency, 193
  rationalism, 50–52
"Karl Barth's *Epistle to the Romans*" (Schlatter), 90–91
kenotic Christology, 138–41
kenoticism, 138n58
kingdom of God, 62–63
knowledge (*Erkenntnis*)
  faith and, 51–52, 80
  of God, 101–4, 108
  historical, 79
  objective, 71, 73, 79
  observation as, 47
  religious, 64, 71–73, 80
  religious experience and, 80
  scientific, 64, 71, 80
Kreuzeswille (will to the cross), 48, 67, 121, 126, 149–52, 150n27

L

language challenges of reading Schlatter's works, 12
Lebensakt (life-act), 27, 118
lecture career, Schlatter's, 2
"Letters on Christian Dogmatics" (Schlatter), 109, 160, 164
liberal, defined, 9n42
liberal Reformed theology, 39
liberal theology, 8–9, 9n43
Life of Jesus Critically Examined (Strauss), 42, 85

life-act (*Lebensakt*), 27, 118
linguistics (language and cognition), 112n32
love
  in giving, 154–61, 158n64
  spiritual, 190
  submission in, 139–41
  Trinitarian, 138–44, 144nn82–83, 150
Luther, Martin, 131–32n32, 160, 174, 182
Lutheranism, 59, 163, 163n75

M

"Manifesto of the Ninety-Three," 87–88, 88n301
Marburg University, 23, 69
mediating theologians, 8, 9n44, 68
Menschendienst (service to humanity)
  overview, 148, 162–63
  relational beings in communion, 163–66
  relational oneness, 169–71
  Trinity and new community, 166–68
"Metaphysics" (Schlatter), 27
miracles, 40, 61n161, 120
mission of Jesus, 121
missionary activities, 34, 34n7
mystical experiences, 192, 192n112

N

National Socialism in Germany, 29, 100, 103
natural revelation, 108
natural theology, 108, 108n7
nature
  God-human, 134–35, 135–36n45, 159–61
  of Jesus, 129, 129n21, 131–32n32
  Schlatter's connection with, 108, 108n4
Nazi ideology, 29–30
new community
  characteristics, 169–71
  establishment of, 166
  as God's gift, 157
  relational beings in communion, 163–66
  Trinity and, 166–68
  See also community
New Testament research
  dogmatic task of, 114–17
  historical task of, 111–14
  unity of, 117–22
New Testament Theology (Schlatter), 6, 11, 28
New Testament theology (Wrede's terminology), 111n24
"new will" (*neuer Wille*), 48

O

obedience, Jesus,' 133–38
objective facts, 79–83, 120
objective faithfulness, 114
objective knowledge, 71, 73, 79
objective scientific research, 80
objectivity, subjective, 115, 125
observation
  facts, 27, 65
  knowledge, 47
  metaphysical congruence between observer and observed, 116
  seeing-act and, 108–10
  source of real science, 109n11, 175
  theology starting point, 64
"On the matter of the Apostles' Creed" (Harnack), 74
ordination, Adolf Schlatter, 4, 20
organic volition
  Christ, 179–81
  cognitive component, 177–78
  ethics, 173
  expressive realism, 191–94
  Gottesdienst and, 189–91
  grace, 181–84, 190
  history and, 178–79
  Holy Spirit, 179–81, 185–89
  human psychology, 185–89
  human volition, 176–79

justification, 184–85
pietism, 174, 174n9
sanctification, 184–85
organic volition *(continued)*
service to God, 185–91
Trinitarian basis for, 179–81
union with Christ, 191–94
volition union, 179–81
works, 181–83
otherness of Christ, 89–90, 93, 103, 128, 130

P

passivity, response to grace, 174, 181–83, 181n50, 194
"Paul and Hellenism" (Schlatter), 85
perception. *See* seeing-act (*Sehakt*)
personal history, theological history as, 15–16, 45n87
personhood of Jesus, 138–43
philosophical concepts, 49–50
"The Philosophical Work since Descartes" (Schlatter), 25
pietism
  Barth and, 92, 95
  cognitive renewal, 177
  contemporary, 174, 174n9
  defined, 4n10
  overlaps with other movements, 35
  social ethics and, 49
  Swiss revival movement, 36
positive theology, 8, 9n45
postmodern individualistic passivism, 194
post-Reformation Protestantism, 52–53, 174
presuppositionless exegesis, 114
protestant theology
  in Germany, 2, 15, 98, 164
  Schlatter's influence on, 2–3
Protestantism
  ethics and, 173–75
  German theology, 2, 15, 98
  Holy Spirit and, 179
  post-Reformation, 52–53, 174
  Schlatter's influence on, 2–3

understanding of the cross, 147–48
publication challenges, Schlatter's, 11–12
pure reason, 19, 19n14

Q

Quest for the Historical Jesus (Schweitzer), 41

R

rationalism, 50–52, 121, 121n88
Ratzinger's *Schülerkreis* (Circle of Alumni), 5, 5n15
realism
  empirical-critical. *See* empirical-critical realism
  expressive, 191–94
  theological, 47–48
realist theology, 42–46
Reformation
  call for completion of, 174–75, 194
  emphasis on passive aspect of grace, 181–83, 181n50
  Enlightenment challenges, 52–53
  post-Reformation Enlightenment challenges, 52–53
  post-Reformation ethics, 174
  total depravity, 189
Reformed Union, Second Theological Week conference (1927), 98
relation (*Anschluss*) with Jesus, ix, x, xn9, 14, 14n58, 18n3, 31, 55, 92, 102, 102n389, 104, 105–6, 115, 122, 125, 165, 176, 178, 179, 198
relational aspects of Christology, 7–8, 63, 126–29
relational beings in communion, 163–66
relational oneness, 169–71
relational terminology, 129–31
relational-volitional agenda, 48
relational-volitional union, 131–33
relationship

God and humankind, 126–27, 126n9
individual with God, 70–71
relative attributes, of Jesus, 140
religion
  attack on, 33
  reemergence and expansion, 34
religions principle and person of Christ, 120n84
religious experience, 80, 81n263, 83
religious knowledge, 64, 71–73
revelation, 96, 98–104, 108n7
revival movement
  Christology and, 33–39
  grandmother as key figure in, 36–37
  idealist critical thought and, 34–39, 52
  parents' influence, 37–38, 37n29
  pietism, 35–36
  school influences, 38–39
  Swiss revival movement, 36
  uncle's influence, 38
Ritschlianism
  background, 61
  community, value of, 61, 63, 65–66n186, 66n187
  Cremer and, 60
  divinity of Christ, 62, 62n168, 66
  kingdom of God, 62–63, 62n169
  liberal theology, 9n43
  Schlatter's critique summary, 67–68, 68–69n199
  soteriological dimension, 66–67, 67n192
  value judgements, 61–65, 62n167
  vocation of Jesus, 62–64, 63n170, 66–67
Roman Catholic Church
  Baader, Franz von, 4, 35, 42, 46–49, 47n96
  Dr. Kurt Hellmich Trust, 5n14
  ecumenical dialogue, 1, 4–5, 5n14
  Enlightenment challenges, 52
  revival movement, 34, 36
Romans epistle, Schlatter-Barth dispute, 88–98
Römerbrief (Barth), 88

S

sacraments, 96–97
salvation. *See* soteriology and Christology
sanctification, 184–85
Schauen. *See* observation
Schlatter, Adolf
  academic studies, 19n10, 22–23, 22nn29–30, 39
  ancestor, 34n8
  career, 2, 20–30, 57–60, 69, 76–79
  children, 26, 26n49, 27, 29, 95, 95n350, 100–101
  death of, 30, 102–3
  doctoral dissertation, 22–23, 22nn29–30
  early life, 17–20
  grandmother, 36–37
  language challenges, 12
  nature, connection with, 108, 108n4
  ordination, 4, 20
  parents, 4, 17–18, 18nn2–3, 37–38
  publication challenges, 11–12
  scholarly interactions, 10–11
  secondary sources, use of, 10–11
  uncles, 38, 77–78
  wife, 20, 26
Schlatter's publications
  "Annotations to the New Testament," 26n49
  Bethel Theological Week lectures, 97
  "The Christian Dogma," 11, 27, 48, 63
  "Christologie und Soteriologie," 11, 63
  "Dienst des Christen" (Schlatter), 182
  Do We Know Jesus? 11, 29–30
  Erlebtes (Schlatter), 163–64
  "Faith in the New Testament," 23, 58
  "God's well-pleasing Sacrifice" (Schlatter), 97
  The History of the Christ, 6, 11, 27, 117–18

Schlatter's publications *(continued)*
  "From the inner life of the Ritschl school," 70
  "Introduction to the Bible," 23
  "Jesus' Divinity and the Cross," 7, 128
  "Karl Barth's *Epistle to the Romans*," 90–91
  "Letters on Christian Dogmatics," 109, 160, 164
  "Metaphysics," 27
  The Modern Theologians: An Introduction to Christian Theology since 1918, 2
  New Testament commentaries, 28–29
  New Testament Theology, 6, 11, 28
  "Paul and Hellenism," 85
  Paul's Letter to the Corinthians, commentary, 100
  "The Philosophical Work since Descartes," 25
  "The Situation of the Proletariat," 48
  "The Teaching of the Apostles," 27
  "The Theology of Karl Barth and the Ministry of the Pastor," 96–97
  The Theology of the Apostles, 6, 11, 118
  "The Word of Jesus," 27
scholarly contribution of Christology, 10–11
scholarly interactions, Schlatter's, 10–11
science
  in broad sense, 109n17
  faith and, 44–45, 80–81
  observation as source of, 109n11, 175
  organic union of dogmatics and ethics, 175
  theology as, 45, 45n81, 88, 109–10, 116
scientific knowledge, 64, 71, 80
scientific research, 80

Second Theological Week conference of the Reformed Union (1927), 98
secondary sources, in Schlatter's works, 10–11
secularization of the European mind, 33
seeing-act (*Sehakt*)
  defined, 23, 108–10
  faith and, 91
  purpose of, 117
  Schlatter's lectures as, 44
  theological development and, 49
  theology of facts component, 27, 108–10
  value judgements and, 65
  wholly other God, 103
self-actualization, of Jesus, 141, 151, 154
self-understanding of Jesus, 122
service to God. *See Gottesdienst*
service to humanity. *See Menschendienst*
sin
  awareness of, 79
  idealism and, 54–55
  Jesus' atonement for, 152n35, 155
  Luther's emphasis on, 174
"The Situation of the Proletariat" (Baader), 48
Sixth Ecumenical Council, 134n41
social ethics, 38, 48–49
Sonship of Christ, 6, 127–28, 127n15, 128nn16–17, 133–34, 137n54, 146n6
soteriology and Christology, 54–55, 66–67, 67n192, 146–49, 191
Spinoza's theology, 39–42
subjective experience, 71–73, 79–80, 83
subjective objectivity, 115, 125
subjectivity of faith, 72
submission in love, 139–41
subordination, 139–40
subordinationism, 166
suffering, 159–61
Swiss revival movement, 36

Subject Index   231

systematic theology, Schlatter on, 109, 125

T

"The Teaching of the Apostles" (Schlatter), 27
temptation, 136–37, 136n50
terminology, 8–10, 129–31
theocentric Christology and soteriology, 146–49
theologians, dogmatic task and, 114–16
theological history, 15, 45n87, 64, 79–83
theological intellectualism, 129n23
theological movements, 8
theological realism, 47–48
theological science, 45, 45n81, 88, 109–10, 116
theological unity, 44
theological-historical research, 80
Theological-Political Treatise (Spinoza), 40
theology
  confessional/conservative, 8
  contemporary emphasis, 164, 179, 183
  defined, 115, 115n57
  dialectical, 8, 9–10n46, 94–98
  ethics and, 175
  faith and, 115
  German Protestant, 2, 15, 98
  Hellenistic, 119n79
  liberal, 8–9, 9n43
  life-act and, 27, 118
  natural, 108, 108n7
  New Testament, 6, 11, 28, 111n24
  observation as starting point, 64
  positive, 8
  realist, 42–46
  Schlatter's view, 124–25
  seeing-act and, 27, 108–10
  systematic, 109, 125
  thinking-act and, 27
  See also specific theological movements

"The Theology of Karl Barth and the Ministry of the Pastor" (Schlatter), 96–97
The Theology of the Apostles (Schlatter), 6, 11, 118
theosis (deification), 191
thinking-act (*Denkakt*)
  Barth's smashing of, 88–95, 103
  faith and, 91
  theology of facts component, 27
  value judgements and, 64–65
  See also Denkakt (I); *Denkakt* (II)
transcendence of God, 88–90, 103
Trinity
  community and, 166–68
  intra-trinitarian love, 138–43, 144nn82–83, 150
  volitional bond between members of, 129n22
  volitional union and, 179–81, 187
truth, faith and, 65
Tübingen University
  Barth as student, 86–87
  Beck's influence, 42–46
  Schlatter's career, 24–30, 82, 84–88
twofold grace, 184

U

unifying grace, 184–85
union, volitional and essential, 129–33
union of will (*Willenseinigung*), 48
unity
  Baader on, 47–48, 47n96
  Beck on, 44
  document content and consciousness, 114
  of essence, 131–33
  individuality and, 141–43
  Jesus Christ in NT account, 117–22
  of Jesus' will, 63, 63n171
  of will, 131
University of Berlin, 24–25, 76
University of Heidelberg, 23, 69

V

value judgements, 61–65, 62n167
vertical fellowship with God, 169–70
vocation of Jesus, 62–64, 63n170, 66–67
volition
   act of the will, 48
   communion of, 131–33
   essence and, 131
   kenosis and, 139–41
volitional union
   essential union and, 129–33
   ethics and, 173–76
   Jesus with the Father, 134–35
   organic. *See* organic volition

W

war
   ethics of, 28n56
   petition supporting Wilhelm II, 87–88
   Schlatter's view of, 28n56, 87

wholly other concept of God, 89–90, 93, 103, 128, 130
will
   act of the, 48
   communion of, 131–33
   to the cross. *See Kreuzeswille*
   of God, 54, 63, 63n171
   good vs. depraved, 137
   human and divine, 134–35, 135–36n45, 159–61
   of Jesus, 121, 133–35
   union of the, 48
   unity of, 131
Willensakt (act of the will), 48
Willenseinigung (union of will), 48
Word of God, 99–101, 100n383
"The Word of Jesus" (Schlatter), 27
work of Christ, 14, 101, 101n385, 176, 180–81, 192

Z

Zwischen den Zeiten (journal), 103

Name Index

A

Alder, Johann Jakob, 38–39, 151, 151n31
Althaus, Paul, 2, 7, 7n33, 25, 25n41, 25n47, 101, 147–48, 147n11, 163n75
Althoff, Friedrich, 76–77
Anselm, 115, 147, 149
Aquinas, 52n125, 186
Aristotle, 52, 52n125, 108, 108n8
Augustine, 142n75
Axt-Piscalar, Christine, 9nn43–44

B

Baader, Franz von, 4, 35, 42, 46–47n91, 46–49, 47nn95–96, 48n100
Bailer, Albert, 5n17, 12n54, 108n6, 189n97
Baird, William, 12, 12n53, 110–11n23, 151, 151n34
Barth, Johann Friedrich "Fritz," 85–86
Barth, Karl, 9–10n46, 25, 28, 68, 68n197, 85nn279–280, 87–103, 87n291, 87n294, 88n301, 88n305, 89n310, 92nn326–28, 93n329, 94nn338–40, 95n350, 97–98n365, 98n369, 113n41
Baur, Ferdinand Christian, 9n45, 25, 61, 61n161, 85, 112n36, 122
Bavinck, Herman, 51n120, 51n122, 109n11, 113n39, 174n9

Bayly, Christopher A., 34, 34n6
Beck, Johann Tobias, 19–20, 35, 42–46, 42nn64–68, 44n77, 45–46nn83–87, 59n155, 84–85, 108, 175n13, 175n15
Bellchambers, Elaine, 198n2
Bender, Julius, 14n57
Benedict XVI (pope), 5
Bengel, Johann Albrecht, 4n10
Benrath, Gustav Adolf, 34n8
Bernard, Emile, 113n41
Bernard of Clairvaux, 137n56
Beyreuther, Erich, 34n11
Biedermann, Alois E., 120n84
Billings, J. Todd, 184n64, 186n74
Bock, Heike, 36n17
Bockmuehl, Markus, 2, 2n1, 6, 6n23
Bodelschwingh, Friedrich von, 24, 93–94, 175n18
Bodelschwingh, Friedrich von, der Jüngere, 95
Boers, Hendrikus, 6
Bolliger, Adolf, 21n20
Bonhoeffer, Dietrich, 2, 26
Boos, Martin, 36
Bornhäuser, Karl, 9n45
Bosse, Friedrich, 9n45
Bosse, Julius R., 76
Bousset, Wilhelm, 9n43, 9n45, 42n64
Bubser, Eberhard, 41n55
Buckley, James J., 171n121
Bultmann, Rudolf, 20, 25, 42n64, 92–94, 94n342, 96, 114, 114n48, 119–20, 119n79
Burk, Carl von, 82

234 Name Index

Busch, Eberhard, 85nn277–78,
    85n281, 86n282, 86nn284–87,
    86nn289–90, 87n291, 87n293,
    88n301, 92, 92n324, 96n352,
    97n359, 100n383
Bütikofer, Kaspar, 36n17

C

Calvin, John, 175n15, 184, 184n63,
    186, 186n74, 186n78
Canlis, Julie, 184, 184n65
Chadwick, Owen, 33, 33n4
Chapman, Mark D., 9n45
Childs, Brevard, 6
Cremer, Ernst, 9n45
Cremer, Hermann, 4, 9n45, 22n30,
    23, 56–60, 59n155, 74n223,
    75–76, 78, 80
Crim, Keith R., 89, 89n308

D

Dintaman, Stephen, viin3, 6, 6n31,
    174, 174nn9–10
Donagan, Alan, 40n45
Dorner, Isaak A., 9n44
Dreher, Matthias, 18n8, 163n75
Dymale, Herbert R., 5n17

E

Egg, Gottfried, 5n17, 107n1
Eglinton, James, 110n18
Ehrman, Bart D., 122, 122n94
Eichhorn, Albert, 9n43, 9n45
Eucken, Rudolf, 19, 108, 108n8

F

Fergusson, David, 33, 33n2
Feuerbach, Ludwig, 33
Fraas, Hans-Jürgen, 5n17
Francke, August Hermann, 4n10

G

Gäbler, Ulrich, 35, 35n15, 36n18,
    36n21
Gasque, Ward, 6n25, 118n72
Gieseler, Johann K. L., 9n44
Gockel, Matthias, 9n44
Gogarten, Friedrich, 96
Gogh, Vincent van, 113n41
Goppelt, Leonhard, 5n19
Gregory of Nazianzus, 135n45
Gregory of Nyssa, 132n34
Grenz, Stanley J., 61n160, 62n166
Güder, Eduard, 57
Gunkel, Hermann, 9n43, 9n45
Guthrie, Donald, 6

H

Hackmann, Heinrich, 9n43, 9n45
Hadorn, Walter, 36n22
Haering, Theodor, 24, 82, 84
Hägele, Clemens, 3n7, 6n28, 45n83
Hake, Claudia., 42n62
Haldane, Robert, 34n10
Hardy, Daniel W., 2n4
Härle, Wilfried, 88nn300–301,
    109n17, 153, 153n40
Harnack, Adolf von, 4, 9n43, 9n45,
    24, 45n81, 68, 73–83, 74nn223–
    28, 75n230, 75n233, 78n248,
    79n250, 80nn253–54, 80n256,
    83n274, 87, 120, 129–30n23
Haupt, Erich, 59
Hegel, Georg W. F., 40, 40n54, 53–54
Heidegger, Martin, 111n27
Heim, Karl, 28
Heitmüller, Wilhelm, 28
Herrmann, Wilhelm, 9n43, 9n45,
    68–73, 69n204, 71n214, 72n219,
    75, 83, 87, 119
Hesse, Hermann Albert, 98, 98n368,
    98n370–371
Hitler, Adolf, 29, 100
Hoffmann, Willi, 42n64, 43n72,
    44n77

Name Index

Hofmann, Johann Christian Konrad von, 59n156
Holl, Karl, 25, 25n38, 88–89, 95, 173–74, 174n4
Holmes, Stephen R., 53, 53n133
Holtzmann, Heinrich, 118, 118n75, 123n95
Hoping, Helmut, 40n52, 134n41

I

Isherwood, Lisa, 198n2
Israel, Jonathan, 39–40, 40n44, 40n46

J

Jaeger, Paul, 45n82
Jäger, Samuel, 93
Jehle-Wildberger, Marianne, 36n24
John, Apostle, 119, 119n78, 127, 182–83
Jung, Carl Gustav, 20
Jung, Paul, 20

K

Kaftan, Julius, 9n43, 9n45, 24, 75, 77
Kähler, Martin, ixn7, 9n45, 59, 59nn155–56, 76
Kaindl, Annemarie, 89n308
Kant, Immanuel, 38–39, 50–52, 51n115, 51n118, 53, 193
Käsemann, Ernst, 2, 5n19, 25
Kattenbusch, Ferdinand, 75
Kindt, Irmgard, 5n17, 47n92, 48n99, 107n1
Kittel, Gerhard, 34–35n13, 110n19
Köberle, Adolf, 42n63
Kögel, Julius, 9n45
Köstenberger, Andreas J., viin1, xn10, ixn5, 2n6, 5–6, 112n36
Kühn, Manfred, 51n117
Kuhn, Thomas K., 36n21
Kuyper, Abraham, 45n81, 175n15

L

Lambert, J. H., 51n115
Larsen, Timothy, 2n5
Lavater, Johann Kaspar, 36
Law, David R., 138n58
Lehman, Hartmut, 35, 35n16
Leontius of Byzantium, 129n21
Lessing, Eckhard, 9n44, 9n45, 15, 15n1, 57n145, 59n155, 107n1
Lessing, Gotthold Ephraim, 35n14, 40–41, 41n56
Loos, Andreas, 6, 6n32, 7, 7n38, 136n47, 138n59, 143, 143n78, 167n105–6, 168n108, 170n119
Lundström, Gösta, 114–15, 115n49
Lüpke, Johannes von, 3, 3n8, 107n1
Lütgert, Wilhelm, 5n19, 9n45, 47n94, 101
Luther, Martin, 131–32n32, 160, 174, 182

M

Macleod, Donald, 139n61, 160–61n70
Marx, Karl, 33
Mausbach, Joseph, 87
Maximus the Confessor, 134, 134n41
McCall, Thomas H., 153n39
McClendon, James Wm., Jr., 15n2
McCormack, Bruce L., 69n204, 72n215, 87n297, 88, 88n302, 90n316, 113n41, 140n67, 192, 192n111
McGrath, Alister E., 52, 52n128, 119n76
McLeod, Hugh, 33, 33n5
McNutt, James E., 29n71
Melanchthon, Philipp, 146, 146n3
Menke, Karl-Heinz, 134n41
Merz, George, 103, 103n394
Meyer-Wieck, Karl, 5n17
Michaelis, Wilhelm, 28n57
Michel, Otto, 3, 5n19, 12, 12n54, 25
Migliore, Daniel L., 179n38

Name Index

Moltmann, Jürgen, 7, 7n39, 133n35, 148, 148n12, 152n36, 153n41, 160–61, 160–61n70
Morgan, Robert, 5, 6n25
Moule, C.F.D., 139n61
Mueller, David L., 65–66n186
Müller, Julius, 59n156
Müller, Karl, 59n155
Mussner, Franz, 4

N

Neuer, Werner, vii, xn10, 2, 4n10, 6, 6n25–27, 7, 7n36, 11n50, 14n57, 17n1, 18nn6–9, 19, 19n10, 19n15, 24n37, 25nn38–39, 25n45, 30n73, 36n23, 36n25, 36n29, 37, 37n26, 38n38, 39n40, 39n43, 43, 43n70, 43n72, 44n75, 44n78, 46n89, 46–47n91, 49, 49n108, 57n141, 57nn146–47, 59n153, 59n158, 69n200, 69n201, 69n205, 77nn242–45, 82nn264–65, 82nn267–69, 83n273, 84n275, 85n277, 86nn282–84, 86n288, 87–88, 87n299, 88n304, 93n330, 93nn332–34, 94nn343–44, 95nn346–48, 96n351, 96n353, 96nn356–57, 97–98nn365–67, 99nn372–77, 100nn378–82, 101nn384–85, 103n393, 107n1, 108n9, 111n27, 151n31, 164n79, 171n127, 173nn1–3, 175n13, 175n18
Neufeld, Karl H., 74n223, 75n231, 76n238
Neugebauer, Matthias, 56n140
Nietzsche, Friedrich, 19
Nippold, Friedrich, 57–58, 57n146, 58n148
Nitzsch, Carl I., 9n44
Noll, Mark, 21–22, 22n24, 34n8
Nowak, Kurt, 74n225

O

Oetinger, Friedrich Christoph, 4n10, 35n14
Oettli, Samuel, 9n45, 21, 57, 57n142
Olson, Roger E., 61n160, 62n166
Orelli, Hans Konrad von, 21n20
Osterhammel, Jürgen, 33, 33n3, 34n7
Osthövener, Claus-Dieter, 74n225

P

Pannenberg, Wolfhart, 147n10
Patterson, D., ixn5
Paul, Apostle, 88–95, 90–91, 96–97, 100, 119, 119n79, 137n54, 141, 177, 180, 184, 185n70, 186, 188, 191
Paulsen, Anna, 14n57
Pfister, Rudolf, 36n21
Pfleiderer, Otto, 24
Pyrrhus I of Constantinople, 134n41

R

Rade, Martin, 9n43, 9n45, 69n204, 75
Rahlfs, Alfred, 9n43, 9n45
Räisänen, Heikki, 115n70, 117
Ratzinger, Joseph, 5n14
Reimarus, Hermann S., 41, 41n56, 52, 119
Reitzenstein, Richard, 9n43
Rengstorf, Karl-Heinrich, 25–26
Renkewitz, Heinz, 34n7
Richmond, James, 61n160, 62n168
Rieger, Hans-Martin, viin3, 5, 5n14, 6n30, 7, 45n84, 149n19, 150n26, 162n74, 165n87, 171n127, 184n68, 185n72
Riggenbach, Christoph, 9n45, 42n64
Ringleben, Joachim, 112n32, 112n35
Ritschl, Albrecht, 9n43, 9n45, 60–68, 61n160, 62–63nn167–72, 63n170, 65–66n186, 66n187, 66n189, 67n192, 68–69n199, 69n204

Root, Michael, 171n121
Rothe, Richard, 57
Rüegg, Daniel, 6n29
Rüetschie, Rudolf A., 57

S

Saint-Martin, Louis Claude de, 46n90
Schaeder, Erich, 9n45
Schäfer, Rolf, 61n160
Schlatter, Adolf, viin2, 2–8, 10–12,
    10nn47–48, 11n51, 12n52,
    14nn57–58, 15nn4–5, 17–30,
    18nn2–5, 18n9, 19–21nn10–23,
    22nn25–30, 23nn33–36, 25n44,
    26–27nn48–55, 28n56, 28n58,
    29–30, 29nn59–70, 29n72,
    30nn74–75, 31n76, 34–35n13,
    37nn29–31, 38nn34–37,
    39, 39n39, 39n42, 41–46,
    41nn58–59, 42–44nn67–76,
    44n79, 45–46nn81–88, 47n93,
    47n96, 47–48nn97–98, 48,
    48–49nn104–7, 50n109,
    50nn113–14, 51n116, 51nn119–
    23, 52n124, 52n126, 53n130,
    53n134, 54n137, 55n139,
    57n144, 58, 58nn149–52,
    59nn153–54, 59n157, 60n159,
    63, 63nn173–74, 64n177, 65–
    66nn179–83, 66n187, 66n190,
    67n192, 69, 69n201, 69n205, 70,
    70nn207–9, 71n210, 71nn212–
    13, 72n216, 72n220, 73–79,
    75n234, 76n237, 76nn239–40,
    77nn242–43, 77n245, 78nn246–
    48, 80nn257–59, 81, 81nn260–
    63, 82nn265–66, 82n271, 85,
    85n276, 87–98, 89nn307–9,
    89n311, 90–103, 90nn312–15,
    90–91n322, 94nn335–37,
    94n341, 94n345, 95n349,
    96nn354–55, 97nn358–64, 97–
    98n365, 100n383, 101nn386–87,
    102nn388–91, 103n395, 107n2,
    108–9, 108nn3–5, 108nn9–10,
    109–10nn11–17, 110nn20–22,
    111nn24–29, 112–13nn30–40,
    113nn42–43, 114nn44–47,
    115nn50–52, 115nn54–56,
    115–16n57, 116nn58–64,
    117–18, 117nn65–68, 118nn72–
    74, 119n77, 119nn79–82,
    120nn83–84, 120nn86–87,
    121nn88–91, 122nn92–93,
    124nn1–2, 125nn3–7,
    126nn8–12, 127nn13–15, 128,
    128nn16–19, 129–30nn22–23,
    130nn24–28, 131–32nn29–32,
    133nn35–38, 134nn39–42,
    135–36nn43–45, 136nn46–51,
    137nn52–57, 139n60,
    139nn62–63, 140n64, 140n68,
    141nn69–71, 142n72–74,
    143nn76–77, 143nn79–81,
    146nn1–2, 146nn4–6,
    147nn8–10, 148nn13–17,
    149nn18–23, 150nn24–28,
    151nn29–33, 152n35, 152n37,
    153n38, 153n41, 154nn42–45,
    155nn46–51, 156nn52–58,
    157nn59–61, 157–58nn62–66,
    160, 160nn67–68, 160–61nn70–
    71, 162nn72–74, 163–64,
    163nn76–77, 164n78, 164nn80–
    85, 165nn88–94, 166nn95–101,
    167nn102–4, 167n107,
    168nn109–10, 169nn111–15,
    170nn116–18, 170n120,
    171nn122–26, 174nn5–8,
    174nn11–12, 175nn14–20,
    176nn21–22, 177nn23–28,
    178nn29–37, 179nn39–40,
    180nn41–47, 181–82nn48–52,
    182, 182nn54–55, 183nn56–62,
    184nn66–67, 185nn69–71,
    186n73, 186nn75–82, 187nn83–
    89, 188–89nn90–96, 189nn98–
    101, 190nn102–6, 191nn107–10,
    192n112, 193–94nn113–118
Schleiermacher, Friedrich D. E., 9n45,
    37, 63, 78, 183n61
Schliesser, Benjamin, 182, 182n53
Schmid, Johannes H., 7, 7n33, 149n19
Schmidt, Kurt Dietrich, 34, 34n12

Name Index

Schniewind, Julius, 59n155
Schreiner, Thomas R., 6
Schrempf, Christoph, 74
Schweitzer, Albert, 41, 41n57
Schwöbel, Christoph, 128–29n20, 131–32n32, 144, 144n83, 196n1
Seeberg, Erich, 2, 25
Seeberg, Reinhold, 76, 87
Semler, Johann S., 9n43, 9n45
Smid, Udo, 84n275, 102n277
Spener, Philipp Jakob, 4n10
Spinoza, Benedict de, 39–42, 40nn48–49, 40n51
Staehelin, Ernst, 36n19, 36n21
Stählin, Gustav, 26
Steffensen, Karl, 19, 39
Strauss, David Friedrich, 9n45, 42, 42n64, 85, 120
Stuhlmacher, Peter, 5n19, 6n25, 12, 12nn55–56, 15, 15n3, 57, 57n143, 68, 77n242, 84n275, 87n292, 115n69
Stupperich, Robert, 23n33, 25n38, 69n203, 79n249, 82, 82n270, 83n272, 89n306, 115n56
Swain, Scott R., viiin4

T

Tanner, Kathryn, 128n16
Tarnow, Martin, 99n372
Thielicke, Helmut, 125n3
Tholuck, August, 59n156
Thomasius, Gottfried, 138, 140, 140n65–66
Thurneysen, Eduard, 68n197
Tillich, Paul, 2, 25, 147n7
Timm, Hermann, 70n206
Troeltsch, Ernst, 9n43, 9n45

U

Ullmann, Carl, 9n44
Umbreit, Friedrich W. C., 9n44

Ungern-Sternberg, Jürgen von, 87n298
Ungern-Sternberg, Wolfgang von, 87n298
Urlsperger, Johann August, 36n19

V

Vadian, Joachim, 17
van Gogh, Vincent, 113n41
Vieweger, Hans-Joachim, 5n16
Volf, Miroslav, 164n83

W

Walldorf, Jochen, viin3, 6n25, 7n35, 50n110, 50n112, 107n1, 110n21, 115, 115n53
Wallmann, Johannes, 4n10
Weber, Hans Emil, 59n155
Weber, Otto, 102
Webster, John, 93n331, 102n392
Weigelt, Horst, 34n9, 36n19
Weinhardt, Joachim, 8, 8n40, 9n42, 56n140, 61n160, 64n176, 68, 68nn195–96, 69n204, 75n232, 76n236, 80n256, 81n263
Weiss, Bernhard, 10, 24, 119, 119n78
Weiss, Johannes, 9n43, 9n45
Weizsäcker, Karl Heinrich, 85
Wellenreuther, Hermann, 34n7
Wette, Wilhelm M. L. de, 37
Wilhelm II, Emperor, 76, 87
Wilson, John E., 2, 2n3
Wischnath, Michael, 43n68
Wrede, William, 9n43, 9n45, 111n24, 119–20, 119n79, 120n85
Wright, N. T., 6, 6n22
Wurm, Theophil, 29

Y

Yarbrough, Robert W., viin1, xn10, 2n2, 5n18, 6, 6n21, 28n57

Z

Zahn-Harnack, Agnes von, 78n248
Zizioulas, John D., 144, 144n82
Zöckler, Otto, 9n45